Dictionary of
Biographical
Quotations

Dictionary of Biographical Quotations

Compiled by Frank S Pepper

Sphere Reference

Sphere Books Ltd.
30-32 Gray's Inn Road
London WC1X 8JL

First published 1985
Copyright © Frank S. Pepper 1985

Reproduced, printed and bound in Great Britain by
Cox & Wyman Ltd, Reading

Phototypeset in Great Britain by
The Word Factory, Rossendale, Lancashire

Preface

In 1922, when I was twelve, I made my first attempt at writing for money. I was sent a paragraph to the *Daily News* and they paid me half-a-crown for it, which was a lot of money in those days, especially to a schoolboy. Obviously I had struck a goldmine. From that time on I was hooked. I was going to be a writer and make a fortune. It didn't quite work out. Nobody told me about beginner's luck. It was four years before I earned my next half-a-crown.

After Matriculation my parents wanted me to go to university, but hearing that Arthur Mee, editor of *Children's Newspaper* and *Children's Encyclopedia*, needed an office boy, I got myself the job, in the firm belief, which future experience did nothing to change, that a few years with Arthur Mee would teach me more about becoming a professional journalist than any university.

I stayed with Arthur Mee for five years, learning my craft. Of all the many things I learnt from my experience on that side of the editorial fence I think the single most valuable lesson was that 'writer' and 'author' are not synonyms. Anyone with a feel for words can be taught to write well enough to get into print. But it's what you write about that counts. A talent for writing is about 10% of the craft. What one is in business to sell is not writing, but ideas.

By 1930 I felt that I knew enough about the trade of giving editors what they wanted and turned freelance. Since then, until semi-retirement a few years ago, I averaged a weekly output of 20,000 words, fact and fiction, for dozens of journals and magazines, under ten pen names. Wrote four non-fiction hardbacks for Nelson's. Was finishing the fifth, on the then new topic of television, when there came that bit of bother with the person Winston Churchill called "that bloodthirsy little guttersnipe". Alexandra Palace shut down abruptly in the middle of a Mickey Mouse film and we all went off to war. I tied a portable typewriter to my kitbag, and managed to knock out a short story every couple of weeks or so.

In 1938 I suggested to Reg Eves, editor of a boys' paper called *Champion*, a series of stories about a fighter pilot called *Rockfist Rogan*. He said he couldn't see much future in it, but commissioned 13 instalments. It ran in weekly episodes for 22 years.

When the paper shortage ended a few years after the war was over American imports had created a market for picture-strip stories. Eves was instructed to produce a rival to *Eagle*. He called me in to devise a character to match *Dan Dare* saying "We've got to have science fiction on the cover. I know nothing about it and am not in the least interested in it. You've got a free hand to do whatever you like – so long as it's successful." I came up with a character called *Captain Condor*. He ran for 12 years.

Two years later Eves launched a picture-strip paper called *Tiger*. It was to specialise in sport. This time my briefing from Reg Eves was "I need a football story for the front page. I want something that will run for years". I produced a character called *Roy of the Rovers*, who is running to this day, although it is now some years since I did a weekly stint on him.

Because I have been, as a writer, so many different people, turning out so many different kinds of work, I have needed to amass a huge quantity of reference material – so much, in fact, that it is now housed in a barn.

It was always my ambition, one day, when I had the time, to use this collection as a source from which to compile some entertaining anthologies. The *Dictionary of Biographical Quotations* is one of them.

Frank S. Pepper

Foreword

Disraeli wrote that biography is "life without theory". Surely life has no theory. It is the biographer who theorises, looking for the whole man, who was somehow unknown even by his intimates. The biographer assembles. The pieces are trimmed to fit. And what they fit was already in mind. The biographer's creation is always artificial, at best plausible.

And the same is true of autobiography. The point from which the life is drawn together tempers the whole. Memories are fashioned in the light of experience.

But what we delight in in a biography is the gossip and irrational behaviour that would strain any theory too far to offer an explanation; and so, perhaps, we should take Clerihew Bentley's "Biography is about chaps" as the best that can be said. For example, there could be no theory to explain the peculiar behaviour of Gladstone: filling his hot water bottle with tea, which he drank the next morning. (This is putting aside his other, well-known, peculiarities.)

Or, of the gourmand Dr. Buckland who had eaten his way straight through the animal kingdom and the worst thing was a mole – and that was utterly horrible. (Later, he changed his mind after eating a bluebottle.) His career reached a climax of exotic gulosity at Nuneham where the relic of the heart of a French king provided too great a temptation, and to the horror of those around, before anyone could stop him, he gobbled it up, exclaiming, "I have eaten many strange things but have never eaten the heart of a king before."

I do not know if Dr. Buckland had any particular aversion to the vegetable kingdom but Beau Brummell, in one of his many poses, forebore to eat any. (Though consciously eccentric he is no less a subject of interest for that.) When asked by a certain lady if he had ever eaten any vegetable in his life, he recalled, "Yes, madam, I once ate a pea."

Beau Brummell is best remembered for his attention to dress. A cravat was rejected if not properly tied at the first attempt. His valet wittily referred to these as "*our* failures". (Carlyle, on the other hand, dressed so badly that Max Beerbohm said, "(that he) should have tried to construct a philosophy of clothes has always seemed to me one of the most pathetic things in literature".)

Matthew Arnold and William Blake shared the same fate, of being caught – though not together – wearing no clothes at all. "Is it possible that you see anything indelicate in the human form divine?" was Arnold's response to being seen in a state of public nudity by a clergyman in a state of shock. Similarly, Mr. and Mrs. Blake were "freed from those 'troublesome disguises' which have prevailed since the Fall" when Mr. Butts made his untimely call. They were reciting passages from *Paradise Lost*, in character – or so they said.

Simply, people are endlessly fascinating, no matter whether their behaviour confirms or denies our suspicions. Consider the plight of Mrs. Dryden, despairing at the neglect suffered from her husband: "Lord, Mr. Dryden, how can you always be poring over these musty books. I wish I were a book, and then I should have more of your company."

"Pray, my dear," Mr. Dryden replied, "if you become a book let it be an almanack, for then I shall change you every year."

Somehow just what one would have expected; satisfying for that.

Editor
Sphere Reference
February 1985

Contents

A

PETER ABELARD (1079–1147)
French theologian and philosopher

1 Older medieval philosophers like Anselm had said "I must believe in order that I may understand." Abelard took the opposite course. "I must understand in order that I may believe." He said "By doubting we come to questioning, and by questioning we perceive the truth." Strange words to have been written in the year 1122.
Sir Kenneth Clark, CIVILISATION 1969

2 Who was there that did not follow you with strained neck and staring eyes as you passed along? What wife, what virgin, did not burn? What queen or noble dame did not envy me my fortune?
Héloise, letter to Abelard

3 So many scholars flocked from all parts of Europe to listen to that nightingale of knowledge that Paris, a mere embryo city when Abelard first came there, had grown bigger and bigger to hold them.
Richard Le Gallienne, OLD LOVE STORIES RETOLD

4 We owe our protestant conscience to Abelard.
George Moore. Quoted Roger B. Lloyd, THE STRICKEN LUTE

LORD ACTON (1834–1902)
(John Emerich Edward Dalberg)
British historian

5 Such men are all vanity; they have the inflation of German professors, and the ruthless talk of undergraduates.
Cardinal Manning. Quoted Lytton Strachey, EMINENT VICTORIANS 1918

6 Lord Acton was totally sane, but in other aspects perhaps the oddest of Victorians. Reputedly the most learned historian in England, he never wrote a book, apart from collected lectures and essays.
Raymond Mortimer, Sunday Times, Rebel Against the Vatican 24 Nov 1968

7 A devout Catholic to the end, he became the most weighty assailant against the Papacy . . . Acton, as a passionate Liberal, not only opposed the Vatican, but feared democracy as potentially the most sinister of despotisms. "It is bad to be oppressed by a minority, but it is worse to be oppressed by a majority." Here he seems to me to be prophetic.
Ibid.

8 When he is in London he is able, if only he is willing, to tell you what Spain intends to do, and what America; the present relations between the Curia and the Secret Societies; how long Lord Salisbury will combine the Premiership with the Foreign Office, and the latest theory about the side of Whitehall on which Charles I was beheaded.
G. W. E. Russell, COLLECTIONS AND RECOLLECTIONS

9 His most conspicuous trait was a sphinx-like mysteriousness which conveyed the sense that he knew a great deal more than he chose to impart and was a walking depository of vital secrets.
G. W. E. Russell, PORTRAITS OF THE SEVENTIES 1916

10 His time, his talents and his fortune were absorbed in the collection of material for a book — a History of Liberty — and it was never written. What he left behind him was a vast collection of disjointed notes, gathered from every age and every land and every tongue. No one had the clue to the labyrinth, or the secret of the plan which would have woven the fragments into one. A spiteful commentator said, when his letters were published, that "he won an immense reputation merely by doing nothing".
Ibid.

11 A historian to whom learning and judgment has not been granted in equal proportions.
Lytton Strachey, EMINENT VICTORIANS 1918

ROBERT ADAM (1728–1792)
Scottish architect in partnership with his brother James

12 The brothers Adam produced one of the finest pieces of town planning in Europe — the new town of Edinburgh. In addition they exploited, and I think one might almost

say invented, the strict, pure classicism that was to influence architecture all over Europe.
Sir Kenneth Clark, CIVILISATION 1969

1 Robert's taste was elegant; he knew how to utilise ornament without overdoing it, and adapted classical styles to modern requirements with great success. The Adam style might be described as rich without being vulgar.
T. P. O'Connor, *T.P's Weekly*, *A Master Builder* 7 *Apr* 1928

2 The chief merit of the Adam variation of the classical style was its recognition of the ancillary trades and crafts. It had moreover the attraction of being economical while retaining the appearance of being costly.
Sir Arthur Richardson, AN INTRODUCTION TO GEORGIAN ARCHITECTURE

3 Adam is all gingerbread, filigrain, and fan painting.
Horace Walpole, letter to Sir Horace Mann 22 *Apr* 1775

HENRY BROOKS ADAMS (1838–1918)
American historian

4 . . . with the wings of a beautiful but in-effectual conscience beating vainly in a vacuum jar.
T. S. Eliot. Quoted J. C. Levinson, THE HEART AND MIND OF HENRY ADAMS

5 Henry Adams, snob, scholar and mis-anthrope.
Alfred Kazin, ON NATIVE GROUNDS

6 Adams, in brief, did not care for truth unless it was amusing; for he was a modern nihilist, and hence a hedonist or nothing.
Yvor Winters, THE ANATOMY OF NONSENSE 1943

JOHN ADAMS (1735–1826)
Second President of the United States

7 His most constantly repeated journal entry is "At home, thinking".
William P. Cuming and Hugh Rankin, THE FATE OF A NATION 1975

8 He is vain, irritable, and a bad calculator of the force and probable effect of the motives which govern men. This is all the ill which can possibly be said of him.
Thomas Jefferson, letter to James Madison 1787

9 He has none of the essential arts which make up a courtier . . . there are thousands who, with a tenth part of his understanding, and without a spark of his honesty, would

distance him infinitely in any court in Europe.
Jonathan Sewell, in 1789. *Quoted Page Smith*, JOHN ADAMS

JOHN QUINCY ADAMS (1767–1848)
Sixth President of the United States

10 Quiet is not his sphere. And when a legiti-mate sphere of action does not present itself it is much to be feared that he will embrace an illegitimate one.
Charles Francis Adams, his son. Quoted Maria B. Hecht, JOHN QUINCY ADAMS, *A Personal History of an Independent Man*

11 When they talk about his old age and venerableness and nearness to the grave he knows better . . . He is an old roué who cannot live on slops and must have sulphuric acid in his tea.
Ralph Waldo Emerson, JOURNALS 1909

12 John Quincy Adams was a short, stout, bald, brilliant and puritanical twig off a short, stout, bald, brilliant and puritanical tree. Little wonder that he took the same view of the office of president as his father.
Alfred Steinberg, THE FIRST TEN

HENRY ADDINGTON (1757–1844)
(First Viscount Sidmouth)
British Prime Minister

13 Pitt is to Addington / As London is to Paddington
George Canning, THE ORACLE 1803

14 My impression of Addington and his col-leagues during this short part of the Session has been pretty much what it has heretofore been. They are, upon my soul, the feeblest — lowest, almost — of Men, still more of Ministers. When there is anything like a general attack on them they look as if they felt it all; they blush and look at one another in despair; they make no fight; or if they offer to defend themselves, no one listens but to laugh at them.
Thomas Creevey, letter to Dr J. Currie 21 *Dec* 1803

15 He was narrow-minded and imbecile beyond any person who has filled such posts since the Revolution. Lord Sidmouth might have made a highly creditable figure if he had continued to be Speaker, as well he might have done, twenty years longer . . . But his sudden elevation to the highest place in the state not only exposed his in-capacity, but turned his head. He began to

think highly of himself at the very moment when everybody else began to think meanly of him.
T. B. Macaulay, JOURNALS
26 *Dec* 1849

1 Addington was the man who opposed all reform in Parliament, who opposed the abolition of the slave trade, and whose sole answer to all the social problems of the period, which experienced hunger, strikes, sabotage, Luddism, the March of the Blanketeers and the massacre of Peterloo, was repression.
Neil McKendrick, *Sunday Times*, *Down With Progress*   12 *Dec* 1965

2 He had the indefinable air of a village apothecary inspecting the tongue of state.
Lord Rosebery, LIFE OF PITT   1891

3 Winchester has never been a school much connected with politics. The only Wyke-hamist Prime Minister, Henry Addington, is remembered only for his insignificance beside William Pitt.
James Saben-Clare, WINCHESTER COLLEGE   1981

4 Progress he viewed at all times with distrust and usually with violent hostility. He hated liberality; nine times out of ten it is cowardice, and the tenth time lack of principle.
Philip Ziegler, ADDINGTON

JOSEPH ADDISON (1672–1719)
English essayist and poet

5 Joseph Addison, essayist, poet, scholar, politician and Christian gentleman, was one of the most perfect men of whom the world has any record. So good was he that critics, in his own day and since, have not been able to make even a scratch on his fair name.
Anon., *Children's Newspaper* 14 *Jun* 1930

6 The style of Mr Addison is adorned by the female graces of elegance and mildness.
Edward Gibbon, AUTOBIOGRAPHY   1796

7 Whoever wishes to attain an English style, familiar but not coarse and elegant but not ostentatious, must give his days and nights to the volumes of Addison.
Samuel Johnson, LIVES OF THE POETS   1779

8 A parson in a tye-wig.
Dr Manderville. Quoted W. Clark Russell, A BOOK OF AUTHORS

9 Addison was the best company in the world.
Lady Mary Wortley Montagu. Quoted Rev. Joseph Spence, OBSERVATIONS, CHARACTERS AND ANECDOTES   1826

10 According to tradition at Holland House, Addison, when composing, used to walk up and down the long gallery there, with a bottle of wine at each end of it, which he finished during the operation.
Thomas Moore, DIARY   23 *Oct* 1818

11 No whiter page than Addison remains / He from the taste obscene reclaims our youth / And sets the passions on the side of Truth / Forms the soft bosom with the gentlest Art / And pours each human virtue in the heart.
Alexander Pope, IMITATIONS OF HORACE'S EPISTLES, BOOK II   1733

12 He was above all men in that talent called humour and enjoyed it in such perfection that I have often reflected, after a night spent with him, that I had had the pleasure of conversing with an intimate of Terence and Catallus, who had all their wit and nature heightened with humour more exquisite and delightful than any other man ever possessed.
Sir Richard Steele

13 Addison, meticulous and elaborate. His paragraphing is a model of precision. The balance and antithesis of his sentences are as carefully contrived as a stonemason's or a carpenter's. His diction, again, is as formal as the costume of his day; never relapsing into full-blooded colloquialism, never robust in its humour. Yet his style is to be analysed and respected — absorbed and forgotten — by anyone who wishes to master the mechanics of good English.
Sir William Emrys Williams, *Introduction to* A BOOK OF ENGLISH ESSAYS

14 It is due to Addison that prose is now prosaic — the medium which makes it possible for people of ordinary intelligence to communicate their ideas to the world.
Virginia Woolf, THE COMMON READER   1925

KONRAD ADENAUER (1876–1967)
West German Chancellor

15 It is certain that if I had not been dismissed by the British from my post as mayor I should not now be Federal Chancellor.
Konrad Adenauer, *Sunday Express* 13 *Nov* 1963

1 About two months ago I personally warned you of your responsibilities [as mayor of Cologne]. You have not fulfilled these responsibilities to my satisfaction. I am

convinced that with proper supervision and
energy on your part more could have been
done . . . you are therefore dismissed today
from your appointment as Oberberger-
meister of Cologne.
*Brigadier John Ashworth Barraclough, letter
of dismissal* 6 Oct 1945

AESCHYLUS (fifth century BC)
Greek dramatist

1 Such was Aeschylus' art that when the
actors playing the Furies began to wriggle
and stir on the theatre floor, whimpering
and snarling like waking hounds of hell
there was panic in the auditorium; we are
told that women screamed, fainted and even
gave birth in their fright. Such a reaction,
such a stupendous suspense of disbelief was
a tribute to Aeschylus' dramatic skill, the
poetic and theatrical skill which marked his
version of the story out from a dozen others.
*Frederic Raphael and Kenneth McLeish,
Observer magazine (of their translation of
the Oresteia for BBC2's production on
7 Mar 1979)*

AESOP (c.650BC)
Greek fabulist

2 As Aesop's fishes, they leap from the frying
pan into the fire.
Robert Burton, THE ANATOMY OF
MELANCHOLY 1621

3 Aesop's fly, sitting on the axle of the chariot,
has been much laughed at for exclaiming
"What a dust I do raise."
Thomas Carlyle on Boswell's THE LIFE OF
JOHNSON

CNAEUS JULIUS AGRICOLA (AD 37–93)
Roman statesman and soldier

4 Plain in his apparel, easy of access, and
never attended by more than one or two
friends, he was remarkable for nothing but
the simplicity of his appearance; insomuch
that they, who knew no criterion of merit
but external show and grandeur, as often as
they saw Agricola, were still to seek for the
great and illustrious character. His modesty
was art, which a few only could understand.
Cornelius Tacitus, LIFE OF AGRICOLA

5 By Agricola's order the Roman fleet sailed
round the Northern point and made the first
certain discovery that Britain is an island.
The cluster of Isles called the Orcades, till
then wholly unknown, was in this expedition added to the Roman Empire.
Ibid.

6 Lest his arrival in Rome should draw
together too great a concourse, he concealed his approach from his friends, and
entered the city privately in the dead of
night. With the same secrecy and in the
night also he went as commanded to present
himself to the emperor. Domitian received
him with a cold salute, and without a word,
left the conqueror of Britain to mix with the
servile creatures of the court.
Ibid.

WILLIAM HARRISON AINSWORTH
(1805–1882)
English novelist

7 His style is artificial and stilted to a degree.
Even in the most appalling crises his characters "reply to one another in the
affirmative" and call a church "the sacred
pile" or "the reverend structure". When a
beautiful girl is being roasted alive in a
burning house one friend says to another "I
will ascertain how the case stands" and
"having learned to his great satisfaction
what had occurred" (i.e. that she had been
saved) "he flew back and briefly explained
the situation to the parties".
CHAMBERS ENCYCLOPEDIA OF ENGLISH
LITERATURE (*edited by David
Patrick*) 1901

8 He had no real knack of arresting and
keeping the interest of those readers who
read merely for excitement; he was decidedly skilful at gleaning from memoirs and
other documents scraps of decoration suitable for his purpose.
George Saintsbury, NINETEENTH-CENTURY
LITERATURE 1896

JELAL-ED-DIN-MOHAMINED AKBAR
(1542–1605)
Mogul emperor

9 His wisdom, vigour and humanity are unex-
ampled in the East. He promoted commerce by constructing roads, establishing a
uniform system of weights and measures,
organising a vigorous police, and adjusting
taxation. For a born Mohammedan his
tolerance was wonderful, and Portuguese
missionaries from Goa were sent at his request to give him an account of the Christian faith. He even attempted to promulgate
a new religion of his own, an eclectic kind
of deism or natural religion.
CHAMBERS BIOGRAPHICAL DICTIONARY
(*edited by David Patrick and F. Hindes
Groome*) 1897

1 Akbar provided the Mogul empire with a
unifying cultural basis. Having made
Persian compulsory for all state officials, he
brought it about that for the first time in
medieval India Moslems and Hindus received their education in common schools
and read the same books on all subjects
from philosophy and history to mathematics
and medicine, translated into Persian from
all languages by a translation department.
Michael Prawdin, THE BUILDERS OF THE
MOGUL EMPIRE 1963

MARK AKENSIDE (1721–1770)
English poet and physician

2 There is another of these tame geniuses, a
Mr Akenside, who writes odes. In one of
them he has lately published he says "Light
the tapers, urge the fire". Had you not
rather make gods jostle in the dark than
light the candles for fear that they should
break their heads?
Horace Walpole

FRANCIS CHARLES AUGUSTUS, PRINCE ALBERT (1819–1861)
Prince Consort to Queen Victoria

3 I am only the husband and not the master in
this house.
Albert, three months after his marriage

4 While I shall be untiring in my efforts and
labours for the country to which I shall in
future belong I shall never cease to be a true
German, a true Coburg and Gotha man.
*Albert, in a letter to Prince Lowenstein, on
the eve of his marriage*

5 He considered that his private life was his
own affair, so lest there should be any evidence on which to found the very slightest
suspicion of anything either for laughter or
for caustic comment, he emitted, like a
cuttlefish, a sort of smoke-screen of
rectitude.
Frank B. Chancellor, PRINCE CONSORT

6 He lived, for over twenty years, a strictly
disciplined life, and since the court set the
fashion in manners, he was largely instrumental in altering the whole tone of English
society.
Ibid.

7 If ever a man killed himself for others it was
this "devout, unselfish and cultivated man".
He died for a country that was never his.
Bernard Darwin, *John o'London's Weekly
reviewing Hector Bolitho's* ALBERT THE
GOOD 2 *Apr* 1932

8 It is one of the puzzles of his life that with all
his conscientious and admirable work and
his really great ability he did not make
people like him.
Ibid.

9 His strength of character and his un-
selfishness attracted the weakness of others
while enabling him to lead himself a
solitary, self-reliant life, but only at terrible
cost. "I go on," he writes, "working at my
treadmill."
Viscountess Dunedin, *John o'London's
Weekly, The Man Who Was Never Young*
2 *Dec* 1933

10 His habit of rigid self-control made
spontaneous self-expression impossible to
him.
Ibid.

11 He made the virtues fashionable, and
though as a result of this he perhaps
increased the sum of human hypocrisy,
he also undoubtedly increased the sum of
human happiness.
W. R. Gordon, *News Chronicle, reviewing
Hector Bolitho's* ALBERT THE GOOD
31 *Mar* 1932

12 Albert was perhaps the first, and certainly
the most conspicuous, man to embark on a
completely new way of living, diametrically
opposed to the heartless manner of his
times.
Ibid.

13 He (Albert) is become so identified with her
(Victoria) that they are one person . . . it is
obvious that while she has the title he
is really discharging the functions of
Sovereign. He is King to all intents and
purposes.
Charles Greville, DIARY 1845

14 He is Victoria's legal husband, but he is not
the legal husband of the British Constitution.
Laurence Housman, HAPPY AND
GLORIOUS 1945

15 We are somehow reluctant to own that his
country owes so great a debt to one who was
always a foreigner and his heart — German.
Laurence Housman, *News Chronicle*
10 *Jul* 1947

16 Unquestionably, he acted in many instances
as a human lightning conductor, providing a
convenient target for those sections of the
Press and Parliament who feared to criticise
the Queen herself.
Robert Rhodes James, *Observer, The
Tightrope Walker* 11 *Jul* 1965

1 Albert helped me with the blotting paper.
Queen Victoria, in her journal, on dealing with state papers

LOUISA MAY ALCOTT (1832–1888)
American author

2 If Miss Alcott's experience of human nature has been small, as we should suppose, her admiration of it is nevertheless great.
Henry James. Quoted Katherine Anthony,
LOUISA MAY ALCOTT

ALEXANDER THE GREAT (356–323 BC)

3 He would wear the sacred robes of the gods at dinner parties, sometimes the purple cloak, the slippers and horns of Artemis, sometimes he would also dress as Hermes, often he carried a lion-skin and a club, like Hercules. A hushed silence fell on all those present as they were frightened; he was murderous and quite unbearable.
Ephippus of Olynthus

4 He spent his life, with legendary success, in the pursuit of personal glory; and until very recent times this was regarded as a wholly laudable aim.
Peter Green, ALEXANDER THE GREAT

5 One globe is all too little for the youth of Pella; he chafes uneasily within the limits of the world.
Juvenal, SATIRES

6 Darius wrote Alexander a letter, and sent friends to intercede with him, requesting him to accept as a ransom for his captives the sum of a thousand talents and offering him in exchange for his amity and alliance all the countries on this side of the Euphrates, together with the hand of one of his daughters in marriage. These propositions Alexander communicated to his friends, and when Parmenio told him that for his part if he were Alexander he would readily embrace them, "So would I", said Alexander "if I were Parmenio."
Plutarch (AD 46–120), PARALLEL LIVES

7 I read in the commentaries of Aristoxenus, that his skin had a marvellous good savour, and that his breath was very sweet, in so much that his body had so sweet a smell that all his apparel that he wore unto his body took thereof a passing delightful savour, as if it had been perfumed.
Ibid.

8 Alexander was himself at last defeated — by a mosquito. "The greatest man the world had ever seen" died in his tent in Babylon,

of malaria. Alexander learned the bitter lesson that it is easier to conquer than to hold. Dying, he was asked to whom he left his kingdom. Bitterly he replied, "to the strongest".
Wilson Pope, The (London) Star, Some Talk of Alexander 23 Feb 1924

9 Why may not imagination trace the noble dust of Alexander till he find it stopping a bung-hole.
Shakespeare, HAMLET (*Act 5 Scene 1*)

10 When in the world I lived I was the world's commander / By east, west, north and south, I spread my conquering might / My scutcheon plain declares that I am Alexander.
Shakespeare, LOVE'S LABOUR LOST (*Act 5 Scene 2*)

11 Alexander at the head of the world never tasted the true pleasure that boys of his own age have enjoyed at the head of school.
Horace Walpole, letter to Montagu 6 May 1736

ALEXANDER I (1777–1825)
Tsar of Russia

12 His judgement of men was execrable. Nowhere is this more apparent than in his initial misreading of Napoleon's character. This he measured in a manner which reminds us somewhat of Neville Chamberlain with Hitler, a mixture of ignorance, obstinacy and conceit. He saw himself as the enlightened monarch who would determine the structure of Europe. In the meantime he rashly believed that he could ride the tiger and, like Chamberlain, was staggered and outraged when the animal bit him.
Earl of Birkenhead, Daily Telegraph, The Inconsistent Tsar 2 May 1974

13 A more virtuous man, I believe, does not exist, nor one who is more enthusiastically devoted to better the condition of mankind.
Thomas Jefferson, letter to William Douane 20 May 1807

14 I have just seen Alexander. I am very satisfied with him; he is an extremely handsome, good young emperor, and he has more intelligence than is commonly thought.
Napoleon, after his first meeting, in a letter to Josephine. He was later to change his view and call Alexander "that shifty Byzantine".

15 Alexander was perpetually looking for a leader, someone who would show him a path through the quicksands of politics or the still more perilous dark nights of the soul. Sometimes he sought him among the warlords or statesmen, sometimes among

the monks and mystics. Always he found that he was pursuing a will-o'-the-whisp and recoiled, hurt and humiliated, yet quick to start off on another tack.
Philip Ziegler, The Times, A Gullible Tsar
28 Apr 1974

ALEXANDER OF TUNIS (1891–1969)
(Harold Rupert Leofric George)
Field Marshal, World War II

1 The nicest and most typical story of Alex is of his response when Winston Churchill went round the Cabinet table asking each individual for his point of view on a certain course of action. Alex's reply was "Well, Prime Minister, if it is right, we should do it." Politics were not his element.
Lord Home, THE WAY THE WIND BLOWS *1976*

2 He was the last of our gentlemanly generals.
Jan Morris, The Times 29 Mar 1973

3 I suppose most of us prefer our generals elegant; and though, as it turns out, Lord Alexander of Tunis got his suits from Montagu Burton, the Tailor of Taste, still no other soldier of our times has seemed so beautifully urbane, so unruffled, so patrician. Even khaki shorts did not look absurd on him.
Ibid.

4 He believed that reticence increases a soldier's authority. It was his nature. A gentleman does not utter everything he thinks.
Nigel Nicolson, ALEX: *The Life of Field Marshal Earl Alexander of Tunis*

5 His laziness was a virtue. It meant a capacity to delegate and in wartime it became a tremendous asset, because it meant that he could relax and unhook.
Field Marshal Sir Gerald Templar. Quoted Ibid.

QUEEN ALEXANDRA (1844–1925)
Consort to Edward VII

6 Sea-king's daughter from over the seas, Alexandra! / Saxon and Norman and Dane are we / But all of us Danes in our welcome to thee, Alexandra.
Alfred, Lord Tennyson, A WELCOME TO ALEXANDRA

7 Alex, good as she is, is not worth the price we have to pay for her in having such a family connection.
Queen Victoria, letter to her daughter, the Crown Princess of Prussia 11 Oct 1864

KING ALFRED (849–901)
King of Wessex

8 From his cradle a longing for wisdom before all things and among all the things of this present life, combined with his noble birth, filled the noble temper of his mind; but alas by the unworthy carelessness of his parents and tutors he remained ignorant of letters until his twelfth year.
Bishop Asser, LIFE OF KING ALFRED *893*

9 The wife of a cowherd with whom Alfred was staying was going to bake bread, and the King was sitting by the fireside making ready his bows and arrows. The woman saw that her bread was burning; she rushed up and removed it from the fire, upbraiding the King with these words; "Alack, man, why have you not turned over the bread when you see it is burning?" The misguided woman little thought she was talking to King Alfred who had fought so vigorously against the heathen and won so many victories over them.
Ibid.

10 Though established in royal power the King was wounded by the nails of many tribulations. From his twentieth to his forty-fifth year (in which he now is) he has been troubled incessantly by the severe visitation of an unknown disease; never an hour passes but he either suffers from it, or is nearly desperate from fear of it.
Ibid.

11 We are given (by Asser) a vision of a man of strong imagination, anxious and temperamental; always afraid of himself, afraid of illness and incapacity to the point of hypochondria, aware of a larger world than he himself lived in, desperately keen to live in it and to enable others to live in it.
Christopher Brooke, THE SAXON AND NORMAN KINGS *1963*

12 Alfred has been compared to Charlemagne who may have been his model. His efforts to revivify learning after wartime devastation and to dignify the common language were most remarkable. He codified the English laws and initiated the Anglo-Saxon Chronicle which recorded each year's events until the Norman Conquest. He made London a strong fortress. Like Charlemagne he fought successfully against the pagans, and

he and his sons made England a united kingdom.
H. J. Fleure and M. Davies, A NATURAL HISTORY OF MAN IN BRITAIN 1951

1   A mythical monarch with many of the gifts of Napoleon, and most of the qualities of Abraham Lincoln.
Philip Guedella, MEN OF AFFAIRS, MEN OF WAR, STILL LIFE

2   The trouble about King Alfred has always been one's complete inability to distinguish him from King Arthur and Prince Albert.
Ibid.

SIR LAWRENCE ALMA-TADEMA
(1836–1912)
Dutch-born Royal Academician

3   The general effect was exactly like a microscopic view of a small detachment of black beetles in search of a dead rat.
John Ruskin of THE PYRRHIC DANCE *in* THE ART OF ENGLAND

ROALD AMUNDSEN (1872–1928)
Norwegian polar explorer

4   Amundsen lived on into a life of anti-climax, to become depressed in his turn, but to die in a gallant venture; an airborne attempt to save General Nobile, stranded on Arctic ice.
Bernard Fergusson, Daily Telegraph, reviewing Roland Hungerford's SCOTT AND AMUNDSEN 11 *Oct* 1979

5   It was three o'clock in the afternoon (Friday 15th December 1911). It was journey's end. They had reached the Pole. Without a word they shook hands with one another. Then Amundsen got out the Norwegian flag, which had been bent to a pair of ski sticks . . . and pronounced these words: "So we plant you, dear flag, on the South Pole and give the plain on which it lies the name King Haakon VI's Plateau."
Roland Hungerford, SCOTT AND AMUNDSEN 1979

6   I must say, that man must have had his head screwed on right.
Captain Oates, in his diary, on hearing that Amundsen had beaten Scott to the South Pole

ELIZABETH GARRETT ANDERSON
(1836–1917)
British pioneer woman doctor

7   She entered much more into my mental state and way of life than any other doctor

could do because I was able to *tell* her so much more than I ever could or would tell to any *man*.
Josephine Butler. Quoted E. M. Bell, JOSEPHINE BUTLER

8   If one regards medicine as a skilled exercise in personal relationships one must rate her very high indeed. It was as a general practitioner that she excelled, with all the qualities of character that calling demands — courage, sense of duty, good judgement and warm humanity.
Naomi Mitchison, REVALUATIONS — STUDIES IN BIOGRAPHY

9   I am much pleased at Miss Garrett's success. She ought to have a vote for Westminster, but not to sit in Parliament. It would make for too much confusion.
Lord John Russell, letter to Lord Amberley 1870

HANS CHRISTIAN ANDERSEN (1805–1875)
Danish fairy-tale writer

10 As you hold a shell to your ear and hear the delicate murmuring, suggesting the untold magic of the sea, so you may hold a book of Hans Christian Andersen's fairy tales and hear between the covers the echoes of a world of creatures and things, all invested with his cunning touch of reality.
G. M. Isherwood Orr, T.P's Weekly, Storyteller of the Nursery 24 *Dec* 1927

11 Apart from his fairy-tales — he wrote 168 in all — his writings included novels, plays, travel books, autobiography and poetry. His best stories are masterpieces of their kind.
J. B. Priestley, LITERATURE AND WESTERN MAN 1960

12 The story goes that after Hans Andersen's famous visit to Dickens, the Dickens children wickedly set up a notice in the bedroom Andersen had occupied. 'Hans Andersen slept here for five weeks. It seemed like five years.'
The Times. Unsigned review of Monica Sterling's THE WILD SWAN: *Life and Times of Hans Christian Andersen* 28 *Oct* 1965

YURI ANDROPOV (1914–1984)
Soviet President

13 Yuri Andropov, who was only three years old in 1917, may be taken as a perfect example of the Soviet man. Brezhnev was nearly that, but being eight years older than his successor he could at least remember the Revolution and the Lenin years. Andropov

grew up under Stalin, the first Russian leader to do so.
Edward Cruickshank, *Observer*, *The Perfect Soviet Man* 26 Jun 1982

FIRST MARQUIS ANGLESEY (1768–1854)
Cavalry Commander at Waterloo

1 Lord Uxbridge (afterwards First Marquis of Anglesey) lost his leg at Waterloo, and afterwards had it coffined and buried in a neighbouring garden. According to tradition he exclaimed to the Duke of Wellington, "By God, sir, I've lost my leg!" to which the Duke is supposed to have replied, "By God, sir, so you have!"
Marquis of Anglesey, ONE-LEG: *the Life and Letters of Henry William Paget, 1st Marquis of Anglesey. The original version of the event is recorded by Creevey, as told to him by Lord Raglan*

QUEEN ANNE (1665–1714)
The last Stuart sovereign

2 Queen Anne was one of the smallest people ever set in a great place.
Walter Bagehot, THE ENGLISH CONSTITUTION 1867

6 Queen Anne had a person and appearance not at all ungraceful, till she grew exceedingly gross and corpulent. There was something of majesty in her look, but mixed with a sullen and constant frown, that plainly betrayed a gloominess of soul and a cloudiness of disposition within.
Sarah Churchill, First Duchess of Marlborough, CHARACTER OF QUEEN ANNE

4 Her friendships were flames of extravagant passion, ending in aversion.
Ibid.

5 Her love for the prince seemed in the eye of the world to be prodigiously great; and great as was the passion of her grief her stomach was greater, for that very day he died she ate three very large and hearty meals, so that one would think that as other people's grief took away their appetite, her appetite took away her grief.
Ibid.

6 She was not very wise, nor clever, but she was very like England.
Winston Churchill, MARLBOROUGH, HIS LIFE AND TIMES 1938

7 When in good humour she was meekly stupid, and when in bad humour was sulkily stupid.
T. B. Macaulay, HISTORY OF ENGLAND 1861

8 If one withholds admiration for Anne, it is impossible to withhold pity. Born to an inheritance of physical pain, the poor woman was also perpetually attending the funerals of her children. She had a genius for maternity but her children had no hold on life.
H. V. Morton, *Daily Express*, *These were our Queens* 16 Apr 1931

9 Here thou, great Anna! whom three realms obey / Does sometimes counsel take — and sometimes tea.
Alexander Pope, RAPE OF THE LOCK 1714

10 The most English of the Stuarts, she had a fund of commonsense so conspicuously lacking in the line. In time she developed a responsiveness to the moods and needs of her people that was wanting in cleverer and more intellectual persons; she was nearer them; it made her right when those were wrong. It was easy to underrate Anne as Sarah Churchill — who did so all her life — found out in the end.
A. L. Rowse, THE EARLY CHURCHILLS

11 Queen Anne was considered rather a remarkable woman and hence was usually referred to as Great Anna, or Annus Mirabilis.
 The queen had many favourites (all women), the most memorable of whom were Sarah Jenkins and Mrs Smashems, who were the first Wig and the first Tory. Sarah Jenkins was really the wife of the Duke of Marlborough, the famous General, inventor of the Ramillies Whig, of which Sarah wore the first example. Meanwhile the Whigs being the first to realize that the Queen had been dead all the time chose George I as King.
W. C. Sellar and R. J. Yeatman, 1066 AND ALL THAT

12 One of her hardest drudgeries was not connected with politics. In those days, when so many offences were punishable by death, the royal prerogative of mercy was constantly being called into action, Queen Anne took great pains in reading the disagreeable literature of such cases, and after faithful examination often directed her ministers to grant a reprieve.
G. M. Trevelyan, ENGLAND UNDER QUEEN ANNE 1930

1 The friendship of Anne Stuart and Sarah Churchill was rooted in genuine human affection. Anne's mind was as slow as a lowland river. Sarah kept her sharp and witty tongue in constant use.
Ibid.

2 Her subjects were pleased to believe that she consoled herself with brandy out of a tea-cup, and jokes were made about Queen Anne's cold tea.
Ibid.

ANNE OF CLEVES (1515–1557)
Fourth wife of Henry VIII

3 Anne of Cleves was the sister of this potential nuisance (the Duke of Cleves). Cromwell saw in her a good match for Henry. The motive was clear cut. But not till Henry saw Holbein's portrait did he allow Cromwell to begin in earnest.
Francis Hackett, HENRY VIII 1929

4 There is no remedy but to put my head into the yoke.
Henry VIII *to Thomas Cromwell on agreeing to marry Anne*

5 By her breasts she should be no maid; which, when I felt them, strake me so to the heart that I had neither will nor courage to prove the rest.
Henry VIII *to Thomas Cromwell after his wedding night*

6 The king found her so different from her picture that he swore they had brought him a Flanders mare.
Tobias Smollett, HISTORY OF ENGLAND 1759

SAINT ANSELM (1033–1109)
Italian-born Archbishop of Canterbury

7 St. Anselm was the sort of man to whom the angels brought messages.
Christopher Brooke, THE SAXON AND NORMAN KINGS 1963

8 One night when Riculfus, who held office of sacristan in the monastery was walking through the cloisters waiting for the moment when he would waken the brethren for vigils, he happened to pass the door of the chapter house. He looked in and saw Anselm standing in prayer in the midst of a great ball of blazing light.
Eadmer, LIFE OF SAINT ANSELM (*first printed* 1691)

GEORGE, LORD ANSON (1697–1762)
English Admiral

9 The settlers of South Carolina gave his name to districts, towns and mines. We still find on our maps Anson County, Anson-ville, Anson's Mines.
Sir John Barrow, LIFE OF ADMIRAL LORD ANSON 1839

10 It was a melancholy day for human nature when that stupid Lord Anson, after beating about for three years, found himself again at Greenwich. The circumnavigation of our globe was accomplished, but the illimitable was annihilated and a fatal blow dealt to all imagination.
Benjamin Disraeli, REMINISCENCES

11 Lord Anson was reserved and proud, and so ignorant that Sir Charles Williams said he had been round the world, but never in it.
Horace Walpole, MEMOIRS 1822

ARCHIMEDES (c.287–212 BC)
Greek mathematician

12 That Greek one then is my hero, who watched the bathwater / Rise above his navel and rushed out naked "I found it / I found it" into the street in all his shining and forgot / That others would only stare at his genitals.
Dannie Abse, WALKING UNDER WATER, *Letter to Alex Comfort*

13 Hiero, king of Syracuse, had given a certain quantity of gold to an artist to make a crown, and suspecting from the lightness of the crown that some silver had been used in making it he begged Archimedes to investi-gate the matter. This great man chanced to observe, in bathing, the water which ran over the side of the bath; and immediately perceived that, as the water was equal to the bulk of his body this would furnish him with the means of detecting the adulteration, by trying how much water a certain weight of silver displaced, and how much a certain weight of gold, and how much a certain mixture of the two. He rushed from his chamber shouting "I have found it! I have found it!"
Anon, THE PURSUIT OF KNOWLEDGE 1830

14 That Archimedes burnt the ships of Marcellus, with speculums of parabolic figures, at three furlongs, sounds hard unto reason.
Sir Thomas Browne, PSEUDOXIA EPIDEMICA 1646

1 Cicero desired to visit the grave of Archimedes, but to his surprise the magistrates of Syracuse denied that it existed. He requested them to assist him in the search. They conducted the obstinate but illustrious stranger to their most ancient burial ground. They observed a small column overhung with brambles. Cicero, looking on while they cleared away the rubbish, suddenly exclaimed "Here is the thing we are looking for!" His eye had caught the geometrical figures on the tomb, a sphere with a cylinder, and the inscription soon confirmed his conjecture.
Isaac D'Israeli, CURIOSITIES OF LITERATURE 1824

2 Archimedes of Syracuse was so great a mathematician that it seems impertinent to praise him. As an engineer and geometer he surpassed all the ancients in originality and brilliance. In all his work, in his study of conoids and spheroids, his analysis of the properties of spirals, his examination of the centres of gravity there can be seen the economy and the beauty that are the marks of mathematical genius.
George Huxley, THE GREEK WORLD, *Greek Mathematics and Astronomy (Edited by Hugh Lloyd-Jones)* 1962

3 Archimedes seems to have turned much of his attention to the construction of machines of extraordinary power, and he boasted of the unlimited extent of his art in the well-known expression "Give me a spot to stand on and I will move the earth."
PERCY ANECDOTES 1820

4 Oftimes his servants got him against his will to the baths, to wash and anoint him and yet being there he would ever be drawing out of the Geometrical figures, even in the very embers of the chimney. And while they were anointing him with oils and sweet savours, with his fingers he did draw lines on his naked body, so far was he taken from himself and brought into an ecstasy or trance with the delight he had in the study of Geometry and truly ravished with the love of the Muses.
Plutarch, PARALLEL LIVES

5 Archimedes being in his study when the city [Syracuse] was taken, busily seeking out for himself the demonstration of some geometrical proposition, he neither saw nor heard any sign of enemies, much less knew the city was taken. He wondered when he saw a soldier by him that bade him go with him to Marcellus. He spoke to the soldier and bade him tarry until he had done his conclusion; but the soldier being angry with

his answer, drew out his sword and killed him.
Ibid.

LUDOVICO ARIOSTO (1474–1533)
Italian poet

6 When Ariosto was rambling through the Apennines he fell in with a band of robbers. They were on the point of taking from him his purse, and perhaps his life, when one of them recognised him as the author of 'Orlando'. They instantly threw themselves at his feet, entreated pardon for their intended injury, and singing his verses, guided him to a place of greater safety.
PERCY ANECDOTES 1820

7 In Ariosto the old legends with which he was ostensibly dealing have arrived in an age very different from the one when they were first conceived, so that, although he retells them with great skill, his narrative glitters with irony and mockery. Early in the sixteenth century he struck a note that is repeated and echoed through much of the literature that followed.
J.B. Priestley, LITERATURE AND WESTERN MAN 1960

8 It is all grace and charm and subtle mockery in his ultra-romantic epic 'Orlando'.
Ibid.

ARISTOPHANES (c.448–388 BC)
Greek dramatist

9 An Aristophanic comedy does not have a 'plot' in the ordinary sense of the word; it builds wild fantasies on the basis of a topical idea, and its humour relies greatly on literary parody and satirical comment on living people.
K. J. Dover, THE GREEK WORLD, *Greek Literature After Homer (Edited by Hugh Lloyd-Jones)* 1962

10 In Aristophanic comedy there was no limit, in word or action, to obscenity. Living men were not only ridiculed, but grossly slandered. Aristophanes seems to have been free to bring any accusation, however monstrous, or cruel, or indecent, against anybody.
Ibid.

ARISTOTLE (384–322 BC)
Greek philosopher

11 Aristotle said melancholy men of all others are the most witty.
Robert Burton, THE ANATOMY OF MELANCHOLY 1621

1   Aristotle was asked how much educated men were superior to uneducated. "As much," said he, "as the living are to the dead."
Diogenes Laertius, LIVES AND OPINIONS OF FAMOUS PHILOSOPHERS: ARISTOTLE (C.250 AD)

2   Aristotle, that hath an oar in every water and meddleth with all things.
Michel de Montaigne, ESSAYS   1588

3   Aristotle was the first, possibly the only, ancient Greek with the true naturalist's passion for minute observation. His description of the habits of the cuttlefish, his accurate account of the life-cycle of the gnat, his observation of the wryneck's tongue or the owl's eyes — all these conjure up a picture of Aristotle spending hour after hour out in the open air in absorbed contemplation of the creatures round him.
J. E. Raven, THE GREEK WORLD: *Greek Science (Edited by Hugh Lloyd-Jones)*   1962

SIR RICHARD ARKWRIGHT (1732–1792)
English inventor

4   He separated from his wife not many years after their marriage because she, convinced that he would starve his family, broke some of his experimental models of machinery.
Edward Baines, HISTORY OF COTTON MANUFACTURE

5   Arkwright's spinning frame, invented about 1770, is always quoted as the beginning of mass production, on the whole, rightly. He and his like gave England a flying start in the economy of the nineteenth century; but they also produced the dehumanisation which obsessed almost every imaginative writer of the time.
Sir Kenneth Clark, CIVILISATION   1969

6   The spinning mule was not the original idea of its patentee, Richard Arkwright, an unscrupulous operator who — unlike most real inventors of the period — died rich.
E. J. Hobsbawm, INDUSTRY AND EMPIRE   1968

7   Arkwright was a tremendous worker and a man of marvellous energy, ardour and application to business . . . At fifty years of age he set to work to learn English grammar and improve himself in writing and orthography.
Samuel Smiles, SELF-HELP   1859

THOMAS AUGUSTINE ARNE (1710–1778)
Composer

8   Thoughtless, dissipated and careless, he neglected, or rather scoffed at all other but musical reputation. And he was so little scrupulous in his ideas of propriety that he took pride rather than shame in being publicly classed, even in his declining years, as a man of pleasure.
Fanny Burney, A MEMOIR OF DR BURNEY   1832

9   Michael Festing, calling in King Street one day, found Arne diligently practising the violin, with his music supported on the lid of a coffin. Horrified with the sight, he declared he could not play under such circumstances, as he would be constantly imagining there might be a corpse in the coffin. "So there is," said Arne, and gave proof by lifting the lid.
W. H. Cummings, DR ARNE AND RULE BRITANNIA

MATTHEW ARNOLD (1822–1888)
English poet

10 I proceeded to Chicago. An evening paper was given me soon after I arrived. I opened it and found the following picture of myself: "He has harsh features, supercilious manners, parts his hair down the middle, wears a single eyeglass and ill-fitting clothes."
Matthew Arnold, writing of an American lecture

11 He is an admirable poet in one sense — an admirable *poetical writer*. But he must break up all his ice of meditation and consent to feel like a child and attain to seeing like a seer, before we can call him a poet in the absolute sense.
Elizabeth Barrett Browning, letter to Mrs David Ogilvy   19 Feb 1854

12 Mr Arnold, when at college, bathed in a river in front of a village. The clergyman came to remonstrate. Matt, quite naked, waved the towel gracefully and with quiet seriousness said, "Is it possible that you see anything indelicate in the human form divine?"
George Eliot, DIARY   10 Apr 1878

13 I met Matthew Arnold and had a few words with him. He is not as handsome as his photographs — or his poetry.
Henry James, letter to Charles Eliot Norton   31 Mar 1873

14 Arnold is a dandy Isaiah, a poet without passion, whose verse, written in a surplice,

is for freshmen and for gentle maidens who will be wooed to the arms of these future rectors.
George Meredith, Fortnightly Review July 1909

1 When Abraham Lincoln was murdered / The one thing that interested Matthew Arnold / Was that the assassin shouted in Latin / As he leapt on the stage / This convinced Matthew / That there was still hope for America.
Christopher Morley, POINTS OF VIEW. *The Latin phrase referred to was "Sic semper tyrannis"*

2 Matthew Arnold who did notable service to the age as a literary and social critic, deliberately tried to steel himself against romanticism, and many of his more ambitious poems read like charming exercises in the classical manner, but in his shorter and more revealing poems, of which "Dover Beach" is a fine example, he expresses with romantic urgency the bewilderment, often darkening to despair, of a sensitive mind in a sadly confused time.
J. B. Priestley, LITERATURE AND WESTERN MAN   1960

3 An Aberdeen granite tomb, with his chilblained, mittened musings.
Edith Sitwell, ALEXANDER POPE   1930

4 Poor Matt! He's gone to Heaven, no doubt — but he won't like God.
Robert Louis Stevenson

THOMAS ARNOLD (1795–1842)
Headmaster of Rugby School

5 My object will be, if possible, to form Christian men, for Christian boys I can hardly hope to make.
Arnold, in a letter, on being appointed headmaster of Rugby in 1828

6 By introducing morals and religion into his scheme of education he altered the whole atmosphere of Public School life. Henceforeward the old rough-and-tumble which was typified by the régime of Keats at Eton became impossible. After Dr Arnold no public school could afford to ignore the virtues of respectability.
Lytton Strachey, EMINENT VICTORIANS: *Dr Arnold*   1918

7 Teachers and prophets have strange afterhistories and that of Dr Arnold has been no exception. The earnest enthusiast who strove to make his pupils Christian gentlemen, and who governed his school according to the principles of the Old

Testament has proved to be the founder of athletics and good form.
Ibid.

ROGER ASCHAM (1515–1568)
English scholar, tutor to Elizabeth I

8 I had rather thrown ten thousand pounds into the sea than have lost my Ascham.
Queen Elizabeth I

9 The first book that can be worth naming at all is Ascham's 'Schoolmaster' published in 1570 and probably written some years before. Ascham is plain and strong in his style but without grace or warmth; his sentences have no harmony of structure. He stands, however, as far as I have seen, above all other writers in the first half of Queen Elizabeth's reign.
Henry Hallam, INTRODUCTION TO THE LITERATURE OF EUROPE   1839

10 It must be owned that Ascham contributed very much to refine and improve the language and, as he was an eminent scholar, to bring the writing of it into repute.
Bishop Richard Hurd, COLLECTED WORKS   1811

11 He is said to have lived and died in poverty owing to an addiction to cockfighting.
Margaret Tubb, THE AGE OF CHAUCER *(edited by Boris Ford)*   1954

HERBERT HENRY ASQUITH (1852–1928)
(Earl of Oxford and Asquith)
British Prime Minister

12 For twenty years he has held a season ticket on the line of least resistance and gone wherever the train of events has carried him, lucidly justifying his position at whatever point he has happened to find himself.
L. S. Amery, speech in the House of Commons (1916)

13 He could stand more in the way of late hours and airless surroundings than any other public man. Until the last few years of his life he had no idea whether a room was hot or cold, and to the last it was a matter of indifference to him whether he inhaled cigar smoke or oxygen.
Cyril Asquith, LIFE OF LORD OXFORD AND ASQUITH

14 Musicians were never left in any doubt that he considered their performances a compound of noise and nuisance which was only tolerable if not too loud.
Ibid.

1 His modesty amounts to a deformity.
Margot Asquith, AUTOBIOGRAPHY   1946

2 He brought to cabinet meetings the cool
calculation that he displayed at the bridge
table.
Robert Cecil, LIFE IN EDWARDIAN
ENGLAND   1969

3 Arthur Balfour is wicked and moral.
Asquith is good and immoral
Winston Churchill. Quoted Ernest Raymond,
MR BALFOUR

4 His mind opened and shut smoothly and
exactly, like the breech of a gun.
Winston Churchill, GREAT
CONTEMPORARIES   1937

5 Black and wicked, and with only a nodding
acquaintance with the truth.
Lady Cunard. Quoted Henry Channon,
DIARY   7 *Jan* 1944

6 Asquith worries too much about small
points. If you were buying a large mansion
he would come to you and say, "Have you
thought there is no accommodation for the
cat?"
*David Lloyd George, letter to Lord
Riddell*   1915

7 Asquith, an unemotional man, wept as he
proposed the (inoperative) Miner's Mini-
mum Wage Bill, which a national coal strike
had forced down the throats of the government.
E. J. Hobshawm, INDUSTRY AND
EMPIRE   1968

8 He struck me as having a head far too large
for his body. His face was of a pleasant, rosy
hue, rather like that of a genial baby, his
body was short and rather inclined to
stoutness. Two things only about him
suggested the sheather of swords — his hair
and his voice. The former was long and
white and so silky that one longed to stroke
it. His voice was deep and rich, with a quality that also suggested silk.
Beverley Nichols, TWENTY-FIVE   1926

EMMA ALICE MARGARET (MARGOT)
ASQUITH (1864–1945)
(Countess of Oxford and Asquith)

9 A café chantant attached to a cathedral.
*Anon. Quoted John Joliffe, The Times,
Yours faithfully*   25 *Nov* 1982

10 I do not say that I was ever what is called
'plain', but I have the sort of face that bores
me when I see it on other people.
Margot Asquith, Lilliput magazine   1938

11 She had a great taste for writing obituaries
and rarely missed an opportunity of doing
so. Once when she was staying with Arthur
Balfour he was surprised to find, written in
Margot's hand on a sheet of paper, an unfinished opening — "So Arthur Balfour is
dead —"
*Mark Bonham Carter. Introduction to
Margot Asquith's* AUTOBIOGRAPHY   1936

12 Beneath a bony, witchlike head, with a big
hooked nose and sharp dark eyes moved
and attitudinised a small skinny body
dressed usually in the height of fashion.
*Lord David Cecil, Observer, Staying with
Margot*   20 *Dec* 1981

13 The affair between Margot Asquith and
Margot Asquith will live on as one of the
prettiest love stories in all history.
*Dorothy Parker, reviewing Margot
Asquith's* AUTOBIOGRAPHY *in the New
Yorker*

14 Her face, except her forehead, is wrinkled
past make-up; she uses a vivid orange lip-
stick not perhaps as an expression of her
vitality but as a gesture to it. Her voice is the
unfaltering instrument of moods that still
seem to be as varying as a debutante's. If an
intelligent man of half her years told me he
had fallen in love with her I should believe
him.
Reginald Pound, THEIR MOODS AND
MINE   1937

15 When Lord and Lady Glenconner and Sir
Edward Grey were staying with the
Asquiths at The Wharf, Lady Glenconner
and Sir Edward were walking in the garden
at an early hour, hearing the bird chorus,
and watching and talking about the small
creatures and their ways, they were startled
to hear a feminine voice unmistakably that
of their hostess observe witheringly just
behind them, "And I know a damned old
robin, too, when I hear one."
Osbert Sitwell, LAUGHTER IN THE NEXT
ROOM   1949

FRED ASTAIRE (1899–   )
American film actor and dancer

1 He is the nearest we are ever likely to get to a human Mickey Mouse.
Graham Greene. Quoted Leslie Halliwell, FILMGOER'S BOOK OF QUOTES 1973

2 I have never met anyone who did not like Fred Astaire. Somewhere in his sad, monkey-sad face, his loose legs, his shy grin, or perhaps the anxious diffidence of his manner, he has found the secret of persuading the world.
C. A. Lejeune. Ibid.

3 The audience meets Mr Astaire and the film at their best when he is adjusting his cravat to an elaborate dance routine or saying delicious things with his flashing feet that a lyricist would have difficulty in putting into words.
André Sennwald, reviewing THE GAY DIVORCEE

NANCY WITCHER, VISCOUNTESS ASTOR (1879–1964)
First woman MP to take her seat in the House of Commons

4 I am a novel principle and have to be endured.
Lady Astor to the House of Commons 1921

5 Lady Astor, born Nancy Langhorne in Greenwood, Virginia, U.S.A., once invited the comedian Will Rogers to her luxurious English country estate. He looked over the establishment and commented "Nancy, you sure have out-married yourself."
Bennett Cerf, SHAKE WELL BEFORE USING 1948

6 When you come into the Debating Chamber, Nancy, I feel as if you had come into my bathroom and I had only a sponge to cover myself with.
Winston Churchill. Quoted John Beavers, Sunday Referee 19 Feb 1939

7 Her uncompromising Protestantism was tenuous but unyielding, like a strand of barbed wire in a hedge.
Walter Eliot. Quoted Christopher Sykes, NANCY

8 Viscount Waldorf Astor owned Britain's two most influential newspapers *The Times* and *The Observer*, but his American wife Nancy had a wider circulation than both papers put together.
Emery Kelen, PEACE IN THEIR TIME

9 Nancy was a devout Christian Scientist, but not a good one. She kept confusing herself with God. She didn't know when to step aside and give God a chance.
Mrs Gordon Smith. Quoted Elizabeth Langhorne, NANCY ASTOR AND HER FRIENDS

10 She wasn't courageous if by courage is meant mastery of fear. She was fearless of physical danger, of criticism, of people.
The Times, Obituary 4 May 1964

CLEMENT RICHARD ATTLEE (1883–1967)
British Prime Minister

11 An empty taxi drew up outside No. 10 and out got Clem Attlee.
Variously attributed

12 Few thought him even a starter / There were many who thought themselves smarter / But he ended PM, CH and OM / An Earl and a Knight of the Garter.
Attlee, of himself

13 He seems determined to make a trumpet sound like a tin whistle.
Aneurin Bevan, Tribune 1945

14 He brings to the fierce struggle of politics the tepid enthusiasm of a lazy summer afternoon at a cricket match.
Ibid.

15 He is a sheep in sheep's clothing.
Winston Churchill

16 Mr Attlee combines a limited outlook with strong qualities of resistance.
Winston Churchill. Speech 27 Sep 1951

17 He is a modest little man with much to be modest about.
Winston Churchill

18 Mr Attlee touches nothing that he does not dehydrate.
The Economist 16 Aug 1947

19 Labour's greatest triumph was scored under Attlee, who had the charisma of an average building society branch manager.
Eric Hobshawm, Observer, Sayings of the Week 9 Oct 1983

20 He is a bourgeois, who is strangling the British bourgeoisie out of existence with a smile.
Peter Howard, Daily Mail 25 May 1947

21 Attlee made no claims to understand technical fields such as economics which he engagingly regarded as a subject similar to medicine, in which one consulted qualified experts and if necessary took a second or third opinion. But his pre-eminent virtue of

mind was his clear knowledge of what he understood and what he did not.
Douglas Jay, CHANGE AND FORTUNE   1980

1   I usually suggested a precise course of action to which he need only reply "Yes" or "No". Among the longest comments I ever extracted from him was "Wouldn't serve any useful purpose."
Ibid.

2   His capacity for saying nothing was absolutely pre-eminent and he avoided all the traps which other people fell into. We used to say that he would never use one syllable where none would do.
Douglas Jay, Thames TV, *The Day Before Yesterday*   1970

3   Charisma? He did not recognise the word except as a clue in his beloved *Times* crossword.
James Margach, THE ABUSE OF POWER   1981

4   He succeeded in presiding over the biggest social, political and economic revolutions of the century. He never lost a single by-election and after five years of ceaseless Press harassment he polled the highest popular vote at any election before or since.
Ibid.

5   He was a man who tucked his personality behind a pipe and left colleagues and public to make what they could of the smoke signals.
Frederick Newman, Daily Sketch. Quoted ibid.

6   Attlee is a charming man, but as a public speaker he is, compared to Winston, like a village fiddler after Paganini.
Harold Nicolson, DIARIES   10 *Nov* 1947

7   He reminds me of nothing so much as a dead fish before it has had time to stiffen.
George Orwell. Quoted Nigel Rees , QUOTE UNQUOTE

8   He must have been pretty shrewd because he managed to survive three conspiracies to throw him out.
Lord Shinwell, Thames TV, *The Day Before Yesterday*   1970

JOHN AUBREY (1626–1697)
English biographer and antiquary

9   About as credulous an old goose as one could hope to find outside of Gotham.
B. G. Johns, Gentleman's Magazine   1893

10   "'Tis time", wrote Sir Thomas Browne "to observe occurrences and let nothing escape us." Nobody took him more literally than his friend John Aubrey, who could never let any part of the past go. He helped to found English archaeology, not by scholarly method but by sheer curiosity, energy, and obsession.
Pat Rogers, Observer, reviewing MONUMENTA BRITANNICA   4 *Apr* 1982

11   He was clever enough to understand the Newtonian system, but he was not clever enough to understand that astrology was an absurdity; and so in his crowded curiosity shop of a brain, astrology and astronomy both found a place and were given equal value.
Lytton Strachey, JOHN AUBREY

12   A shiftless person, roving and maggotie-headed, and sometimes little better than crazed. And being exceedingly credulous, would stuff his many letters with follities and misinformations, which would sometimes guide him into the paths of error.
Anthony à Wood (1632–1695)

WYSTAN HUGH AUDEN (1907–1973)
British poet

13   My face looks like a wedding cake that has been left out in the rain.
Auden. Quoted Humphrey Carpenter, AUDEN: A BIOGRAPHY

14   In a century of the symbolist, surreal and absurd, W. H. Auden is essentially a poet of the reasonable.
James D. Brophy, W. H. AUDEN

15   I heard you read; no dramatist / More interested in what you said / Than how you said it: Airless stateside vowels / Ricocheting off the kippered panelling / Like custard pies, yet more telling / Than bullets or blood transfusions.
Charles Causley, LETTER FROM JERICHO

16   We have one poet of genius in Auden who is able to write prolifically, carelessly and exquisitely, nor does he seem to have to pay any price for his inspiration. It is as if he worked under the influence of some mysterious drug, which presents him with a private vision, a mastery of form and vocabulary.
Cyril Connolly, ENEMIES OF PROMISE   1938

17   I see him striding towards me along Yarmouth Pier, a tall figure with loose, violent, impatient movements, dressed in dirty grey flannels and a black evening bow

tie. On his straw-coloured hair was planted a very broad-brimmed black hat.
Christopher Isherwood. Quoted Charles Osborne, W. H. AUDEN   1980

1 He drank innumerable cups of tea each day as if his large white, apparently bloodless body needed continual reinforcement of warmth.
Ibid.

2 One never steps twice into the same Auden.
Randall Jarrell, THE THIRD BOOK OF CRITICISM   1969

3 An engaging, bookish, American talent, too verbose to be memorable and too intellectual to be moving.
Philip Larkin. Quoted George T. Wright, W. H. AUDEN

4 Auden killed his own poetry by going to America where, having sacrificed the capacity to make art out of life, he tried to make art out of art instead.
Philip Larkin, REQUIRED WRITING   1983

5 A man like Auden, with his fierce repudiation of half-way houses, and his gentle integrity makes one feel terribly discontented with one's own smug successfulness. I go to bed feeling terribly Edwardian and back-number and yet, thank God, delighted that people like Wystan Auden should actually exist.
Harold Nicolson, DIARY   4 Aug 1933

6 The high watermark, so to speak, of Socialist literature is W. H. Auden, a sort of gutless Kipling.
George Orwell, THE ROAD TO WIGAN PIER   1937

7 Interviewed by his future English tutor, Nevill Coghill, he was asked what he intended to do when he left university. "I am going to be a poet" he replied.
Charles Osborne, W. H. AUDEN   1980

8 Throughout his summer holiday he liked to have a fire in the sitting room whenever possible and he invariably slept with two thick blankets and an eiderdown, both his and Isherwood's overcoats and all the rugs in his bedroom piled on his bed.
Ibid.

9 Isherwood found his visitor stimulating, exasperating and also disturbing. Stimulating was the literary talk, exasperating the nicotine stains and dirty thumb marks on his precious books, not to speak of the hole burnt in his only overcoat by a cigar; disturbing were Auden's shameless descriptions of his sexual adventures, and his amateur psycho-analysis of his host.
Ibid.

10 Auden, a real and often powerful poet even though apt to keep his cleverness showing, was sometimes obscure because his poetry used private references, private jokes, so that at these times the reader seems only an outsider at a private party of old friends.
J. B. Priestley, LITERATURE AND WESTERN MAN   1960

11 He is English in his toughness, his richness, his obstinacy, his adventurousness, his eccentricity. What America has done for Auden is to help him to acquire a mind that feels itself at the centre of things. It has given him a point of view that is inter- or super-national
Edmund Wilson, THE BIT BETWEEN MY TEETH   1965

12 Mr Auden seems to have been arrested at the mentality of an adolescent schoolboy. His mind has always been haunted, as the minds of boys at prep school still are, by parents and uncles and aunts. His love poems seem unreal and ambiguous as if they were the product of adolescent flirtations and prep-school homosexuality.
Edmund Wilson, THE SHORES OF LIGHT   1952

JOHN JAMES AUDUBON (1780–1851)
American ornithologist

13 I take a bird neatly killed, put him up with wires and when satisfied with the truth of the position, I take my palette and finish off the bird at one sitting — often, it is true, of fourteen hours.
Audubon describing his method of working, which differed from all previous bird-artists, who used stuffed specimens as models

14 He prattled about himself like an infant, gloried in his long hair, he admired the fine curve of his nose, thought 'blood' a great thing and reverenced the great. Well, happy is the man who has no greater errors than these.
Robert Buchanan, LIFE AND ADVENTURES OF AUDUBON THE NATURALIST

15 A bounder, a bankrupt in his early days, Audubon became in his mid-forties an institution, his expeditions regarded as part of the advancement of American science — with the Great Cham no doubt talking nineteen to the dozen every step of the way.
Michael Maxwell Scott, Daily Telegraph, reviewing John Chancellor's AUDUBON, A BIOGRAPHY   8 Feb 1979

SAINT AUGUSTINE (354–430)
Italian divine

1 I am interested in the shape of ideas even if I do not believe in them. There is a wonderful sentence in Augustine, "Do not despair; one of the thieves was saved; do not presume, one of the thieves was damned." That sentence has a wonderful shape. It is the shape that matters.
Samuel Beckett. Quoted John Lahr, UP AGAINST THE FOURTH WALL

2 The conscious mind allows itself to be trained, like a parrot, but the unconscious does not — which is why St. Augustine thanked God for not making him responsible for his dreams
Carl Jung, PSYCHOLOGY AND ALCHEMY 1953

AUGUSTUS CAESAR (63 BC–14 AD)
First Roman emperor

3 He was wont to say a battle or a war ought never to be undertaken unless the prospect of gain overbalanced the fear of loss. For men who pursue small advantages with no small hazard resemble those who fish with a golden hook, the loss of which, if the line should break, could never be compensated by all the fish they might take.
Caius Tranquillus Suetonius (75–160 AD), LIVES OF THE FIRST TWELVE CAESARS

4 That he was guilty of several acts of adultery is not denied, even by his friends; but they allege in excuse for it, that he engaged in these intrigues, not from lewdness, but from policy, in order to discover more easily the designs of his enemies, through their wives.
Ibid.

5 The cohorts which yielded their ground in time of action he decimated, and fed on barley. Centurions, as well as common sentinels, who deserted their post when on guard he punished with death. For other misdemeanours he inflicted upon them various kinds of disgrace, such as obliging them to stand all day before the praetorium, sometimes in their tunics only, and without their belts, sometimes to carry poles ten feet long, or sods of turf.
Ibid.

6 The city (Rome) which was not built in a manner suitable to the grandeur of the empire, and was liable to inundations of the Tiber, as well as to fires, was so much improved under his administration that he boasted, not without reason, that he "found it of brick, but left it of marble".
Ibid.

JANE AUSTEN (1775–1817)
English novelist

7 She knew exactly what she was doing. Perfection is not obtained by blundering; and even if it were, to blunder into perfection in six consecutive works would be inconceivable. Miss Austen was a highly sophisticated artist.
Walter Allen, THE ENGLISH NOVEL 1954

8 More can be learnt from Miss Austen about the nature of the novel than from almost any other writer.
Ibid.

9 The scope of her art is not in fact lessened by her ignoring of the major events in the history of her times; the reality of her world would not in any way have been intensified had she dragged in references to the Napoleonic wars or the Industrial Revolution.
Ibid.

10 Beside her Joyce seems as innocent as grass / It makes me most uncomfortable to see / An English spinster of the middle class / Describe the amorous effects of "brass" / Reveal so frankly and with such sobriety / The economic basis of society.
W. H. Auden, LETTER TO LORD BYRON

11 I could no more write a romance than an epic poem. I could not sit seriously down to write a serious romance under any other motive than to save my life; and if it were indispensable to me to keep it up, and never relax into laughing at myself or other people, I am sure I should be hung before I had finished the first chapter.
Jane Austen in a letter to James Stainer Clarke, who had suggested she write a historical romance illustrative of the House of Coburg, 1 Apr 1816

12 No one ever made less fuss about the pains of authorship. There was nothing of the thwarted genius about Jane Austen.
Kenneth Bell, Teacher's World 4 Dec 1929

13 "Tell me," said Madame la Duchesse in a lecherous whisper, "where may I get a book by the nottee Miss Austen."
Caryl Brahms and S. J. Simon, NO NIGHTINGALES

1   I should hardly like to live with her ladies and gentlemen in their elegant but confined homes.
Charlotte Brontë, letter to G. H. Lewes 12 Jan 1848

2   Miss Austen is only shrewd and observant.
Ibid.

3   Jane Austen is slandered if she is called either a miniaturistic or a naturalistic novelist. Her books are domestic in the sense that *Oedipus Rex* is domestic. Her moral dilemmas are often drawn in precisely oedipal terms.
Brigid Brophy, DON'T NEVER FORGET

4   A child of the high-spirited, unsqueamish eighteenth century.
David Cecil, A PORTRAIT OF JANE AUSTEN 1978

5   Jane Austen — it is one of the most important facts about her — was born in the eighteenth century and spiritually she stayed there. A contemporary of Coleridge and Wordsworth, her view of things had much more in common with that of Dr Johnson.
Ibid.

6   Some people are well worth knowing, even as acquaintances. Jane Austen is one of them.
Ibid.

7   Mr Wordsworth used to say that though he admitted that her novels were an admirable copy of life he could not be interested in productions of that kind; unless truth to nature were presented to him clarified, as it were, by the pervading light of imagination it had scarce any attraction in his eyes.
Sara Coleridge, letter to Emily Trevenen Aug 1838

8   Scott misunderstood it when he congratulated her for painting on a square of ivory. She is a miniaturist, but never two-dimensional. All her characters are round, or capable of rotundity.
E. M. Forster, ASPECTS OF THE NOVEL 1927

9   She has given us a multitude of characters, all in a certain sense common-place, all such as we meet every day. Yet they are all as perfectly discriminated from each other as if they were the most eccentric of human beings.
T. B. Macaulay, Edinburgh Review Jan 1843

10 Home, and finished *Persuasion*. I have now read over again all Miss Austen's novels. Charming they are, but I found a little more to criticise than formerly. Yet there are in this world no compositions which approach nearer to perfection.
T. B. Macaulay, Journals 1 May 1851

11 Nothing much happens in her books, and yet, when you come to the bottom of the page, you eagerly turn it to learn what will happen next. The novelist who has the power to achieve this has the most precious gift a novelist can possess.
W. Somerset Maugham, TEN NOVELS AND THEIR AUTHORS 1955

12 Till *Pride and Prejudice* showed what a precious gem was hidden in that unbending case she was no more regarded in society than a poker or a firescreen or any other thin upright piece of wood or iron that fills its corner in peace and quietness. The case is very different now, she is still a poker — but a poker of whom everyone is afraid.
Mary Russell Mitford, letter to Sir William Elford 3 Apr 1815

13 Mamma says she was then the prettiest, silliest, most affected husband-hunting woman she ever remembers and a friend of mine who visits her now says she has stiffened into the most perpendicular, precise, taciturn piece of single blessedness that ever existed.
Ibid.

14 Miss Austen has no romance — none at all. What vile creatures her parsons are.
John Henry Newman, letter to Mrs John Mozley 10 Jan 1837

15 I love Jane Austen, but when her admirers call themselves "Jane-ites" and begin smirking and making masonic grimaces at one another, whether in speech or in print, I rush for consolation to some splendid but cultless old girl. Maria Edgeworth would do nicely.
William Plomer, AN ALPHABET OF LITERARY PREJUDICES

16 It is no valid objection to Jane Austen as a writer that she limits her field; limitation is the condition of good art. One of her strengths was that she knew perfectly well what she could do and what she could not do.
A. L. Rowse, PORTRAITS AND VIEWS: Jane Austen as Social Realist 1979

17 That young lady has a talent for describing the involvements and feelings and characters of ordinary life which is to me the most wonderful thing I ever met with.
Sir Walter Scott, Journals 14 Mar 1826

1 I think *Pride and Prejudice* a very superior
   work. It depends not on any of the common
   resources of novel-writers, no drownings,
   no conflagrations, no runaway horses, no
   rencontres and disguises. I really think it is
   the *most probable* I have ever read. It is not
   a crying book, but the interest is very
   strong.
   Charlotte Smith,
   letter to her mother   1 May 1813

2 The extraordinary thing about Emma is that
   she has a moral life as a man has a moral life
   . . . It is the presumption of our society that
   women's moral life is not as men's.
   Lionel Trilling, BEYOND CULTURE

B

CHARLES BABBAGE (1792–1871)
English mathematician, inventor of calculating machines

1 He once tried to investigate statistically the credibility of the biblical miracles. In the course of his analysis he made the assumption that the chance of a man rising from the dead is one in ten to the power of twelve.
B. V. Bowden, FASTER THAN THOUGHT

2 Rational cost-accounting, or industrial management were rare in the mid-nineteenth century, and those who recommended them, like the scientist Charles Babbage, were regarded as unpractical eccentrics.
E. J. Hobshawm, INDUSTRY AND EMPIRE 1968

3 He was the nearest thing to a whizz-kid that the 19th century produced.
John Naughton, Observer, Babbage and Chips 24 Oct 1982

4 Hundreds of mechanical appliances in the factories and workshops of Europe and America, scores of ingenious expedients in mining and architecture, the construction of bridges and the boring of tunnels, and a world of tools by which labour is benefited and the arts improved — all the overflowings of a mind so rich that its very waste became valuable to utilise — came from Charles Babbage.
The Director of the Smithsonian Institution 1877

JOHANN SEBASTIAN BACH (1685–1750)
German musician

5 All Bach's last movements are like the running of a sewing machine.
Arnold Bax. Quoted Basil Maine, Morning Post 21 Aug 1930

6 Too much counterpoint, and what is worse — Protestant counterpoint.
Sir Thomas Beecham. Quoted Harold Atkins and Archie Newman, BEECHAM STORIES

7 Bach is Bach, as God is God.
Hector Berlioz

8 Bach is the foundation of piano playing.
Feruccio Busoni, RULES FOR PRACTISING THE PIANO 1898

9 To make divine things human, and human things divine; such is Bach, the greatest and purest moment in music of all times.
Pablo Casals. Speech, Prades Bach Festival 1950

10 Bach is like an astronomer who, with the aid of ciphers, finds the most wonderful stars.
Chopin, letter to Delphine Potocka

11 Some of the great moments in Bach's oratorios of the Passion have the solemn simplicity and deep religious feeling of Giotto's frescoes.
Sir Kenneth Clark, CIVILISATION 1969

12 Bach almost persuades me to be a Christian.
Roger Fry. Quoted Virginia Woolf, ROGER FRY 1940

13 Bach, sir? Bach's concert? And pray sir who is Bach? A piper?
Samuel Johnson. Quoted Fanny Burney, MEMOIRS OF DR BURNEY

14 I find that I never lose Bach. I don't know why I love him so. Except that he is so pure, so relentless and incorruptible, like a principle in geometry.
Edna St. Vincent Millay, LETTERS

15 Music owes as much to Bach as religion to its founder.
Robert Schumann

16 I like to play Bach because it is interesting to play a good fugue, but I do not regard him as a great genius.
P. I. Tchaikovsky, DIARY 1880

17 Departed Bach! Long since thy splendid organ playing / Alone brought thee the cognomen "The Great" / And what thy pen has writ, the highest art displaying / Did some with joy and some with envy contemplate.
G. P. Telemann, POEM IN PRAISE OF BACH 1751

FRANCIS BACON (1561–1626)
(Viscount St. Albans)
*English author, philosopher and
statesman*

1 He had the sound, distinct, comprehensive
knowledge of Aristotle, with all beautiful
lights, graces and embellishments of Cicero.
Joseph Addison

2 He had a delicate, lively Eie; Dr Harvey
told me it was like the eie of a viper.
John Aubrey, BRIEF LIVES 1680

3 In April, in the springtime his lordship
would, when it rayned, take his open coach
to receive the benefit of the irrigation,
which he was wont to say was very wholesome because of the nitre in the aire and the
universall spirit of the world.
Ibid.

4 He was taking the air in a coach with Dr
Witherborne. Snow lay on the ground and it
came into my Lord's thoughts why flesh
might not be preserved in snow as in salt.
They went into a poor woman's house at the
bottom of Highgate Hill and bought a hen,
then stuffed it with snow. The snow so chilled
him that he immediately fell seriously ill. He
went to the Earl of Arundel's house at Highgate, where they put him into a good bed
warmed with a pan, but it was a damp bed
that had not been lain in about a year before,
which gave him such a cold that in two or
three days he died of suffocation.
Ibid.

5 I have taken all knowledge to be my province.
Bacon in a letter to Lord Burghley 1591

6 When their lordships asked Bacon / How
many bribes he had taken / He had at least
grace / To get very red in the face.
E. C. Bentley, BASELESS BIOGRAPHY

7 In Bacon see the culminating prime / Of
British intellect and British crime. / He died,
and Nature, settling his affairs / Parted
his powers among us, his heirs / To each a
pinch of common sense for seed / And, to
develop it, a pinch of greed. / Each frugal
heir, to make the gift suffice / Buries the
talent to manure the vice.
Ambrose Bierce, THE LANTERN: *Sir Francis
Bacon* 15 *Jul* 1874

8 The curtain parted. Bacon had come back.
He pulled out a sheaf of papers from his
pocket and laid them on the desk. "Oh by
the way, Will," he said. "I almost forgot. If
you've got a moment to spare you might
polish up this essay."
Caryl Brahms and S. J. Simon, NO BED FOR
BACON

9 There is something faintly disreputable

about Bacon, not because of his politics, but
because he lacked the dominating faith of
the seventeenth century — the faith in
mathematics.
Sir Kenneth Clark, CIVILISATION 1969

10 His strength was in reflection, not in pro-
duction; he was the surveyor, not the
builder of science.
William Hazlitt, LECTURES ON THE AGE OF
ELIZABETH: *Character of Lord Bacon's
Work* 1820

11 My Lord Chancellor Bacon is lately dead of a
long languishing illness; he died so poor he
scarcely left money to bury him, which,
although he had great wit, did argue no great
wisdom; it being one of the essential properties of man to provide for the main chance.
James Howell, FAMILIAR LETTERS 1644

12 This great man, by an extraordinary force of
nature, compass of thought and indefatig-
able study had amassed to himself such
stores of knowledge as we can only look
upon with amazement. His capacity seems to
have grasped all that was revealed in books
before his time; and not satisfied with that he
began to strike out new tracks of science, too
many to be travelled over by one man, in the
compass of the longest lifetime.
John Hughes, HISTORY OF
ENGLAND c.1720

13 His hearers could not cough, or look aside
from him, without loss. The fear of every
man that heard him was that he should
make an end.
Ben Jonson, DISCOVERIES: *On the Lord St.
Albans*

14 In his adversity I ever prayed that God
would give him strength; for greatness he
could not want.
Ibid.

15 With the same pen which demolished the
Aristotelianism of the schoolmen he writes
a treatise on the laws, a cure for gout, the
translation of a psalm, and an essay on the
plantations.
Lord Lytton. Quoted W. Clark Russell, A
BOOK OF AUTHORS

16 Lord Bacon was the greatest genius Eng-
land, or perhaps any other country, ever
produced.
*Alexander Pope. Quoted Rev. Joseph
Spence*, OBSERVATIONS, CHARACTERS AND
ANECDOTES 1820

17 Bacon's sentence bends beneath the weight
of his thought, like a branch beneath the
weight of its fruit.
Alexander Smith, DREAMTHORP: *On the
Writing of Essays* 1863

1   It was not by the juxtaposition of a few opposites, but by the infiltration of a multitude of highly varied elements that his mental composition was made up. He was no striped frieze, he was shot silk.
Lytton Strachey, ELIZABETH AND ESSEX   1928

ROGER BACON (1214–1292)
English scientist

2   Our great Roger Bacon by a degree of penetration which perhaps has never been equalled discovered some of the most occult secrets of nature. His honours have been stolen from him by more modern authors who have appeared inventors when they were copying Bacon. Yet, for the reward of all his intense studies, the holy brethren and the infallible majesty of Rome occasioned him to languish in prison for the greater part of his life.
Isaac D'Israeli, CURIOSITIES OF LITERATURE   1824

3   Bacon discovered the art of making reading-glasses, the *camera obscura*, microscopes, telescopes and various other mathematical and astronomical instruments. He discovered a method of performing all the chemical operations that are now in use. He combined the mechanical powers in such a wonderful manner that it was for this he was accused of magic. His discoveries in medicine were by no means unimportant. That the ingredients of gunpowder and the art of making it were known to him is now undeniable; but the *humane philosopher* dreading the consequences of communicating the discovery to the world, transposed the letters of the Latin words which signify charcoal, which made the whole obscure.
Robert Henry, HISTORY OF ENGLAND   1771

ROBERT STEPHENSON SMYTH BADEN-POWELL (1857–1941)
Founder of the Boy Scout Movement. Defender of Mafeking during the Boer War

4   In his messages from Mafeking to the outside world Baden-Powell played the stereotype of the stiff-upper-lip Englishman to perfection: "All well. Four hours' bombardment. One dog killed."
Thomas Packenham, THE BOER WAR   1979

5   He was neat, dapper and bald; his favourite coat a coat of many colours. He was a man of parts; the conventional pig-sticking colonel (he had commanded the 5th Dragoons in India); the exhibitionist (he revelled in wearing a wig and a girl's dress in amateur theatricals); the military eccentric (he had ideas about the importance of scouting that most officers would have considered laughable). He had a boyish enthusiasm for hard work and new knowledge.
Ibid.

STANLEY BALDWIN (1867–1947)
(Earl of Bewdley)
British Prime Minister

6   Nothing sharpens the intellect of a manufacturer like losing a market. I have lost two in my life and it so sharpened my intellect I am standing proof of the gospel according to Manchester.
Stanley Baldwin. Quoted William Rapley, Sunday Despatch   30 May 1937

7   His successive attempts to find a policy remind me of the chorus of a third-rate review. His evasions reappear in different scenes and in new dresses and every time they dance with renewed and despairing vigour. But it is the same old jig.
Lord Beaverbrook, advocating his Empire Free Trade policy   Oct 1930

8   It is medicine man talk . . . Murmurs of admiration break out as this second-rate orator trails his tawdry wisps of mist over the parliamentary scene.
Aneurin Bevan, Tribune   1937

9   I think Baldwin has gone mad. He simply takes one jump in the dark, looks round, and takes another.
Lord Birkenhead, letter to Austen Chamberlain   Aug 1923

10   The candle in that great turnip has gone out.
Winson Churchill on Baldwin's retirement. Quoted Harold Nicolson, DIARIES   17 Aug 1950

11   At times I could have murdered S.B., but I would always have voted him a state funeral.
Colin R. Coote, Daily Telegraph, A New Judgement on Baldwin   15 Nov 1973

12   Had he been completely incompetent he could never have kept his high position. It was that fatal touch of talent that England and the Empire and the world are suffering from now in consequence.
J. L. Garvin. Quoted Henry Channon, DIARY   24 Mar 1942

1 His fame endures; we shall not forget the name of Baldwin until we are out of debt.
Kensal Green, PREMATURE EPITAPHS

2 When the history of this century is written and the peace-time Prime Ministers weighed I believe Baldwin will top the list in domestic achievement; and his handling of the Abdication crisis will heavily tip the balance, for he saved our constitutional monarchy. His ear was closer to the groundroots of the feelings of ordinary men and women than any politician whom I have ever known.
Lord Home, THE WAY THE WIND BLOWS 1976

3 His career lasted two years too long and yet ended two years too soon. Had he retired in 1934 or 1935 he would have escaped much of the odium that fell upon him. But had he remained in office until 1938 it is improbable that affairs would have degenerated as they did; certainly, as he himself said, he would never have gone to Godisberg or Munich.
Robert Rhodes James, *The Times* 14 Jul 1967

4 Baldwin was never quite sure that anybody was right, especially himself.
Harold Macmillan, THE PAST MASTERS

5 As a man he was unattractive, with unpleasant habits, always scratching himself.
Diana Mosley, THE DUCHESS OF WINDSOR

6 Stanley Baldwin always hits the nail on the head, but it doesn't go in any further.
G. M. Young. Quoted G.W. Lyttelton, THE LYTTELTON HART-DAVIS LETTERS 2 May 1958

ARTHUR JAMES, EARL BALFOUR (1848–1930)
British Prime Minister

7 Mr Balfour was difficult to understand because of his formidable detachment. The most that many of us could hope for was that he had a taste in us as one might have in clocks or china.
Margot Asquith, AUTOBIOGRAPHY 1936

8 I am more or less happy when being praised, not very uncomfortable when being abused, but I have moments of uneasiness when being explained.
A. J. Balfour. Quoted Kenneth Rose, *Daily Telegraph* 9 Nov 1960

9 He played politics in the same spirit as he played golf.
Robert Cecil, LIFE IN EDWARDIAN ENGLAND 1969

10 A powerful, graceful cat, walking delicately and unsoiled across a rather muddy street.
Winston Churchill, GREAT CONTEMPORARIES 1937

11 When Arthur Balfour launched his scheme for peopling Palestine with Jewish immigrants I am credibly informed that he did not know there were Arabs in the country.
Dean W. R. Inge, *The Evening Standard*

12 The House of Lords is not the watchdog of the constitution, it is Mr Balfour's poodle. It fetches and carries for him, it barks for him, it bites anyone he sets it on to.
David Lloyd George. Speech, *House of Commons* 22 Oct 1908

13 All he will leave behind in history is the scent of a pocket handkerchief.
David Lloyd George. Quoted A. J. P. Taylor, *Observer*, *From Embassy to Grub Street* 26 Oct 1981

HONORÉ DE BALZAC (1799–1850)
French novelist

14 All Balzac's novels occupy one shelf / The new edition fifty volumes long.
Robert Browning, BISHOP BLOUGRAM'S APOLOGY 1855

15 Balzac with his prodigious understanding of human motives scorns conventional values, defies fashionable opinion, as Beethoven did, and should inspire us to defy all those forces that threaten to impair our humanity; lies, tanks, tear-gas, ideologies, opinion polls, mechanisation, planners, computers — the whole lot
Sir Kenneth Clark, CIVILISATION 1969

16 Balzac amused himself with a collection of crayon portraits.
Isaac D'Israeli, CURIOSITIES OF LITERATURE 1824

17 One evening at Gavarni's Balzac said "I should like one of these days to be so well known, so popular, so celebrated, so famous that it would permit me —" [Try to imagine the most enormous ambition that has entered the head of man since time began. The most impossible. The most unattainable, the most monstrous, the most Olympian ambition; an ambition forbidden to a dictator, to a nation's saviour, to a pope, to a master of the world. Balzac said simply] "— so celebrated, so famous that it

would permit me to break wind in society, and society would think it the most natural thing in the world."
GONCOURT JOURNALS 18 *Oct* 1855

1 There exists a book containing biographies of two thousand Balzac characters.
J. B. Priestley, LITERATURE AND WESTERN MAN 1960

2 Balzac was consistently deprecated and undervalued. But though his work, often written in a great hurry, is unequal and he has obvious faults of manner and style Balzac by his sheer creative force and his large grasp on life cannot be denied his original reputation as a great novelist, a genuine master, though fundamentally a Romantic and not a realist as he was once thought to be.
Ibid.

TALLULAH BROCKMAN BANKHEAD
(1903–1968)
American actress

3 I am as pure as the driven slush.
Tallulah Bankhead. Quoted Observer 24 *Feb* 1957

4 Tallulah is always skating on thin ice. Everyone wants to be there when it breaks.
Mrs Patrick Campbell, The Times, Obituary 13 *Dec* 1968

SIR JOSEPH BANKS (1743–1820)
English naturalist. President of the Royal Society

5 Sir Joseph refused to go on Captain Cook's second voyage unless he was allowed to have *two* horn players to make music for him during dinner.
Sir Kenneth Clark, CIVILISATION 1969

6 He was not himself a genius who, by his discoveries, astonished and delighted the world but he was one who, in his early youth, without a guide, discovered the path that led to Science, and from that moment never deviated from it to the end of his life.
Sir Everard Home, LECTURE ON BANKS 1822

7 That wild man Banks, who is drawing naked savages and poaching in every ocean for the fry of little islands that escaped the drag-net of Spain.
Horace Walpole, letter to Sir Horace Mann 20 *Sept* 1772

SIR JAMES MATTHEW BARRIE
(1860–1937)
Scottish playwright and novelist

8 A friend once said to me "Everyone is famous for something, and you are famous for living opposite Bernard Shaw."
J. M. Barrie, Presidential Address to the Society of Authors 28 *Nov* 1928

9 When I began writing novels, people said they were not real novels. When I began writing plays folk said they were not real plays. I expect they are going about now saying I am not a real baronet.
J. M. Barrie, on receiving a knighthood. Quoted J. A. Hammerton, BARRIE: *The Story of a Genius* 1929

10 "You'll be sick tomorrow, Jack, if you eat any more chocolates," Sylvia Llewelyn-Davies remarked to her small son during a picnic at which Barrie was a guest. "I'll be sick tonight," replied the child helping himself to another sweetmeat. So delighted was Barrie at this epigram that he offered the child a royalty of a halfpenny a performance for the copyright. The offer was promptly taken up and must have proved a good financial investment for the youngster.
Mrs J. Comyns Carr, REMINISCENCES 1930

11 Like all sentimentalists he took refuge at times in ferocious cynicism.
Hamilton Fyfe, John o' London's Weekly 2 *Jul* 1937

12 The cheerful clatter of Sir James Barrie's cans as he went round with the milk of human kindness.
Philip Guedella, SOME CRITICS

13 Oh for an hour of Herod.
Anthony Hope, after the first night of Peter Pan 1904

14 Peter Pan is a charming play for children. It is not a rule of conduct for a great nation.
Edith Shackleton. Quoted James Agate EGO 3 4 *Dec* 1936

15 William Nicholson, noticing that J. M. Barrie always ordered Brussels sprouts and never ate them, asked him why. J.M.B. replied, "I cannot resist ordering them. The words are so lovely to say."
Sunday Referee 5 *Dec* 1927

BELA BARTOK (1881–1945)
Hungarian composer

16 Béla Bartók's compositions consist of unmeaning bunches of notes, apparently representing the composer promenading the

keyboard in his boots. Some can be played better with the elbows, others with the fists. None require fingers to perform or ears to listen to.
Anon., Musical Quarterly Jul 1915

1 The opening *Allegro* [of Bartók's Fourth Quartet] took me straight back to childhood and gave me in turn the rusty windlass of a well, the inter-linking noises of a goods train being shunted, then the belly-rumblings of a little boy acutely ill after robbing an orchard, and finally the singularly alarming noise of poultry being worried to death by a Scotch terrier.
Alan Dent, letter to James Agate
26 Nov 1945

2 And the fifth movement reminded me immediately and persistently and vividly of something I have never thought of since the only time I heard it; the noise of a Zulu village in the Glasgow Exhibition, a hub-hub more singular because it had a background of skirling Highland bagpipes.
Ibid.

3 I cannot imagine anyone "quite liking" Bartók's music — as a pleasant background to a game of bridge. Either his works — I am thinking particularly of his later ones — give you perhaps the greatest thrill that contemporary music has to offer; or you will have absolutely nothing to do with the fellow.
'A.F.', Radio Times 30 Sept 1938

4 It is of no use to approach Bartók with preconceptions concerning harmony, or even musical form, derived from our experience of the practice of western European composers. It may help if we look on Hungary as being musically as well as geographically, well on the way to China.
Dyneley Hussey, Radio Times 11 Jul 1946

CHARLES BAUDELAIRE (1821–1867)
French poet and critic

5 To glorify the cult of images is my single great passion.
Baudelaire, of himself

6 Himself a poet of great originality, power and depth, as an influence it is almost impossible to over-estimate him. He is one of the key figures of the whole modern movement in literature.
J. B. Priestley, LITERATURE AND WESTERN MAN 1960

7 Behind the fastidious poet and critic, the coolly impudent social poseur, half dandy, half priest who yet wastes his slender stock of money on a coarse and vindictive mulatto

mistress, is little Charles Baudelaire, his mother's boy, defying all the archangels and turning his back on heaven.
Ibid.

RICHARD BAXTER (1615–1691)
English Nonconformist divine and author

8 He had a very moving and pathetic way of writing and was his whole life a man of great zeal and much simplicity, but was most unhappily subtle and metaphysical in everything.
Gilbert Burnet, HISTORY OF HIS OWN TIMES 1734

9 I may not unfrequently doubt Baxter's memory, or even his competence, in consequence of his particular modes of thinking, but I could almost as soon doubt the Gospel verity as his veracity.
Samuel Taylor Coleridge, NOTES ON ENGLISH DIVINES

10 Richard, thou art an old knave. Thou hast written books enough to load a cart and every book as full of sedition as an egg is full of meat.
Judge Jeffreys to Baxter when prosecuted for seditious libel 1685

11 Dr Johnson said he was not angry with me at all for liking Baxter. He liked him himself "but then" he said, "Baxter was bred up to the establishment and would have died in it if he could have got the living of Kidderminster. He was a very good man." Here he was wrong, for Baxter was offered a bishopric after the restoration.
Hannah More, letter to her sister 1780

PIERRE DE TERRAIL, CHEVALIER DE BAYARD (1476–1524)
French knight

12 The knight without fear and without reproach (*Chevalier sans peur et sans reproche*).
Anon., contemporary French description

13 The noblest man in Europe. The man for whom his very enemies would weep.
Francis Hackett, HENRY VIII 1929

14 Chevalier Bayard, as noble a human being as ever gave model to Cervantes.
Ibid.

15 His device was a porcupine with the motto "One man possesses the power of a whole troop." This was given him in consequence of his having singly defended a bridge against two hundred Spaniards.
PERCY ANECDOTES 1820

1   At the defeat of Romagnans Bayard as
    usual performed prodigies of valour, until
    he was wounded by a musket shot which
    broke the vertebrae of his back. He then
    caused himself to be helped off his horse
    and to be placed at the foot of a tree. "At
    least," said he, "I may die facing the
    enemy." Thus fell the brave Bayard.
    Ibid.

AUBREY VINCENT BEARDSLEY
(1872–1898)
English artist and author

2   He had a passion for reality, he hated the
    people who denied the existence of evil and
    so, being young, he filled his pictures with
    evil.
    *Mabel Beardsley (his sister) to W. B. Yeats.
    Quoted Miriam J. Benkovitz,* AUBREY
    BEARDSLEY *1981*

3   Beardsley always seemed to know, by in-
    stinctive erudition, all about everything.
    *Max Beerbohm, The Listener, First Meeting
    With W. B. Yeats* 6 *Jan* 1955

4   I've always wondered what people saw in
    Beardsley's drawings. Lust does frighten
    me. I say it looks like such despair — des-
    pair of any happiness and search for it in
    new degradation.
    Sir F. Burne-Jones. Quoted Mary Lago,
    BURNE-JONES TALKING *1982*

5   The Fra Angelico of Satanism.
    Roger Fry. Quoted Stanley Weintraub,
    AUBREY BEARDSLEY

6   He had a sort of innocent familiarity with
    evil, he communed with leering dwarfs,
    the bloated epicene figures that peopled the
    depraved landscapes and grotesque inter-
    iors designed by his pen, as a child might
    talk to fairies.
    William Gaunt, THE AESTHETIC ADVENTURE

7   With the art of Beardsley we enter the
    realm of pure intellect, the beauty of the
    work is wholly independent of the thing
    portrayed.
    Ezra Pound, FORUM *1912*

THE BEATLES
Liverpudlian pop group

8   *Q.* How do you rate your music?
    A. We're good musicians. Just adequate.
    Q. Then why are you so popular?
    A. Maybe people just like adequate music.
    *The Beatles in an interview.
    Quoted Nat Shapiro,* AN ENCYCLOPEDIA OF
    QUOTATIONS ABOUT MUSIC

9   Four in many ways ordinary young men,
    subjected to unprecedented pressures are
    granted unprecedented freedoms. They
    could have anything money could buy, but
    they couldn't walk down the street.
    Peter Brown and Steven Gaines, THE LOVE
    YOU MAKE: THE INSIDE STORY
    OF THE BEATLES *1983*

10 Their vulgar prodigality is impossible to
    summarise.
    Philip Larkin, Observer, Fighting the Fab
    9 *Oct* 1983

11 When you get to the top there is nowhere to
    go but down, but the Beatles could not get
    down. There they remain, unreachable,
    frozen, fabulous.
    Ibid.

12 What kind of phenomenon? Musical, socio-
    logical, political even? Or a phenomenal
    spoof, made up of adolescent hysteria and
    shrewd publicity?
    Ibid.

13 We are more popular than Jesus.
    John Lennon in an interview 1966

14 Lots of people who complained about us
    receiving the MBE received theirs for
    heroism in war — for killing people. I'd say
    we deserved ours more.
    John Lennon, BEATLES ILLUSTRATED
    LYRICS

15 Do you remember when everyone began
    analysing Beatle songs? I don't think I
    understood what some of them were
    supposed to be about.
    Ringo Starr. Quoted Nat Shapiro,
    AN ENCYCLOPEDIA OF QUOTATIONS
    ABOUT MUSIC

PIERRE-AUGUSTIN CARON DE
BEAUMARCHAIS (1732–1799)
French playwright

16 A strange ambiguous figure, Beaumarchais
    is immensely lively and inventive in his com-
    edy, and its aggressively satirical attitude
    towards aristocratic privilege had some
    influence on revolutionary feeling.
    J. B. Priestley, LITERATURE AND WESTERN
    MAN *1960*

17 He was a great many other things as well as
    an author; watchmaker, musician, specu-
    lator, political agent, and adventurer, very
    much an impudent, cool card, to whom

dramatic authors owe something, for he was one of the first to fight for their rights.
Ibid.

FRANCIS BEAUMONT (1584–1616) and JOHN FLETCHER (1579–1625)
English collaborating dramatists

1 There was a wonderful co-similarity between Mr Francis Beaumont and Mr John Fletcher which caused that dearness of friendship between them. I have heard Dr John Earles, since Bishop of Sarum, say, who knew them, that Beaumont's chief business was to lop the overflowings of Mr Fletcher's luxuriant fancy and flowing wit.
John Aubrey, BRIEF LIVES 1813

2 They lived together on the Bankside, not far from the Playhouse; both bachelors; lay together; had one wench in the house between them which they did so admire; the same clothes, cloaks etc. between them.
Ibid.

3 John Fletcher, invited to go with a Knight into Norfolk or Suffolk in the plague-time, 1625, stayed but to make himself a suit of clothes, and while it was in the making, fell sick of the plague and died. This I had from his tailor who is now a very old man.
Ibid.

4 All their women are represented with the minds of strumpets, except a few irrational Humourists far less capable of exciting our sympathy than a Hindoo who had had a basin of cow-broth thrown over him.
Samuel Taylor Coleridge, ANNOTATION TO THE WORKS OF BEAUMONT AND FLETCHER 1811

5 They represented all the passions very lively, but above all, love. I am apt to believe that the English language in them rose to its highest perfection.
John Dryden, AN ESSAY ON DRAMATIC POETRY

6 The blossoms of Beaumont and Fletcher's imagination draw no sustenance from the soil, but are cut and slightly withered flowers stuck in sand.
T. S. Eliot, ESSAYS, *Ben Jonson*

7 The comic talents of these authors far exceeded their skill in tragedy. In comedy they founded a new school, at least in England, the vestiges of which are still to be traced in our theatre. Their plays are at once distinguishable from those of their contem-poraries by the regard to dramatic effect which influenced the writers' imaginations.
Henry Hallam, THE LITERATURE OF EUROPE 1838

8 They are not safe teachers of morality, they tamper with it and seem to regard the decomposition of the common affections and the dissolution of the strict bonds of society as an agreeable study and a careless pastime.
William Hazlitt, LECTURES ON THE AGE OF ELIZABETH 1820

9 The pair wrote a good deal that was pretty disgraceful, but at least they had been educated out of the possibility of writing *Titus Andronicus. George Bernard Shaw*, *Saturday Review* 19 Feb 1898

LORD BEAVERBROOK (1879–1964)
(William Maxwell Aitken)
Canadian-born newspaper proprietor

10 He is a magnet to all young men, and I warn you that if you talk to him no good will come of it.
Clement Attlee, at a meeting of his junior ministers Jun 1945

11 I suppose one cannot help it if Birkenhead and Winston will dine with Beaverbrook. There is no accounting for taste.
Stanley Baldwin in 1924. *Quoted Thomas Jones*, WHITEHALL DIARY VOL. 1 1916–1925

12 Beaverbrook is so pleased to be in the Government that he is like the town tart who has finally married the Mayor.
Beverley Baxter. Quoted Henry Channon, DIARY 12 *Jun* 1940

13 The Beaver is not a bad man; he's a bad boy.
John Buchan. Quoted Observer 29 May 1949

14 Churchill's devotion to Beaverbrook always puzzled Ernest Bevin. In the end he decided that Churchill was "like a man who is married to a whore; he knows she's a whore, but he loves her just the same".
Alan Bullock, LIFE AND TIMES OF ERNEST BEVIN

15 David Lloyd George called at Cherkley Court, near Leatherhead, where Beaverbrook lived, to consult his friend about a current political conspiracy. "Is the Lord at home?" he asked the butler. "No, sir, the

Lord is out walking." "Ah," said Lloyd George, "on the water, I presume."
Hugh Cudlipp, WALKING ON THE WATER

1 He was in his bedroom stark naked, with his hairy little body covered with moles and blotches, shaving himself with a Schick razor. He had not slept, had diarrhoea. I felt sorry for him.
Sir Robert Bruce Lockhart, DIARIES 1939–1965

2 His pugnacity destroys both his judgement and his decent feelings. He lives only by opposition. If he cannot find an opposition, he creates one.
Harold Nicolson, DIARY 6 *Nov* 1930

3 If he has been as great a sinner as some people want us to think his nature will call him in the end to a startling repentance.
Reginald Pound, THEIR MOODS AND MINE 1935

4 A strange and complicated character, it seemed to me he had the queer belief which grows, sometimes, in his kind of journalism, that a thing can be made true by saying it.
Vincent Sheean, BETWEEN THE THUNDER AND THE SUN 1943

5 If Max gets to heaven he won't last long. He will be chucked out for trying to bring off a merger between heaven and hell — after having secured a controlling interest in key subsidiary companies in both places.
H. G. Wells. Quoted *A. J. P. Taylor*, BEAVERBROOK

6 He was like a fierce small monkey strewing nutshells around the cage.
Andrew Wilson, *Observer*, *Hallelujah Travels With the Beaver* 20 *May* 1979

THOMAS À BECKET (?1118–1170)
Martyred Archbishop of Canterbury

7 As may appear from the accounts in the ledger-books of the offerings made to the three great altars in Christ's Church Canterbury, in one year was offered at Christ's altar £31 2s 6d; to the Virgin's altar £631 5s 6d, but to St. Thomas's altar £8321 12s 6d.
Gilbert Burnet, HISTORY OF THE REFORMATION 1679

8 Your Becket was a noisy egoist and hypocrite; getting his brains spilt on the floor of Canterbury cathedral to secure the main chance — somewhat uncertain how!
Thomas Carlyle, PAST AND PRESENT 1843

9 This is the man who was the tradesman's son, the backstairs creeper from Cheapside; /
This is the creature that crawled upon the king; swollen with blood and swollen with pride. / Creeping out of the London dirt / Crawling up like a louse on your shirt / The man who swindled, lied; broke his oath and betrayed his king.
T. S. Eliot, MURDER IN THE CATHEDRAL 1935

10 Nothing could be more misleading than the notion of a saintly man of God ill-treated by a tyrannical potentate. It was said that Henry was never known to choose an unworthy friend, but Becket's worthiness is a matter of opinion.
John Harvey, THE PLANTAGENETS 1949

11 Extraordinary mixture of man-about-town, witty and extravagant, and self-willed, self-torturing, and it must be said, self-advertising churchman, Thomas à Becket won for himself an outstanding place in history by his genius for manoeuvring other parties into the wrong.
Ibid.

12 I have nourished and raised up in my kingdom indolent and wretched fellows, faithless to their master whom they allow to be mocked so shamefully by a certain low-born clerk.
Henry II *to members of his court, Dec* 1170
(*NB The oft-quoted "Who will rid me of this turbulent priest?" appears to be apocryphal. No contemporary source has been traced*)

13 Meanwhile the boldness of this man wore out his victims, and others in England; they fell upon him and killed him (I say it with sorrow). I fear the anger I had recently shown against him may be the cause of this misdeed. I call God to witness that I am extremely disturbed, but more with anxiety about my reputation than qualms of conscience.
Henry II, *letter to Pope Alexander* III 1171

14 Other saints have borne testimony by their suffering to the general doctrine of Christianity; but Becket had sacrificed his life to the power of the clergy; and this peculiar merit challenged, and not in vain, a suitable acknowledgement of his memory.
David Hume, HISTORY OF ENGLAND 1754

15 Robert of Merton, the dead archbishop's confessor, showed those around him the hairshirt and drawers, sewn tightly around the body and thighs but could be opened at the back for the daily scourging. The whole garment was alive with vermin, and the monks remarked to each other that the

martyrdom by the sword was more tolerable than this other never-ceasing martyrdom.
Ibid.

1 In the seven years that he held that office [1155–1162] the Angevin chancery became the most perfect piece of administrative machinery that Europe had yet known.
T. F. TOUT, THE PLACE OF ST. THOMAS OF CANTERBURY IN HISTORY

SAMUEL BECKETT (1906–   )
Irish-born dramatist

2 His characters typically advance through worsening stages of decrepitude or paralysis. Such human bonds as they form are the coupling of tyrant and victim, or at best of two pathetically groping dependencies.
William Rose Benét, THE READER'S ENCYCLOPEDIA (*Revised edition* 1975)

3 His greatest success (*En attendant Godot* 1952; *translated by Beckett as Waiting For Godot*, 1954) with the two tramps forever waiting in a bare symbolic landscape for the arrival of the unidentified Godot, and their encounter with the disturbingly symbolic rich man and his slave is saved from bleak nihilism by the vulgar colloquial humour and the ritualistic overtones of the situation.
David Daiches, PENGUIN COMPANION TO LITERATURE   1971

4 You either like Samuel Beckett's plays or you think they are a heap of twaddle. They remind me of something Sir John Betjeman might do if you filled him up with benzedrine and then force-fed him intravenously with Guinness.
Tom Davies, *Observer*   17 *Jun* 1979

WILLIAM BECKFORD (1760–1844)
English author and eccentric

5 Mr Beckford travelled and resided abroad until his twenty-second year, when he wrote *Vathek*, a work of startling beauty. More than fifty years afterwards he told Mr Cyrus Redding that he wrote it at one sitting. "It took me," he said, "three days and two nights of hard labour. I never took off my clothes the whole time. This severe application made me very ill."
John Timbs, ENGLISH ECCENTRICS   1875

6 Mr Beckford had sworn that he would have his Christmas dinner cooked in his new Abbey kitchen. The apartment was indeed finished by Christmas morning, but the bricks had no time to settle, the beams were not secure, the mortar had not dried. The fire was lit, the splendid repast was cooked,

the servants were carrying the dishes through the long passages into the dining room when the kitchen fell with a loud crash; but it was not a misfortune of any consequence; no one was hurt, the master had kept his word, and he had money enough to build another kitchen.
Ibid.

7 Mr Beckford seldom rode out beyond his gates, but when he did he was generally asked for charity by the poor people. Sometimes he used to throw a one-pound note or a guinea to them, or he would turn round and give the supplicants a severe horse-whipping. When the last was the case, soon after he had ridden away, he generally sent back a guinea or two to the persons he had whipped.
Ibid.

THE VENERABLE BEDE (673–735)
English historian and monk

8 Bede, or Baeda, was a monk at the Northumbrian monastery at Jarrow. He wrote over thirty works of history, grammar, science, theological commentary etc. His *Ecclesiastical History of the English People*, written in Latin and translated into Old English under King Alfred provided the material for the earlier part of the *Anglo-Saxon Chronicle*.
William Rose Benét, THE READER'S ENCYCLOPEDIA   1949

9 The most famous of his works was the *Ecclesiastical History of the English Nation* — the story of the Conversion. Lucid, just, immensely learned, it is a monument to his age, his Faith, and his country.
Arthur Bryant, MAKERS OF THE REALM   1953

10 Bede, a monk of high ability, working unknown in the recesses of the church, now comes forward as the most effective and almost the only audible voice from the British Isles in those dim times.
Winston Churchill, HISTORY OF THE ENGLISH-SPEAKING PEOPLES   1956

11 O venerable Bede / The saint, the scholar from a circle freed / Of toil stupendous in a hallowed seat / Of learning where thou heardst the billows beat / On a wild coast, rough monitors to feed / Perpetual industry. Sublime Recluse! / The recreant soul, that dares to shun the debt / Imposed on human kind, must first forget / Thy diligence, thy unrelaxing use / Of a long life, and in the

hour of death / The last dear service of they passing breath!
William Wordsworth, ECCLESIASTIC SONNETS

SIR THOMAS BEECHAM (1879–1961)
Conductor

1 I was always touched by the friendliness and humility beneath the brilliant exterior. Remember he always bowed *first* to the *orchestra* and only secondly to the audience.
Richard Arnell, BEECHAM REMEMBERED (*Edited by Humphrey Proctor-Gregg*)

2 There was a break in a recording session of an opera in the Kingsway Hall. Sir Thomas was alone when some recording engineers entered and one asked how things were going. "Reasonably well," said Sir Thomas, "but I sometimes long for the days of the old castrati. You knew where you were with them."
Harold Atkins and Archie Norman, BEECHAM STORIES

3 Beecham was deeply rooted in provincial England. In this respect and in others he resembled Arnold Bennett. One from Lancashire, one from the Potteries. Both enjoyed being thought of as 'cards' which indeed they were. *Lord Boothby*, MY YESTERDAY, YOUR TOMORROW

4 A complex character — Falstaff, Puck, Malvolio all mixed up, each likely to overwhelm the others. Witty, then waggish, supercilious, then genial, kindly, and sometimes cruel, an artist in affectation, yet somehow always himself. Lancashire in his bones, yet a man of the world.
Neville Cardus, SIR THOMAS BEECHAM

HENRY WARD BEECHER (1815–1887)
American clergyman and abolitionist

5 Mankind fell in Adam and has been falling ever since, but never touched bottom till it got to Henry Ward Beecher.
Tom Appleton, MORE UNCENSORED RECOLLECTIONS

6 A dunghill covered with flowers.
Henry Wallerson, THE BEECHER–TILTON SCANDAL

MAX BEERBOHM (1872–1956)
English author and cartoonist

7 It is rather terrible to know that the successful Somerset Maugham criticised Sir Max as being someone whose shirt-cuffs were generally dirty.
Cecil Beaton, THE STRENUOUS YEARS

8 The public knows me to be a child author and likes to picture me at my desk, dressed in black velveteen with legs dangling towards the floor.
Max Beerbohm. Quoted S. C. Roberts, THE INCOMPARABLE MAX

9 Behind Beerbohm's façade of a Yellow Book aesthete there lurked a frightened rabbi.
Malcolm Muggeridge, TREAD SOFTLY FOR YOU TREAD ON MY JOKES 1966

10 He is a shallow, affected, self-conscious fribble.
Vita Sackville-West, letter to Harold Nicolson 8 Dec 1959

11 He has the most remarkable and seductive genius — and I should say about the smallest in the world.
Lytton Strachey, letter to Clive Bell 4 Dec 1917

12 A delicious little old dandy, very quick in mind still.
Evelyn Waugh, DIARY   17 May 1947

13 The Gods have bestowed on Max the gift of perpetual old age.
Oscar Wilde. Quoted Vincent O'Sullivan, ASPECTS OF OSCAR WILDE

14 Tell me, when you are alone with Max, does he take off his face and reveal his mask?
Oscar Wilde. Quoted W. H. Auden, FOREWORDS AND AFTERWORDS

LUDWIG VAN BEETHOVEN (1770–1827)
German composer

15 Even Beethoven thumped the tub. The Ninth Symphony was composed by a sort of Mr Gladstone of music.
Sir Thomas Beecham. Quoted Harold Atkins and Archie Newman, BEECHAM STORIES

16 What can you do with the Seventh Symphony? It's like a lot of yaks jumping about.
Ibid.

17 Bach is the foundation of piano playing; Liszt is the summit. The two make Beethoven possible.
Ferruccio Busoni, RULES FOR PRACTISING THE PIANO   1898

18 He said that if he knew as much about strategy as he knew about counterpoint he would give Napoleon a run for his money.
Sir Kenneth Clark, CIVILISATION   1969

31

1 Beethoven embraced the universe with the power of his spirit.
Frederic Chopin, letter to Delphine Potocka

2 Beethoven's Fifth Symphony is the most sublime noise that has ever penetrated the human ear. All sorts and conditions are satisfied by it. The passion of your life becomes more vivid, and you are bound to admit that such a noise is cheap at two shillings.
E. M. Forster, HOWARD'S END 1910

3 Beethoven was so deaf he thought he was a painter.
Grafitto. Quoted BBC Radio 4, Quote Unquote

4 Beethoven is the father of all megalomaniacs who, looking into their own souls, write what they see therein — misery, corruption, slighting, selfishness and ugliness.
James Huneker, OLD FOGY 1912

5 Beethoven is not beautiful. He is dramatic, powerful, a maker of storms, a subduer of tempests; but his speech is the speech of a self-centred egoist.
Ibid.

6 There can no more be a new Beethoven than there can be a new Christopher Columbus.
René Leonormond, ETUDE SUR L'HARMONIE MODERNE 1913

7 Having adapted Beethoven's Sixth Symphony for *Fantasia*, Walt Disney commented, "Gee, this'll make Beethoven."
Marshall McLuhan, CULTURE IS OUR BUSINESS 1970

8 The last movement of Beethoven's Ninth Symphony is the song of the angels sung by earthly spirits.
E. H. W. Meyerstein, letter to his mother 21 *Oct* 1908

9 You can chase a Beethoven symphony all your life and never catch up.
André Previn

10 Beethoven's Fifth Symphony may be Fate — or Kate — knocking at the door. It's up to you.
C. B. Rees, Penguin Music Magazine, The Purpose of Music

11 The only entirely creditable incident in English history is the sending of £100 to Beethoven on his deathbed by the London Philharmonic Society, and it is the only one historians never mention.
George Bernard Shaw, letter to The Times 20 *Dec* 1832

12 I love Beethoven, especially the poems.
Ringo Starr

13 If melody were all of music, what could one prize in the various forces which make up the immense work of Beethoven, in which melody is assuredly the least?
Igor Stravinsky, POETICS OF MUSIC

APHRA BEHN (1640–1689)
First English professional woman writer

14 She seems to have been the kind of woman as common in the age of liberation as heretofore, who was a glutton for amorous punishment. We need not be surprised that she caught syphilis.
Anthony Burgess, Observer, reviewing Angeline Goreau's RECONSTRUCTING APHRA 30 *Dec* 1980

15 She was involved in an insurrection of slaves, thus going one better than Harriet Beecher Stowe, who merely preached abolitionism. *Oronooko* unfortunately is inferior as art to *Uncle Tom's Cabin* but it is the first anti-slavery fiction and it merits a certain reverence.
Ibid.

16 Aphra did not confine herself to simple dirty jokes. Her amorous verses, amiably bi-sexual, had a philosophic under-pinning. Her prose pieces spoke not merely of passionate adventure but of social squalor and psychological niceties. Beneath the maniacal intrigues her plays flaunted not merely licentiousness, but intellectual libertinism.
J. W. Lambert, Sunday Times, A Bluestocking at the Court of King James 6 *Nov* 1977

17 Mrs Behn, daughter of a barber, spent a while spying for Charles II in Antwerp rather unsuccessfully — she did manage to warn the government that the Dutch were about to send a fleet up the Medway but nobody took any notice of her — and she also introduced milk punch into England.
Frank Muir, THE FRANK MUIR BOOK 1975

18 *Oroonnoko* was said to have given Rousseau the germ of his philosophy of the Noble Savage.
Ibid.

19 Mrs Behn was the first woman in history to earn her living as an author and her remains were appropriately entombed in the cloisters of Westminster Abbey.
Ibid.

ALEXANDER GRAHAM BELL (1847–1922)
Scottish-born inventor

1   It was on March 10 1876, over a line extending between two rooms at No. 5, Exeter Place, Boston, that the first complete sentence was ever spoken by Bell and heard by his assistant Thomas A. Watson, who recorded it in his notebook at the time. It consisted of these words: "Mr Watson, come here, I want you." Thus the telephone was born.
John J. Carty, SMITHSONIAN REPORT   1922

GERTRUDE (MARGARET LOWTHIAN) BELL (1868–1936)
English traveller, author and archaeologist

2   A staunch liberal by upbringing, she was a firm believer in early independence for the Arabs and was influential in bringing it about. Both her fame and her writing helped to create public interest in the problems and romance of Arabia, in a way similar to the achievements of T. E. Lawrence
Jan Marsh, PENGUIN COMPANION TO LITERATURE   1971

3   She was the first woman to get a first class degree in modern history.
Ibid.

4   Gertrude Bell, after a decade of globe-trotting and mountain climbing, settled in Arabia. She became, to a whole sub-continent, its gadfly conscience, its self-appointed step-mother, a tireless meddler, busybody and architect of schemes and dreams.
Jonathan Raban, Sunday Times, reviewing H. V. E. Winstone's GERTRUDE BELL   15 *Oct* 1978

5   She was a supremely talented, supremely dangerous amateur who brought to the politics of Arabia a kind of artistic genius which the Arabs could well have done without.
Ibid.

JOSEPH HILAIRE PIERRE BELLOC (1870–1953)
English author, French born

6   Mr Hilaire Belloc / Is a case for legislation *ad hoc* / He seems to think nobody minds / His books being all of different kinds.
E. C. Bentley, BIOGRAPHY FOR BEGINNERS

7   He has grown a splendid white beard and in his cloak, which with his hat he wore in-doors and always, he seemed an archimandrite.
Evelyn Waugh, DIARY   1 *May* 1945

8   With face alight with simple joy and many lapses of memory he quavered out old French marching songs and snatches from the music hall of his youth. He is conscious of being decrepit and forgetful, but not of being a bore.
Ibid.

ANTHONY WEDGWOOD BENN (1925–   )
English politician

9   The Bertie Wooster of Marxism.
Malcolm Bradbury, BBC Radio 4, *Quote Unquote*   12 *Sept* 1979

10   He flung himself into the Sixties technology with the enthusiasm (not to say language) of a newly enrolled Boy Scout demonstrating knot-tying to indulgent parents.
Bernard Levin   1976

11   He led the left, not through any rigorous approach, but through dazzling rhetoric and instinctive popularism, owing much of his appeal to his ability to always appear thoroughly English, reasonable and Christian.
Anthony Sampson, THE CHANGING ANATOMY OF BRITAIN   1982

12   "I've been trying to work out," said one of his civil servants, "which has cost Britain more. The Second World War or Tony Benn."
Ibid.

13   I have always said about Tony that he immatures with age.
Sir Harold Wilson, THE CHARIOT OF ISRAEL

ENOCH ARNOLD BENNETT (1867–1931)
English novelist

14   Arnold Bennett was assuredly the super-realist of his age.
Lilian Arnold

15   His genial sea-lion figure seemed poured into his tail-coat, larded and trussed by the famous white waistcoat, the epitome of the fat dandy, oil without vinegar — so much more difficult to carry off, as the Prince Regent found, than the Baudelairean, Brummellesque thin one.
Dudley Barker, A WRITER BY TRADE: *A View of Arnold Bennett*

16   He was avuncular to the Sitwells and Aldous Huxley, a talent-spotter and friend of the young. He was neither so grand as

Shaw nor so philistine as Wells, so aloof as Galsworthy, so critical as Eliot, so envious as Wyndham Lewis, so feline as Gosse.
Ibid.

1 This establishment entertainer was the son of a pawnbroker who had brought his stammer with him like an old wound from his struggle against poverty and parental authority in the Five Towns. He had been gifted with a good mind, a marvellous memory, enormous industry, a love of the best French authors and a shorthand speed of 130 words a minute.
Cyril Connolly, Sunday Times 26 *Jun* 1966

2 What was so remarkable about this ageing epicure and critic-impresario festooned like a yacht laid up in harbour for cocktail parties, was that it should ever have gone to sea and fought through storms and angry seas to land a cargo.
Ibid.

3 Bennett — a sort of pig in clover.
D. H. Lawrence, letter to Aldous Huxley 27 *Mar* 1928

4 He has described how, when as a young dramatic critic he went to a Lyceum first-night, he would saunter into the stalls and glance at the front rows of the pit with cold disdain, thinking, "Don't you wish you were me?"
Robert Lynd, News Chronicle, Obituary 28 *Mar* 1931

5 He never outgrew the provincialism that made the Savoy Hotel in his eyes the Earthly Paradise.
S. P. B. Mais, ALL THE DAYS OF MY LIFE

6 I remember that once, beating his knee with his clenched fist to force the words through his writhing lips, he said, "I am a nice man." He was.
W. Somerset Maugham, THE VAGRANT MOOD

7 Bennett, who had a quiff like a cockatoo, looked like an untidy butler, and had a squeaky voice that grated on the ear, was probably the most successful playwright, author and journalist of the decade. He loved "high life", expensive restaurants, good wine and Lucullian meals. He came from the lower classes but he lived like an overblown and somewhat vulgar duke.
L. W. Needham, FIFTY YEARS IN FLEET STREET

8 Arnold Bennett knew his eggs. Whatever his interest in good writing, he never showed his public anything but his avarice. consequently they adored him.
Ezra Pound, Criterion magazine 1937

9 *The Old Wives Tale* after Dickens is perhaps England's first record of ordinary people's lives. It is a work of genius. I cannot imagine its author writing, as he does, such drivelling journalism — "How to Get Thin" and that sort of thing — at £100 a time. Still, the rich must live, I suppose.
Hannen Swaffer, of Bennett's contributions to the Evening Standard. Quoted L. W. Needham, FIFTY YEARS IN FLEET STREET

10 Is Dickens of no more value to the world because Mr Arnold Bennett has found it impossible to finish one of his novels?
Hugh Walpole, T.P's and Cassell's Weekly, Literary Dogmatists 6 *Aug* 1927

11 "The scene where Darius Clayhanger dies that lingering death could not be bettered — and why?" says Bennett. "Because I took infinite pains over it. All the time my father was dying I was at the bedside making copious notes. You can't just slap these things down. You have to take trouble."
P. G. Wodehouse, BRING ON THE GIRLS 1954

12 "Art is long, life is short" save when it / Is applied to Arnold Bennett / Whose Art was aimed (unless we wrong her) / To prove that life's a damned sight longer.
Humbert Wolfe, LAMPOONS 1925

JEREMY BENTHAM (1745–1842)
English writer on jurisprudence and ethics

13 The awe which his admirers had of Bentham was carried so far as to make them think everything he said or thought was a miracle. Once he came to see Leigh Hunt in Surrey Gaol and played battledore and shuttlecock with him. Hunt told me after of the prodigious power of Bentham's mind. "He proposed," said Hunt, "a reform in the handle of the battledore, taking in, you see, everything, like an elephant's trunk, which lifts alike a pin or twelve hundredweight. Extraordinary mind!" "Extraordinary," I echoed.
B. R. Haydon, AUTOBIOGRAPHY 1853

14 He sees and hears only what suits his purpose and looks out for facts and passing occurrences in order to put them in his logical machinery and grind them into the

dust and powder and subtle theory, as the miller looks out for grist to his mill.
William Hazlitt,
THE SPIRIT OF THE AGE   1825

1 The arch-philistine Jeremy Bentham was the insipid, pedantic, leather-tongued oracle of the bourgeois intelligence of the nineteenth century.
Karl Marx, DAS KAPITAL   1894

2 The father of innovation, both in doctrines and institutions, is Bentham. He is the greatest *subversive*, or in the language of continental philosophers the great *critical* thinker of his age and country.
John Stuart Mill, DISSERTATIONS: BENTHAM

3 Bentham's adoption of the principle of "the greatest good for the greatest number" was no doubt due to democratic feeling, but it involved opposition to the doctrine of the rights of man, which he bluntly characterised as "nonsense".
Bertrand Russell, HISTORY OF WESTERN PHILOSOPHY   1945

4 Apparently Bentham thought that human beings had but two desires, gain and pleasure. He would have been at home in New York.
Gore Vidal, BURR

BERNARD BERENSON (1865–1959)
German-born art historian and connoisseur

5 Bernard Berenson was the most powerful connoisseur who ever lived. Cribbing Nietzsche, he preached the doctrine of judging works of art by judging whether they were 'life-enhancing' or 'life-diminishing'; he also persuaded critics to look for 'tactile value' in pictures. With Lord Duveen he formed the basic collections of several national galleries and of many newly rich collectors.
Paul Levy, *Observer*, *reviewing Ernest Samuels'* BERNARD BERENSON, *the Making of a Connoisseur*   17 Aug 1979

6 His nose is well-taught, he has the true critic's sense of quality. His observation is acute, his deduction logical. He has scholarship, perception, a good memory, and the indispensable training in method.
Eric Linklater, THE ART OF ADVENTURE

7 . . . he looked like a miniature banker on Wall Street, though his voice was gentler.
Ibid.

8 It has now been fully established that Berenson must have authenticated large numbers of paintings for Duveen which he cannot have believed to be genuine.
Philip Toynbee, *Observer*, *reviewing Meryle Secrest's* BEING BERNARD BERENSON
20 Jan 1980

9 Berenson was always a haunted and guilt-ridden man, always aware that the great edifice of his gracious living was built over a sewer. He might, he believed, have been a Goethe, but he chose to be a Mephistopheles instead.
Ibid.

10 In the world of modern art history he surely did far more good than harm, for though he may have corrupted himself by deliberately false ascriptions, the art world can no more be corrupted than Don Juan could be seduced.
Ibid.

11 The last years of his life had become so precious to him that, as he said, he would willingly stand at street corners hat in hand, begging passers-by to drop their unused minutes in it.
John Walker, THE BERNARD BERENSON TREASURY

HENRI BERGSON (1859–1941)
French philosopher

12 His influence upon modern philosophy and thought has been profoundly significant. Bergson's philosophy is complex, but the basic premise of his intellectual system is a faith in direct intuition as a means of attaining knowledge.
William Rose Benét, THE READER'S ENCYCLOPEDIA   1948

13 His interest in biological evolution led to the formulation of his theory of *élan vital*, a spirit of energy and life that moves all living things.
Ibid.

14 True reality, in Bergson's view, is an endless becoming, an unceasing flow and flux, that can be perceived and understood only by intuition, and not by the inferior function of intellect, compelled to halt the flow, to abstract something static from it, in order to analyse it.
Ibid.

GEORGE, BISHOP BERKELEY (1684–1753)
Philosopher

15 Being in company with a gentleman who thought fit to maintain Dr Berkeley's

ingenious philosophy, that nothing exists but as perceived by some mind, when the gentleman was going away Dr Johnson said to him, "Pray sir, don't leave us, for we may perhaps cease to think of you, and then you will cease to exist."
James Boswell, LIFE OF THE JOHNSON   1791

1   I observed that though we are satisfied his doctrine is not true, it is impossible to refute it. I shall never forget the alacrity with which Johnson answered, striking his foot with mighty force against a large stone till he rebounded from it, "I refute it thus."
Ibid.

2   The celebrated and ingenious Bishop of Cloyne, in his *Principles of Human Knowledge*, denies without any ceremony the existence of every kind of matter whatever . . . According to that theory we perceive nothing but ideas which are present in the mind, and which have no dependence at all on external things, so that we have no evidence of the existence of anything external to our minds. Berkeley seems to have been altogether in earnest in maintaining his scepticism concerning the existence of matter; and the more so because he conceived this system to be highly favourable to the doctrines of religion.
Sir David Brewster Quoted W. Clark Russell, A BOOK OF AUTHORS

3   When Bishop Berkeley said "There is no matter" / And proved it — 'twas no matter what he said / They say his system 'tis in vain to batter / Too subtle for the airiest human head: / And yet who can believe it? I would shatter / Gladly all matter down to stone and lead / Or adamant to find the world a spirit / And wear my head, denying that I wear it.
Lord Byron, DON JUAN, *Canto* XI   1824

4   Bishop Berkeley destroyed this world in one volume octavo; and nothing remained, after his time, but mind.
Sydney Smith, SKETCHES OF MORAL PHILOSOPHY

5   We now know much about tar-water on the publication of a book I will send you, written by Dr Berkeley, Bishop of Cloyne. The book contains every subject from tar-water to the trinity; however all the women read it and understand it no more than they would if it were intelligible.
Horace Walpole. Quoted W. Clark Russell, A BOOK OF AUTHORS

1   And God-appointed Berkeley, that proved all things a dream / That this pragmatical preposterous pig of a world, its farrow that so solid seem / Must vanish on the instant if the mind but change its theme.
W. B. Yeats, BLOOD AND THE MOON

HECTOR BERLIOZ (1803–1869)
French composer, pioneer of romanticism

2   Berlioz, musically speaking, is a lunatic; a classical composer only in Paris, the great city of quacks. His music is simply and undisguisedly nonsense.
Anon., *Dramatic and Musical Review* 7 *Jan* 1843

3   The remarkable inequality of his composition may be explained, at least in part, as the work of a vivid imagination, striving to explain itself in a tongue which he never perfectly understood.
Sir W. Henry Haddow, GROVE'S DICTIONARY OF MUSIC AND MUSICIANS (*third edition*)   1929

4   That he possessed genius is beyond all question or controversy. No composer has ever been more original in the true sense of the term; noone has ever written with more spontaneous force or with more vehement and volcanic energy.
Ibid.

5   His imagination seems always at white heat; his eloquence pours forth in a turbid, impetuous torrent which levels all obstacles and overpowers all restraints.
Ibid.

6   He was one of the first musicians in Europe who really appreciated Beethoven.
Ibid.

7   He knew the composition of the various instruments better than the virtuosi who played them. He could foresee by intuition the effect of every possible composition or arrangement. He had inexhaustible invention, boundless audacity, an unerring sense of colour and that highest economy of resource which knows when to spare and when to lavish.
Ibid.

8   Berlioz says nothing in his music, and says it magnificently.
James Gibbons Huneker

SARAH BERNHARDT (1844-1923)
French actress

1 Even in her best days at the Théatre Français refinement was not one of Sarah Bernhardt's strong points. She was ever inclined to emphasise the shrewish part of a woman's temperament, but the discipline and surroundings of the Comédie Française held her in some sort of bondage. Left to herself, alone and uninfluenced she is more inclined to forget the refinement and dignity that are the essentials of her art.
Anon., The Graphic 21 Jul 1894

2 You cannot praise her for knowing how to say verse. She is the Muse of poetry incarnate. Neither intelligence nor art has anything to do with it. She is guided by a secret instinct. She recites verse as the nightingale sings, as Lamartine in the old days used to recite verse.
An anonymous critic in 1868. *Quoted Henry and Dana Lee Thomas,* LIVING BIOGRAPHIES OF FAMOUS WOMEN

3 She is a bit of smoke, a breath of the mist — a fugitive vision of delicate features under a shower of hair and a cloud of lace.
Ibid.

4 Sarah took it for granted that she was the greatest actress in the world, just as Queen Victoria took it for granted that she was Queen of England.
Maurice Baring, SARAH BERNHARDT

5 What can I say of Sarah, so slight, so slim; of Sarah luckily unpossessed of the haunches and thighs which make the usual impersonation of male parts so unrealistic and indeed so offensive — of Sarah with all the suppleness, the lightness and grace of a young man.
François Coppée, of her performance in his play Le Passant

6 She has the head of a virgin and the body of a broomstick.
Alexandre Dumas, of her début at the Comédie Française 1866

7 I remember Sarah Bernhardt's funeral perfectly. I have never had to wait so long to cross the street.
Eric Dunstan. Quoted James Agate, Ego 9 14 Oct 1946

8 She had a great talent but a small nature and a foul tongue.
Frank Harris. Quoted Joanna Richardson, SARAH BERNHARDT AND HER WORLD

9 On her initial visit to America, when the crowds went wild over her, one reporter exclaimed, "Why, New York didn't give Don Pedro of Brazil such an ovation." Sarah serenely announced, "Yes, but he was only an emperor."
Cornelia Otis Skinner, MADAM SARAH

10 She was a great tragic actress everywhere, it seemed, but on the stage in those early years. She was morbid to the point of artistic passion. She fell deeply in love with an undertaker's assistant but refused to marry him when he would not permit her to be present at an embalming. Between the hours of her rehearsals she visited the cemeteries of Paris and sat among the tombstones like a sister of the departed.
Henry and Dana Lee Thomas, LIVING BIOGRAPHIES OF FAMOUS WOMEN

11 You are too stupid to be much of an actress, but it will keep you out of mischief.
Her mother, Julie Von Hard, on entering her as a pupil at the Paris Conservatory

GIOVANNI LORENZO BERNINI (1598-1680)
Italian architect, sculptor and painter; embellisher of St. Peter's, Rome

12 Bernini frequently went into retreats and practised the spiritual exercises of St. Ignatius.
Sir Kenneth Clark, CIVILISATION 1969

13 Bernini was dazzlingly precocious. At the age of sixteen one of his carvings was bought by the Borghese family, and by the time he was twenty he was already commissioned to do a portrait of the Borghese Pope Paul V. In the next three years he became more skilful in the carving of marble than has ever been known before or since.
Ibid.

14 The work of Bernini is ideal and eternal. He not only gave Baroque Rome its character, but he was the chief source of an international style that spread all over Europe.
Ibid.

15 One of the reasons why medieval and renaissance architecture is so much better than our own is that the architects were artists. Bernini, one of the great artists of seventeenth-century Rome, was a sculptor.
Ibid.

16 Bernini's design of the Louvre I would have given my skin for, but the old reserved Italian would give me only a few minutes' view.
Sir Christopher Wren, letter to a friend during a visit to France 1665

SIR JOHN BETJEMAN (1906–1984)
English poet

1 Betjeman's genius lies in his ability to render nebulous or transient states of feeling in a direct and simple manner, so that life itself seems simple; in that sense he is close to the spirit of popular song.
Peter Ackroyd, Sunday Times, reviewing Frank Delany's BETJEMAN COUNTRY 20 *Nov* 1983

2 His poems celebrate the English countryside and ordinary provincial and suburban life. They nostalgically evoke the Victorian era and a past or passing English culture.
William Rose Benét, THE READER'S ENCYCLOPEDIA 1948

3 You've no idea how original it was to write like Tennyson in the 1930s, rather than Eliot or Auden.
Lord David Cecil

4 We invite people like that to tea, but we don't marry them.
Lady Chetwode, mother of Penelope who later became Lady Betjeman

5 Some critics consider Betjeman a trivial, snobbish and sentimental poet, but he has a uniquely individual flavour, and his admirers include W. H. Auden and Philip Larkin.
G. S. Fraser, PENGUIN COMPANION TO LITERATURE (*edited by David Daiches*) 1971

6 He has a passion for Victoriana / Nostalgia flows like lava from his quill / How lovely the remembered dreams of Cornwall / How long the golden days of Muswell Hill.
Roger Woddis, Radio Times, Far More Than Freckled Girls 12 *Feb* 1983

ANEURIN BEVAN (1897–1960)
Welsh-born British politician

7 That squalid nuisance and Welsh soapbox buccaneer.
James Robertson Armstrong, founder of the Vermin Club. Quoted News Review 19 *Aug* 1948

8 If thy Nye offend thee, pluck it out.
Clement Attlee. Speech, Labour NEC Mar 1955

9 Bevan was the greatest parliamentary orator since Charles James Fox.
R. A. Butler, THE ART OF THE POSSIBLE 1982

10 Bevan was an unorthodox Minister. His chief civil servant, Sir William Douglas, started by saying "I would never work with a man like that, who attacked Churchill in the war." But later, when asked how the Minister had got on, he replied with a complete volte-face "He is the best Minister we have ever had."
Ibid.

11 Bevan first heard impassioned rhetoric from the chapels to which his mother and father took him as a child. It is Hazlitt who says that without the background of dissent you cannot become an honest politician, and Aneurin certainly came from a background of dissent.
Ibid.

12 Before his speeches Aneurin became intense and withdrawn, as Bagehot says, to gain inspiration. But there is no doubt that when on his feet he spoke almost completely extempore and as he himself has acknowledged, he sometimes surprised himself by what he said.
Ibid.

13 He will be as great a curse to this country in peace as he was a squalid nuisance in time of war.
Winston Churchill. Quoted Robert Lewis Taylor, THE AMAZING MR CHURCHILL

14 A merchant of discourtesy.
Winston Churchill. Quoted Michael Foot, ANEURIN BEVAN, VOL 1

15 He is one of the few people I would sit still and listen to.
Winston Churchill. Quoted R. A. Butler, THE ART OF THE POSSIBLE 1982

16 Nye wasn't cut out to be a leader. He was cut out to be a prophet. It's no joke being leader of the Labour party, and Nye didn't want the bother; he just wanted to have it all led for him.
Richard Crossman, Thames TV, The Day Before Yesterday 1970

17 He was like a fire in a room on a cold day.
Constance Cummings. Quoted Michael Foot, ANEURIN BEVAN, VOL 1

18 Repent, for the kingdom of Bevan is Nye,
Election slogan, Northampton 1959

19 Bevan could be possessed by Lloyd George's terrible urge to claw down the enemy.
Michael Foot, ANEURIN BEVAN, VOL 2

20 He should have been a poet. Political parties only chain such spirits.
Ibid.

21 Aneurin Bevan was a true orator in the sense that even on quite important issues he

did not know what he was going to say until he had said it.
Paul Johnson, Daily Telegraph, Searching for a Phrase 27 Jul 1979

1 He could boil blood with the evidences of misery, split sides with his jests, and make spirits soar with his visions.
Neil Kinnock, The Times 3 May 1982

2 Nye was born old and died young.
Jennie Lee, his wife. Quoted Michael Foot, ANEURIN BEVAN, VOL 1

3 He enjoys prophesying the imminent fall of the capitalist system and is prepared to play a part, any part, in its burial except that of mute.
Harold Macmillan, Ibid.

4 An ideal Welsh type, the Prophet Aneurin; fatal charm, magic voice, exquisite sensitiveness to beauty, and a liability to break loose and create fifteen different kinds of roaring hell.
Timothy Shy, News Chronicle. Quoted News Review Dec 1946

ERNEST BEVIN (1881–1951)
British politician

5 His strength lay in himself; his weakness in his relation with others.
Alan Bullock, LIFE AND TIMES OF ERNEST BEVIN

6 Somebody once observed of one of his *bêtes noires* "he is his own worst enemy". Bevin growled, "Not while I'm alive he isn't."
Ibid.

7 Beaverbrook once described himself as "the cat that walks alone". Ernest Bevin was a tiger who walked alone, and woe betide anyone who came near him. He often bullied in a good cause; he was a bully just the same.
Ibid.

8 His aim had been to bring the working class within the national community on equal terms. He sought not to raise himself, but the class from which he came, and we are still trying to come to terms with what he achieved.
Alan Bullock, Observer, The Importance of being Ernie 8 Mar 1981

9 Bevin did not understand the Commons much. "I gets up when they nudges me and I sits down when they pulls my coat."
Alan Bullock, ERNEST BEVIN, FOREIGN SECRETARY 1983

10 A speech from Ernest Bevin on a major occasion had all the horrific fascination of a public execution. If the mind was left immune, eyes and ears and emotions were riveted.
Michael Foot, ANEURIN BEVAN, VOL 2

11 He was one of the few men in modern British political history who could have been Prime Minister, but did not think the place worth the effort. He preferred the power he was already exercising.
Roy Jenkins, Observer, reviewing Alan Bullock's ERNEST BEVIN, FOREIGN SECRETARY
6 Nov 1983

12 Bevin always treated the Soviet Union as if it were a breakaway faction of the Transport and General Workers' Union.
Kingsley Martin, HAROLD LASKI

13 He objected to ideas only when others had them.
A. J. P. Taylor, ENGLISH HISTORY 1914–1945

14 Like Churchill he seemed a visitor from the eighteenth century — of the company of Chatham and Samuel Johnson, men of strong hearts and strong opinions.
The Times, obituary

15 Bevin thought he was Palmerston wearing Keir Hardy's cloth cap, whereas he was really the Foreign Office's Charlie McCarthy.
Konni Zilliacus. Quoted Kingsley Martin, HAROLD LASKI

FIRST EARL OF BIRKENHEAD (1872–1930)
(Fredrick Edwin Smith)
British statesman

16 Lord Birkenhead is very clever, but sometimes his brains go to his head.
Margot Asquith, AUTOBIOGRAPHY 1936

17 The trouble with Lord Birkenhead is that he is so un-Christlike.
Margot Asquith. Quoted C.M. Bowra, MEMORIES

18 A most fluent and plausible bounder.
Raymond Asquith

19 He was an orator in an age of mutterers.
Second Earl of Birkenhead, F. E. SMITH, *First Earl of Birkenhead*

20 "Who is this Effie Smith?" asked an old lady when the country was ringing with his maiden speech. "She can't be a modest girl to be talked about so much."
Ibid.

21 He had no idea of the value of money. He refused to attend to his income tax returns

and encountered an enormous overdraft. When remonstrated with he would buy another car or a new motor launch.
Ibid.

1 Smith thought might was right in Ireland, regarded women as mere playthings who should not have the vote, and would not take Indians seriously at all.
Piers Brendon, The Times, reviewing John Campell's F.E. SMITH   24 *Nov* 1983

2 An outstanding Lord Chancellor who distributed the ecclesiastical patronage in his gift on the basis of the cricketing skills of the clerics concerned.
Ibid.

3 A man with the vision of an eagle, but with a blind spot in his eye.
A. Bonar Law. Quoted A. J. P. Taylor, BEAVERBROOK

4 He would sooner keep hot coals in his mouth than a witticism.
Ibid.

KARL OTTO EDUARD LEOPOLD, FÜRST VON BISMARCK (1815–1898)
(Prince von Bismarck-Schönhausen)
German chancellor

5 If the sole duty of a statesman is to do the best he can for his country then Bismarck did his duty. If, between nations, honour and justice count for anything, then Bismarck was a bandit.
Kenneth Bell, Teachers' World, The Iron Chancellor   Sept 1929

6 The soul of Bismarck was a cask of beer.
E. C. Bentley, A BALLADE OF SOULS

7 He lied with consistency and with enjoyment although unlike Lenin he did not actually prefer lying to telling the truth.
Edward Crankshaw, BISMARCK   1981

8 Of vast physical strength, a powerful orator, a gay companion, a brilliant linguist, and born to every subtlety of the diplomatic art, Bismarck united all the qualities of the consummate politician with the breadth and simplicity of purpose which is essential to the highest forms of statesmanship.
H. A. L. Fisher, A HISTORY OF EUROPE 1934

9 Who in hell wants to see a picture about a herring?
Sam Goldwyn, when it was suggested he make a film on the life of Bismarck. Quoted Reginald Pound, THEIR MOODS AND MINE   1937

10 If he was never foolish enough to say "power transcends right", that, nevertheless, was his belief.
Emil Ludwig, BISMARCK; *The Story of a Fighter*

11 Bismarck prepared the way for Hitler by his political demoralisation of Germany.
Anthony Quinton, Observer, reviewing Edward Crankshaw's BISMARCK
17 *Dec* 1981

12 He had been as ruthless and unscrupulous as any other politician. What had distinguished him was his moderation.
A. J. P. Taylor, THE COURSE OF GERMAN HISTORY   1950

13 The most mischievous and dangerous person alive.
Queen Victoria, letter to the Crown Princess of Prussia

WILLIAM BLAKE (1757–1827)
English poet and artist

14 Sanity (in the everyday sense of the word) is not an essential quality of great art. Indeed William Blake's insanity was worth more than the sanity of any number of artistic mediocrities.
Gerald Abraham, Radio Times, The Genius of William Blake   10 *Dec* 1937

15 Blake saw a treeful of angels at Peckham Rye / And his hands could lay hold on the tiger's terrible heart / Blake knew how deep is Hell, and Heaven how high / And could build the universe from one tiny part.
William Rose Benét, MAD BLAKE

16 He approached everything with a mind unclouded by current opinions. There was nothing of the superior person about him. This makes him terrifying.
T. S. Eliot, THE SACRED WOOD   1920

17 Mr Butts calling one day found Mr and Mrs Blake sitting in their summerhouse freed from those "troublesome disguises" which have prevailed since the Fall. "Come in," cried Blake. "It's only Adam and Eve, you know." Husband and wife had been reciting passages from *Paradise Lost*, in character, and the garden had to represent the Garden of Eden.
Gilchrist, LIFE OF WILLIAM BLAKE   1863

18 This seer's ambition soared too far / He sank, on pinions backward blown; / But tho' he touched not sun or star / He made a world his own.
Edmund Gosse, WILLIAM BLAKE

1 He has no sense of the ludicrous, and, as to God, a worm crawling in a privy is as worthy an object as any other, all being to him indifferent. So to Blake the Chimney Sweeper, etc. He is ruined by vain struggles to get rid of what presses on his brain – he attempts impossibles.
William Hazlitt. Quoted Henry Crabb Robinson, DIARY 1811

2 Children, as creatures of delight, are a comparatively recent discovery. It was left for Blake first to see that the child was not merely the young man, but a separate creature, filled with fugitive and exquisite charm.
E. V. Lucas, 365 DAYS AND ONE MORE

3 How shall a wise man babbling like a child / Tame jungle tigers and make lambkins wild?
John Macy, COUPLETS IN CRITICISM, BLAKE

4 Thought by some to be insane, he died in poverty. He is now regarded as one of England's major poets, and one who, despite his difficult private mythology, repays study if only for the sake of his profound intuitive wisdom.
J. B. Priestley, LITERATURE AND WESTERN MAN 1960

5 His paintings are copies of what he saw in his visions. His books are dictations from the spirits. He told me yesterday that when he writes it is for the spirits only; he sees the words fly about the room the moment he has put them on paper, and his book is then published. A man so favoured, of course, has sources of wisdom peculiar to himself.
Henry Crabb Robinson, letter to Dorothy Wordsworth 1828

6 All poetry, to be poetry at all, must have the power of making one now and then involuntarily ejaculate; "What made him think of that?" With Blake one is asking the question all the time.
Lytton Strachey, BOOKS AND CHARACTERS 1922

7 In his earlier work Blake is satisfied with nature as a symbol; in his later work — the Prophetic Books — his meaning is no longer apparent in the ordinary meaning of the words he uses; we have to read him with a key, and the key is not always in our hands; he forgets he is talking to men on earth in some language which he has learnt in heavenly places.
Arthur Symons, WILLIAM BLAKE 1907

8 Where other poets use reality as a springboard into space, he uses it as a foothold when he returns from flight.
Ibid.

9 I called on Blake one evening and found him more than usually excited. He told me he had just seen a wonderful thing — the ghost of a flea! "And did you make a drawing of him?" I enquired. "No indeed," said he. "I wish I had, but I shall if he appears again". He looked earnestly into the corner of the room and then said, "Here he is — reach me my things. I shall keep an eye on him. There he comes! His eager tongue whisking out of his mouth, a cup in his hand to hold blood, and covered in a scaly skin of gold and green" — as he described him, so he drew him.
John Varley. Quoted Allan Cunningham, LIVES OF THE MOST EMINENT BRITISH PAINTERS

10 That he was trained as a pictorial artist is a fact of central importance in Blake's poetry. He was neither a draughtsman and painter who wrote poetry nor a poet who also drew and painted; he was essentially an artist-poet, single and inseparable.
A. C. Ward, ILLUSTRATED HISTORY OF ENGLISH LITERATURE 1955

11 Almost from infancy Blake was beset by visions; when he was four he spoke of God looking in at him through a window; and at the age of eight he declared he saw "a tree filled with angels, bright angelic wings bespangling every bough like stars".
Ibid.

12 Things are in their essence what we choose to make them. A thing is according to the mode in which one looks at it. "Where others," says Blake, "see but the dawn coming over the hill I see the sons of God shouting for joy."
Oscar Wilde, DE PROFUNDIS 1905

13 There is no doubt that this poor man was mad, but there is something in the madness of this man which interests me more than the sanity of Lord Byron or Sir Walter Scott.
William Wordsworth. Quoted Henry Crabb Robinson, REMINISCENCES

14 That William Blake / Who beat upon the wall / Till truth obeyed his call.
W. B. Yeats, AN ACRE OF GRASS 1936

LOUIS BLERIOT (1872–1936)
French pioneer aviator

1 I have to report that M. Bleriot, with his monoplane, crossed the Channel from Calais this morning. I issued to him a Quarantine Certificate, thereby treating it as a yacht and the aviator as Master and owner.
The Collector of Customs at Dover   25 Jul 1909

MARGUERITE, COUNTESS BLESSINGTON (1798–1849)
Irish-born authoress and society hostess

2 A degraded wretch connected with a low and scurrilous Sunday print waited on her and producing an MS sketch of her life, had the audacity to demand one hundred pounds for its suppression. Her ladyship politely told the gentleman that she could not give one hundred pounds for its suppression but would undertake to pay two hundred pounds, if he would print it and bring a copy in person. It is scarcely necessary to say that the scoundrel took the hint and made his bow.
The Crim-Con Gazette   4 May 1839

3 She has an abundant command of language, speaking, in my opinion, more eloquently than she wrote, and in tones in which now and then the delicate flavour of the Irish accent could be detected — that accent which gives great emphasis and expression to kind words, and is wholly different from what is called brogue. She told a good story capitally and was quite the best *raconteuse* I ever heard.
Mrs Newton Crossland, MEMOIRS

4 Lady Blessington's existence is a curiosity and her house and society have at least the merit of being singular, though the latter is not so agreeable as from its composition it ought to be. The reason for this is that the woman herself, who must give the tone to her own society, and influence its character, is ignorant, vulgar and commonplace.
Charles Greville, DIARY   Feb 1839

5 I have no means of knowing whether what the world said of this most beautiful woman was true or false, but I am sure *God* intended her to be good, and there was a deep-seated good intent in whatever she did that came under my observation. She never lost an opportunity of doing a gracious act or saying a gracious word.
Mrs S. C. Hall, letter to R. R. Madden   1853

6 Lady Blessington has grown old, coarse and unattractive — she is fighting against wrinkles and scorbutic complexion and a very unwieldy person and her contemptible paramour is growing too old to be the glass of fashion and is overwhelmed with debt. What an old age theirs must be!
Mrs M. W. Hughes (grandmother to T. Hughes, author of Tom Brown's Schooldays), letter to Mrs Southey   1842

7 "Lady Blessington!" cried the usher aloud / As she swam through the doorway like moon through a cloud / I know not which most her face beamed with — fine creature! / Enjoyment or judgment, or wit or good nature.
Leigh Hunt, BLUE STOCKING REVELS

8 Her perception of the ridiculous was quick and keen. If there was anything absurd in a subject or object presented to her, she was sure to seize on it, and to represent it to others in the most ridiculous aspect possible.
Dr R. R. Madden, THE LITERARY LIFE AND CORRESPONDENCE OF THE COUNTESS OF BLESSINGTON   1855

9 I have seen no other so striking instance of the inferiority of art to nature as in the celebrated portrait of Lady Blessington (by Lawrence). As the original stood before it she fairly "killed" the copy, and this no less in the individual details than in the general effect.
P. G. Patmore, BENTLEY'S MISCELLANY, VOL XXII

10 She was a fine woman; she had understood too well how to captivate the other sex. She had won hearts, never having had a heart to return. No one could be more bland and polished, when she pleased. She knew from no short practice, when it was politic to be amiable, and yet no one could be less amiable when her temper was roused; her language then being well suited to the circumstances of the provocation, both in style and epithet.
Cyrus Redding, FIFTY YEARS' RECOLLECTIONS

11 Widowed, she for more than fifteen years presided over a brilliant salon in Seymour Place, and at Gore House, Kensington, to which every man of talent was proud to come. Every *man* — but virtually no women. For Lady Blessington throughout her years of gorgeous hospitality was a figure of scandal and was ostracised by correct society on account of her supposed

relationship with the fascinating young Frenchman, Alfred Count D'Orsay.
Michael Sadleir, BLESSINGTON–D'ORSAY: A MASQUERADE 1933

1 That she was happy appears nowhere, either in her letters or her diaries; yet hers was a life diffusing happiness. Her kindness was instinct, yet ardent as though it had been passion; and above all women of her time was fascinated, and fascination is a moral grace, for it has origin in the soul.
Lady Wilde, *Dublin University Magazine* Mar 1855

2 She did not write absolute trash — on the contrary she sometimes uttered very shrewd commonsense opinions. But there was such a total lack of elevation of feeling or depth of thought in her works that it was impossible to read them with profit or remember them with interest.
Ibid.

3 The great fault in her character seemed to be an incapacity for profound thought on any subject. She lived on passionately from day to day — excitement the very breath of her existence; never caring or thinking whither it was all tending, but purposing, some day or other when she had time, to think seriously about religion — and thus it was until the end came. There is therefore no tragedy in her life: no deep earnestness and therefore no despair.
Ibid.

BOADICEA (d. 61 AD)
(*or Boudicca as we are now expected to call her*) *Queen of Iceni*

4 Edmund Bolton, a respected historian and friend of Inigo Jones, decided Stonehenge was the tomb of Boadicea, although most archaeologists believe she is buried under platform 10 at King's Cross station.
Glyn Daniels, *The Times*, *Oldest Cathedral* 25 Jul 1983

5 Seneca amassed a huge fortune, much of it acquired by lending money in Britain. The excessive rates of interest that he exacted were among the causes of revolt in that country. The heroic Queen Boadicea, if this is true, was heading a rebellion against capitalism.
Bertrand Russell, HISTORY OF WESTERN PHILOSOPHY 1945

6 Great glory, equal to that of our old victories, were won on that day. Some indeed say that there fell little less than eighty thousand of the Britons, with a loss to our

soldiers of about four hundred, and only as many wounded. Boadicea put an end to her life by poison.
Tacitus, ANNALS

12 The rising of Boadicea is the exception that proves the rule of the easy submission of East and South to Roman influence.
G. M. Trevelyan, HISTORY OF ENGLAND 1926

ANNE BOLEYN (1507–1536)
Henry VIII*'s second queen*

13 You may not imagine that this coronation was before her marriage for she was married much about St. Paul's day last, as the condition thereof doth well appear by reason she is now big with child. Notwithstanding it hath been reported throughout a great part of the realm that I married her; which is plainly false, for I knew not thereof a fortnight after it was done.
Thomas Cranmer, *to Nicholas Hawkins* 17 Jun 1533

1 At my coming she said "Mr Kingston I hear I shall not die afore noon, and I am very sorry therefore, for I thought to be dead by this time, and past my pain." I told her it should be no pain, it was so little. And then she said "I heard say the executioner is very good and I have a little neck" and then, putting her hands about it, laughed heartily, I have seen many men and women executed, and that they have been in great sorrow, and to my knowledge this lady had great joy in death.
Sir W. Kingston, *Constable of the Tower*, *in a letter to Thomas Cromwell* 19 May 1536

2 The unfortunate queen insisted that all her attendants should employ their leisure in making clothes for the poor, which she took care to see were properly distributed.
PERCY ANECDOTES 1820

3 Queen Anne Boleyn is said to have been provided daily with a purse, the contents of which were entirely appropriated to the poor; when she casually met with proper objects, justly thinking no week well passed which did not afford her pleasure in retrospect.
Ibid.

4 She is not one of the handsomest women in the world. She has a swarthy complexion, long neck, wide mouth, bosom not much raised, and in fact has nothing but the king's

great appetite, and her eyes, which are black and beautiful and take great effect.
Report of the Venetian ambassador

HENRY ST. JOHN, VISCOUNT BOLINGBROKE (1678–1751)
English statesman

1 He was ambitious without fortitude, and enterprising without resolution, he was fawning without insinuation and insincere without art; he had admirers without friendship and followers without attachment; parts without probity, knowledge without conduct and experience without judgement.
Lord Hervey, MEMOIRS

2 He was a scoundrel and a coward, a scoundrel for charging a blunderbuss against religion and morality, a coward because he had not the resolution to fire it off himself, but left half-a-crown to a beggarly Scotsman to draw the trigger after his death.
Samuel Johnson, referring to Bolingbroke's posthumously published writings edited by David Mallet. Quoted Boswell, THE LIFE OF JOHNSON

CESARE BORGIA (1476–1507)
Italian administrator and ecclesiastic

3 He was, by his twenty-seventh year, the most feared, hated and envied man of his day, courted by the rulers of France, Spain and the Empire, admired by Machiavelli who immortalised him in *The Prince*. At thirty-one he was dead, dying in an ambush in northern Spain as violently and spectacularly as he had lived.
Sarah Bradford, CESARE BORGIA, HIS LIFE AND TIMES 1976

4 The real Cesare Borgia was a fascinating figure in the mould of the great Shakespearean hero. During the brief space of time that he occupied the stage he shocked and stunned his contemporaries by the loftiness of his ambitions, the boldness and daring of their execution.
Ibid.

5 That Machiavelli, dazzled by the temporary good fortune of Cesare, should boldly hold him up as a model to be copied only makes us realise the cynical despair of the Italians as to the the possibility of success in their country by any other means, and the depth of degradation to which the people had fallen.
A. H. Johnson, EUROPE IN THE SIXTEENTH CENTURY 1879

LUCREZIA BORGIA (1480–1519)
Sister of Cesare Borgia, Duchess of Ferrara

6 Far from being the poisoning Messalina of legend she was a gay, charming pleasure-loving girl whose high spirits made her the centre of the Vatican circle.
Sarah Bradford, CESARE BORGIA, HIS LIFE AND TIMES 1976

7 This beautiful woman, whose character has been the subject of so much controversy and who has been accused, probably unjustly, of the most unmentionable crimes, seems to have been a person of colourless disposition who was made the puppet of the schemes of her father and brother.
A. H. Johnson, EUROPE IN THE SIXTEENTH CENTURY 1897

JAMES BOSWELL (1740–1795)
Scottish-born author. Biographer of Samuel Johnson

8 His clothes were always too large for him; his hair or wig was constantly in a state of negligence; and he never for a moment sat still or upright in a chair. Every look and movement displayed either intentional or involuntary imitation of Johnson.
Fanny Burney, DIARIES 1846

9 He needed Johnson as ivy needs oak.
Cyril Connolly, THE EVENING COLONNADE

10 The incarnation of toadyism.
Washington Irving. Quoted W. Clark Russell, A BOOK OF AUTHORS

11 Sir, you have but two topics, yourself and me. I am sick of both.
Samuel Johnson. Quoted Hester Thrale, ANECDOTES OF JOHNSON 1786

12 Many of the greatest men that have ever lived have written biography. Boswell is one of the smallest men that ever lived and he has beaten them all.
T. B. Macaulay, Edinburgh Review, Samuel Johnson Sep 1831

13 Servile and impertinent, shallow and pedantic, a bigot and a sot, bloated with family pride, and eternally blustering about the dignity of a born gentleman, yet stooping to being a tale-bearer, an eavesdropper, a common butt in the taverns of London.
Ibid.

14 Everything which another man would have hidden, everything the publication of which would have made another man hang himself, was a matter of exaltation of his weak and diseased mind.
Ibid.

1 Boswell certainly looked very badly when dressed; for as he seldom washed himself his clean ruffles served as a striking contrast to his dirty flesh.
J. T. Smith, NOLLEKENS AND HIS TIMES

2 It would be difficult to find a more shattering refutation of the lessons of cheap morality than the life of James Boswell. One of the most extraordinary successes in the history of civilisation was achieved by an idler, a lecher, a drunkard and a snob.
Lytton Strachey, PORTRAITS IN MINIATURE

3 Have you got Boswell's most absurd enormous book [Tour of the Hebrides]? Boswell is the ape of most of Johnson's faults, without a grain of his sense. It is the story of a mountebank and his zany.
Horace Walpole, letter to the Hon. H. S. Conway 6 Oct 1785

SANDRO BOTTICELLI (1444–1510)
Italian artist

4 Nearly all the Madonnas of Botticelli have that expression which has been referred to as 'peevish', but they are more humanly impressive than some of Raphael's apathetic Virgins, whose beauty is often inexpressive and conventional.
Julia de Wolf Addison, THE ART OF THE NATIONAL GALLERY 1905

5 Savonarola persuaded his hearers to make a bonfire of their so-called vanities, including pictures by Botticelli; a heavy price to pay for religious conviction.
Sir Kenneth Clark, CIVILISATION 1969

6 Botticelli's Venus is not at all the amorous strumpet of paganism, but pale and withdrawn, dissolves into his image of the Virgin Mary.
Ibid.

7 The culmination of mediaevalism, the inception of modernism, centre in him.
R. A. Cram, RELIGIOUS PAINTING IN ITALY

8 Surrounded by all the luxury and vice of an epoch of enormous glory, he yet turned and followed the fierce prophet (Savonarola) who cursed it all in the name of Christ; loving the newly discovered art and literature of Greece and Rome, he linked himself with the man who condemned them all to the flames.
Ibid.

9 If Botticelli were alive today he'd be working for *Vogue*.
Peter Ustinov, Observer, Sayings of the Week 21 Oct 1968

ROBERT BOYLE (1627–1691)
English physicist

10 His greatest delight is Chymistry. He has at his sister's a noble laboratory and several servants (prentices to him) to look to it. Foreign Chymists have had large proof of his bounty, for he will spare no expense to get any rare secret.
John Aubrey, BRIEF LIVES 1690

11 He was looked on by all who knew him as a very perfect pattern. He was a devout Christian, humble and modest, almost to a fault, of most spotless and exemplary life in all respects. He neglected his person, despised the world, and lived abstracted from all pleasures, designs and interests.
Gilbert Burnet, HISTORY OF HIS OWN TIMES 1734

12 I went to the Society where were divers experiments in Mr Boyle's Pneumatic Engine. We put in a snake but could not kill it by exhausting the air, only making it extremely sick, but a chick died of convulsions in a short space.
John Evelyn, DIARY 22 Apr 1661

13 The excellent Mr Boyle was the person who seems to have been designed by nature to succeed to the labours and enquiries of the extraordinary genius I have just mentioned (Bacon). By innumerable experiments he, in great measure, filled out those plans and outlines of science which his predecessor had sketched out. His life was spent in the pursuit of nature, through a great variety of forms and changes, and in the most rational as well as devout admiration of its Divine Author.
John Hughes, Spectator

14 Boyle was a great partisan of the mechanical philosophy; a theory which, by discovering some of the secrets of nature, and allowed us to imagine the rest, is so agreeable to the natural vanity and curiosity of men.
David Hume, CONCERNING HUMAN UNDERSTANDING 1748

15 I took boat to the Old Swan and up the river as high as Putney and back again, all the while reading Mr Boyle's book of Colours, which is so chymical that I can understand but little of it, but understand enough to see that he is a most excellent man.
Samuel Pepys, DIARY 2 Jun 1667

16 "Which", says Boerhaave, "of all Mr Boyle's writings shall I recommend?" All of them. To him we owe the secrets of fire, air, water, animals, vegetables, fossils; so that

from his works may be deduced the whole system of natural knowledge.
PERCY ANECDOTES 1820

1   The only attack that the writings of this great and good man ever provoked came from the pen of the irascible Swift. Boyle had published "Occasional Reflections upon several Subjects, whereto is prefixed a Discourse about such kinds of thought" and to ridicule this production Swift wrote his "Pious Meditations on a Broomstick, in the style of the Honourable Mr Boyle". "To what a height", says Boyle's noble relation, the late Lord Orrery, "must the spirit of sarcasm arise in an author who could prevail on himself to ridicule so good a man as Mr Boyle."
Ibid.

2   He was the son of the Earl of Cork and the father of modern chemistry.
George Wilson, British Quarterly Review 1849

TYCHO BRAHE (1546–1601)
Swedish-born astronomer

3   A young Danish astrologer with a golden nose, Tycho Brahe had been partly defaced in a German duel.
Nigel Calder, THE COMET IS COMING 1980

4   On a Baltic island Tycho Brahe was launching comet science by establishing that the comet so 1577 was a long way off in space . . . As soon as someone as skilled as Tycho took the trouble to check Aristotle's fable about comets being sublunary exhalations the observations falsified it.
Ibid.

5   Tycho Brahe diverted himself with polishing glasses for all kinds of spectacles, and making mathematical instruments.
Isaac D'Israeli, CURIOSITIES OF LITERATURE 1824

6   Tycho had a strong belief in the predictions of astrology. When he lived at Uraniaburg he had at his house a madman whom he placed at his feet at table, and fed himself. As he imagined that everything spoken by mad persons presaged something, he carefully observed all this man said; and because it sometimes proved true he imagined it might always be depended on. But credulity, so unworthy of a man so deeply versed in real science, is certainly to be set down less to his own account than to the age in which he lived.
PERCY ANECDOTES 1820

7   Yet Tycho with his knowledge of astronomy and having made observations more

numerous and more accurate than all the astronomers who went before him, continued to reject the system of Copernicus, and to deny the motion of the earth. If Tycho had lived before Copernicus his system would have been a step in the advancement of knowledge; coming after him it was a step back.
Ibid.

JOHANNES BRAHMS (1833–1897)
German composer

8   The Third Symphony is an example of the height of music because the work gives no clue to what it means. It is simply a piece of music.
Sir Edward Elgar: Quoted Basil Maine, ELGAR: HIS LIFE AND WORKS

9   In him the illustrious line of German composers of the first rank seems to have come to an end. Whatever may be the future history of that nation's music, the last of her great masters is in no way unworthy of association with her most illustrious names.
J. A. Fuller-Maitland, GROVE'S DICTIONARY OF MUSIC AND MUSICIANS (*third edition*) 1927

10 One truth you taught us outlived / All the rest; / Music has Brahms to soothe / the savage breast.
Daniel G. Mason, LINES TO PERCY GOETSCHIUS ON HIS 82ND BIRTHDAY

11 Brahms is just like Tennyson, an extraordinary musician with the brains of a third-rate village policeman.
George Bernard Shaw, letter to Packenham Beatty 4 Apr 1893

12 To me it seems quite obvious that the real Brahms is nothing more than a sentimental voluptuary. He is the most wanton of composers, only his wantonness is not vicious; it is that of a great baby, rather tiresomely addicted to dressing himself up as Handel or Beethoven and making a prolonged and intolerable noise.
George Bernard Shaw, The World 21 Jun 1893

13 I played over the music of that scoundrel Brahms. What a giftless bastard.
Tchaikovsky, DIARY 19 Oct 1886

BERTOLT BRECHT (1896–1956)
German dramatist

14 Brecht! If it hadn't been for Adolf Hitler he'd still be behind the bacon counter at Oberammergau.
Anon. Quoted Frank Muir, THE FRANK MUIR BOOK 1975

1 The state of alienation known as Brechtism, but what we used to call bored stiff.
John Coleman, Ibid.

2 I don't regard Brecht as a man of iron-grey purpose and intellect. I think he is a theatrical whore of the first quality.
Peter Hall, Ibid.

3 He could make a horse act.
Lotte Lenya, BBC 1 TV   24 May 1979

4 *The Days of the Commune* has the eloquence of a conversation between a speak-your-weight machine and a whoopee-cushion.
Bernard Levin, Sunday Times   6 Nov 1977

LEONID ILYICH BREZHNEV (1906–1982)
Soviet leader

5 The inexhaustible energy, the principled stand of the party leader, and the indissoluble connection with the nation's life, which are all inherent in L. I. Brezhnev's work have gained him the universal affection and profound respect of the working people.
Tass News Agency, on his 75th birthday   18 Dec 1981

6 Under Brezhnev's leadership the Soviet Union achieved its most prolonged period of internal stability even though many problems were pushed out of sight rather than solved.
The Times, obituary   17 Nov 1982

7 It is hardly surprising that he put a stop to discussions of the crimes of the Stalin era in Soviet publications, for a closer examination of his own rapid promotion under Stalin would doubtless have revealed some of the less edifying chapters in his career.
Ibid.

8 One of the things for which he will be remembered is the "Brezhnev doctrine" which held that "socialist states could not remain inactive in the name of some abstract idea of sovereignty" when they saw socialism (as they defined it) threatened in another socialist state. They had, rather, the right and duty to intervene "to defend socialism wherever and whenever it was threatened".
Ibid.

9 There can be no doubt that Brezhnev bore the prime responsibility for both of the two major acts of policy which disheartened those of us in the West who look forward to a period of calm and of improving East–West relations — the invasion of Czechoslovakia in 1968, and the more recent military intervention in Poland.
Sir Harold Wilson, The Times   12 Nov 1982

JOHN BRIGHT (1811–1889)
English politician and orator

10 In English politics the importance of Bright was that he turned liberalism into a creed, that he made men seek reform because reform was 'right', and that he refused to separate the spheres of morality and politics.
Asa Briggs, VICTORIAN PEOPLE   1954

11 It is true that throughout his life Bright was a bitter critic of the establishment, both ecclesiastical and civil, and that he thundered against the privileges of parsons and squires; but he never wished to see a complete transformation of English institutions, even a complete middle class transformation.
Ibid.

12 I do not pretend myself to be a democrat. I never accepted that title and I believe those who knew me and spoke honestly of me never applied it to me. What I am in favour of is such freedom as will give security to people, but I am not in favour of that freedom which will destroy it.
Of himself. Quoted Asa Briggs, VICTORIAN PEOPLE   1954

13 He was a self-made man and worshipped his creator.
Benjamin Disraeli

14 It was his work to cut down forest trees and he had nothing to do with the subsequent cultivation of the land.
Anthony Trollope

BENJAMIN BRITTEN (1913–1978)
English composer

15 What immediately struck me, as someone who warms to languages, about Britten the composer was his extraordinary musical sensibility in relation to the English language.
W. H. Auden of his co-operation with Britten in the making of The Night Mail for the GPO Film Unit   1935

16 I may not be the best living composer, but I am certainly the busiest.
Benjamin Britten. Quoted William Plomer, ELECTRIC DELIGHTS

17 Composing is like driving down a foggy road towards a house. Slowly you can make out

more details of the house — the colour of the slates and bricks; the shape of the windows. The notes are the bricks and mortar of the house.
Benjamin Britten

ANNE BRONTË (1820–1849)
English novelist

1 She was a very sincere and practical Christian, but the tinge of religious melancholy communicated a sad shade to her brief, blameless life.
Charlotte Brontë

2 A sort of literary Cinderella.
George Moore, CONVERSATIONS IN EBURY STREET 1924

3 Anne Brontë was a gentle, quiet, rather subdued person, by no means pretty, yet of a pleasing appearance. Her manner was curiously expressive of a wish for protection and encouragement, a kind of constant appeal which invited sympathy.
George Smith, employee of her publishers Smith Elder, Cornhill Magazine 1900

4 Her gentle and delicate presence, her sad short, short story, her hard life and early death entered deeply into the poetry and tragedy that have always been entwined with the memory of the Brontës, as women and as writers.
Mrs Humphrey Ward. Preface to the collected edition of the Brontës' works

5 The books and poems that she wrote serve as a matter of comparison by which to test the greatness of her two sisters. She is the measure of their genius — like them but not with them.
Ibid.

CHARLOTTE BRONTË (1816–1855)
English novelist

6 She showed that abysses may exist inside a governess, and eternities inside a manufacturer.
G. K. Chesterton, TWELVE TYPES

7 A coarse, brilliant, selfish waif.
Angus Eassonn, ELIZABETH GASKELL 1979

8 *Jane Eyre* is interesting — but I wish the characters would talk a little less like the heroes and heroines of police reports.
George Eliot, letter to Charles Bray 11 Jun 1848

9 She had been entrusted with the care of a little boy . . . Instigated by his brother he began throwing stones at her and one of

them hit her so severe a blow on the temple that the lads were alarmed into obedience. The next day the mother asked Miss Brontë what occasioned the mark on her forehead. She simply replied "An accident ma'am" and no further enquiry was made: the truant, in a little demonstrative gush, said, putting his hand in hers, "I love 'ou, Miss Brontë." Whereupon the mother exclaimed before all the other children "Love the *governess*, dear?"
Mrs Gaskell, LIFE OF CHARLOTTE BRONTË 1857

10 Charlotte Brontë, one cannot but feel after comparing her early work with modern best sellers, was only unlike them in being fortunate in her circumstances which gave her a cultured background, and in the age in which she lived, which did not get between her and her spontateities.
Q. D. Leavis, FICTION AND THE READING PUBLIC

11 If these remarkable works are the productions of a woman we shall only say she must be a woman pretty nearly unsexed; and Jane Eyre strikes us as a personage much more likely to have sprung ready-armed from the head of a man, and that head a pretty hard one, than to have experienced, in any shape, the softening influence of a female creation.
James Lorimer, North British Review Aug 1849

12 If there is to be an award for one who specialised in love then undoubtedly it must go to Charlotte Brontë. I have the uneasy feeling that the award itself might take the form of a blackthorn crucifix. She belongs to the breed of women who are slaves to love. She was plain, so plain that when members of the opposite sex looked at her she feared they would never look again. She wore black. Black coats and black mantles.
Edna O'Brien, Observer, Love and Punishment 13 Feb 1983

13 Two gentlemen came in leading a tiny, delicate, serious little lady with fair straight hair and steady eyes. She may be a little over thirty; she is dressed in a little barège dress with a pattern of faint green moss. She enters in mittens, in silence, in seriousness; our hearts are beating with wild excitement. This then is the authoress, the unknown power whose books have set all London talking, reading, speculating.
Anne, Lady Ritchie (Thackeray's daughter), CHAPTERS FROM SOME MEMOIRS 1895

1 After breakfast on Sunday morning I took the MS of *Jane Eyre* to my little study, and began to read it. The story took me captive. When the servant came to tell me that luncheon was ready I asked him to bring me in a sandwich and a glass of wine, and still went on with *Jane Eyre*. Dinner came; for me the meal was a very hasty one; and before I went to bed that night I had finished reading the manuscript.
George Smith, employee of her publishers Smith Elder, Cornhill Magazine 1900

2 I believe she would have given all her genius and all her fame to be beautiful. Perhaps few women ever existed more anxious to be pretty than she, and more angrily conscious of the circumstance that she was *not* pretty.
George Smith, The Critic Jan 1901

3 She wants some Tomkins or other to love her and be in love with. But you see she is a little bit of a creature without a pennyworth of good looks, thirty years old, I should say, buried in the country and eating up her own heart there, and no Tomkins will come.
William Makepeace Thackeray, letter to Lucy Baxter 11 *Mar* 1853

4 Though the end of the book is weak, and the beginning not very good, I venture to predict that *Jane Eyre* will be read among English novels when many whose names are now better known shall be forgotten.
Anthony Trollope, AUTOBIOGRAPHY 1883

5 She does not attempt to solve the problems of human life; she is even unaware that such problems exist; all her force, and it is all the more tremendous for being constricted, goes into the assertion "I love, I hate, I suffer".
Virginia Woolf, THE COMMON READER 1925

EMILY JANE BRONTË (1818–1848)
English novelist

6 *Wuthering Heights* sadly wants relief. A few glimpses of sunshine would have increased the reality of the picture and given strength rather than weakness to the whole. There is not, in the entire *dramatis personae*, a single character which is not utterly hateful or thoroughly contemptible.
Anonymous contemporary reviewer. Quoted Charles Simpson, EMILY BRONTË 1929

7 Indeed, I have never seen her parallel in anything, stronger than a man, simpler than a child, her nature stood alone.
Charlotte Brontë, Preface to WUTHERING HEIGHTS

8 Posterity has paid its debt to her too generously, and with too little understanding.
Ivy Compton-Burnett, letter to Anthony Powell

9 Emily is of the company of Blake, not indeed in manner nor in faith, but in her capacity for spiritual absolutism.
Charles Morgan, THE GREAT VICTORIANS (*edited by H.J. and Hugh Massingham*)

10 Emily Brontë remains the sphinx of literature.
W. Robertson Nicoll, CHAMBERS ENCYCLOPEDIA OF ENGLISH LITERATURE 1903

11 Few people have the gift of looking and smiling as she could look and smile. One of her rare impressive looks was something to remember through life.
Ellen Nussey. Letter quoted T. Wemyss Reid, CHARLOTTE BRONTË, A MONOGRAPH 1877

12 *Wuthering Heights* is a fiend of a book, an incredible monster, combining all the strong female tendencies from Mrs Browning to Mrs Brownrigg. The action is laid in Hell — only it seems places and people have English names there.
Dante Gabriel Rossetti, letter to William Allingham 19 *Sept* 1845

13 None can comprehend her genius who does not himself, with passion and sincerity, embrace the illusory nature of time and of material happiness.
May Sinclair, THE THREE BRONTËS 1912

14 She was in love with the Absolute. She was a mystic, not by religious vocation, but by temperament and by ultimate vision.
Ibid.

RUPERT CHAWNER BROOKE (1887–1915)
English poet

15 He energised the Garden-Suburb ethos with a certain original talent and the vigour of a prolonged adolescence.
F. R. Leavis, NEW BEARINGS IN ENGLISH POETRY 1932

16 His verse exhibits something that is rather like Keats' vulgarity with a public school accent.
Ibid.

17 His immensely popular war verses, expressing a mood that was soon to change, have not only removed critical favour from his earlier and much better work but have also

obscured the undoubted fact that he was a writer — maturing slowly, and no worse for that — of great promise in several possible forms, prose as well as verse.
J. B. Priestley, LITERATURE AND WESTERN MAN   1960

1   His attitude towards all other males within a short radius of any attractive female was ridiculously jealous — the attitude of a farmyard cock among hens.
Leonard Woolf, BEGINNING AGAIN   1964

JOHN BROWN (1800–1859)
American abolitionist

2   I am fully persuaded that I am worth inconceivably more to hang than for any other purpose.
Speech at his trial   2 *Nov* 1859

3   I, John Brown, am now quite certain that the crimes of this guilty land can never be purged away, but with blood.
On the day of his execution   2 *Dec* 1859

4   John Brown died on the scaffold for the slave; / Dark was the hour when we dug his shallow grave; / Now God avenges the life he gladly gave, / Freedom reigns today!
Edna Dean Proctor, JOHN BROWN

5   John Brown of Ossawatomie, they led him out to die / And lo! a poor slave-mother with her little child pressed nigh / Then the bold blue eye grew tender, and the old harsh face grew wild / As he stopped between the jeering ranks and kissed the little child.
J. G. Whittier, BROWN OF OSSAWATOMIE

LANCELOT (CAPABILITY) BROWN (1716–1783)
English landscape gardener

6   Brown never hesitated to divert roads, rivers, and demolish villages. His work mirrored both an aggressive ownership of land and the dramatic changes taking place in land usage in his lifetime. Then, a Brown landscape was a symbol of progress or of deprivation — depending on one's point of view.
Peter Levi, *The Times*, *Capability's Fading Glory*   6 *Dec* 1983

7   You can't understand Brown's work if you don't believe in art.
Ibid.

8   Known as 'Capability' because he referred to the capability of a landscape to his clients, he had a meteoric rise from obscure

gardener to friend and adviser to kings and dukes.
Ibid.

SIR THOMAS BROWNE (1605–1682)
English physician and writer

9   He is a pre-eminent example of the class of writer with whom it is form, not substance, that is of the first importance. He is interesting almost exclusively to the student and lover of style.
Edmund Gosse, SIR THOMAS BROWNE   1905

10 Sir Thomas Browne seemed to be of the opinion that the only business of life was to think and that the proper object of speculation was, by darkening knowledge, to breed more speculation and "find no end in wandering mazes lost".
William Hazlitt, CHARACTER OF SIR T. BROWNE AS A WRITER

11 Who would not be curious to see the lineaments of a man who, having himself been twice married, wished that mankind were propagated like trees.
Charles Lamb. Quoted W. Hazlitt, *New Monthly Magazine*   *Jan* 1826

12 Browne's works are unsystematic and unequal; his thought is strikingly original, often expressed with quaint humour or searching pathos. His favourite theme is ever the mystery of death. His style is too idiomatic and difficult to be popular and his studied brevity often falls into absurdity.
David Patrick and F. Hindes Groome, CHAMBERS BIOGRAPHICAL DICTIONARY   1897

13 It is interesting to consider what are the most appropriate places in which different authors should be read. Sir Thomas Browne demands an exotic atmosphere. One could read him floating down the Euphrates, or past the shores of Arabia, and it would be pleasant to open the *Vulgar Errors* in Constantinople, or to get by heart a chapter of the *Christian Morals* between the paws of the Sphinx.
Lytton Strachey, BOOKS AND CHARACTERS   1922

14 His immense egotism has paved the way for all psychological novelists, autobiographers, confession-mongers and dealers in the curious shades of our private life. It was who first turned from the contacts of man with man to their lonely life within.
Virginia Woolf, THE COMMON READER   1923

ELIZABETH BARRETT BROWNING
(1806–1861)
English poet

1 Mrs Browning's death is rather a relief to me, I must say. No more *Aurora Leigh*, thank God. A woman of real genius, I know. But what is the upshot of it all? She and her sex had better mind the kitchen and the children, and perhaps the poor.
Edward Fitzgerald, in a letter. To which Robert Browning replied —

2 That you, Fitzgerald, whom by ear and eye / She never knew, "thanked God my wife was dead". / Aye, dead! and were yourself alive, good Fitz / How to return your thanks would tax my wits / Kicking you seems the lot of common curs — / While more appropriate greeting lends you grace; / Surely to spit there glorifies your face — / Spitting — from lips once sanctified by hers.
Robert Browning, Athenaeum 13 *Jul* 1889

3 The poetess was everything I did not like. She had great cavernous eyes, glowering out under two big bushes of black ringlets, a fashion I had not beheld before. She never laughed, or even smiled, once, during the conversation, and through all the gloom of the shuttered room I could see that her face was hollow and ghastly pale. I was glad when I got out into the sunshine again.
Mrs Hugh Fraser, A DIPLOMAT'S LIFE IN MANY LANDS

4 Her physique was peculiar; curls like the pendant ears of a water spaniel and poor little hands — so thin that when she welcomed you she gave you something like the foot of a young bird.
Frederick Locker, MY CONFIDENCES

5 She was just like a King Charles spaniel; the same large soft brown eyes, the full silky curls falling round her face like a spaniel's ears, the same pathetic wistfulness of expression.
Mrs David Ogilvy, RECOLLECTIONS OF MRS BROWNING

6 Her mouth was too large for beauty, but full of eloquent curves and movements. Her voice was expressive, her manner gentle but full of energy. At times she became intense in tone and gesture, but it was so spontaneous that nobody could ever have thought it assumed.
Ibid.

7 Fate has not been kind to Mrs Browning. Nobody reads her, nobody discusses her, nobody troubles to put her in her place.
Virginia Woolf, SECOND COMMON READER 1932

ROBERT BROWNING (1812–1889)
English poet

8 Metrically he gives the impression of a rhyme, but determined to have one at all costs.
Raymond Asquith, LIFE AND LETTERS

9 Robert Browning / Immediately stopped frowning / And started to blush / When fawned on by Flush.
W. H. Auden, ACADEMIC GRAFFITI

10 Browning was a bit of a grocer in real life.
A. C. Benson, DIARIES 1926

11 Browning used words with the violence of a horse-breaker, giving out the scent of a he-goat. But he got them to do their work.
Ford Madox Ford, THE MARCH OF LITERATURE

12 I like Browning. He isn't at all like a damned literary man.
James Lockhart, LIFE AND LETTERS

13 Many people assert he is hardly a poet at all. An aphorist, a maker of proverbs, a dramatist of sorts, a technical contortionist — but at the core of his work there is a mind of prose. So runs the indictment and it is unfortunately helped by the opportunity his work offers to the drier sort of scholarship.
Peter Porter, Observer, THE POET AS STORYTELLER 20 *Dec* 1981

14 He might have passed for a politician, or a financier, or a diplomatist or, indeed, for anything but a poet.
G. W. E. Russell, PORTRAITS OF THE SEVENTIES 1916

15 And did you once find Browning plain? / And did he really seem quite clear? / And did you read the book again? / How strange it seems, and queer.
Charles W. Stubbs, Parody on Browning's AND DID YOU ONCE SEE SHELLEY PLAIN?

16 Meredith is a prose Browning, and so is Browning.
Oscar Wilde, THE CRITIC AS ARTIST

ANTON BRUCKNER (1824–1896)
Austrian composer

17 In the first movement alone, of the Seventh Symphony, I took note of six pregnancies and at least four miscarriages.
Sir Thomas Beecham. Quoted Harold Atkins and Archie Newman, BEECHAM STORIES

1 As a composer Bruckner can only be understood through his own country, Upper
Austria (much as Schubert can only be
completely understood through his country,
Lower Austria) and through his attributes
as a devout Catholic. His patriotism led him
to mirth and love of the world; his
Catholicism to deep mysticism.
Dr Alfred Einstein, GROVE'S DICTIONARY
OF MUSIC AND MUSICIANS
(*third edition*) 1927

GEORGE BRYAN (BEAU) BRUMMELL
(1778–1840)
Arbiter of fashion. Dandy.

2 A number of us lined the entrance-passage
to the Dandy Club to receive the Prince
who, as he passed along, turned from side to
side to shake hands with each of us; but
when he came to Brummell, he passed him
without the smallest notice and turned to
shake hands with the man opposite
Brummell. As the Prince turned from that
man Brummell leaned forward across the
passage and said in a loud voice, "Alvanley,
who's your fat friend?" We were all dis-
mayed, but in those days Brummell could
do no wrong.
Grantley Berkeley, LIFE AND
RECOLLECTIONS

3 He managed in the end to do that which no
one else could do; he ruined himself. The
gaming table, in the long run, deprived him
of his fortune.
Sir Bernard Burke, FAMILY ROMANCE

4 Speaking lightly of a man to convey contempt he said "He's a fellow who would
send up his plate twice for soup."
Daniel George, A BOOK OF
ANECDOTES 1952

5 Having taken it into his head, at one time,
to eat no vegetables, and being asked by a
lady if he had never eaten any in his life he
said "Yes madam, I once ate a pea."
Ibid.

6 If the cravat was not properly tied at the first
effort it was always rejected. His valet was
coming downstairs one day with a quantity
of tumbled neckcloths under his arms, and
on being interrogated on the subject
solemnly replied. "Oh, these, sir, are *our*
failures."
Captain Jesse, LIFE OF BEAU
BRUMMELL 1844

7 An acquaintance, having bored him dread-
fully about some tour he made in the North
of England, inquired of his impatient listener
which of the lakes he preferred. Brummell
turned his head imploringly towards his
valet, "Robinson, which of the lakes do I
admire?" "Windermere, sir." "Ah yes,
Windermere," repeated Brummell. "So it
is. Windermere."
John Timbs, ENGLISH ECCENTRICS 1875

8 Brummell's sayings are not brilliant in
point. They owe their success to the inimitable impudence with which they were
uttered. Dining at a gentleman's house in
Hampshire where the champagne was far
from being good, he waited for a pause in
the conversation, and saying loud enough to
be heard by everyone at the table, "John,
give me some more of that cider."
Ibid.

GEORGE VILLIERS, FIRST DUKE OF
BUCKINGHAM (1592–1628)
English statesman and royal favourite

9 It was no more in his power to be without
promotion and titles and wealth than for a
healthy man to sit in the sun in the brightest
dog-days and remain without any warmth.
Earl of Clarendon, HISTORY OF THE
REBELLION 1704

10 His ascent was so quick that it seemed
rather a flight than a growth, and he was
such a darling of fortune that he was at the
top before he was seen at the bottom.
Ibid.

11 It is generally given to him who is the little
god at court, to be the great devil in the
country. The commonality hated him with a
perfect hatred; and all the miscarriages in
church and state, at home, abroad, at sea
and on land, were charged on his want of
wisdom, valour or loyalty.
Thomas Fuller, WORTHIES OF
ENGLAND 1662

12 John Felton, a melancholy, mal-contented
gentleman, and a sullen soldier, apprehending himself injured, could find no other way
to revenge his conceived wrongs, than by
writing them with a point on a knife in the
heart of the Duke, whom he stabbed at
Portsmouth Anno Domini 1628.
Ibid.

1   At the age of 22 George Villiers had that rather over-ripe masculine attraction that trembles on the verge of femininity; tall and beautifully proportioned, he had a heart-shaped face framed in dark chestnut hair and short beard, an exquisitely-curved mouth, and the dark blue eyes of the highly-sexed.
J. P. Kenyon, THE STUARTS 1958

2   James was head over heels in love with his "sweet Steenie gossip", his "sweetheart", his "sweet child and wife" and a few days' absence was enough to set him throbbing with desire. "My only sweet and dear child" he drooled "I pray thee hasten thee home to thy dear dad by sunsetting at the furthest."
Ibid.

3   No one dances better, no man runs or jumps better. Indeed he jumped higher than ever Englishman did in so short a time from a private gentleman to a dukedom.
Arthur Wilson, LIFE AND REIGN OF JAMES I 1653

GEORGE VILLIERS, SECOND DUKE OF BUCKINGHAM (1627–1687)
Statesman

4   The madness of vice appeared in his person in very eminent instances, since at the last he became contemptible and poor, sickly and sunk in his parts, as well as in all other respects, so that his conversation was as much avoided as it had ever been courted.
Gilbert Burnet, HISTORY OF HIS OWN TIMES 1734

5   A man so various that he seemed to be / Not one, but all mankind's epitome.
John Dryden, ABSALOM AND ARCHITOPHEL 1682

6   The Duke of Buckingham possessed all the advantages which a graceful person, a high rank, a splendid fortune and a lively wit could bestow; but by his wild conduct, unrestrained either by prudence or principle, he found means in the end to render himself odious, and even insignificant. The least interest could make him abandon his honour, the smallest pleasure could seduce him from his interest, the most frivolous caprice was sufficient to counterbalance his pleasure.
David Hume, HISTORY OF THE STUARTS 1754

7   By his want of secrecy and constancy he destroyed his character in public life; by his contempt of order and economy he dissipated his private fortune; by riot and debauchery he ruined his health; and he remained at least as incapable of doing hurt as he had ever been little desirous of doing good to mankind.
Ibid.

8   When he came into the presence-chamber it was impossible for you not to follow him with your eye as he went along, he moved so gracefully. He got the better of his vast estate and died between two common girls at a little ale-house in Yorkshire.
Dr Lockier. Quoted Rev. Joseph Spence, OBSERVATIONS, ANECDOTES AND CHARACTERS 1820

9   The witty Duke of Buckingham was an extremely bad man. His duel with Lord Shrewsbury was concerted between him and Lady Shrewsbury. All that morning she was trembling for her gallant, and wishing for the death of her husband; and after his fall, it is said, the Duke lay with her in his bloody shirt.
Alexander Pope, Ibid.

FRANCIS TREVELYAN BUCKLAND
(1826–1880)
British naturalist and zoologist

10   Tiglath Pileser the bear was about six months old when he entered Christ Church, where he lived in a corner of a court beside Fell's Buildings. He was provided with a cap and gown, and in this costume was taken to wine parties, or went boating with his master, to the wonderment of the children in Christ Church meadows . . . Tig took part in the proceedings of the British Association in Oxford in 1847, receiving a visit from Lord Houghton, then Mr Monckton Milnes, who attempted to mesmerise him. Tig at last fell under the censure of the Dean of Christ Church. "Mr Buckland," the Dean is reported to have said, "I hear you keep a bear in college, either it or you must go."
George C. Bompas, LIFE OF FRANCIS BUCKLAND 1885

WILLIAM BUCKLAND (1784–1856)
Geologist. Father of the above

11   Dr Buckland used to say that he had eaten his way straight through the animal kingdom and the worst thing was a mole — that was utterly horrible.
August T. C. Hare, THE STORY OF MY LIFE 1896

1 Talk of strange relics led to mention of the heart of a French king preserved at Nuneham in a silver casket. Dr Buckland, looking at it exclaimed, "I have eaten many strange things but have never eaten the heart of a king before" and before anyone could stop him he had gobbled it up, and the precious relic was lost for ever.
Ibid.

2 Dr Buckland used to say that the worst thing he had eaten was a mole, but he afterwards told Lady Lyndhurst that there was one thing worse than a mole, and that was a bluebottle fly.
Ibid.

3 One day, when Dr Buckland was away on holiday a leopard died at the zoo and was interred, as was then the custom, beneath a rose bush. On his return Dr Buckland seized a spade and enjoyed a somewhat gamey leopard steak.
Frank Muir, THE FRANK MUIR BOOK 1975

JOHN BUNYAN (1622–1688)
English author

4 Bunyan's English is tinker's and soldier's and preacher's English. It is the English of the Bible, of the Ironsides and of the village green.
Robert Blatchford, MY FAVOURITE BOOKS

5 Then I set pen to paper with delight / And quickly had my thoughts in black and white / For having now my method by the end / Still as I pulled it came; and so I penned / It down, until at last it came to be / For length and breadth the bigness that you see.
John Bunyan, THE AUTHOR'S APOLOGY FOR HIS BOOK, THE PILGRIM'S PROGRESS 1678

6 To pass away the gloomy hours in prison Bunyan took a rail out of the stool belonging to his cell, and, with his knife, fashioned it into a flute. The keeper, hearing music, followed the sound to Bunyan's cell; but while they were unlocking the door the ingenious prisoner replaced the rail in the stool so that the searchers were unable to solve the mystery; nor, during the remainder of Bunyan's residence in the jail, did they ever discover how the music had been produced.
Robert Chambers, THE BOOK OF DAYS 1864

7 Nowhere perhaps, except in Homer, is there such perfect description by the use of merely plain words. The Elstow tinker produced an original thing, if an original thing was ever produced.
G. K. Chesterton, INTRODUCTION TO PILGRIM'S PROGRESS

8 He was the first man that I ever heard preach to my unenlightened understanding and experience, for methought all his sermons were adapted to my condition and had apt similitudes, being full of the love of God and the manner of its secret working upon the soul, and of the soul under the sense of it, that I could weep for joy, most part of his sermons.
Charles Doe, EXPERIENCES OF CHARLES DOE

9 John Bunyan is the greatest representative of the "common man", and common speech, in English literature.
P. J. Kavanagh, *Radio Times*, *Still Making Progress*

10 He may be supposed to have been always vehement and vigorous in delivery as he frequently is in his language. One day when he had preached "with peculiar warmth and enlargement" some of his friends came to shake hands with him after the service and observed what a "sweet sermon" he had delivered. "Aye," he replied, "you need not remind me of that, for the Devil told me of it before I was out of the pulpit."
Robert Southey, LIFE OF JOHN BUNYAN 1830

11 Why do you call John Bunyan a mystic? It is not possible to make a description of mysticism to include him.
W. B. Yeats, *letter to his father* 24 Jun 1918

EDMUND BURKE (1729–1797)
Irish-born politician and author

12 Burke was a damned wrong-headed fellow, through his whole life jealous and obstinate.
Charles James Fox

13 He prescribed Christian resignation for the poor, to keep them in their place; avarice for the bourgeoisie, to create wealth; and Christian duty for the ruling class, to legitimise the whole system.
Michael Freeman, EDMUND BURKE AND THE CRITIQUE OF POLITICAL RADICALISM 1981

14 I admire his eloquence, I approve his politics, I adore his chivalry and I can almost excuse his reverence for Church establishments.
Edward Gibbon, MEMOIRS 1796

1 Though equal to all things, for all things unfit; / Too nice for a statesman. Too proud for a wit; / For a patriot too cool, for a drudge disobedient, / And too fond of the right to pursue the expedient / In short was his fate, unemployed or in place Sir, / To eat mutton cold and cut blocks with a razor.
Oliver Goldsmith, RETALIATION 1774

2 Burke, sir, is such a man that if you met him for the first time in the street where you were stopped by a drove of oxen and you and he stepped aside to take shelter but for five minutes he'd talk to you in such a manner that when you parted you'd say "This is an extraordinary man."
Samuel Johnson. Quoted Boswell, THE LIFE OF JOHNSON 1791

3 The ideal politician in whom the desire for progress is held in check by a profound regard for the principles of order and continuity.
Hector Macpherson, CHAMBERS ENCYCLOPEDIA OF ENGLISH LITERATURE: *John Morley* 1903

4 Burke always disappointed me as a speaker. I have heard him, during his speeches in the House, make use of the most vulgar expressions, such as "three nips of a straw", "three skips of a louse" etc. and on one occasion when I was present he introduced, as an illustration, a most indelicate story about a French king who asked his physician why his natural children were so much finer than his legitimate.
William Maltby. Quoted Samuel Rogers, TABLE TALK 1856

5 He pities the plumage, but forgets the dying bird.
Thomas Paine, THE RIGHTS OF MAN: *Reflections on the Revolution in France* 1791

6 He was oppressed by metaphor, dislocated by parenthesis, and debilitated by amplification.
Samuel Parr

7 Sheridan once said to me, "When posterity read the speeches of Burke they will hardly be able to believe that, during his life-time, he was not considered a first-rate speaker; nor even a second rate one."
Samuel Rogers, TABLE TALK 1856

8 Burke did not do himself justice as a speaker; his manner was hurried, and he always seemed to be in a passion.
Ibid.

9 Fox once said to me that "Burke was a most impractical person, a most unmanageable colleague — he never would support any measure, however convinced in his heart he might be of its utility, if it has first been proposed by another."
Ibid.

10 Malone was one day walking down Dover Street with Burke when the latter all at once drew himself up and carried his head aloft with an air of great hauteur. Malone perceived that this was occasioned by the approach of Fox who presently passed them on the other side of the street. After Fox had gone by, Burke asked Malone very eagerly "Did he look at me?"
Ibid.

11 Edmund Burke's *Reflections on the Revolution in France*, became the Bible of Conservatives.
David Thomson, ENGLAND IN THE NINETEENTH CENTURY 1950

SIR EDWARD COLEY BURNE-JONES
(1833–1898)
English painter

12 When J. W. M. Turner sent a picture to the Academy it was frequently unfinished; he waited until varnishing day to put in the last touches, planning these according to the proximity of other paintings. On one occasion Burne-Jones had a vividly coloured picture close to Turner's. Turner, murmuring "I'll out-blue you, Jonesy" painted in a brilliant sky. Burne-Jones, to baffle him, changed his own picture to a low tone, which made Turner's look absurd.
Julia de Wolf Addison, THE ART OF THE NATIONAL GALLERY 1905

13 His diligence was stupendous, not only in painting his pictures, but in the constant drawing and sketching by which he sought patiently and humbly to perfect his powers. His pencil drawings are miracles of delicate accuracy; I have heard he never erased, and from the sureness of his touch I can well believe this to be true.
Martin Armstrong, THE GREAT VICTORIANS: *Edward Burne-Jones (Edited by H.J. and Hugh Massingham)*

14 He cured her, he remembered, of a passion for Burne-Jones, but never, alas, of a passion for virtue.
Aldous Huxley, POINT COUNTER POINT 1928

15 Mr Burne-Jones' figures have a way of looking rather sick; but if illness is capable of being amiable — and most of us have had some happy intimation that it is — Mr

Burne-Jones accentuates this side of the case.
Henry James, Atlantic Monthly, London Pictures   Aug 1882

1   I generally go and see Burne-Jones when there is a fog. He looks so angelic, painting away there by candlelight.
Ellen Terry, letter to G. B. Shaw 29 Oct 1896

FANNY (MADAME D'ARBLAY) BURNEY (1752–1842)
English novelist and diarist

2   Miss Burney is a real wonder. What she is, she is intuitively. Dr Burney told me she had had the fewest advantages of any of his daughters, from some peculiar circumstances. And such had been her timidity that he himself had not any suspicion of her powers.
Samuel Johnson, to Mrs Thrale. Quoted Fanny Burney, DIARY   20 June 1779

3   The variety of humour which is to be found in her novels is immense; and though the talk of each person separately is monotonous, the general effect is not monotonous, but a very lively and agreeable diversity. Her plots are rudely construed improbable if we consider them in themselves. But they are admirably framed for exhibiting striking groups of eccentrical characters.
T. B. Macaulay, Edinburgh Review Jan 1843

4   When her best novels were produced her knowledge of books was very small. It is particularly deserving of observation that she appears to have been by no means a novel reader. Her father's library was large, but in the whole collection there was but a single novel, Fielding's *Amelia*.
Ibid.

5   All those whom we have been accustomed to revere as intellectual patriarchs seemed children when compared to her; for Burke sat up all night to read her writings, and Johnson had pronounced her superior to Fielding.
Ibid.

6   Madame D'Arblay is an elderly lady with no remains of personal beauty but a gentle manner.
Sir Walter Scott, Journal   18 Nov 1826

ROBERT BURNS (1759–1796)
Scottish poet

7   A Burns is infinitely better educated than a Byron.
Thomas Carlyle, NOTEBOOK   2 Apr 1831

8   If you can imagine a Scotch commercial traveller in a Scotch commercial hotel leaning on the bar and calling the barmaid "Dearie" then you will know the keynote of Burns' verse.
A. E. Housman in an unpublished essay. Quoted William Plumer, ELECTRIC DELIGHTS

9   Burns had too many love affairs, he drank too much, and he died too soon. If he had loved less, drunk less, and lived longer he would have been a more respectable citizen, a more reliable father, and either a worthy farmer or a worthy exciseman. Whether it would have been more desirable thus than that he should be a great poet is fortunately an unanswerable question.
A. C. Ward, ILLUSTRATED HISTORY OF ENGLISH LITERATURE   1955

SIR RICHARD FRANCIS BURTON (1821–1890)
English explorer

10   I struggled for 47 years. I distinguished myself in every way I possibly could. I never had a compliment, or a "thank you" nor a single farthing. I translated a doubtful book in my old age and I immediately made 16,000 guineas. Now that I know the taste of England we need never be without money.
Richard Burton. Quoted Philip Howard, The Times, For Sale, the Mind of Richard Burton   17 Jun 1983

11   It was his own commander-in-chief, General C. J. Napier who commissioned Burton to investigate the pederast brothels of Karachi, so firing his lifelong interest in oriental erotica.
Philip Howard, Ibid.

ROBERT BURTON (1577–1640)
English author

12   "Burton's *Anatomy of Melancholy* is a valuable book," he said. "It is perhaps overloaded with quotation, but there is a great spirit and a great power in what Burton says when he writes from his own mind. It is the only book that ever took me out of bed two hours sooner than I wished to rise."
Boswell, THE LIFE OF JOHNSON   1791

13   The book in my opinion most useful to a man wishing to acquire a reputation for being well read, with the least trouble, is

Burton's *Anatomy of Melancholy*, the most amusing and instructive medley of quotations and anecdotes I ever perused. But a superficial reader must take care, or his intricacies will bewilder him. If, however, he has patience to go through his volume he will be more improved for literary conversation than by the perusal of any twenty other works with which I am acquainted — at least in the English language.
Lord Byron. Quoted Lady Blessington,
CONVERSATIONS WITH BYRON

1 The author of the *Anatomy of Melancholy* is said to have laboured long in the writing of this book to suppress his own melancholy, and yet but did improve it. I have heard that nothing at last could make him laugh but going down to the Bridge-foot in Oxford, and hearing the barge-men scold and storm and swear at each other, at which he would set his hands to his sides and laugh most profusely.
W. Kennet, A REGISTER AND CHRONICLE ECCLESIASTICAL AND CIVIL 1728

SAMUEL BUTLER (1612–1680)
English author

2 The allusions in Butler are often dark and far fetched, and though scarcely any author was ever able to express his thoughts in so few words, he often employs too many thoughts on one subject and thereby becomes prolix after an unusual manner. It is surprising how much erudition Butler has introduced with so good a grace into a work of pleasantry and humour; *Hudibras* is perhaps one of the most learned compositions that is to be found in any language.
David Hume, PHILOSOPHICAL ESSAYS CONCERNING HUMAN UNDERSTANDING 1748

3 Of all his gains by verse he could not save /
Enough to purchase flannel and a grave.
John Oldham

4 To the Wardrobe; hither comes Mr Battersby; and we falling into discourse on a new book of drollery in use called *Hudibras* I would needs go find it out and met with it at the Temple; cost me 2s 6d. But when I came to read it, it is so silly and abusive of the Presbyter Knight going to the wars, that I am ashamed of it; and by and by meeting at Mr Townsend's for dinner, I sold it to him for 18d.
Samuel Pepys, DIARY 1663

JOHN BYNG (1704–1757)
English Admiral

5 To the perpetual disgrace of Public Justice / The Hon John Byng Esq / Admiral of the Fleet / Fell a Martyr to Political Persecution / March 14th in the year 1757 when / Bravery and Loyalty / Were insufficient securities for the Life and Honour / of a Naval Officer.
Inscription on his monument, Southill, Bedfordshire

6 On Monday March 14, 1757, Mr Byng accompanied by a clergyman who attended him during his confinement and two gentlemen of his relations, about 12 came on the quarterdeck, when he threw his hat on the deck, kneeled on a cushion, tied a handkerchief over his eyes, and dropping another which he held in his hand as a signal, a volley from six marines was fired, five of whose bullets went through him and he was no more. He died with great resolution and composure, not showing the least sign of timidity in the awful moment.
NAVAL HISTORY OF GREAT BRITAIN VOL IV

7 Disgrace and death on the quarter-deck were Byng's lot for allowing caution and wisdom to prevail.
J. H. Plumb, THE FIRST FOUR GEORGES 1956

8 In England it is thought well to kill an Admiral from time to time in order to encourage the others.
Voltaire, CANDIDE 1759

GEORGE GORDON NOEL, LORD BYRON (1788–1824)
English poet

9 Aside from the impossibility of equalling Dryden and Pope in their medium, Byron was really a comedian, not a satirist.
W. H. Auden, THE DYER'S HAND 1963

10 Byron would be forgotten today if he had lived to be a florid old gentleman with iron-grey whiskers, writing very long, very able letters to *The Times* about the Repeal of the Corn Laws.
Max Beerbohm, ZULEIKA DOBSON 1911

11 Talking one day of his domestic misfortunes, as he likes to call his separation from Lady Byron, he dwelt in a kind of unmanly strain of lamentation in that all felt to be unworthy of him . . . I wrote a few lines of verse expressive of my sentiments. He read them, became red and pale by turns with

anger, and threw them down on the table with an expression of countenance which is not to be forgotten. The following are the lines: "And canst thou bare thy breast to vulgar eyes? / And canst thou show them wounds that rankle there? / Methought in noble hearts that sorrow lies / Too deep to suffer coarser minds to share / No! Byron spurn such vain, such weak relief; / And if thy tears must fall — in secret weep."
Lady Blessington, CONVERSATIONS WITH BYRON 1834

1 And poor, proud Byron, sad as grave, / And salt as life forlornly brave, / And quivering with the dart he gave.
Elizabeth Barrett Browning, A VISION OF POETS

2 Even I — albeit I did not know it, / Nor sought of foolscap subjects to be king — / Was reckon'd a considerable time / The grand Napoleon of the realms of rhyme.
Byron, DON JUAN 1824

3 He added nothing to the language, he discovered nothing in the sounds, developed nothing in the meaning, of individual words.
T. S. Eliot, BYRON

4 He writes the thoughts of a city clerk in a metropolitan clerical vernacular.
Ford Madox Ford, THE MARCH OF LITERATURE

5 Lord Byron is only great as a poet. As soon as he reflects he is a child.
Goethe, CONVERSATIONS WITH ECKERMANN 18 *Jan* 1825

6 Luncheon was brought in — veal cutlets etc. Lady Byron began to eat. Byron turned round in disgust and said "Gormandizing beast!" and taking up the tray threw the whole luncheon into the hall.
B. R. Haydon, letter to Miss Mitford 13 *May* 1824

7 I loved him as if he were a favourite and sometimes forward sister.
John Cam Hobhouse. Quoted Michael Joyce, MY FRIEND H

8 Lord Byron did not like to see women eat — and he had another reason for not liking to dine with them, which was, they always had the wings of the chicken.
Leigh Hunt, LORD BYRON AND SOME OF HIS CONTEMPORARIES 1828

9 Byron dealt chiefly in felt and furbelow, wavy Damascus daggers and pocket pistols studded with paste. He threw out frequent and brilliant sparks but his forge burnt to no

purpose; it blazed furiously when it caught muslin and hurried many a pretty wearer into an untimely blanket.
Walter Savage Landor

10 After Byron had become the rage I was frequently amused at the manoeuvres of certain noble ladies to get acquainted with him by means of me; for instance I would receive a note requesting the pleasure of my company on a certain evening, with a postscript "Pray could you not contrive to bring Lord Byron with you."
Samuel Rogers, TABLE TALK 1856

11 Byron had prodigious faculties of composition. He was fond of suppers and used often to sup at my house and eat heartily. After going home he would throw off sixty or eighty verses, which he would send to press next morning.
Ibid.

12 Byron one evening took me to the green room of Drury Lane Theatre where I was much entertained. When the play began I went round to the front of the house, and desired the box-keeper to show me into Lord Byron's box. I had been there about a minute, thinking myself alone when suddenly Byron and Miss Boyce (the actress) emerged from the shadows.
Ibid.

13 One of his fancies (or affectations) was that he could not endure to see a woman eat. I recollect that he once refused to meet Madame de Stael at my house *at dinner*, but came in the evening; and when I asked him to dinner without mentioning what company I was to have, he would write me a note to inquire "if I had invited any women".
Ibid.

14 Byron was without any feeling for the fine arts. He accompanied me to the Pitti Palace in Florence, but soon growing tired of looking at the pictures, sat down in a corner.
Ibid.

15 Such was the insanity of Lady Caroline Lamb's passion for Byron that sometimes when not invited to a party where he was to be, she would wait for him in the street until it was over!
Ibid.

16 Byron sent me *Childe Harold* in the printed sheets before it was published and I read it to my sister. "This," I said "in spite of all its beauty, will never please the public; they will dislike the querulous repining tone that

pervades it, and the dissolute character of the hero." But I quickly found that I was mistaken.
Ibid.

1 The Pilgrim of Eternity.
Percy Bysshe Shelley, ADONIS XXX

2 Lord Byron's establishment consists, besides servants, of ten horses, eight enormous dogs, three monkeys, five cats, an eagle, a crow and a falcon; and all these, except the horses, walk about the house as if they were the masters of it . . . After I have sealed my letter I find that my enumeration of the animals in this Circean Palace was defective. I have just met on the grand staircase five peacocks, two guinea-hens and an Egyptian crane.
Percy Bysshe Shelley, LETTERS, *Ravenna* 10 *Aug* 1821

3 A denaturalised being who, having exhausted every species of sensual gratification and drained the cup of sin to its bitterest dregs, is resolved to show that he is no longer human, even in his frailties, but a cool, unconcerned fiend.
Rev. John Styles, SERMON PREACHED ON LORD BYRON'S WORKS VIEWED IN CONNECTION WITH CHRISTIANITY AND THE OBLIGATIONS OF SOCIAL LIFE

4 A gentleman's children are expected to conform in all things, and academic brilliance is not an acceptable deviation from the norm. The fact that Lord Byron showed promise as a poet was due to the fact that he was brought up by his nurse.
Douglas Sutherland, THE ENGLISH GENTLEMAN   1978

5 He was the most affected of sensualists and the most pretentious of profligates.
Algernon Swinburne, BYRON

6 There lay the enbalmed body of the Pilgrim . . . To confirm or remove my doubts as to the cause of his lameness I uncovered the Pilgrim's feet and was answered — the great mystery was solved. Both his feet were clubbed and his legs withered to the knee — the form and features of an Apollo, with the feet and legs of a sylvan satyr.
E. J. Trelawny, RECOLLECTIONS OF THE LAST DAYS OF SHELLEY AND BYRON   1858

7 My friend the apothecary over the way / Doth in his window Byron's bust display / Once, at Childe Harold's voice, did Europe bow / He wears a patent lung-protector now.
William Watson, THE FALL OF HEROES

8 There never existed a more worthless set than Byron and his friends.
Duke of Wellington

C

CAEDMON (seventh century)
First known English poet

1 In a dream he saw a man standing beside him who called him by name, "Caedmon, sing me a song." "I don't know how to sing," came the reply. The man who addressed him then said "You shall sing for me," and Caedmon immediately began to sing verses in praise of God the Creator that he had never heard before. When he awoke he remembered everything he had sung in the dream. When he told the reeve of the gift he had received the reeve took him before the abbess who ordered him to repeat the verses in the presence of learned men. All agreed that Caedmon's gift had been given him by the Lord.
Bede, ECCLESIASTICAL HISTORY OF THE ENGLISH NATION

CAIUS CAESAR AUGUSTUS GERMANICUS CALIGULA (12–41 AD)
Roman emperor

2 Caligula loved Prasinus the coachman so well that for good will towards the master he bid his horse to supper, gave him wine to drink in cups of state, set barley grains of gold before him to eat, and swore that he would make him consul; which thing had been performed had he not been prevented by sudden death.
Stephen Gosson, THE SCHOOLE OF ABUSE   1579

3 Besides squandering in one year the enormous wealth left by Tiberius he banished or murdered his relatives, excepting his uncle Claudius and his sister Drusilia (with whom he carried on an incestuous intercourse); filled Rome with executions and confiscations; amused himself when dining by having victims tortured and slain in his presence; and uttered the hideous wish that all the Roman people had but one neck, that he might strike it off at a blow.
David Patrick and F. Hindes Groome, CHAMBERS BIOGRAPHICAL DICTIONARY   1897

4 As for his horse, which he called Incitatus, for whose sake before the Circensian Games he would always order the soldiers to give notice to the neighbourhood not to make a noise for fear of disturbing his rest, he built him up a marble stable, with a manger of ivory, and richly furnished it with purple housing clothes, and a collar of precious stones to come round the horse's neck. More than that he allowed him a house and attendants, with costly furniture, for the more splendid entertainment of such as might be invited in the horse's name. And some report that he intended to have made his horse a Consul.
Suetonius, LIVES OF THE CAESARS

JAMES CALLAGHAN (1912–   )
Former British Prime Minister

00 If Hugh Gaitskell's motto was "fight and fight and fight again" then Jim Callaghan's is "manoeuvre and manoeuver and man-oeuvre again."
Ian Bradley, The Times   16 Oct 1980

6 When I am shaving in the morning I say to myself that if I were a young man I would emigrate. By the time I am sitting down to breakfast I ask myself "Where would I go?"
Callaghan at a cabinet meeting. Quoted Barbara Castle, THE CASTLE DIARIES 1974–1976

7 He is not merely a schemer, he's also got a very nice side to him and I like him because he can't resist talking to me. His feelings about me are very much divided. He's attracted by my ability and probably knows that ultimately I'm not nearly as thrusting and ambitious as he is and that unlike him I am intellectually honest. So he talks to me in the friendliest way and fights me ruthlessly behind my back. It is not an attractive combination but in politics it is sometimes inevitable.
Richard Crossman, DIARIES   21 Jul 1968

8 I am more interested in new policies and Jim is more interested in the drama of decision-taking. He hasn't a good policy mind, but he is terribly good at public opinion and

at wisely playing the role of the link between the public and Whitehall.
Ibid. 17 *Aug* 1969

1 There is nobody in politics I can remember, and no case I can think of in history where a man combined such a powerful political personality with so little intelligence.
Roy Jenkins. Ibid. 5 *Sep* 1969

2 He's inordinately ambitious and inordinately weak. So weak that as Chancellor of the Exchequer he used to weep on my shoulder and then go away and intrigue against me. That's a pretty fair analysis.
Harold Wilson. Ibid 4 *Sep* 1968

3 That fellow is getting above himself. We must teach him a lesson. I'll do it after Cabinet tomorrow.
Ibid. 28 *May* 1969

4 I'm having to hold his hand. His nerve is very poor these days.
Harold Wilson 1964

CALLIMACHUS (third century BC)
Alexandrian poet

5 This is the tomb of Callimachus thou are passing. He could sing well and laugh well at the right time, over the wine.
Callimachus, epitaph written for himself

6 Yet weep not for Callimachus; if few the days I lived, few were my sorrows, too.
Lucian (C 150 AD), GREEK ANTHOLOGY

JOHN CALVIN (1509–1564)
French Protestant reformer

7 None can dispute Calvin's intellectual greatness or the powerful services which he rendered to the cause of Protestantism. Stern in spirit and unyielding in will, he is never selfish or petty in his motives. He rendered a double service to Protestantism; he systematised its doctrine and he organised its ecclesiastical discipline
David Patrick and F. Hindes Groome,
CHAMBERS BIOGRAPHICAL
DICTIONARY 1897

WILLIAM CAMDEN (1551–1623)
English historian and antiquary

8 What I have performed I leave to men of judgement. I have travelled over all England; I have conferred with most skilful observers; I have studiously read our own country's writers, old and new; all Greek and Latin authors which have made mention of Britain; I have been diligent in the Records of this Realm; I have looked into most Libraries, Registers and Memorials of Churches, Cities and Corporations; I have pored over many an old Roll and Evidence and produced their testimony when the cause required.
Camden, preface to BRITANNIA 1610

9 His *Annals of the Reign of Queen Elizabeth* is written with a simplicity of expression very rare in that age, and with regard to truth.
David Hume, HISTORY OF ENGLAND 1761

ALBERT CAMUS (1913–1960)
Algerian-born French philosopher, novelist, dramatist

10 His work presents the feeling of the *Absurd*, the plight of man's need for clarity and rationality in confrontation with the unreasonable silence of the universe, and various tragedies of man's failure to assume proper consciousness of his condition or, if he does, to find the human values by which he can shape his life.
William Rose Benét, THE READER'S
ENCYCLOPEDIA 1948

11 His refusal to take solace in a concept of divine or cosmic meaning for human life did not conflict with Camus' humanistic attitude that man is capable of a certain degree of dignity in honestly facing his solitary condition and trying to find and assert the human values such as the maximum possible individual freedom, intercommunication and even love within the limits of that condition.
Ibid.

12 The Humphrey Bogart of Absurdism.
Herbert R. Lottmann, ALBERT
CAMUS 1979

GEORGE CANNING (1770–1827)
British statesman

13 Certainly a very great statesman, he had the vulgarity to use without mercy his splendid aptitude for ridicule. The lash of his tongue, as his friend Sir Walter Scott put it, "fetched away both skin and flesh and would have penetrated the hide of a rhinoceros".
T. Charles Edwards and Brian Richardson,
THEY SAW IT HAPPEN 1958

14 Any difference of opinion or dissent from his views threw him into an ungovernable rage, and on such occasions he flew out with a violence which, the Duke of Wellington said, had often compelled him to be silent

that he might not be involved in bitter altercation.
Charles Greville, MEMOIRS 10 *Aug* 1816

1 The Duke of Wellington talked of Canning the other day a great deal at my mother's. He said his talents were astonishing, his compositions admirable, that he possessed the art of saying exactly what was necessary and passing over those topics on which it was not advisable to touch, his fertility and resources inexhaustible.
Ibid. 10 *Aug* 1817

2 Mr Canning has the luckless ambition to play off the tricks of a political rope-dancer and he chooses to do it on the nerves of humanity.
William Hazlitt, THE SPIRIT OF THE AGE 1824

3 I have not strength and nerves to bear Mr Canning's perpetual notes. He sends me a dozen a day; every trifle, a remark from one of his secretaries, a pamphlet, a paragraph in a newspaper, is cause for his firing off a note; and I live in continual dread every time the door opens that it is to bring a note from Mr Canning.
Lord Liverpool, Prime Minister, of Canning, his Foreign Minister. Ibid. 15 *Dec* 1826

4 He exhibited no extremes. His evening dress was in the plainer fashion of the times. A handsome man in feature, compact in person moulded between activity and strength. His countenance indicated firmness of character, with a good-natured cast over all. He was "bald as the first Caesar".
Sir Charles Petrie, GEORGE CANNING 1946

5 Canning, the hero of the day, now rose. If his predecessor might be compared to an elegant and dexterous boxer, Canning presented the image of a finished antique gladiator. All was noble, refined, simple; then, suddenly, at one splendid point, his eloquence burst forth like lightning — grand and all-subduing.
Prince von Puckler-Moskau, A TOUR IN GERMANY, HOLLAND AND ENGLAND 1826–28

ANTONIO CANOVA (1757–1822)
Italian sculptor and painter

6 The Princess Borghese, Buonaparte's sister, who was no saint, sat to Canova as a reclining Venus, and being asked if she did not feel a little uncomfortable, replied "No. There was a fire in the room."
William Hazlitt, CONVERSATIONS OF JAMES NORTHCOTE ESQ R.A. 1830

CANUTE (994–1035)
King of England, Denmark and Norway

7 Cnut was feared; but he was also respected and admired as a just king who ruled equitably, as a man who strove to emphasise his position as the successor to the dynasty of Alfred, and especially to Edgar the peaceful, and as a pious man who fostered the church.
Christopher Brooke, THE SAXON AND NORMAN KINGS 1963

8 Cnut was not a man to trifle with. Before leaving England in 1014 he dispensed with the hostages his father had collected, but he mutilated them in the process.
Ibid.

9 From 1016 until his death in 1035, when he was aged about forty Cnut was undisputed master of England; for most of the time he was king of Denmark, too, for some of it king of Norway and lord of part of Sweden. He was the greatest figure in the Northern world, and he entered into legend in his lifetime.
Ibid.

10 King Canutus, commonly called Knute, walking on the sea-sands near to Southampton, was extolled by some of his flattering followers and told by them that he was King of Kings. Thereupon he made this demonstration to repel their flattery. He took off his cloak and by wrapping it round together sat down upon it saying, "Sea, I command that thou touch not my feet." But he had no sooner spoken the words but the surging waves dashed him. He then rising up and going back said, "You see now what cause you have to call me King that I am not able by my commandments to stay one wave. No man hath such command, but one King ruleth all. Let us honour him, call him King of Kings, profess him to be the Ruler of the Heavens, Sea and Land."
William Camden, REMAINS CONCERNING BRITAIN 1580

11 A noble figure he was, that great and wise Canute, trying to expiate by justice and mercy the dark deeds of his bloodstained youth; trying (and not in vain) to blend the two races over whom he ruled; rebuilding

the churches and monasteries which his father had destroyed.
Charles Kingsley, HEREWARD THE WAKE 1865

MICHAEL ANGELO MERISI CARAVAGGIO (1569–1609)
Italian painter

1 Carracci extols him for "grinding flesh instead of painting it" — which sounds to our ears like a doubtful compliment, though given with the best intentions.
Julia de Wolf Addison, THE ART OF THE NATIONAL GALLERY 1905

2 He constantly quarrelled with people high in power, and was obliged to flee at various times from various places. He committed homicide in Rome and immediately withdrew discreetly to Naples. After a time he went to Malta, where he was accomplishing good work when he had a misunderstanding with a cavalier which made it necessary for him to disappear at once, so he went to Sicily. On his returning to Rome in 1609 he was overtaken on the road by a malignant fever, which soon put an end to his adventurous life.
Ibid.

3 The earliest, and, on the whole, the greatest Italian painter of the period, experimented with the kind of lighting fashionable in highbrow films in the 1920s, and gained thereby a new dramatic impact.
Sir Kenneth Clark, CIVILISATION 1969

THOMAS CARLYLE (1796–1881)
Scottish-born essayist and historian

4 That anyone who dressed as badly as did Thomas Carlyle should have tried to construct a philosophy of clothes has always seemed to me one of the most pathetic things in literature.
Max Beerbohm

5 It was very good of God to let Carlyle and Mrs Carlyle marry one another and so make only two people miserable instead of four.
Samuel Butler

6 I married for ambition. Carlyle has exceeded all that my wildest hopes ever imagined of him — and I am miserable.
Jane Carlyle. Quoted J. A. Froude, LIFE OF CARLYLE 1884

7 The infatuated little beast dances round him on its hind legs as I ought to do and can't;

and he feels flattered and surprised by such unwonted capers to his honour and glory.
Jane Carlyle. Quoted Elizabeth Drew, THE LITERATURE OF GOSSIP

8 A spectre moving in a world of spectres.
Carlyle, description of himself

9 Carlyle's talk was very racey and interesting, just like his writings, but he sometimes went on too long on the same subject. I remember a funny dinner at my brother's where, among a few others, were Babbage and Lyell, both of whom liked to talk. Carlyle, however, silenced everyone by haranguing during the whole dinner on the advantage of silence. After dinner Babbage, in his grimmest manner, thanked Carlyle for his most interesting lecture on silence.
Charles Darwin, AUTOBIOGRAPHY 1882

10 I must tell you a story Miss Bremer got from Emerson. Carlyle was very angry with him for not believing in the devil, and to convert him took him amongst all the horrors of London — the gin shops etc. — and finally to the House of Commons, plying him at every turn with the question, "Do ye believe in the devil noo?"
George Eliot, letter to Sara Hennell 19 Oct 1851

11 A trip-hammer with an Aeolian attachment.
R. W. Emerson, after meeting Carlyle 1848

12 Swim on his pages, take the poetry and the fine grisly humour, the manly independence.
George Meredith. Quoted G. W. Lyttelton, THE LYTTELTON HART-DAVIS LETTERS 1978

13 His is a wind-in-the-orchard style.
George Meredith. Quoted Sir William Beach Thomas, THE GREAT VICTORIANS: *George Meredith (edited by H.J. and Hugh Massingham)*

14 He had an infallible nose for humbug of all kinds, political, philosophical, logical — and that was something in the Victorian age, which was full of it.
A. L. Rowse, The Times, Fallen Idol: Thomas Carlyle 21 Jan 1981

15 . . . the immaculate Calvinism of so fiery and forcible a champion of slave-holding and slave-torture as Mr Carlyle.
Algernon Swinburne, AFTER LOOKING INTO CARLYLE'S REMINISCENCES

16 Carlyle was the greatest of all historical novelists. He deserves to be remembered by

the *French Revolution* rather than for his failings as a husband, though these, too, are quite interesting.
A. J. P. Taylor, Observer, Carlyle Warts and All 23 Sep 1979

1 Carlyle is a poet to whom nature has denied the faculty of verse.
Alfred, Lord Tennyson, letter to W. E. Gladstone

2 Over-emphasis was habitual in Carlyle's conversation (he once confessed that he was not actually dying every time he cried "Murder!")
A. Wyatt-Tilby, THE GREAT VICTORIANS; Carlyle (edited by H. J. and Hugh Massingham

3 He was an iconoclast in religion, but he distrusted the clergy who would have followed him in modernising the doctrines of Christianity ("There goes Dean Stanley, boring holes in the bottom of the Church of England.")
Ibid.

ANDREW CARNEGIE (1835-1919)
American industrialist and philanthropist

4 He had no ears for any charity unless labelled with his name. He would have given millions to Greece had she labelled the Parthenon Carnegopolis.
Poultney Bigelow, SEVENTY SUMMERS

5 Never before in the history of plutocratic America had any man purchased by mere money so much social advertising and flattery.
Ibid.

6 "How much did you say I had given away?" he asked his secretary. "324,657,399 dollars," said the secretary, his taste for figures being precise. "Good Heavens!" answered Carnegie. "Where did I get all that money?"
Burton J. Hendrick, LIFE OF ANDREW CARNEGIE

CAROLINE OF ANSPACH (1683-1737)
Queen consort of George II

7 Her predominant passion was pride and the darling passion of her soul was power. She was at least seven or eight hours tête-à-tête with the king every day, during which time she was generally saying what she did not think, assenting to what she did not believe and praising what she did not approve. Her single consolation was in reflecting she had

power and that people in coffee-houses were saying she governed the country, without knowing how dear the government of it cost her.
John, Lord Hervey, MEMOIRS OF THE REIGN OF GEORGE II 1848

8 The queen loved reading, and the conversation of men of wit and learning. But she dared not indulge herself so much as she wished to do in this pleasure for fear of the king, who often rebuked her for dabbling in all that lettered nonsense (as he called it).
Ibid.

9 Through force of circumstances her proceedings were often devious, but in a certain robust integrity she never failed and though she dissimulated she remained obstinately and grandly herself.
Peter Quennell, CAROLINE OF ENGLAND 1939

CAROLINE OF BRUNSWICK (1766-1821)
Queen consort of George IV

10 Poor woman. I shall support her for as long as I can because she *is* a woman . . . I am resolved at least always to think that she would have been respectable, if the Prince had behaved only tolerably towards her at first.
Jane Austen, letter to Martha Lloyd 16 Feb 1813

11 Fate wrote her a most tremendous tragedy, and she played it in tights.
Max Beerbohm, KING GEORGE THE FOURTH

12 Harris, I am not well, pray get me a glass of brandy.
George, Prince Regent, on his first sight of Caroline 5 Apr 1795, three days before their marriage

13 Never, so long as she drew breath — and she survived until 1821, the year of her consort's coronation from which, having failed to divorce her, he had her forcibly excluded — was she either respectable or well-behaved.
Peter Quennell, Observer, reviewing Thea Holmes' CAROLINE 1 Jul 1979

14 There was usually a spy behind the door; and Caroline, who was both a hot-headed, pleasure-loving woman and an incorrigible exhibitionist, seldom failed to supply the kind of scandalous details that the British government required.
Ibid.

LEWIS CARROLL (1832–1898)
(Charles Lutwidge Dodgson)
English author and mathematician

1 Boys are not in my line. I think they are a mistake.
Lewis Carroll, LETTERS, VOL I 1837–1885

2 Although remembered chiefly for his two *Alice* books (1865 and 1871) and *The Hunting of the Snark* (1876) the eccentric mathematics don of Christ Church, Oxford also published 252 other books, pamphlets and articles, including his *Symbolic Logic*, his rules for circular billiards, and his proposals for a system of proportional representation.
Richard Holmes, The Times, O Frabjous Day 15 Dec 1982

3 He was as fond of me as he could be of anyone over the age of ten.
Ellen Terry. Quoted Derek Hudson, LEWIS CARROLL 1954

ENRICO CARUSO (1873–1921)
Italian singer

4 He lived his own life so noiselessly, with such concentration, such intensity, such inner stillness that he had no need to draw on the lives of others to replenish it. When I am asked what Caruso thought of his contemporaries I cannot answer. He didn't think of them — he greeted them.
Dorothy Caruso, ENRICO CARUSO; HIS LIFE AND DEATH

5 I am a great singer because I am a bachelor. No man can sing unless he smiles and I should never smile if I was married.
Enrico Caruso. Quoted John Fisher, Everybody's Weekly 3 Sept 1931 (*words which he later disproved by marrying*)

6 The beaming smile, lit by flashing white teeth, radiated an urchin exuberance. Only Caruso would dare to go before the Metropolitan curtain, pat his stomach and implore the audience to go home, "because I am so hungry and want my supper".
Stanley Johnson, CARUSO

GIOVANNI DE SEINGALT CASANOVA (1725–1785)
Italian adventurer

7 A man of finer moral fibre could scarcely have loved so many women; a man of coarser fibre could never have left so many women happy.
Havelock Ellis, SELECTED ESSAYS

8 A self-made man if ever there was one, Casanova is not revered by those who worship self-help.
Ibid.

9 In 1750 he had been abbé, secretary to Cardinal Aquaviva, ensign, and violinist at Rome, Constantinople, Corfu and his own birthplace, Venice, where he cured a senator of apoplexy.
David Patrick and F. Hindes Groome, CHAMBER'S BIOGRAPHICAL DICTIONARY 1897

10 For twenty years he wandered through Europe making the acquaintance of the greatest men of the day, from the pope to Madame Pompadour, and from Cagliostro to Frederick the Great. Alchemist, cabalist, knight of the papal order of the Golden Spur and spy he was everywhere introduced to the best society and had always to 'vanish' after a brief period of felicity.
Ibid.

VISCOUNT CASTLEREAGH (1739–1821)
(Robert Stewart, Marquis of Londonderry)
Irish-born British politician

11 It appears he had an interview with the king on the same day that he saw the Duke and had talked in so strange a way that the king sent for Lord Liverpool in the middle of the night and told him Castlereagh was mad.
Mrs Arbuthnot, JOURNAL

12 He was forbidden to eat hot buttered toast, to a healthy stomach indigestible, to a diseased one ruin. His servant the last morning brought it to him ignorantly; Lord Castlereagh ate heartily of it, his brain filled with more blood; he became insane and cut the carotid artery.
R. B. Haydon, CORRESPONDENCE AND TABLE TALK, *of Castlereagh's suicide* 1853

13 Lord Grenville has more than once said to me at Dropmore "What a frightful mistake it was to send Castlereagh to the Congress of Vienna — a man who was so ignorant he did not know the map of Europe; and who could be won over to make any concessions by only being asked to breakfast with the Emperor."
Samuel Rogers, TABLE TALK 1856

CATHERINE OF ARAGON (1485–1536)
First wife of Henry VIII

14 Henry's wife never laughed, seeing she was the heavy and rather torpid Spaniard,

immersed in Saints' days and expert in indulgencies, grave in her communication with servants and rustling with her crucifix and keys.
Francis Hackett, HENRY THE EIGHTH   1929

1   She had married Henry VIII in the course of dynastic duty. Had Arthur survived Catherine would have marshalled her fidelity and her devotion with the same cruel thoroughness, and entombed him under the same mound of obligation.
Ibid.

MARCUS PORCIUS CATO (234-149 BC)
Roman statesman

2   Physicians will tell us that some food makes turbulence, some gives quiet dreams. Cato, who doted upon cabbage, might find the crude effects thereof in his sleep.
Sir Thomas Browne, ON DREAMS

3   Heroic, stoic Cato the sententious / Who lent his lady to his friend Hortensius.
Lord Byron, DON JUAN   1819

4   The destruction of Carthage became an obsession with Cato and he concluded all speeches and even signed letters with the formula "Carthage must be destroyed".
Bergen Evans, DICTIONARY OF QUOTATIONS

5   He preferred to be, rather than to seem, good; hence the less he sought fame, the more it pursued him.
Sallust, BELLUM SATILINAE

WILLIAM CAXTON (1422-1491)
English translator, and first printer

6   What Caxton chose to print naturally became the staple reading matter of the English reading public of his time. He published nearly 80 titles.
William Rose Benét, THE READER'S ENCYCLOPEDIA   1948

7   The manuscript of the *Morte D'Arthur* has disappeared and the book is thus the first English classic for which we are dependent on a printed text, Caxton's edition, printed in 1485, being itself so rare that only two copies are known, one of these imperfect.
David Patrick, CHAMBERS ENCYCLOPEDIA OF ENGLISH LITERATURE   1903

BENVENUTO CELLINI (1500-1571)
Italian goldsmith, sculptor and author

8   A fairly complete picture of the times emerges from his *Autobiography*, though exaggerated by the author's distortion of his own role in events. Its realism, vivid descriptions, racy style, and above all its portrait of a genuine personality have exerted a strong influence on historians of the Renaissance.
William Rose Benét, THE READER'S ENCYCLOPEDIA   1948

9   When I was about five years old my father, happening to look into the fire, spied in the middle of those most burning flames, a little creature like a lizard, which was sporting in the core of the most intense flames. Pointing it out, he gave me a great box on the ear, which caused me to howl and weep with all my might. Then he pacified me good humouredly and spoke as follows, "My dear little boy I am not striking you for any wrong you may have done, but only to make you remember that the lizard which you see in the fire is a salamander, a creature which has never been seen before by anyone of whom we have creditable information." So saying he kissed me and gave me some pieces of money.
Benvenuto Cellini, AUTOBIOGRAPHY   1558

MIGUEL DE CERVANTES SAAVEDRA (1547-1616)
Spanish novelist, dramatist and poet

10   The ridiculous, for the first time in European literature, became a technique for confronting the spiritual. Cervantes originated an artistic tradition that is still with us.
Anthony Burgess, *Observer*, reviewing *William Byron's* CERVANTES   25 Nov 1979

11   Casting my mind's eye over the whole of fiction, the only absolutely original creation that I can think of is *Don Quixote*.
W. Somerset Maugham, NOVELS AND THEIR AUTHORS   1955

12   In many respects *Don Quixote* is a work of fiction that has never been excelled, for it can be read with equal satisfaction on many different levels. It is at once romance and satire, realism and mythology, one of the most amusing, most pathetic, the wittiest tale ever written.
J. B. Priestley, LITERATURE AND WESTERN MAN   1960

13   The peerless Knight of La Mancha, whom, by the bye, with all his follies, I love more and would actually have gone farther to have paid a visit to, than the greatest hero of antiquity.
Laurence Sterne, TRISTRAM SHANDY   1759

1   I only desire to have follies that are amusing, and am sorry Cervantes laughed chivalry out of fashion.
Horace Walpole, letter to Sir Horace Mann 19 *Jul* 1774

PAUL CÉZANNE (1839–1906)
French post-impressionist painter

2   Trust nature in terms of the cylinder, the sphere, the cone, all in perspective.
Paul Cézanne. Quoted Emile Bernard, PAUL CÉZANNE

3   M. Cézanne gives the impression of being a sort of madman who paints in fits of *delirium tremens . . .* in reality it is only one of the weird shapes generated by hashish.
Marc de Montifond, L'ARTISTE

4   Cézanne was the embodiment of the modern concept of the Artist as Genius, totally preoccupied with his talent and quite indifferent to considerations of social esteem, his own personal comfort and other people's feelings. He was unkempt, foul-mouthed and filthy; he once refused to shake hands with Manet on the grounds that he had not washed for eight days.
Frank Muir, THE FRANK MUIR BOOK 1975

5   He was a nervy, brooding figure, sometimes trundling his canvasses to the Salon, where they were refused, in a cart. When someone asked him politely what was the subject of his new submission to the Salon he replied "A pot of shit".
Ibid.

SIR AUSTEN CHAMBERLAIN (1863–1937)
British politician

6   He is more loyal to his friends than to his convictions.
Margot Asquith, AUTOBIOGRAPHY 1936

7   He always plays the game — and he always loses it.
Winston Churchill

8   He had the mind and manners of a clothes brush.
Harold Nicolson, DIARIES 6 *Jun* 1936

JOSEPH CHAMBERLAIN (1836–1914)
British politician

9   The master of the feast has the manners of a cad and the tongue of a bargee.
H. H. Asquith, letter to Herbert Gladstone Oct 1900

10 Like many successful organisers, his was an uninteresting mind.
Margot Asquith, AUTOBIOGRAPHY 1936

11 Mr Chamberlain loves the working-class man; he loves to see him work.
Winston Churchill

12 His characteristic sally was the sneer, delivered with a poker face broken by a distinct curl of the lip.
Richard Jay, JOSEPH CHAMBERLAIN; *A Political Study*

13 Chamberlain had energy without principle. His aim was Napoleonic — to do great things. The method of getting there was of less importance.
Ibid.

14 Gladstone, when asked in extreme old age why he had clung to public office so long replied in surprise, "Why, don't you know? To keep Mr Chamberlain out, of course."
Ibid.

15 Dangerous as an enemy, untrustworthy as a friend, but fatal as a colleague.
Sir Hercules Robinson

16 For literature he had not the slightest feeling. He rented from Lord Acton a house in Prince's Gate which had a considerable library. When he left I remarked "You will miss the library." to which he replied with indescribable emphasis, "Library? I don't call that a library. There isn't a single book of reference in it."
G. W. E. Russell, PORTRAITS OF THE SEVENTIES 1916

NEVILLE CHAMBERLAIN (1869–1940)
British Prime Minister

17 You have sat too long for any good you have been doing. Depart I say, and let us have done with you. In the name of God — *go!*
L. S. Amery, House of Commons May 1940

18 Chamberlain thought he could run things himself, but he knew nothing of how things go in the world. Stubborn and narrow, and always convinced he was right, he wouldn't listen to advice.
Clement Attlee. Quoted Francis Williams, A PRIME MINISTER REMEMBERS 1961

19 It was like a visit to Woolworth's. Everything in its place and nothing over sixpence.
Aneurin Bevan, of a speech by Neville Chamberlain

20 In the funeral service of capitalism the honeyed and soothing platitudes of the clergyman (Stanley Baldwin) are finished and the cortège is now under the sombre and impressive guidance of the undertaker.
Aneurin Bevan, on Chamberlain becoming Prime Minister

1 Neville Chamberlain is no better than a Mayor of Birmingham, and in a lean year at that. Furthermore, he is too old. He thinks he knows the modern world. What should an old hunks like that know of the modern world?
Lord Hugh Cecil. Quoted David Cecil, THE CECILS OF HATFIELD HOUSE

2 That old town clerk, looking at foreign affairs through the wrong end of a municipal drainpipe.
Attributed to Churchill, after Munich, by A. J. P. Taylor in THE AMAZING MR CHURCHILL; *but to David Lloyd George by Leon Harris in* THE FINE ART OF POLITICAL WIT

3 In the depths of that dusty heart there is nothing but abject surrender.
Winston Churchill

4 The people of Birmingham have a specially heavy burden for they have given the world the curse of the present British Prime Minister.
Sir Stafford Cripps. Speech in Birmingham 18 Mar 1938

5 He seemed such a nice old gentleman that I thought I would give my autograph as a souvenir.
Adolf Hitler, after Munich 1938

6 He was a meticulous housemaid, great at tidying up.
A. J. P. Taylor, ENGLISH HISTORY 1914–1945

SIR CHARLES CHAPLIN (1889–1977)
English-born film actor

7 I remain one thing and one thing only, and this is a clown. It places me on a much higher plane than any politician.
Charles Chaplin, MY AUTOBIOGRAPHY 1965

8 Chaplin is no business man. All he knows that he can't take less.
Sam Goldwyn. Quoted Chaplin, MY AUTOBIOGRAPHY 1964

9 . . . somehow importing to the peeling of a banana the elegant nonchalance of a duke drawing a monogrammed cigarette from a platinum case.
Alexander Woollcott, WHILE ROME BURNS 1834

CHARLEMAGNE (742–814)
King of the Franks and Roman emperor

10 Charlemagne is the first great man of action to emerge from the darkness since the collapse of the Roman world. He was a tireless administrator. The lands he conquered — Bavaria, Saxony, Lombardy — were organised a good deal beyond the capacity of a semi-barbarous age. His empire was an artificial construction and didn't survive him, but the old idea that he saved civilisation isn't so far wrong, because it was through him that the Atlantic world re-established contact with the Mediterranean world.
Sir Kenneth Clark, CIVILISATION 1969

11 He tried to read and write, and used to keep tablets and blanks in bed under his pillow that at leisure hours he might accustom his hand to form letters; however as he did not begin his efforts in due season, but late in life, they met with ill success.
Eginhard (770–820), LIFE OF THE EMPEROR CHARLES

12 He abominated drunkenness in anybody, much more in himself and those of his household; but he could not easily abstain from food, and often complained that fasts injured his health.
Ibid.

13 Charles was large and strong and of lofty stature, though not disproportionately tall (his height is well known to have been seven times the length of his foot.)
Ibid.

CHARLES I (1600–1649)
King

14 He was always an immoderate lover of the Scottish nation, having not only been born there, but educated by that people and besieged by them always, having few English people about him till he was king.
Earl of Clarendon, HISTORY OF THE REBELLION 1704

15 He was very fearless in his person, but not enterprising, and had an excellent understanding, but was not confident enough of it; which made him often times change his opinion for a worse, and follow the advice of a man that did not judge so well as himself.
Ibid.

16 He was, if ever any, the most worthy of the title of an honest man; so great a lover of justice that no temptation could dispose him

to a wrongful action, except that it was so disguised from him that he believed it to be just.
Ibid.

1   We will cut off his head with the Crown upon it.
Oliver Cromwell to Algernon Sidney Jan 1649

2   In spite of his intelligence and cultivation Charles was curiously inept in his contacts with human beings. Socially he was tactless and diffident, and his manner was not helped by his stammer and thick Scottish accent, while in public he was seldom able to make a happy impression.
Ralph Dutton, ENGLISH COURT LIFE   1963

3   A mild and gracious prince who knew not how to be, or how to be made, great.
Archbishop Laud. Quoted Peter Heylin (his chaplain), CYPRIANUS ANGELICUS   1688

4   Though he was as slow of pen as of speech, yet both were very significant; and he had that modesty of his own parts that he was wont usually to say he would willingly make his own despatches, but that he found it better to be a cobbler than a shoemaker.
Sir Philip Warwick, MEMOIRS   1701

5   There were few gentlemen in the world that knew more of useful or necessary learning than the prince did, and yet his proportion of books was small, having like Francis the First of France learnt more by ear than by study.
Ibid.

CHARLES II (1630–1685)
King

6   He said to me once that he was no atheist, but he could not think God would make a man miserable only for taking a little pleasure out of the way.
Gilbert Burnet, HISTORY OF HIS OWN TIMES   1703

7   He has a strange command of himself; he can pass from business to pleasure, and from pleasure to business in so easy a manner that all things seem to come alike to him; he has the greatest art of concealing himself of any man alive, so that those about him cannot tell when he is ill and when he is pleased.
Ibid.

8   The royal refugee our breed restores / With foreign courtiers and with foreign whores, /

And carefully repeopled us again / Throughout his lazy, long, lascivious reign.
Daniel Defoe, THE TRUE-BORN ENGLISHMAN   1701

9   He took delight in having a number of little spaniels follow him and lie in his bedchamber, where he often suffered the bitches to puppy and give suck, which rendered it very offensive, and indeed made the whole court nasty and stinking.
John Evelyn, DIARY   4 *Feb* 1685

10   Charlest II changed his ministers almost as often as he changed his linen, and much of his immunity must be attributed to this sanitary precaution.
J. P. Kenyon, THE STUARTS   1958

11   He was utterly without ambition. He detested business, and would sooner have abdicated his crown than have really undergone the trouble of directing the administration.
T. B. Macaulay, HISTORY OF ENGLAND   1848

12   Charles II was always very merry and was therefore not so much a king as a Monarch. During the civil war he had rendered valuable assistance to his father's side by hiding in all the oak-trees he could find. He was thus very romantic and popular and was able after the death of Cromwell to descend to the throne.
W. C. Sellar and R. J. Yeatman, 1066 AND ALL THAT

13   Here lies our Sovereign Lord, the King / Whose word no man relies on / He never says a foolish thing / Nor ever does a wise one.
John Wilmot, Earl of Rochester, written on the door of the king's bedchamber, 1670. *Charles replied, "True, for my sayings are my own and my actions are my ministers'".*

CHARLES V (1500–1558)
Holy Roman Emperor and King of Spain

14   I came, I saw, God conquered.
Charles, after winning the battle of Muhlberg 23 *Apr* 1547

15   Of middle height and slouching gait, his fine forehead and powerful aquiline nose were spoilt by the underhanging jaw of the Hapsburg and small, bad teeth.
A. H. Johnson, EUROPE IN THE SIXTEENTH CENTURY   1897

THOMAS CHATTERTON (1752–1770)
English poet

1 All think now Chatterton is dead his works are worth preserving: yet no one when he was alive would keep the bard from starving.
Anon., THE ROLLIAD 1785

2 An addiction to poetry is very generally the result of "an uneasy mind in an uneasy body" — Chatterton, *I* think, is mad.
Lord Byron, letter to Leigh Hunt Nov 1815

3 I cannot find in Chatterton's works anything so extraordinary as the age at which they were written. They have a facility, vigour and knowledge which was prodigious in a boy of sixteen, but which would not have been so in a man of twenty. He did not show extraordinary powers of genius, but of precocity.
William Hazlitt, LECTURES ON THE ENGLISH POETS 1818

4 This is the most extraordinary young man that has encountered my knowledge. It is wonderful how the whelp has written such things.
Samuel Johnson. Quoted Boswell, THE LIFE OF JOHNSON 1791

5 He was an instance that a complete genius and a complete rogue can be formed before a man is of age.
Horace Walpole, letter to William Mason 24 Jul 1778

GEOFFREY CHAUCER (1340–1400)
English poet

6 He lacks the high seriousness of the great classics, and therewith an important part of their virtue.
Matthew Arnold, ESSAYS IN CRITICISM 1865

7 And Chaucer, with his infantine / Familiar clasp of things divine / That mark upon his lip is wine.
Elizabeth Barrett Browning, A VISION OF POETS

8 Chaucer, notwithstanding the praises bestowed on him, I think obscene and contemptible; he owes his celebrity merely to his antiquity.
Lord Byron

9 Redith his werkis fol of pleasaunce / Clere in sentence, in language excellent / Briefly to wryte such was his suffysuance / What eyer he saye he tooke in his entente / His language was so fayre and pertynente / It seemeth unto manny's heerynge / Not only the words but verely the thing.
William Caxton, Proem to his edition of CANTERBURY TALES

10 Chaucer is glad and erect.
R. W. Emerson, REPRESENTATIVE MEN 1860

11 In serious and moral poetry he is frequently languid and diffuse; but he springs like Antaeus from the earth, when his subject changes to coarse satire or to merry narrative.
Henry Hallam

12 His words point as an index to the objects like an eye or a finger. There were none of the commonplaces of poetic diction in our author's time; no reflected lights of fancy; no borrowed roseate tints: he was obliged to inspect things for himself; to look narrowly, almost to handle the object. Chaucer had an equal eye for truth of nature and discrimination and character; and his interest in what he saw gave new distinctness and force to what he said.
William Hazlitt, LECTURES ON THE ENGLISH POETS 1818

13 For many historians of literature, and for all general readers, the great mass of Chaucer's work is simply a background to the *Canterbury Tales*, and the whole output of the fourteenth century is simply a background to Chaucer.
C. S. Lewis, ALLEGORY OF LOVE 1936

14 Nothing is too late / Till the tired heart shall cease to palpitate / Chaucer at Woodstock with the nightingales / At sixty wrote the *Canterbury Tales*.
Henry Wadsworth Longfellow, MORITURI SALUTAMUS 1875

15 Sith of our language he was the lode star.
John Lydgate, THE FALLS OF PRINCES 1430

16 Sith he in Englishmaking was the best / Pray unto God to give his soul good rest.
Ibid.

17 I read Chaucer still with as much pleasure as any of our poets. He is a master of manners and of description and the first tale-teller in the true enlivened, natural way.
Alexander Pope. Quoted Rev. Joseph Spence, OBSERVATIONS, ANECDOTES AND CHARACTERS 1820

18 Dan Chaucer, well of English undefiled / On Fame's eternal beedroll worthy to be filed.
Edmund Spenser, FAERIE QUEENE, BOOK IV, CANTO 2 1596

1 Dan Chaucer, the first warbler, whose sweet breath / Precluded those melodious bursts that fill / The spacious times of Elizabeth / With sounds that echo still.
Alfred, Lord Tennyson, A DREAM OF FAIR WOMEN

2 He was a staunch churchman but he laughed at priests. He was an able public servant and courtier, but his views upon sexual morality were very lax. He sympathised with poverty but did nothing to improve the lot of the poor — and yet, as we read him, we are absorbing morality at every pore.
Virginia Woolf, THE COMMON READER   1925

ANTON PAVLOVICH CHEKHOV
(1860–1904)
Russian author

3 I have bought Chekhov's stories. How delightful they are. You buy them, too.
Anton Chekhov, SELECTED LETTERS

EARL OF CHESTERFIELD (1694–1773)
(Philip Dormer Stanhope),
English politician

4 Chesterfield is a little tea-table scoundrel that tells little womanish lies to make quarrels in their families, and tries to make women lose their reputations and make their husbands beat them, without any object but to give himself airs; as if anybody could believe that a woman could like such a dwarf balloon.
George II. *Quoted W. Clark Russell*, A BOOK OF AUTHORS

5 Chesterfield's letters to his son teach the morals of a whore and the manners of a dancing master.
Samuel Johnson. Quoted Boswell, THE LIFE OF JOHNSON

6 Lord Chesterfield's eloquence, the fruit of much study, was less characterised by force and compass than by eloquence and perspicuity and especially by good taste and urbanity and a vein of delicate irony which, while it sometimes inflicted severe strokes, never passed the limits of decency and propriety. It was that of a man who, in the union of wit and good sense with politeness, had no competitor.
Lord Mahon. Quoted W. Clark Russell, A BOOK OF AUTHORS

7 The only Englishman who ever argued for the art of pleasing as the first duty in life.
Voltaire, letter to Frederick the Great
16 *Aug* 1774

8 He had early in his life announced his claim to wit, and the women believed it. He had besides given himself out as a man of great intrigue, with as slender pretensions; yet the women believed in that too — one should have thought that they had been more competent judges of merit in that particular! It was not his fault if he had not wit; nobody excelled his efforts in that point; and though they were far from producing the wit, they at least amply yielded the applause he aimed at.
Horace Walpole, LETTERS

9 Truth he sets at absolute defiance. He continually guards his son against it. Half his letters inculcate deep dissimulation as the most necessary of accomplishments. Add to this his studiously instilling into the young man all the principles of debauchery, when he himself was between seventy and eighty years old; if he is rewarded according to his deserts his name will stink to all generations.
John Wesley, DIARY   11 *Oct* 1775

10 He was a man of much wit, middling sense, and some learning; but as absolutely void of virtue as any Jew, Turk or Heathen that ever lived.
Ibid.

GILBERT KEITH CHESTERTON
(1874–1936)
English novelist, poet and critic

11 Remote and ineffectual don / That dared attack my Chesterton.
Hilaire Belloc, LINES ON A DON

12 One has been told so often that Chesterton is an enormous elephantine creature that the actual sight of him is a little disappointing. He *is* a big man, of course, but not as big as all that; if it were not for his cloak, and his longish hair, and the bow tie he sometimes wears, one would not say he was an exceptional figure in any way. It seemed to me that he took a secret joy in making himself as large as possible, like some little boy who stuffs his overcoat with cushions.
Beverley Nichols, TWENTY-FIVE   1926

13 Chesterton's resolute conviviality is about as genial as an *auto da fé* of teetotallers.
George Bernard Shaw, PEN PORTRAITS AND REVIEWS

FREDERIC CHOPIN (1809–1849)
Polish composer

1 A friend said to Chopin / It would be topin / If only you'd / Write an étude.
Anon., Punch, Moment Musicale

2 Only one man knew how to compose quasi-improvised music; or at least what seemed such. That is Chopin. Here is a charming personality, strange, unique, inimitable.
Georges Bizet

3 The entire works of Chopin present a motley surface of ranting hyperbole and excruciating cacophony. There is an excuse at present for Chopin's delinquencies; he is entrammelled in the enthralling bonds of that arch-enchantress, George Sand; celebrated equally for the number and excellence of her romances and her lovers.
Musical World   28 Oct 1841

4 The piano bard, the piano rhapsodist, the piano mind, the piano soul is Chopin. Tragic, romantic, lyric, heroic, dramatic, fantastic, soulful, sweet, dreamy, brilliant, grand, simple; all possible expressions are found in his compositions, and all are sung by him upon his instrument.
Arthur Rubinstein

DAME AGATHA CHRISTIE (1890–1976)
English thriller writer

5 Outsold only by the Bible and Shakespeare, and translated into over a hundred foreign languages, writer of the longest-running play on the British stage and the most popular entertainer the world has ever known.
Robert Barnard, A TALENT TO DECEIVE 1980

6 You know that, relaxing with a Christie, for an hour or two you can forget the nastiness of life and submerge yourself in a world where, no matter how many murders take place, you are essentially in never-never land.
Edmund Crispin. Quoted H. R. F. Keating, AGATHA CHRISTIE, FIRST LADY OF CRIME

LORD RANDOLPH HENRY SPENCER CHURCHILL (1849–1895)
British statesman

7 Winston Churchill represented his father immortally as a misunderstood Prometheus; hostile opinion retaliated by seeing him as a thwarted Lucifer.
R. F. Forster, LORD RANDOLPH CHURCHILL 1981

8 His cheeks and chin were shaved but he cultivated a ponderous moustache which he turned up at the ends; and this appendage illustrated what Mr Gladstone always urged — that to disguise the mouth, which is one of the most expressive features of the face, is to obscure the whole expression.
G. W. E. Russell, PORTRAITS OF THE SEVENTIES 1916

9 He might have been a great leader. In retrospect he appears a great nuisance.
A. J. P. Taylor, Observer, Winston's Father 22 Nov 1981

SIR WINSTON LEONARD SPENCER CHURCHILL (1874–1965)
British Prime Minister

10 Winston's back.
Admiralty message to Royal Navy on Churchill's appointment as First Sea Lord 3 Sep 1939

11 Trouble with Winston; he nails his trousers to the mast and can't climb down.
Clement Attlee. Quoted Harold Wilson, A PRIME MINISTER ON PRIME MINITERS 1977

12 Lloyd George said to me once, "There's Winston Churchill. He's got ten ideas and one of them is right, but he doesn't know which one."
Clement Attlee. Quoted Francis Williams, A PRIME MINISTER REMEMBERS 1961

13 Then comes Winston with his hundred horse-power mind and what can I do?
Stanley Baldwin. Quoted G. M. Young, STANLEY BALDWIN

14 Dreadful legends were told about Winston Churchill who had been taken away from the school. His naughtiness appeared to have surpassed anything. He had been flogged for taking sugar from the pantry, and so far from being penitent he had taken the Headmaster's sacred straw hat from where it hung over the door, and kicked it to pieces.
Maurice Baring, THE PUPPET SHOW OF MEMORY 1922

15 Churchill has the habit of breaking the rungs of any ladder he puts his foot to.
Lord Beaverbrook, letter to Arthur Brisbane 20 Oct 1932

1 Churchill on top of the wave has in him the stuff of which tyrants are made.
Lord Beaverbrook, POLITICIANS AND THE WAR 1959

2 He never spares himself in conversation. He gives himself so generously that hardly anybody else is permitted to give anything in his presence.
Aneurin Bevan

3 He is a man suffering from petrified adolescence.
Aneurin Bevan. Quoted Vincent Broome, ANEURIN BEVAN

4 He does not like the language of the twentieth century; he talks the language of the eighteenth century. He is still fighting Blenheim all over again. His only answer to a difficult diplomatic situation is to send a gunboat.
Aneurin Bevan. Speech, Labour Party Conference 2 Oct 1951

5 Winston has devoted the best years of his life to preparing his impromptu speeches.
Lord Birkenhead

6 Englishman, 25 years old, about five feet eight inches tall, indifferent build, walks with a forward stoop, pale appearance, reddish brown hair, small and hardly noticeable moustache, talks through his nose and cannot pronounce the letter 's' properly.
Boer description of Churchill after his escape from them

7 The man who may be the wrecker of the Tory party, but was certainly the saviour of the civilised world.
Henry Channon, DIARIES 9 *Apr* 1952

8 In private conversation he tries on speeches like a man trying on ties in his bedroom to see how he would look in them.
Lionel Curtis in a letter to Nancy Astor 1912

9 Churchill is one of the born organists of the English language.
J. L. Garvin, Observer, reviewing THE WORLD CRISIS 1922

10 He has spoiled himself by reading about Napoleon.
David Lloyd George. Quoted Frances Stevenson, DIARIES 19 *May* 1917

11 Winston would go up to his Creator and say he would very much like to meet His Son, about Whom he had heard a great deal and, if possible, would like to call on the Holy Ghost. Winston *loves* meeting people.
David Lloyd George. Quoted A. J. Sylvester, DIARY 2 *Jan* 1937

12 The first time you meet Winston Churchill you see all his faults and the rest of your life you spend in discovering all his virtues.
Lady Lytton. Quoted Christopher Hassall, EDWARD MARSH

13 Sir Winston Churchill *always* wore a watch-chain of a design which most gentlemen would have considered more appropriate to a civic dignitary who had made his money out of hosiery. But then, there were many gentlemen who did not consider Churchill to be quite a gentleman.
Douglas Sutherland, THE ENGLISH GENTLEMAN 1978

14 The Russians in the late war were enormously impressed by Churchill at the table. His appetite for caviar and vodka convinced them they were fighting on the right side.
Robert Lewis Taylor, THE AMAZING MR CHURCHILL

15 By his father he is an Englishman, by his mother an American. Behold the perfect man.
Mark Twain, when Churchill was on a lecture tour in the USA

COLLEY CIBBER (1671–1757)
English actor-manager, dramatist and poet laureate

16 Colley Cibber, they say, was extremely haughty as a theatrical manager, and very insolent to dramatists. When he had rejected a play, if the author desired him to point out the particular parts that displeased him, he took a pinch of snuff and answered in general terms, "Sir, there is nothing in it to *coerce my passions*."
George Coleman the Younger, RANDOM RECORDS 1830

17 He was a strong Hanoverian and as poet laureate from 1730 onwards wrote some sufficiently tiresome and absurd odes.
David Patrick, CHAMBERS ENCYCLOPEDIA OF ENGLISH LITERATURE 1903

18 Cibber had the misfortune to have Fielding as a persistent enemy. Fielding was severe on him for his alterations to Shakespeare's plays, of one of which Cibber self-complacently said "I have endeavoured to make it more like a play than I found in Shakespeare."
Ibid.

19 Less human genius than God gives an ape.
Alexander Pope, DUNCIAD 1743

GIOVANNI CIMABUE (1240–1302)
Italian painter

1 Cimabue has always been regarded as the founder of the great Tuscan school . . . Everyone knows the story of the famous Rucellai Madonna which he painted, and which was escorted to its place over the altar by an enthusiastic multitude, shouting and singing for joy.
Julia de Wolf Addison, THE ART OF THE NATIONAL GALLERY 1905

GEORGE DUKE OF CLARENCE (1449–1478)
Brother of Edward IV

2 This year; that is to mean ye 18th day of February, the Duke of Clarence and brother to the King, then being a prisoner in ye Tower, was secretly put to death and drowned in a barrel of malmesye within ye said Tower.
Robert Fabyan, CHRONICLES 1478

EDWARD HYDE, EARL OF CLARENDON (1608–1674)
English statesman and historian

3 In ordinary times he would have been known during his life merely to his family, his personal friends, and his profession; and would have been forgotten as soon as the tomb closed over him; but amidst civil strife and revolutions he was qualified to take a leading part, and to influence the opinions and conduct of mankind. For delicacy of observation and felicity of delineation of the character of contemporaries he is almost without rival.
Lord John Campbell, LIVES OF THE CHANCELLORS 1845

4 Visited the Lord Chancellor, to whom His Majesty had sent for the seals a few days before. I found him in his bedchamber very sad. The Parliament had accused him and he had enemies at court, especially the buffoons and ladies of pleasure because he thwarted some of them and stood in their way. The truth is he made few friends during his grandeur, among the royal sufferers, but advanced the old rebels.
John Evelyn, DIARY 27 *Aug* 1667

5 To visit the late Lord Chancellor. I found him in his garden at his new-built palace, sitting in his gout wheel-chair, and seeing the gales setting up towards the north-east and the fields. He looked and spake very disconsolately. After some while deploring his condition to me, I took my leave. Next morning I heard he was gone (to live in exile in France) though I am persuaded that had he gone sooner, though but to Canterbury, and there lain quiet, it would have satisfied Parliament.
John Evelyn, DIARY 9 *Dec* 1667

GEORGES CLEMENCEAU (1841–1929)
French Prime Minister

6 There the old Tiger would be sitting, in his grey gloves and grey skull-cap, usually wearing grey slippers, looking like a grey cat.
Bernard Baruch, THE PUBLIC YEARS

7 One day he said to me, "I have no political system, and I have abandoned all political principles. I am a man dealing with events as they come in the light of my experience."
Winston Churchill, GREAT CONTEMPORARIES 1937

8 Monet would never have achieved his last great masterpieces without the support of his friend Georges Clemenceau. That great old warrior had will to spare from saving his country for keeping Monet at work. Time and again Monet, who was going blind, wrote that he could do no more. Whereupon Clemenceau would leave his cabinet room and drive down to Monet's studio and bid him take up his brush.
Sir Kenneth Clark, CIVILISATION 1969

9 My home policy? I wage war. My foreign policy? I wage war. Always, everywhere, I wage war, and I shall continue to wage war until the last quarter of an hour.
Georges Clemenceau. Speech to French Chamber of Deputies 8 *Mar* 1918

10 One could not despise Clemenceau, or dislike him, but only take a different view as to the nature of civilised man or indulge, at least, a different hope.
John Maynard Keynes, THE ECONOMIC CONSEQUENCES OF THE PEACE

CLEOPATRA (69–30 BC)
Queen of Egypt

11 If Cleopatra's nose had been shorter the whole face of the earth would have changed.
Blaise Pascal, PENSÉES

12 Gaius Octavius had a desire to have reserved Cleopatra as a captive to adorn his Triumph; therefore he sent for the Psylli, a people whose faculty and employment is to suck out poison, and made them apply themselves to her wounds, to see if they

could draw forth that venom which her asps had infused there, and which was thought to be the occasion of her death. He did Anthony and Cleopatra that favour as to let them be buried together, and ordered that monument to be finished which was begun by themselves.
Suetonius, LIVES OF THE CAESARS

ROBERT, LORD CLIVE (1725–1774)
British imperial administrator

1 It appears I am destined for something; I will live.
Clive after his failed suicide attempt 1744

2 Robert Clive was charged with having abused his position as Governor of Bengal. During a parliamentary cross-examination he made his famous reply "By God, Mr Chairman, at this moment I stand astonished at my own moderation."
Daniel George, A BOOK OF ANECDOTES 1957

3 A savage old Nabob, with an immense fortune, a tawny complexion, a bad liver and a worse heart.
T. B. Macaulay, Edinburgh Review Jan 1840

WILLIAM COBBETT (1763–1835)
Author, publisher, agricultural reformist

4 In digging up your bones, Tom Paine / Will Cobbett has done well; / You visit him on earth again / He'll visit you in Hell.
Lord Byron

5 There was something cool about Cobbett, for all his fire; and that was his educational instinct, his love of alphabetical and objective teaching. He was a furious debater; but he was a mild and patient schoolmaster. His dogmaticism left off where most dogmaticism begins. He would always bully an equal; but he would never have bullied a pupil.
G. K. Chesterton, WILLIAM COBBETT

6 When I am asked what books a young man or a young woman ought to read I always answer let him or her read *all that I have written* . . . Experience has taught me that it is my duty to give that recommendation.
William Cobbett, ADVICE TO YOUNG MEN

7 He is a kind of fourth estate in the politics of the country. He is not only unquestionably the most powerful political writer of the day; but one of the best writers in the language. He thinks and speaks plain,

broad, downright English. He might be said to have the clearness of Swift, the naturalness of Defoe, and the picturesque satirical description of Mandeville.
William Hazlitt, CHARACTER OF W. COBBETT

8 He was a tall stout man, fair and sunburnt, with a bright smile and an air compounded of the soldier and the farmer, to which his habit of wearing an eternal red waistcoat contributed not a little.
Mary Russell Mitford

RICHARD COBDEN (1804–1865)
British politician. Free Trade advocate

9 You cannot find the man who says "Mr Cobden said this of me", and it is not true.
Walter Bagehot, obituary

10 The greatest political character the pure middle class of this country has yet produced.
Benjamin Disraeli, House of Commons 3 Apr 1864

11 He saw the economic disorder of the world in the same vivid light in which Gladstone saw its political confusion and he pursued his remedy with the same single-minded devotion.
J. L. Hammond, THE GREAT VICTORIANS

SAMUEL TAYLOR COLERIDGE (1772–1834)
English poet and critic

12 Coleridge, poet and philosopher, wrecked in a mist of opium.
Matthew Arnold, ESSAYS IN CRITICISM *(second Series)* 1888

13 Though themes of innocence amuse him best, / Yet still absurdity's a welcome guest.
Lord Byron, ENGLISH BARDS AND SCOTTISH REVIEWERS 1809

14 Never did I see so much apparatus got ready for thinking, and so little thought. He mounts scaffolding, pulleys and tackle, gathers all the tools in the neighbourhood with labour, with noise, demonstration, precept, abuse, and sets three bricks.
Thomas Carlyle

15 A weak, diffusive, weltering, ineffectual man.
Ibid.

16 Stop, Christian passer-by! Stop, child of God / And read with gentle breast! Beneath this sod / A poet lies, or that which once seemed he. / O, lift one thought in prayer for S.T.C. / That he who many a year with

toil of breath / Found death in life, may here find life in death! / Mercy for praise — to be forgiven for fame / He ask'd, and hoped through Christ. Do thou the same.
Coleridge, EPITAPH ON HIMSELF

1 He talked on for ever: and you wished him to talk on for ever.
William Hazlitt, THE LIVING POETS

2 He has only to draw the sliders of his imagination and a thousand subjects expand before him . . . he revolves in his wayward soul, or utters to the passing wind, or discourses in his own shadow . . . and so has sunk into uneasy torpid repose, tantalised by vain imaginings, his lips idly moving, but his heart for ever still, or, as the shattered cords vibrate of themselves, waking melancholy music to the ear of memory.
William Hazlitt

3 I dislike his tergiversation, and his subtleties. I *admire* his genius but not the manner in which, on the whole, he has used it; I think him a martyr to indolence, to extremes, and to disappointed enthusiasm, to a ready metaphysical faculty of over-refining, and talking on any side of any subject.
Leigh Hunt

4 An archangel a little damaged.
Charles Lamb in a letter to William Wordsworth 1816

5 Coleridge holds that a man cannot have a pure mind who refused apple dumplings. I am not sure but he is right.
Charles Lamb, letters of Charles and Mary Lamb

6 Wordsworth and I called upon Coleridge one forenoon when he was lodging off Pall Mall. He talked uninterruptedly for about two hours during which Wordsworth listened to him with profound attention, every now and then nodding his head in assent. On quitting the lodging I said to Wordsworth, "Well, for my own part I could not make head or tail of Coleridge's oration; pray did you understand it?" "Not one syllable," was Wordsworth's reply.
Samuel Rogers, TABLE TALK 1856

7 I have heard Coleridge talk, with eager musical energy, two stricken hours, his face radiant and moist, and communicate no meaning at all to any individual of his hearers.
Sir Walter Scott

8 That extraordinary man Coleridge, after eating a hearty dinner during which he spoke not a word, began a most learned harangue on the Samothracian Mysteries, which he considered as affording the germ

of all stories about fairies, past present and to come. He then diverged to Homer, whose *Iliad* he considered as a collection of poems by different authors at different times during a century.
Sir Walter Scott, DIARY 22 *Apr* 1828

9 Coleridge's ballad of *The Ancient Mariner* is, I think, the clumsiest attempt at German sublimity I ever saw.
Robert Southey

CHRISTOPHER COLUMBUS (1446–1506)
Genoese explorer

10 When news was brought that Dom Christoph Colonus Genoese had discovered the coasts of India all men with great admiration affirmed it to be a thing more divine than human, to sail by the West into the East where spices grow, by a way that was never known before. By this fame and report there increased in my heart a great flame of desire to attempt some notable thing.
Sebastian Cabot. Quoted Hakluyt's VOYAGES

11 Here the men could bear no more, they complained of the length of the voyage. But the Admiral Columbus encouraged them as best he could, holding out high hopes of the gains they could make. He added that it was no use their complaining, because he had reached the Indies and must sail on until with the help of our Lord he discovered land.
Bartolomé de las Casas, quoting from Columbus's log book for 10 *Oct* 1942, *the day before land was sighted*

12 When I reached Cuba I followed its North coast Westward, and found it so extensive I thought that this must be the mainland, the province of Cathay.
Columbus, letter to Ferdinand and Isabella 15 *Feb* 1493

13 Pedro Gonzalo de Mendoza, the grand cardinal of Spain, invited Columbus to a banquet. A shallow courtier present, impatient of the honours paid to Columbus, abruptly asked him whether he thought that in case he had not discovered the Indies, there were not other men who were capable of the enterprise. To this Columbus made no answer, but taking an egg, invited the company to make it stand on one end. Everyone attempted it, but in vain: whereupon he struck it on the table so as to break the end, and left it standing on the broken part, illustrating in this simple manner, that

when he had once shown the way to the New World nothing was easier than to follow it.
Washington Irving, LIFE OF COLUMBUS 1828, *translated from Benzoni*, HISTORIA DEL MONDO NUOVO 1565

1 Columbus, when asked by the Spanish queen to describe the appearance of the newly discovered land (Dominica) had shown her its likeness by crumpling a sheet of parchment in his hand.
Rayner Unwin, THE DEFEAT OF JOHN HAWKINS 1959

WILLIAM CONGREVE (1670–1729)
English dramatist

2 Wickedness is no subject for comedy; to forget this was Congreve's great error, and almost peculiar to him.
Samuel Taylor Coleridge

3 Mirabel, the fine gentleman of *Way of the World* is, I believe, not far distant from the real character of Congreve.
Thomas Davies, DRAMATIC MISCELLANIES

4 He spoke of his works as trifles that were beneath him, and hinted to me at our first conversation that I should visit him upon no other foot than that of a gentleman who led a life of plainness and simplicity. I answered that had he been so unfortunate as to be a mere gentleman, I should never have come to visit him, and I was very much disgusted at so unseasonable a piece of vanity.
Voltaire, LETTERS CONCERNING THE ENGLISH NATION 1733

JOSEPH CONRAD (1857–1924)
(Jozef Korzeniowski)
Polish-born novelist, writing in English

5 I had to work like a coal-miner in his pit, quarrying all my English sentences out of a black night.
Conrad, letter to Edward Garnett 28 Aug 1908

6 I can spell and I can understand English. I may not always speak it very well, but I have no need of a dictionary.
Conrad to Hugh Walpole, who had presented him with a dictionary. Quoted John Conrad, JOSEPH CONRAD: TIMES REMEMBERED

7 When one of the dogs jumped on Hugh Walpole and made him indulge in a querulous blasphemy Conrad was quick with a rebuke. He did not go to church, but he never took God's name in vain. He had

heard the voice of God too often, howling in the rigging.
John Conrad, JOSEPH CONRAD: TIMES REMEMBERED

8 Conrad spent a day finding the *mot juste*, and then killed it.
Ford Madox Ford. Quoted Robert Lowell, NOTEBOOK

9 The first mate is a Pole called Conrad, and is a capital chap though queer to look at; he is a man of travel and experience in many parts of the world, and has a fund of yarns on which I draw freely.
John Galsworthy in a letter written, age 26, when travelling home in a clipper from Australia. Quoted Dudley Barker, JOHN GALSWORTHY: MAN OF PRINCIPLE

10 That a foreigner should write English like this is one of the miracles of literature.
George Gissing, letter to Miss Collet 24 Dec 1908

11 What is Conrad but the wreck of Stevenson, floating about on the slip-slop of Henry James?
George Moore. Quoted G. W. Lyttelton, THE LYTTELTON HART-DAVIS LETTERS 8 Mar 1950

12 One of the surest signs of his genius is that women dislike his books.
George Orwell, New English Weekly 23 Aug 1936

13 He thought of civilised and morally tolerable human life as a dangerous walk on a thin crust of barely cooled lava which at any moment might break and let the unwary sink into fiery depths.
Bertrand Russell. Quoted Norman Sherry, CONRAD AND HIS WORLD

JOHN CONSTABLE (1776–1837)
English painter

14 Constable had no large fame in his own day, but he knew that he painted truth, and his simple heart was satisfied with his own honesty. He used to say "My pictures will never be popular for they have no handling, but I do not see handling in nature."
Julia de Wolf Addison, THE ART OF THE NATIONAL GALLERY 1905

15 His life may be said to have been bounded on the south by Salisbury for he never went abroad, not even to visit Italy.
Ibid.

16 The painters of the 'brown-fiddle school' used to laugh at his 'dampness' which is neither more nor less than virility, and

Fuseli called one day to the Academy porter, "Bring my umbrella — I am going to see Mr Constable's pictures."
Ibid.

1 I have got my picture [*Valley Farm*] into a very beautiful state; I have kept my brightness without my spottiness, and I have preserved God Almighty's daylight, which is enjoyed by all mankind except only lovers of old dirty canvas and snuff of candle.
Constable, DIARY

2 My first lesson was when Benjamin West told me not to forget that "light and shadow never stand still".
Ibid.

3 When real business is to be done you are the most energetic and punctual of men. In smaller matters, such as putting on your breeches, you are apt to lose time in deciding which leg shall go in first.
John Fisher, letter to Constable 3 *Jul* 1823

4 I have seen him admire a fine tree with an ecstasy like that with which he could catch up a beautiful child into his arms.
C. R. Leslie, LIFE OF JOHN CONSTABLE 1843

5 Don't be disheartened young man, we shall hear from you again. You must have loved nature very much before you could have painted this.
Benjamin West to Constable when one of his early landscapes was rejected by the Academy

CAPTAIN JAMES COOK (1728–1779)
English navigator and explorer

6 At daylight in the morning we discovered a bay which appeared to be tolerably well sheltered from all winds, into which I resolved to go with the ship.
Cook, recording the discovery of Botany Bay in his journal 20 *Apr* 1770

7 The story of his life does not lend itself to exploitation by cheap biographers. He was no 'great lover'; he was a great worker; there was nothing scandalous, or equivocal, or cheaply sensational in his career; and nobody ever made fewer mistakes.
William Plomer, ANNE TO VICTORIA (*edited by Bonamy Dabreé*)

JOHN CALVIN COOLIDGE (1872–1935)
Thirtieth President of the United States

8 Nobody has worked harder at inactivity with such a force of character, with such unremitting attention to detail, with such conscientious devotion to the task.
Walter Lippmann, obituary of Coolidge

9 He looks as if he had been weaned on a pickle.
Alice Roosevelt Longworth

10 He had one really notable talent. He slept more than any other president.
H. L. Mencken, obituary of Coolidge

11 There were no thrills while he reigned, but neither were there any headaches. He had no ideas and he was not a nuisance.
Ibid.

12 Why, I never even knew that he was alive.
Dorothy Parker, on being told that Coolidge had died

13 "You must talk to me Mr Coolidge," said a woman at a party. "I've made a bet that I can get more than two words out of you." "You lose," he answered, poker-faced.
Isabel Ross, GRACE COOLIDGE AND HER ERA

NICOLAS COPERNICUS (1473–1543)
Polish astronomer

14 It was objected to Copernicus, in his own day, that if his scheme was true, Venus must appear to us with different phases, just as the Moon does. "So she would I believe," he replied, "if we could see her aright." This was a noble guess for the time and what has proved actually to be the case, since Galileo has found out new eyes for us.
Dr Cocchi. Quoted Rev. Joseph Spence, OBSERVATIONS, ANECDOTES AND CHARACTERS 1820

15 An upstart astrologer who strove to show that the earth revolves, not the heavens or firmament, the sun and the moon. This fool wishes to reverse the entire science of astronomy; but sacred scriptures tell us that Joshua commanded the sun to stand still, not the earth.
Martin Luther

16 Modern neurosis began with the discoveries of Copernicus. Science made men feel small by showing them the earth was not at the centre of the universe.
Mary McCarthy, ON THE CONTRARY 1961

17 Calvin, after quoting the text 'The world also is established that it cannot be moved' (Psalms xciii) triumphantly concluded "Who will venture to place the authority of Copernicus above that of the Holy Spirit?"
Bertrand Russell

MARIE CORELLI (1855–1924)
(Mary Mackay)
English novelist

1 At first ambitious to be a musician, she turned to literature after a "psychical experience".
William Rose Benét, THE READER'S ENCYCLOPEDIA 1948

2 I had no need to marry. I had three pets at home which answered the same purpose as a husband. I have a dog which growls every morning, a parrot which swears all the afternoon, and a cat which comes home late at night.
Marie Corelli. Quoted Sir James Crichton Brown, WHAT THE DOCTOR THOUGHT

3 Her work is marked by an earnestness and an attempt to make the fruits of scientific discovery more palatable to readers who still wished uncritically to be left with their old comfortable moral, ethical and cosmological pictures.
Angus Ross, PENGUIN COMPANION TO LITERATURE (*edited by David Daiches*) 1971

4 Though she has no place in serious literary history she is still read with attention, especially on the fringes of Western culture (in the West Indies, for example).
Ibid.

5 I am not saying anything against her morals, but judging from her style she ought to be here.
Oscar Wilde, to the librarian warder in Reading gaol

ANTONIO CORREGGIO (1489–1531)
Italian painter

6 This picture of a Muleteeer was drawn by Correggio and served a great while as a sign to a little public house by the roadside. It has all the marks in the upper corners of it having been doubled in for that purpose. The man who kept the house had been a muleteer, and had on some occasion obliged Correggio a good deal on the road. He set him up and painted his sign for him. The persons who were sent into Italy to collect pictures for the Regent, met with this sign and bought it of the inn-keeper. It cost 500 guineas.
Guide at the Palais Royal, Paris. Quoted Rev. Joseph Spence, OBSERVATIONS, ANECDOTES AND CHARACTERS 1820

7 The corregiosity of Correggio.
Laurence Sterne, TRISTRAM SHANDY 1767

BARONESS ANGELA BURDETT COUTTS (1814–1906)
English philanthropist

8 She did not mind obscurity. Few women can have gone to a court ball in a hundred thousand pounds' worth of jewellery, including Marie Antoinette's tiara, with less éclat.
Edna Healey, LADY UNKNOWN: THE LIFE OF ANGELA BURDETT COUTTS 1978

9 She was a paragon, the richest heiress of her age. She gave away about £3 million. She was justly called 'The Queen of the Poor' or 'The Queen of the Costers'. She was the first woman to win a peerage on her own merits.
John Vincent, Observer, reviewing Diana Orton's A BIOGRAPHY OF ANGELA BURDETT COUTTS 3 *Feb* 1980

10 She was the last person, other then the Unknown Warrior, to be buried uncremated in Westminster Abbey.
Ibid.

11 She was a female Lord Shaftesbury, a financial Florence Nightingale, a rival in longevity and popularity to Queen Victoria.
Ibid.

12 The Duke of Wellington, getting on for 80, wrote her 850 letters but was distinctly rattled when she proposed marriage. The Duke retreated in some disorder.
Ibid.

SIR NOËL PIERCE COWARD (1899–1973)
English dramatist and actor

13 Emotionally she was unimportant, like a play by Noël Coward; but her construction was faultless, like a play by Noël Coward.
Michael Arlen, PORTRAIT OF A LADY IN PARK AVENUE

14 Edna Furber turned up sporting a tailored suit similar to one Noël Coward was wearing. "You look almost like a man," said Coward. "So," Miss Furber replied, "do you."
Robert E. Brennan, WIT'S END 1968

15 He was his own greatest invention.
John Osborne. Quoted William Marchant, THE PLEASURE OF HIS COMPANY

16 If his face suggested an old boot it was unquestionable hand made.
Kenneth Tynan, THE SOUND OF TWO HANDS CLAPPING

WILLIAM COWPER (1731–1800)
English poet

1 His taste lay in smiling, colloquial, good-natured humour; his melancholy was a black and diseased melancholy, not a grave and rich contemplativeness.
Sir E. Brydges, RECOLLECTION OF FOREIGN TRAVEL

2 That maniacal Calvinist and coddled poet.
Lord Byron

3 He was a lunatic of the melancholy kind, with occasional lucid intervals. He firmly believed that good and evil spirits haunted his couch every night, and that the influence of the last largely prevailed. For the last five years of his life a perpetual gloom hung over him — he was never observed to smile — he had dreadful stomach complaints and drank immense quantities of tea. He was indulged in everything, even in his wildest imaginings. It would have been better had he been regulated in all respects.
Dr J. Currie to W. Roscoe. Quoted W. Clark Russell, A BOOK OF AUTHORS

4 He shakes hands with nature with a pair of fashionable gloves on.
William Hazlitt, LECTURES ON THE ENGLISH POETS 1818

5 I can forgive a man for not enjoying Milton; but I would not call that man my friend who should be offended by the "divine chit-chat" of Cowper.
Charles Lamb, letter to Coleridge 5 Dec 1796

6 *The Task* was incomparably the best poem that any Englishman then living had produced — a poem, too, which could hardly fail to excite in a well-constituted mind a feeling of esteem and compassion for the poet, a man of genius and virtue whose means were scanty and whom the most cruel of calamities incident to humanity had made incapable of supporting himself by vigorous and sustained effort.
T. B. Macaulay. Quoted W. Clark Russell, A BOOK OF AUTHORS

7 The gentle, shy, melancholy Calvinist, whose spirit had been broken by fagging at school, who had not courage to earn a livelihood by reading the titles of bills in the House of Lords, and whose favourite associates were a blind old lady and an evangelising divine.
T. B. Macaulay, Edinburgh Review, MOORE'S LIFE OF LORD BYRON *Jun 1831*

THOMAS CRANMER (1489–1556)
Archbishop of Canterbury

8 A name which deserves to be held in everlasting execration, a name which we could not pronounce without almost doubting the justice of God, were it not for our knowledge of the fact that the cold-blooded, most perfidious, most impious, most blasphemous caitiff expired, at last, among those flames which he himself had been the chief cause of kindling.
William Cobbett, HISTORY OF THE PROTESTANT REFORMATION 1827

9 Stretching out his arm, he put his right hand into the flame, which he held so steadfast and unmoveable (save that once with the same hand he wiped his face) that all men might see his hand burned before his body was touched.
John Foxe, BOOK OF MARTYRS 1563

10 It is no wonder his notions of Christian liberty were in those times imperfect, which made him, against the natural bent of his mind, in some few instances a persecutor. It is but late we have understood the doctrine of toleration in its full extent. His greatest failing was his recantation at Oxford, that effect of a natural constitutional timidity which yet he repaired as well as he could by giving the sincerest marks of repentance. On the whole, he lived in trying times and was, with the exception of a few faults, an eminently great and good man.
Bishop Richard Hurd, DIALOGUES ON SINCERITY 1759

SIR RICHARD STAFFORD CRIPPS (1889–1952)
British politician

11 He has a brilliant mind, until he makes it up.
Margot Asquith, AUTOBIOGRAPHY 1936

12 There, but for the grace of God, goes God.
Winston Churchill. Quoted Bennet Cerf, SHAKE WELL BEFORE USING 1948

13 He has all the virtues I dislike and none of the vices I admire.
Winston Churchill. Quoted Leon Harris, THE FINE ART OF POLITICAL WIT

14 Sir Stafford has built a high stone wall around his mind, as if it were an intellectual nudist colony.
Tribune. Quoted News Review 18 Mar 1948

15 No one likes Cripps. He does not allow it.
Alain Verney, Tribune des Nations (Paris) Nov 1947

OLIVER CROMWELL (1599–1658)
Lord Protector

1 One that I knew that was at the battle of Dunbar, told me that Cromwell was carried on with a Divine Impulse; he did laugh so excessively as if he had been drunk; his Eyes sparkled with Spirits. He obtained a great Victory; but the Action was said to be contrary to Human Prudence. The same fit of Laughter seiz'd Oliver Cromwell, just before the Battle of Naseby, as a Kinsman of mine, Colonel J.P. then present, testified Cardinal Mazarine said he was a lucky Fool.
John Aubrey, MISCELLANIES   1696

2 A perfect master of all the arts of simulation, who, turning up the whites of his eyes, and seeking the Lord with pious gestures, will weep and cant and pray most devoutly till an opportunity offers to dealing his dupe a knock-down blow under the short ribs.
George Bate

3 Cromwell was a man in whom ambition had not wholly suppressed, but only suspended, the sentiments of religion.
Edmund Burke, in a letter   1791

4 He will be looked upon by posterity as a brave, bad man.
Earl of Clarendon, HISTORY OF THE REBELLION   1704

5 I would have been glad to have lived under my woodside, and to have kept a flock of sheep, rather than to have undertaken this government.
Cromwell. Speech to Parliament   1658

6 If I were ten years younger there is not a king in Europe I would not have made to tremble.
Cromwell at the age of 54

7 Mr Lely I desire you would use all your skill to paint your picture truly like me and not flatter me at all; but remark all those roughnesses, pimples, warts and everything as you see me, otherwise I will never pay a farthing for it.
Cromwell to Sir Peter Lely   1657

8 O Oliver hadst thou been faithful, the King of France should have bowed his neck under thee, the Pope should have withered as in winter, the Turk in all his fatness should have smoked.
George Fox (founder of the Quakers)   1654

9 His foreign enterprises, though full of intrepidity were pernicious to the national interest and seem more the result of impetuous fury or narrow prejudices than of cool foresight and deliberation.
David Hume, HISTORY OF ENGLAND   1754

10 Cromwell our chief of men, who through a cloud / Not of war only, but detractions rude, / Guided by faith and matchless fortitude / To peace and truth thy glorious way has ploughed.
John Milton, SONNET XVI, *To the Lord General Cromwell*

11 Or, ravished with the whistling of a name / See Cromwell damn'd to everlasting fame.
Alexander Pope, ESSAY ON MAN   1733

GEORGE NATHANIEL CURZON (1859–1925)
(Marquess Curzon of Kedleston)
British statesman

12 My name is George Nathaniel Curzon / I am a most superior person.
Anon, THE BALLIOL MASQUE

13 Very bad tempered in the forenoon, but better as the day advances.
Stanley Baldwin. Quoted Thomas Jones, WHITEHALL DIARY   1916–1925

D

SALVADOR DALI (1904–   )
Spanish-born surrealist artist

1   The famous soft watches are nothing else than the tender, extravagant solitary, paranoaic-critical camembert of time and space.
Dali, CONQUEST OF THE IRRATIONAL

2   There is only one difference between a madman and me. I am not mad.
Dali, The American   *Jul* 1956

GABRIEL D'ANNUNZIO (1863–1938)
Italian poet

3   Restless, half-sincere charlatans like D'Annunzio have an undying attraction for those whose day-dreams need stimulating.
Sir Kenneth Clark, CIVILISATION   1969

4   The astonishing D'Annunzio, half genius and half mountebank, ready to imitate whatever was fashionable in literary Europe and yet able to bring new sensuous life to Italian poetry, a Fascist caricature of a great writer.
J. B. Priestley, LITERATURE AND WESTERN MAN   1969

DANTE ALIGHIERI (1265–1321)
Italian poet

5   A hyena that wrote poetry in tombs.
Friedrich Nietzsche

6   A Methodist parson in bedlam.
Horace Walpole

GEORGES-JACQUES DANTON (1749–1794)
French revolutionary statesman

7   Don't forget to show my head to the people. It's worth seeing.
Danton to his executioner at the guillotine

CHARLES ROBERT DARWIN (1809–1882)
Naturalist and evolutionist

8   I have no patience whatever with these gorilla damnifications of humanity.
Thomas Carlyle

9   The more one knew of him, the more he seemed the incorporated ideal of a man of science.
T. H. Huxley, Nature, obituary of Darwin

SIR HUMPHRY DAVY (1778–1829)
English chemist

10 Sir Humphry Davy / Detested gravy / He died in the odium / Of having discovered sodium.
E. C. Bentley, BIOGRAPHY FOR BEGINNERS   1921

11 I was introduced to Mr Davy, who has rooms adjoining mine in the Royal Institution; he is a very agreeable young man, and we have interesting conversations in an evening; the principal failing in his character is that he does not smoke.
John Dalton, letter to John Rothwell
10 *Jan* 1804

CLAUDE ACHILLE DEBUSSY (1862–1918)
French composer

12 I love music passionately, and because I love it I try to free it from the barren conditions that stifle it.
Debussy

13 The century of aeroplanes deserves its own music. As there are no precedents I must create anew.
Ibid.

14 Technically he is the inventor (so far as any individual can claim such a title) of a new pianism. He demands from both the fingers and the feet of his interpreters (as well as from their rhythmical sense) all sorts of refinements previously unexploited, and his influence has been amazingly fertile — no composer in musical history has taught the pianist more new and permanently valuable things.
Ernest Walker, GROVE'S DICTIONARY OF MUSIC AND MUSICIANS (*third edition*)   1927

DANIEL DEFOE (1663–1731)
English author

15 He is a middle-sized, spare man, about forty years old, of a dark complexion and dark

brown-coloured hair, but wears a wig. A hooked nose, a sharp chin, grey eyes, and a large mole near his mouth; was born in London and for many years was a hose-factor in Freeman's Yard in Cornhill, and is now owner of the brick and pantile works near Tilbury Fort, Essex.
Advertisement accompanying a reward of £50 for Defoe's apprehension 1703

1 Nobody ever laid down the book of *Robinson Crusoe* without wishing it longer.
Samuel Johnson. Quoted James Boswell,
THE LIFE OF JOHNSON 1791

2 The first part of *Robinson Crusoe* is good. De Foe wrote a vast many things and none of them bad, though none excellent. There's something good in all he writ.
Alexander Pope. Quoted Rev. Joseph Spence, OBSERVATIONS, ANECDOTES AND CHARACTERS 1820

3 One of those authors (the fellow was pilloried, I have forgot his name) is indeed so grave, sententious, dogmatic a rogue that there is no enduring him.
Jonathan Swift

GENERAL CHARLES DE GAULLE
(1890–1970)
French President

4 I have every sympathy with General de Gaulle and his violent tantrums but let us conquer some of his country before we start squabbling about how it is to be governed. Yes, let's give him a bit of land to govern first.
Winston Churchill, at an invasion conference. Quoted Michael Pertwee, NAME DROPPING

5 Just look at him! He might be Stalin with 200 divisions.
Winston Churchill 1943

6 The hardest cross I have to bear is the Cross of Lorraine.
Winston Churchill. Quoted Harold Wilson, A PRIME MINISTER ON PRIME MINISTERS 1977

7 I respect only those who resist me; but I cannot tolerate them.
De Gaulle. Quoted New York Times Magazine 12 May 1966

8 Intelligent — brilliant — resourceful — he spoils his undoubted talents by his excessive assurance, his contempt for other people's point of view, and his attitude of a king in exile.
Report of French War College 1922

9 An improbable creature, like a human giraffe, sniffing down his nostril at mortals beneath his gaze.
Richard Wilson. Quoted Nancy McPhee, THE SECOND BOOK OF INSULTS

FREDERICK DELIUS (1863–1934)
English composer

10 Delius is all intoxication, but it is all the same intoxication. Wagner has a hundred ways of making you tight.
James Agate, EGO 7 17 *Sep* 1944

11 It is only that which cannot be expressed otherwise that is worth expressing in music.
Delius, AT THE CROSSROADS 1920

12 Delius said he thought it was a great pity that Elgar had wasted so much of his time and energy in writing long-winded oratorios. "That," said Elgar, "is the penalty of my English environment." "Well, anyhow," said Delius, "you're not as bad as Parry. *He* would have set the whole Bible to music had he lived long enough."
Eric Fenby, DELIUS AS I KNEW HIM

13 One feels that all Delius' music is evolved out of the emotions of a past that was never fully realised when it was present, emotions which only became real after they had ceased to be experienced.
Philip Heseltine, DELIUS

14 It is dangerous to hear Delius' music too often, for its sensuous autumnal beauty induces a profound nostalgia, a passionate and fruitless desire to stop the clocks, to recapture the past.
Alec Robertson, MORE THAN MUSIC

CECIL BLOUNT DE MILLE (1881–1959)
American film director

15 Cecil B. de Mille / Rather against his will / Was persuaded to leave Moses / Out of the Wars of the Roses.
E. C. Bentley, CLERIHEWS

16 His success was a world success and he enjoyed every minute of it, and it lasted. He kept sex, sadism, patriotism, real estate, religion and public relations dancing in mid-air like jugglers' balls for fifty years.
Agnes de Mille, SPEAK TO ME, DANCE WITH ME

17 The trouble with Cecil is that he bites off more than he can chew — and chews it.
William de Mille (his brother)

18 I once asked Gary Cooper how on earth he could read those goddam lines. "Well," he said, "when De Mille finishes talking to you

they don't seem so bad. But when you see the picture, then you kind of hang your head."
Howard Hawkes. Quoted Kevin Brownlow, THE PARADE'S GONE BY

GERMAINE DE STAEL (1766–1817)
French authoress

1 She thinks like a man, but alas! she feels like a woman.
Lord Byron, in a letter to a friend on first meeting her

2 Germaine de Stael was the first woman of Europe during the cataclysmic eruptions of the French Revolution and the Napoleonic Wars. It is a rueful measure of her greatness that her own voice was heard above the roar.
J. Christopher Herold, MISTRESS TO AN AGE   1959

EAMON DE VALERA (1882–1975)
First President, Irish Free State

3 Lloyd George once remarked that negotiating with De Valera was like trying to pluck up mercury with a fork. De Valera replied, "Why doesn't he use a spoon?"
Bernard Baruch, THE PUBLIC YEARS

CHARLES DICKENS (1812–1870)
English novelist

4 In literary matters my dividing line is; Do you like Dickens or do you not? If you do not I am sorry for you and that is an end of the matter.
Stanley Baldwin. Speech, Spectator centenary   30 Oct 1928

5 We were put to Dickens as children, but it never quite took. That unremitting humanity soon had me cheesed off.
Alan Bennett, THE OLD COUNTRY

6 The good, the gentle, the highly-gifted, ever-friendly, noble Dickens, every inch of him an Honest Man.
Thomas Carlyle. Quoted John Forster's LIFE OF DICKENS   1874

7 Dickens saved himself for his books, there was nothing to be learned in private — he never talked.
Philip Collins, DICKENS, INTERVIEWS AND RECOLLECTIONS   1981

8 The operation of flogging a dead horse is always popular and is very congenial to Rhetoricians. Dickens was careful to castigate abuses that were being reformed.
W. R. Inge, THE END OF AN AGE   1948

9 I could never see why people were so happy about Dickens's *Christmas Carol* because I never had any confidence that Scrooge was going to be any different next day.
Dr Karl Menninger, A PSYCHIATRIST'S WORLD

10 Dickens was not the first or the last to find virtue more difficult to portray than the wish for it.
V. S. Pritchett, BOOKS IN GENERAL

11 One must have a heart of stone to read the death of Little Nell without laughing.
Oscar Wilde

12 It has often been said of Charles Dickens (not quite accurately, by the way), that though he created scores of immortal characters, there was not a gentleman among the lot.
Alexander Woollcott, WHILE ROME BURNS   1934

DIOGENES (412–323 BC)
Cynic, philosopher

13 Diogenes struck the father when the son swore.
Robert Burton, ANATOMY OF MELANCHOLY   1621

14 Alexander the Great found Diogenes lying in the sun. When he saw so much company near him Diogenes raised himself a little to look upon Alexander who kindly asked him whether he wanted anything. "Yes," said he, "I would have you stand from between me and the sun."
Plutarch, PARALLEL LIVES

WALT DISNEY (1901–1966)
American film producer

15 Soft little faces turned stony when I dealt out books by such counterfeit authors as Barrie, Collodi and Salten. Was I really so dumb, their withering looks asked plainly, as not to know that Walt Disney had written *Peter Pan* and *Pinocchio* and *Bambi*?
Wanda Burgan, Punch, Librarian   12 Sep 1962

16 I love Mickey Mouse more than any woman I've ever known.
Disney. Quoted Walter Wagner, YOU MUST REMEMBER THIS

BENJAMIN DISRAELI (1804–1881)
(Earl of Beaconsfield)
British Prime Minister

17 Never in my life had I been so struck by a face as I was by that of Disraeli. It was

lividly pale, and from beneath two finely arched eyebrows blazed out a pair of intensely black eyes. His physiognomy was strictly Jewish. Over a broad, high forehead were ringlets of coal-black glossy hair. There was a sort of half-smile, half-sneer playing about his beautifully formed mouth, the lips of which were curved, as we see it in portraits of Byron.
Anon. Quoted Moneypenny and Buckle,
LIFE OF BENJAMIN DISRAELI 1910

1 The soul of Dizzy was a chandelier.
E. C. Bentley, A BALLAD OF SOULS

2 I have climbed to the top of the greasy pole.
Disraeli on first being appointed Prime Minister 27 Feb 1868

3 He was, without any rival whatever, the first comic genius who ever installed himself in Downing Street.
Michael Foot, DEBTS OF HONOUR: *The Good Tory* 1982

4 Disraeli got up as soon as Lord Hartington finished and he delivered a twenty-minute speech of the most scathing invective and ridicule I ever heard. The House was worked up to a great pitch of excitement by this performance; for the speech was full of telling epigrams, namely "You have legalised confiscation . . . you have condoned high treason . . . you have emptied the gaols of Ireland . . . you are making Government ridiculous."
Lord George Hamilton, PARLIAMENTARY REMINISCENCES AND REFLECTIONS 1868–1885

5 In the most effective part of his speech he suddenly put his handkerchief to his mouth and turning to his neighbour, Lord John Manners, apparently asked him a question. The young men behind the Front Opposition Bench could not make out the purpose of this bit of by-play. What happened was that in the middle of a sentence his teeth fell out and he caught them up with extraordinary rapidity in his right hand, turned round apparently to ask a question of his neighbour, put them in, and resumed his speech at the exact word where he had left off.
Ibid.

6 Gladstone once described him as "the greatest master of Parliamentary sarcasm and irony for the past two centuries", and the knowledge that at any moment, if provoked, he might have recourse to his armoury of inimitable satire kept many turbulent and self-advertising sparks quiet.
Ibid.

7 Disraeli was nearly always in the House and he listened most attentively to the Under Secretaries doing their work, and if you glided successfully over thin ice, or counteracted a difficult attack, a quiet "Hear, hear" fell from his lips — a great encouragement to a young official.
Ibid.

8 The attitude he found most conducive to happy delivery was to stand balancing himself on heel and toe, with hands in his coat-tail pockets. In this pose, with head hung down as if mentally debating how best to express a thought just born to him, he slowly uttered the polished and poisoned sentences over which he had spent laborious hours in the study.
Henry Lucy, SIXTY YEARS IN THE WILDERNESS 1909

9 Disraeli lacked two qualities, failing which true eloquence is impossible. He was never quite in earnest, and he was not troubled by dominating conviction. Only on the rarest occasions did he affect to be roused to righteous indignation and then he was amusing rather than impressive.
Ibid.

10 He possesses just the qualities of the impenitent thief who died upon the cross, whose name, I verily believe, was Disraeli.
Daniel O'Connor. Speech in Dublin 1835

11 Mrs Disraeli, famous for her conversational oddities, once said to a friend of mine "Dizzy has the most wonderful courage, but no physical courage. When he has his shower-bath I always have to pull the string."
George W. E. Russell, PORTRAITS OF THE SEVENTIES 1916

12 Disraeli very generously purchased the Panama Canal from the Khalif and presented it to Queen Victoria with a huge bunch of primroses (his favourite flower) thus becoming Lord Beaconsfield and a romantic minister.
W. C. Sellar and R. J. Yeatman, 1066 AND ALL THAT 1930

JOHN DONNE (1573–1631)
English poet, Dean of St. Paul's

13 In Donne's satires when carefully inspected, there appear some flashes of wit and ingenuity; but these totally buried and

suffocated by the hardest and most uncouth expression that is anywhere met with.
David Hume, ESSAYS MORAL AND POLITICAL 1742

1 Dr Donne's verses are like the peace of God;they pass all understanding.
King James I

2 Dr Donne, the poet, in 1602 married the daughter of Sir George Moore who was so enraged that he not only turned Donne and his wife out of the house but got Lord Chancellor Egerton to turn him out of his office as Great Seal. They took refuge in a house in Pyrford, Surrey where the first thing he did was to write on a pane of glass "John Donne — An Donne — Undone." The words were visible at the house in 1749.
Sir James Prior, LIFE OF EDMOND MALONE 1860

3 The king appointed Dr Donne to wait on him at dinner next day; and His Majesty (being set down) before he eat any meat said (after his pleasant manner) "Doctor Donne, and though you are not down with me, I will carve to you a dish that I know you love; you love London well, I do therefore make you Dean of St. Paul's, and, when I have dined, take your meat home with you to your study, say grace, and much good may it do you."
Izaak Walton, LIFE OF JOHN DONNE 1640

4 He abounds in false thoughts, in far-fetched sentiments, in forced unnatural conceits. He was the corrupter of Cowley. Dryden was the first to call him a metaphysical poet. He had a considerable share of learning; and though he entered late into orders, yet was esteemed a good divine.
Thomas Warton HISTORY OF ENGLISH POETRY 1774

FYODOR MIKHAILOVICH DOSTOEVSKY (1821–1881)
Russian novelist

5 A waiter in a Leningrad restaurant said to me, "It was a crime to write it and a punishment to read it."
Anthony Burgess, *Observer*, reviewing John Jones' DOSTOEVSKY, 15 May 1983

SIR FRANCIS DRAKE (1540–1596)
English admiral and circumnavigator

6 I remember Drake, in the vaunting style of a soldier, would call the enterprise "the singeing of the King of Spain's beard".
Francis Bacon, CONSIDERATIONS TOUCHING A WAR WITH SPAIN (*referring to the raid on Cadiz*)

7 Drake was never to know what failure meant; he died at sea at Porto Bello; his vice-admiral (Sir John Hawkins) having passed on a few days before him. Once more he followed in the wake of his old leader; two more perplexing spirits can seldom have appeared before the Recording Angel.
Laurence Irving, *biographical note for Heinemann edition of Hakluyt's* VOYAGES 1927

8 He was more skilful in all points of Navigation than any that ever was before his time, in his time, or since his death. He was also of a perfect memory, great observation, eloquent by nature, skilful in Artillery, expert and apt to let blood and give physick to his people according to the climate. He was low of stature, of strong limbs, broad-breasted, round-headed, brown hair, full-bearded, his eyes round, large and clear, well-favoured, fair and of a cheerful countenance.
John Stowe, ANNALS 1580

THEODORE DREISER (1871–1945)
American novelist

9 I spent the better part of forty years trying to induce him to reform and electrify the manner of his writing, but so far as I am aware with no more effect than if I had tried to persuade him to take up golf or abandon his belief in non-Euclidian arcana.
H. L. Mencken. Quoted Philip L. Gerber, THEODORE DREISER

10 His style is atrocious, his sentences are chaotic, his grammar and syntax faulty; he has no feeling for words, no sense of diction. His wordiness and his repetitions are unbearable, his cacophanies incredible.
T. K. Whipple, SPOKESMEN

JOHN DRYDEN (1631–1700)
English poet

11 A monster of immodesty and of impurity of all sorts.
Bishop Gilbert Burnet, HISTORY OF HIS OWN TIMES 1734

12 We feel that he never heartily and sincerely praised any human being, or felt any real enthusiasm for any subject he took up.
John Keble, LECTURES ON POETRY

1 Waller was smooth, but Dryden taught to join / The varying verse, the full resounding line / The long majestic march, and energy divine.
Alexander Pope, IMITATIONS OF HORACE 1739

2 Ev'n copious Dryden wanted, or forgot / The last and greatest art — the art to blot.
Ibid.

3 His wife, thinking herself neglected, and that he spent too much time in his study, one day exclaimed, "Lord, Mr Dryden, how can you always be poring over these musty books. I wish I were a book, and then I should have more of your company." "Pray, my dear," replied old John, "if you become a book let it be an almanack, for then I shall change you every year."
Sir James Prior, LIFE OF EDMOND MALONE 1860

4 He is a rarity which I cannot but be fond of, as one would be of a hog that could fiddle, or a singing owl.
Earl of Rochester. Quoted W. Clark Russell, A BOOK OF AUTHORS

ALEXANDRE DUMAS (1802–1870)
French novelist and dramatist

5 Alexandre Dumas published, according to his own testimony, 1200 volumes. He hired a corps of ghost writers and put the production of books on an assembly-line basis. One day he met his son, the author of *Camille,* and asked "Have you read my new novel yet?" "No," said his son, "have you?"
Bennett Cerf, SHAKE WELL BEFORE USING

6 Dumas owned a theatre, a newspaper and a magazine, slept only four hours out of twenty-four, and was involved in over a hundred lawsuits. For pets he had twelve dogs, three apes, two parrots, two peacocks, a vulture, a pheasant and a cat. He entertained so lavishly that, when he rented a chateau in the country, the railroad's receipts for the local station increased by 20,000 francs the first summer. He lived like a prince in the *Arabian Nights* — and died a pauper.
Ibid.

7 He dissipated a huge fortune by unbridled extravagance and on his deathbed in 1870 he wryly remarked, "I came to Paris with twenty-four francs. That is exactly the sum with which I die."
Ibid.

8 My father was a Creole, his father was a Negro, his father a monkey; my family, it seems, begins where yours left off.
Dumas to one who sneered at his ancestry

ISADORA DUNCAN (1878–1927)
American dancer

9 I am the enemy of the ballet, which I look upon as false, absurd, and outside the domain of art.
Isadora Duncan, MY LIFE 1927

10 As she stepped into the machine that was to be her final enemy, Isadora's last spoken words were, by chance, "Je vois la gloire".
Janet Flanner, PARIS WAS YESTERDAY
(*Isadora was accidentally strangled when her long scarf was caught in the wheel of a car*)

11 A woman whose face looked as if it had been made out of sugar, and someone had licked it.
George Bernard Shaw. Quoted Hesketh Pearson, BERNARD SHAW 1961

12 In less inspired moments she followed the music as a bear might follow a mouse.
Adrian Stokes, TONIGHT THE BALLET

13 Once her mother took her to a ballet teacher for dancing lessons. When he told her to stand on her toes she asked "Why?" "Because it is beautiful," he answered. "No, it is ugly and against nature," she answered. She walked out of the room and never came back.
Henry and Dana Lee Thomas, LIVING BIOGRAPHIES OF FAMOUS WOMEN: ISADORA DUNCAN

14 I beheld the dance I had always dreamed of, a flowing of movement into movement, an endless interweaving of motion and movement, satisfying every sense as a flower does, or a phrase of Mozart's.
Edith Wharton. Quoted Edward Wagenknecht, SEVEN DAUGHTERS OF THE THEATRE

SAINT DUNSTAN (909–988)
Archbishop of Canterbury

15 The present coronation rites of the English sovereign derive from that compiled and used by Dunstan for the sacring of Edgar as King of all England at Bath in 973.
Donald Attwater, PENGUIN DICTIONARY OF SAINTS 1965

16 St. Dunstan, as the story goes / Once pulled the Devil by the nose / With red hot tongs which made him roar / That could be heard a mile or more.
Traditional children's rhyme. Origin unknown

E

SIR ANTHONY EDEN (1897–1977)
(First Earl of Avon)
British Prime Minister

1 He is more pathetic than sinister. Beneath the sophistication of his appearance and manner he has all the unplumbable stupidies and unawareness of his class and type.
Aneurin Bevan, Tribune 15 Jan 1943

2 The charming milksop who became the blood-lusting monster.
Brendan Bracken. Quoted David Carlton, ANTHONY EDEN 1981

3 That's Anthony for you — half mad baronet, half beautiful woman.
Lord Butler

4 He is an over-ripe banana, yellow outside, squishy within.
Reginald Paget

5 He will be the worst prime minister since Lord North.
Lord Swinton to Winston Churchill. Quoted J. A. Cross, LORD SWINTON 1983

6 The best advertisement the Fifty Shilling Tailors ever had.
Bonar Thompson. Quoted Michael Foot, DEBTS OF HONOUR 1981

MARIA EDGEWORTH (1767–1849)
Irish novelist

7 Maria Edgeworth writes all the while she laughs, talks, eats and drinks — and I believe, though I do not pretend to be so far in the secret, while she sleeps, too.
Sir Walters Scott, letter to Joanna Baillie 1825

8 Miss Edgeworth was delightful — so clever and sensible! She does not say witty things, but there is such a perfume of wit runs through her conversation as makes it very brilliant.
Rev. Sydney Smith

EDWARD THE CONFESSOR (c. 1003–1066)
King

9 The most kindly Kind Edward passed his life in security and peace, and spent much of his time in the glades and woods in the pleasures of hunting. After divine service which he gladly and devoutly attended each day, he took much pleasure in hawks and birds of that kind which they brought before him and was really delighted by the baying and scrambling of the hounds.
VITA AEDWARDI REGIS (LIFE OF KING EDWARD) *translated from a medieval text by F. Barlow*

10 He used to stand with a lamb-like meekness and tranquil mind at the holy offices of the divine mysteries and masses, a worshipper of Christ manifest to all the faithful, and at these times, unless he was addressed, he rarely spoke to anyone.
Ibid.

EDWARD II (1284–1327)
King

11 Edward somme tyme kyng was brought from Kenelworthe to the castell of Berkeley, where he was slayne with a hoote brooche putt thro the secrete place posterialle.
Ranulf Higden of Chester (fourteenth-century monk), POLYCHRONICON

12 He is one of the best medieval examples of the brutal and brainless athlete established on the throne. He was not exceptionally vicious or depraved. He was just incompetent, idle, frivolous and incurious.
T. F. Tout, THE CAPTIVITY AND DEATH OF EDWARD OF CARNARVON

13 Every president of the US has somehow been found to descend from Edward II.
Gore Vidal. Quoted John Heilpern, Observer 26 Apr 1981

EDWARD IV (1442–1483)
King

14 This Monarch was famous only for his Beauty and his Courage, of which the Picture we have here given of him, and his undaunted Behaviour in marrying one Woman while he was engaged to another, are sufficient proofs. His Wife was Elizabeth Woodville, a Widow who, poor Woman! was afterwards confined in a Convent by that Monster of Iniquity and Avarice Henry the 7th. One of Edward's

Mistresses was Jane Shore, who had had a play written about her, but it is a tragedy and therefore not worth reading. Having performed all these noble actions, his Majesty died, and was succeeded by his son.

Jane Austen, THE HISTORY OF ENGLAND BY A PARTIAL, PREJUDICED AND IGNORANT HISTORIAN

1 That which greatly contributed to his entering London as soon as he appeared at its gates was the great debts this prince had contracted, which made his creditors gladly assist him.

Philip de Comines, MEMOIRS 1524

2 Many ladies and rich citizens' wives, of whom he formerly had great privacies and familiar acquaintance, gained over to him their friends and relations.

Ibid.

3 He had been during the last twelve years more accustomed to his ease and pleasure than any other princes who lived in his time. He had nothing in his thoughts but *les dames* and of them more than was *reasonable*, and hunting matches, good eating, and great care of his person.

Ibid.

4 He always carried with him great pavilions for *les dames*, and at the same time gave great entertainments, so it was not surprising that his person was as jolly a one as ever I saw. He was then young, and as handsome as any man of his age; but he has since become enormously fat.

Ibid.

EDWARD V (1570–1583)
King

5 He is commonly called King Edward the Fifth, tho' his head was ask'd but never *married* to the English crown, and therefore in all the pictures made of him, a distance interposed, *forbiddeth* the *banes* betwixt them.

Thomas Fuller, THE WORTHIES OF ENGLAND 1662

EDWARD VI (1537–1553)
King

6 As this prince was only nine years old at the time of his Father's death, he was considered by many people as too young to govern, and the late King happening to be of the same opinion, his mother's Brother the Duke of Somerset was chosen Protector of the realm during his minority. This Man was on the whole of a very amiable Character, and is somewhat of a favourite with me,

tho' I would by no means pretend to affirm that he was equal to those first of Men Robert Earl of Essex, Delamere, or Gilpin. He was beheaded, of which he might with reason have been proud, had he known that such was the death of Mary Queen of Scotland; but as it was impossible that he should be conscious of what had never happened, it does not appear that he felt particularly delighted with the manner of it. After his decease the Duke of Northumberland had the care of the King and the Kingdom, and performed his trust of both so well that the King died and the Kingdom was left to his daughter in law the Lady Jane Grey, who has been already mentioned as reading Greek. Whether she really understood that language or whether such a study proceeded only from an excess of vanity for which I believe she was always rather remarkable, is uncertain. Whatever might be the cause, she preserved the same appearance of knowledge, and contempt of what was generally esteemed pleasure, during the whole of her life, for she declared herself displeased with being appointed Queen, and while conducting to the scaffold, she wrote a sentence in Latin and another in Greek on seeing the dead Body of her Husband accidentally passing that way.

Jane Austen, THE HISTORY OF ENGLAND BY A PARTIAL, PREJUDICED AND IGNORANT HISTORIAN

7 All the graces were in him. He had many tongues when yet but a child; together with the English, his natural tongue, he had both Latin and French; nor was he ignorant, as I hear, of the Greek, Italian and Spanish. But for the English, French and Latin, he was great in them and apt to learn everything. Nor was he ignorant of logic, of the principles of natural philosophy, nor of music.

Giralamo Cardano, a Milanese physician, who visited Edward in 1552

8 He hath made already forty or fifty pretty Latin verses, is now ready to enter into Cato, to some proper and profitable fables of Aesop. Every day readeth a portion of Solomon's proverbs, wherein he delighteth much and learneth there to beware of strange women, and to be thankful to him who telleth him of his faults.

Richard Cox, tutor to Edward when he was eight years old

9 You have never seen in the world for these thousand years so much erudition united with piety and sweetness of disposition.

Should he live and grow up with these virtues, he will be a terror to all the sovereigns of the earth.
John Hooper, Bishop of Gloucester, letter to a friend in Switzerland 27 Mar 1550

1 He receives with his own hand a copy of every sermon he hears, and most diligently requires an account of them after dinner from those who study with him.
Ibid.

EDWARD VII (1841–1910)
King

2 The leader writer in a great Northern daily said on the morning after King Edward died that if he had not been a king he would have been the best type of sporting publican.
James Agate, EGO I 1935

3 Edward the Caresser — Edward the Peacemaker — and the piece he caressed was Lily Langtree.
Arthur Askey. Quoted BBC Radio 4, Quote Unquote 21 Jul 1980

4 I wouldn't know the king from the knave.
Nancy Astor, declining an invitation to play bridge with Edward VII. Quoted Geoffrey Bocca, Sunday Express, Nancy the Incredible Astor 8 Jan 1956

5 Flashed from his bed, the electric tidings came / He is no better, he is much the same.
Alfred Austin, of the illness of Edward when Prince of Wales 1871

6 He had a passion for pageantry and ceremonial and dressing up and he was never tired of putting on uniforms and taking them off, and receiving princes and ambassadors and opening museums and hospitals, and attending cattle shows and military shows and shows of every kind while every night of his life he was to be seen at theatres and operas and music halls.
Wilfrid Scawen Blunt, MY DIARIES

7 Mr Fildes, to whom I am sitting for my portrait, is under the impression that I am a short, stout man.
Edward. Quoted L. V. Fildes, LUKE FILDES, A VICTORIAN PAINTER

8 A capable, amiable, but very crafty man, with a remarkably sinister look in his eyes — *not* our friend.
Prince Eulenberg to Kaiser Wilhelm II. Quoted Dr Johannes Haller, PRINCE EULENBERG, THE KAISER'S FRIEND

9 He wasn't clever, but he always did the right thing, which is better than brains.
Lord Fisher, letter to Reginald McKenna 14 May 1910

10 He was the best king we ever had — on the racecourse.
Attributed to Lord Northcliffe

11 He had many romantic occupations. He went betting and visited Paris and was sometimes late for dinner; in addition he was merry with actresses and kind to gipsies.
W. C. Sellar and R. J. Yeatman, 1066 AND ALL THAT 1930

12 Edward VII smoked cigars and was addicted to entente cordials, married a Sea King's daughter and invented appendicitis.
Ibid.

13 We shall not pretend that there is nothing in his long career which those who respect and admire him would wish otherwise.
Times leader on Edward's accession 23 Jan 1901

EDWARD VIII (1894–1972)
(Duke of Windsor)
King

14 I pray to God that my eldest son will never marry and have children and that nothing will come between Bertie and Lilibet and the throne.
George V. Quoted Elizabeth Longford, THE QUEEN MOTHER

15 The Prince of Wales embodied some of the more conspicuous qualities of his time; gaiety that was not really light hearted; social concern that sprang from an uneasy conscience rather than any profound conviction; acceptance of the privileges that go with great wealth, coupled with unreadiness to carry the corresponding burden of duty.
George Malcolm Thomson, LORD CASTLEROSSE AND HIS TIMES

16 He was born to be a salesman. He would be an admirable representative of Rolls-Royce; but an ex-king cannot start selling motor cars.
Duchess of Windsor. Quoted Harold Nicolson, DIARIES 28 May 1947

ALBERT EINSTEIN (1879–1955)
German–Swiss–American physicist

17 A Nazi professor once called a public meeting to denounce the relativity theory. Isaac Newton would have shunned such a

meeting in mortification. Einstein went along to heckle
Adrian Berry, Daily Telegraph, Sir Isaac in his Orbit 18 Jun 1979

1 If my theory of relativity is proved successful Germany will claim me as a German and France will declare I am a citizen of the whole world. Should my theory prove untrue France will say I am a German and Germany will say I am a Jew.
Einstein, News Review 8 May 1947

2 I want to know how God created this world. I am not interested in this or that phenomenon. I want to know His thoughts; the rest are details.
Einstein. Quoted Ronald W. Clark, EINSTEIN, HIS LIFE AND TIMES

3 When I was doing Einstein's bust he had many a jibe at the Nazi professors, one hundred of whom had condemned his theory of relativity in a book. "Were I wrong," he said, "one professor would have been enough."
Jacob Epstein, LET THERE BE SCULPTURE

4 The genius of Einstein leads to Hiroshima.
Pablo Picasso. Quoted Françoise Gilot and Carlton Lake, LIFE WITH PICASSO

5 Einstein was the creative philosophic mind of the century and I have been the creative literary mind of the century.
Gertrude Stein. Quoted J. M. Brinnin, THE THIRD ROSE

DWIGHT DAVID EISENHOWER
(1890–1969)
Thirty-fourth President of the United States

6 As an intellectual he bestowed upon·the games of golf and bridge all the enthusiasm and perseverance that he withheld from books and ideas.
Emmet John Hughes, THE ORDEAL OF POWER

7 Eisenhower is the only living unknown soldier.
Senator Kerr of Oklahoma. Quoted Groucho Marx, LETTER TO GOODMAN ACE

8 The best clerk I ever fired.
General MacArthur. Quoted Marquis Childs, EISENHOWER, CAPTIVE HERO

SIR EDWARD WILLIAM ELGAR
(1857–1934),
English composer

9 Elgar's A flat Symphony is the musical equivalent of St. Pancras station.
Sir Thomas Beecham. Quoted Neville Cardus, SIR THOMAS BEECHAM

10 Elgar's *Gerontius* has been rightly described by George Moore as holy water in a German beer barrel.
Sir Thomas Beecham. Quoted Lord Boothby, MY YESTERDAY YOUR TOMORROW

11 Elgar was the last serious composer to be in touch with the great public.
Constant Lambert, MUSIC HO!

12 Elgar's music, through no fault of his own, has for the present generation an almost intolerable air of smugness, self-assurance and autocratic benevolence.
Ibid.

GEORGE ELIOT (1819–1880)
(Mary Ann or Marian Evans)
English novelist

13 I began *Romola* a young woman. I finished it an old woman.
George Eliot. Quoted Ruby V. Redinger, GEORGE ELIOT: *The Emergent Self*

14 A large, thick-set sybil, dreamy and immobile, whose massive features, somewhat grim when seen in repose, were incongruously bordered by a hat, always in the height of Paris fashion, which in those days commonly included an immense ostrich feather; that was George Eliot. The contrast between the solemnity of the face and the frivolity of the headgear had something pathetic and provincial about it.
Sir Edmund Gosse, HISTORY OF MODERN LITERATURE 1898

15 She had, even in her sixties, a remarkable fascination. Famous, benign in appearance, like the poet Dante draped in lace, she drove several lesbian admirers to distraction.
Margaret Lane, Daily Telegraph, Postscript to George Eliot 15 Mar 1979

16 There is something daunting about the image she was at such pains to project, the intellectual pretentiousness, the "holier than thou" stance in the sexual relationships in which she landed herself; the liking for being addressed as "Madonna", the dichotomy between her masculine intellectual powers, and her over-emotional femininity.
Ibid.

1 Bishop-like.
Lord Morley, STUDIES IN
LITERATURE 1891

2 The rest of the characters are the sweepings
out of a Pentonville omnibus.
John Ruskin, of The Mill on the Floss,
FICTION FAIR AND FOUL

3 Outwardly serene she was inwardly
tormented by ill-health, religious doubt,
headaches and night terrors. She appears
herself to have been aware of some dis-
crepancy in her make-up, for she hated
herself "for caring about carpets, easy
chairs and coal fires — one's soul is under a
curse and can preach no truth while one is in
bondage to the flesh in this way. We are
reprobates and shall never enter into the
kingdom of heaven."
V. Sackville-West, THE GREAT VICTORIANS:
GEORGE ELIOT

4 A new acquaintance having enjoyed an
hour's conversation with George Eliot came
away under the impression that she was
beautiful, though later, seeing her in repose, could hardly believe her to be the
same person.
Ibid.

THOMAS STEARNS ELIOT (1888–1965)
American-born English poet

5 How unpleasant to meet Mr Eliot / With his
features of clerical cut / And his brow so
grim / And his mouth so prim / And his
conversation so nicely / Restricted to What
Precisely / and If and Perhaps and But.
T. S. Eliot, SELF PORTRAIT

6 He is very yellow and glum. Perfect manners. Dyspeptic, ascetic, eclectic. Inhibi-
tions. Yet obviously a nice man and a great
poet. He is without pose and full of poise.
He makes one feel that all cleverness is an
excuse for thinking hard.
Harold Nicolson, DIARY 2 *May* 1932

7 Pale marmoreal Eliot was there last week,
like a chapped office boy on a high stool,
with a cold in his head.
Virginia Woolf

ELIZABETH I (1533–1603)
Queen

8 It was the peculiar misfortune of this
Woman to have bad Ministers — Since
wicked as she herself was, she could not
have committed such extensive mischief,
had not these vile and abandoned Men con-
nived at, and encouraged her in her Crimes.
I know that it has by many people been
asserted and believed that Lord Burleigh,
Sir Francis Walsingham, and the rest of
those who filled the chief offices of State
were deserving, experienced, and able
Ministers. But oh! how blinded such writers
and such Readers must be to true Merit, to
Merit despised, neglected and defamed; if
they can persist in such opinions when they
reflect that these men, these boasted men
were such scandals to their Country and
their sex to allow and assist their Queen in
confining for the space of nineteen years, a
Woman who if the claims of Relationship
and Merit were of no avail, yet as a Queen
and as one who condescended to place confidence in her, had every reason to expect
assistance and protection; and at length in
allowing Elizabeth to bring this amiable
Woman to an untimely, unmerited, and
scandalous Death.
Jane Austen, HISTORY OF ENGLAND BY A
PARTIAL, PREJUDICED AND IGNORANT
HISTORIAN

9 I am attracted to perpetual spinsterhood not
by prejudice but rather by natural inclination.
*Elizabeth to the ambassador of the Duke of
Württemberg*

10 I know I have the body of a weak and feeble
woman but I have the heart and stomach of
a king, and a king of England, too; and
think foul scorn that Parma or Spain, or any
prince of Europe, should dare invade the
borders of my realm.
*Elizabeth, speech to the troops at Tilbury
8 Aug 1588*

11 She converted her reign through the
perpetual love-tricks that passed between
her and her people into a kind of Romance,
wholly neglecting the Nobility.
James Harrington, THE COMMONWEALTH
OF OCEANS 1656

12 The queen did fish for men's souls, and had
so sweet a bait that no one could escape her
network.
Sir Christopher Hatton

13 Her virtues were such as might suffice to
make an Ethiopian beautiful, which, the
more a man knows and understands, the
more he shall admire and love. In life, she
was most innocent; in desires, moderate; in
purpose, just; of spirit, above credit and
almost capacity for her sex; of divine wit, so
well for depth of judgement as for quick
conceit and speedy expedition; of eloquence, so sweet in the utterance, so ready

and easy to come to the utterance; of wonderful knowledge both in learning and affairs; skilful not only in the Latin and Greek, but also in divers other foreign languages; none knew better the hardest art of all others, that of commanding men.
Sir John Hayward, ANNALS OF QUEEN ELIZABETH

1 She was a lady upon whom nature had bestowed and well-placed many of her fairest favours; of stature mean [medium] slender, straight and amiably composed; of such state in her carriage as every motion of her seemed to bear majesty; her hair was inclined to pale yellow, her forehead large and fair, a seeming seat for princely Grace; her eyes lively and sweet but short-sighted; her nose somewhat rising in the midst; the whole compass of her countenance somewhat long, yet of admirable beauty, not so much in that which is termed the flower of youth, as in a most delightful composition of majesty and modesty in equal mixture.
Ibid.

2 All her faculties were in motion, and every motion seemed a well-guided action; her eye was set upon one, her ear listened to another; her judgement ran upon a third, to a fourth she addressed her speech; her spirit seemed to be everywhere, and yet so entire in herself as it seemed to be nowhere else.
Ibid.

3 Her face oblong, fair but wrinkled; her eyes small, yet black and pleasant; her nose a little hooked, her lips narrow and her teeth black (a defect the English seem subject to from their too great use of sugar). She wore false hair, and that red.
Paul Hentzner, JOURNEY INTO ENGLAND   1598

4 Her teeth are very yellow and unequal. Many of them are missing so that one cannot understand her easily when she speaks quickly.
André Hurault, reporting to Henry IV *of France*   1597

5 She keeps the front of her dress open and one can see the whole of her bosom, and passing low and often she would open the front of this robe as if she were too hot . . . Her bosom is somewhat wrinkled, as well as one can see from the collar which she wears round her neck, but lower down her flesh is exceedingly white and delicate so far as one could see.
Ibid.

6 She thinks highly of herself and has little regard for her servants and Council being of opinion that she is far wiser than they; she mocks them and often cries out upon them.
Ibid.

7 When a man speaks to her, and especially when he says something displeasing she interrupts not seldom; and by reason of her interruptions very often she misunderstands what is said to her and misreports it to her Council. Hence comes the custom of delivering to the Council what has been said to her. She is a haughty woman, falling easily into rebuke.
Ibid.

8 So secret were her amours that even to the present day their mysteries cannot be penetrated; but the utility she drew from them is public, and always operated for the good of her people. Her lovers were her ministers and her ministers were her lovers. Love commanded, and love was obeyed, and the reign of the princess was happy because it was a reign of *love* in which its chains and its slavery are liked.
Sir Philip Marville   MEMOIRS

9 When she came to the throne, a knight of the realm, who had insolently behaved to her when she was Lady Elizabeth, fell upon his knees to her and besought her pardon, expecting to be sent to the Tower; she replied mildly, "Do you not know we are descended of the *lion*, whose nature is not to prey upon the mouse, or any other small vermin."
George Puttenham, THE ART OF POESY   1589

10 There is no evidence that Elizabeth had much taste for painting, but she loved pictures of herself.
Horace Walpole, ANECDOTES OF PAINTING IN ENGLAND   1771

ELIZABETH II (1926–)
Queen

11 At the age of two she had an air of authority and reflectiveness, astonishing in an infant.
Winston Churchill, letter to his wife   1928

12 She doesn't make all that difference between Labour and Conservative, and for her an election simply means that, just when she has begun to know us, she has to meet another terrible lot of politicians.
Richard Crossman, DIARIES   22 *Jun* 1970

1   It always frightens me that people should
    love her so much.
    *Elizabeth, The Queen Mother, of her
    daughter as a child*

2   My chief claim to fame seems to be that I
    am the father of Princess Elizabeth.
    King George VI

3   The Queen is a very pleasant middle to
    upper class type of lady, with a talkative
    retired Navy husband.
    *Malcolm Muggeridge, Saturday Evening
    Post*

4   She knows more about world affairs than
    most diplomats who visit her, and has com-
    plained to her Foreign Office about its
    elementary briefings.
    Anthony Sampson, THE CHANGING
    ANATOMY OF BRITAIN   1982

5   The Queen showed herself able to come to
    terms with each new lurch of the political
    system. When Harold Wilson came to
    power in 1964 the palace was apprehensive
    about the Labour revolutionaries . . . But
    the Queen was soon having friendly talks
    every Tuesday afternoon with Wilson, who
    later paid tribute to her helpfulness and
    commonsense.
    Ibid.

6   The weekly meetings between the Queen
    and Mrs Thatcher — both the same age —
    are dreaded by at least one of them. The
    relationship is the more difficult because the
    roles seem confused; the Queen's style is
    more matter-of-fact and domestic, while it is
    Mrs Thatcher (who is taller) who bears
    herself like a queen.
    Ibid.

HAVELOCK ELLIS (1859–1939)
English psychologist, essayist and critic

7   He has the air of a fake prophet, like a
    Santa Claus at Selfridge's.
    *Graham Greene. Quoted Phyllis Gross
    Kurth*, HAVELOCK ELLIS, *a biography*

8   You are the first human being who has been
    a perfect rest to me.
    Olive Schreiner, in a letter to Ellis

RALPH WALDO EMERSON (1803–1882)
*American essayist, poet and
philosopher*

9   I could readily see in Emerson a gaping
    flaw. It was the insinuation that had he lived
    in those days when the world was made, he
    might have offered some valuable
    suggestions.
    Herman Melville

10 Emerson is one who lives instinctively on
    ambrosia — and leaves everything indi-
    gestible on his plate.
    Friedrich Nietzsche

SIR JACOB EPSTEIN (1880–1959)
English sculptor

11 They are a form of statuary which no careful
    father would wish his daughter, or no dis-
    cerning young man his fiancée, to see.
    *Evening Standard and St. James
    Gazette* 1908

12 The Epstein makes me feel physically sick.
    The wretched woman has two sets of breasts
    and a hip joint like a merrythought.
    *John Galsworthy, letter to
    Edward Garnett* 14 Jun 1925

13 Epstein is a great sculptor. I wish he would
    wash, but I understand Michaelangelo *never*
    did, so I suppose it is part of the tradition.
    Ezra Pound. Quoted Charles Norman,
    EZRA POUND

JOHN EVELYN (1620–1706)
English diarist

14 He read me part of a play or two of his own
    making, very good, but not as he conceits
    them, I think, to be . . . In fine, a most
    excellent person he is, and must be allowed
    a little conceitedness, but he may well be so,
    being a man so much above others.
    Samuel Pepys, DIARY   5 Nov 1665

15 Somehow or other the bygone gentleman
    sets up, through three centuries, a
    perceptible tingle of communication, so that
    without laying stress on anything in particu-
    lar, stopping to dream, stopping to laugh,
    stopping merely to look, we are yet taking
    notice all the time.
    Virginia Woolf, THE COMMON
    READER   1925

F

MICHAEL FARADAY (1791–1867)
English physicist

1 The prince of scientific expositors, Faraday, was once asked, "How much may a popular lecturer suppose his audience knows?" He replied emphatically, "Nothing."
T. H. Huxley. Quoted L. Huxley, LIFE AND LETTERS OF THOMAS HUXLEY   1900

WILLIAM FAULKNER (1897–1962)
American novelist

2 Poor Faulkner! Does he really think big emotions come from big words?
Ernest Hemingway. Quoted A. E. Hotchner, PAPA HEMINGWAY

GUY FAWKES (1570–1606)
Gunpowder Plot conspirator

3 Being thus taken in the fact he both confessed and defended it, adding; "That if he had happened to be within the house, as he was without, he would, by putting fire to the train, have put an end to their enquiry."
Evidence given after his arrest   5 Nov 1605

4 One Johnson (alias of Fawkes) was found in the vault when the Gunpowder Plot was discovered. He was asked if he was sorry. He answered that he was only sorry that it had not taken place.
Sir Edward Hoby, letter to Sir Thomas Edmondes, ambassador to Brussels
19 Nov 1605

5 When Johnson (alias of Fawkes) was brought into the King's presence the king asked him how he could conspire so hideous a treason against his children and so many innocent souls who had never offended him? He answered that dangerous diseases required a desperate remedy, and he told some of the Scots that his intent was to have blown them back to Scotland.
Ibid.

6 When the party himself was taken he was but newly come out of his house from working, having his Firework for kindling ready in his pocket, wherewith, as he confesseth, if he had been taken but immediately before

when he was in the House, he was resolved to have blown up himself with his takers.
King James I. *Speech to Parliament*
Dec 1605

HENRY FIELDING (1707–1754)
English novelist

7 A novel should always be kept moving on. Nobody knew this better than Fielding, whose novels, like most good ones, are full of inns.
Augustine Birrell, THE OFFICE OF LITERATURE

8 The most singular genius that this country ever produced, whose works it has long been the fashion to abuse in public and read in private.
George Borrow, THE BIBLE IN SPAIN   1843

9 Fielding being mentioned, Johnson exclaimed "He was a blockhead" and upon my expressing surprise at so strange an assertion he said: "What I mean by his being a blockhead is that he was a barren rascal
Boswell, THE LIFE OF JOHNSON   1791

10 There are many kinds of laughter; you [Samuel Richardson] make me laugh with pleasure, but I often laugh, and am angry at the same time, at the facetious Mr Fielding.
Lady Dorothy Bradshaigh, letter to Samuel Richardson   29 Mar 1750

11 Who would venture to read one of his works aloud to a modest woman?
Dr Charles Burney

12 To take Fielding up after Richardson is like emerging from a sick-room heated by stoves into an open lawn on a breezy day in May.
Samuel Taylor Coleridge, TABLE TALK
5 Jul 1834

13 Richardson picked the kernel of life while Fielding was content with the husk.
Samuel Johnson. Quoted Mrs Thrale, ANECDOTES OF THE LATE SAMUEL JOHNSON   1786

14 His happy constitution (even when he had half demolished it) made him forget everything when he was before a venison pasty or over a flask of champagne, and I am

persuaded he had known more happy moments than any prince on earth.
Lady Mary Wortley Montagu (his cousin)

1 He had either to be a hackney driver, or a hack writer
Ibid., of his improvidence

2 I never saw Johnson really angry with me but once. I alluded, rather flippantly, I fear, to some witty passage in *Tom Jones*; he replied "I am shocked to hear you quote from so vicious a book. I am sorry to hear you have read it; a confession which no modest lady should ever make." I thanked him for his correction; assured him I thought full as ill of it now as he did, and had only read it at an age when I was more subject to be caught by the wit than able to discern the mischief.
Hannah More, in a letter to her sister 1780

3 *Tom Jones* is an epic of life, of the healthy average life of the average natural man, not faultless by any means, but human and actual, as no one else but Shakespeare has shown him in the mimic world.
George Saintsbury

4 The genius of Cervantes was transferred into the novels of Fielding who painted the characters and ridiculed the follies of life with equal strength, honour and propriety.
Tobias Smollett, HISTORY OF ENGLAND 1758

5 Fielding has as much humour, perhaps, as Addison, but having no idea of grace, is perpetually disgusting.
Horace Walpole, letter to Mr Pinkerton Jun 1785

ARTHUR ANNESLEY RONALD FIRBANK (1886–1926)
English novelist

6 He received us in a closely-curtained room lighted by numerous candles and filled with a profusion of exotic flowers. A large table was set with a banquet of rich confectionery and hot-house fruits. Firbank, whose appearance was as orchidaceous as his fictional fantasies, behaved so strangely that all attempts at ordinary conversation became almost farcical. For instance, when Sacheverell spoke appreciatively of his latest novel *Caprice* he turned his head away and remarked in a choking voice, "I can't bear calceolarias! Can you?"
Siegfried Sassoon, SIEGFRIED'S JOURNEY 1945

7 Anxious to entertain him properly I bought a monumental bunch of grapes and a glutinous chocolate cake. Powdered, ninetyish, and insuperably shy, he sat with eyes averted from me and my well-meaning repast. His most rational response to my attempts at drawing him out about literature and art was "I adore italics, don't you?" His cup of tea remained untasted and he quailed when I drew his attention to my large and cosy pile of crumpets. As a gesture of politeness he slowly absorbed a single grape.
Ibid.

8 When after a dozen or so examinations the War Office finally rejected him as totally unfit for service and then — in its usual muddled way — immediately called him up again, he replied through his lawyer with a threat of a suit for libel. The War Office, at a time when it governed the world, was so startled by this simple piece of initiative that it at once sent back to him a humble apology.
Sir Osbert Sitwell, NOBLE ESSENCES AND COURTEOUS REVELATIONS 1950

EDWARD FITZGERALD (1809–1883)
English poet and translator

9 Fitzgerald's *Omar* is worth all the Persian scholarship of the century.
Ezra Pound, THE NEW AGE 1917

10 Edward Fitzgerald had one of the strangest fates in literature. By freely translating the *Rubaiyat* of Omar Khayyam into English he perpetuated his own name, and gave a twelfth century collection of Persian verses a unique place in the poetry of this country.
Anthony Powell, Daily Telegraph, Fitzgerald's Other Works 17 Aug 1962

11 Mr Quaritch, finding that the British public unanimously declined to give a shilling for it [the *Rubaiyat*], had relegated it to be disposed of for a penny. Having read it Rossetti and I invested upwards of sixpence apiece. In a week or two, if I'm not mistaken, the remaining copies were sold at a guinea. I have since seen copies offered for still more absurd prices. I kept my own pennyworth, and have it still.
Algernon Swinburne, letter to A. C. Benson

FRANCIS SCOTT KEY FITZGERALD (1896–1940)
American author

12 F. Scott Fitzgerald; Hack Writer and Plagiarist. St. Paul, Minnesota.
Fitzgerald's letter heading 1922

1 Mr Fitzgerald is a novelist. Mrs Fitzgerald is a novelty.
   Ring Lardner, THE OTHER SIDE

2 Of good social standing and addicted to strong liquor, he had neither the stamina of a Hemingway nor the peasant goodness of a Faulkner to withstand the corrupting influences attendant on success in the materialistic USA. He wasted his energies on the glossier magazines, wrote rubbishy film scripts, and died in his forties a bitter, exhausted man.
   News Review reviewing THIS SIDE OF PARADISE   9 *Dec* 1948

3 Although he would write a bad story, he could not write badly.
   Dorothy Parker. Quoted Anthony Burgess, Daily Telegraph, Dollars and Dolours 2 *Dec* 1979

GUSTAVE FLAUBERT (1821–1880)
French novelist

4 The other day Flaubert said to me, "It's finished. I have only ten more pages to write. But I've already got the ends of the sentences." You see? He already had the music of the ends of the sentences which he had not yet begun.
   Théophile Gautier. Quoted Goncourt Journals   3 *Mar* 1862

5 An interviewer asked me what book I thought best represented the modern American woman. All I could think of to answer was *Madame Bovary*.
   Mary McCarthy, ON THE CONTRARY: CHARACTERS IN FICTION   1962

6 Flaubert was married to his work, lived with his mother in the provinces, and when he fell in love, as he often did, he succumbed to all the glorious idiocies — violets, handkerchiefs, tears, letters and separation simply for the sake of experiencing the sweet suffering that attends the contemplation of the absent one. He committed it all to paper, employing the heart of the poet and the scalpel of the surgeon. At 50 he wondered if he should marry but realised he had left it too late.
   Edna O'Brien, Observer, Love and Punishment   13 *Feb* 1983

GERALD FORD (1913–)
Thirty-seventh President of the United States

7 He looks like the guy in the science fiction movie who is the first to see 'The Creature'.
   David Frye

8 Jerry Ford is so dumb that he can't fart and chew gum at the same time.
   Lyndon Johnson

9 He played too much football without a helmet.
   Ibid.

EDWARD MORGAN FORSTER (1879–1970)
English novelist and essayist

10 Forster's world seemed a comedy, neatly layered and staged in a garden whose trim privet hedges were delicate with gossamer conventions. About its lawns he rolled thunderstorms in teacups, most lightly, beautifully.
   T. E. Lawrence, Spectator   6 *Aug* 1927

11 Forster never gets any further than warming the teapot. He's a rare hand at that. Feel this teapot. Is it not beautifully warm? Yes, but there ain't going to be no tea.
   Katherine Mansfield, JOURNAL   May 1917

12 Leonard Woolf said he thought *Passage to India* much the best of Morgan Forster's books, but remarked that on re-reading it he had been struck anew by the oppressively feminine influences under which M. had grown up. I said that if one grew up with a lot of old women it must do a good deal to one's outlook. "But Morgan *is* an old woman," he said. "He always has been."
   William Plomer, ELECTRIC DELIGHTS

CHARLES JAMES FOX (1749–1808)
British statesman

13 That young man has so thoroughly cast off every principle of common honour and honesty, that he must become as contemptible as he is odious.
   George III, *letter to Lord North*   26 *Jul* 1775

14 He talked to me at the club one day concerning Cataline's conspiracy — so I withdrew my attention and thought about Tom Thumb.
   Samuel Johnson, MISCELLANIES (*edited Birkbeck Hill*)   1897

15 It is impossible for me to describe with what fire and persuasive eloquence he spoke, and how the speaker in the chair incessantly nodded approbation from beneath his solemn wig; and innumerable voices cried out "Hear him! Hear him!" and when there was the least sign that he intended to leave

off speaking they no less vociferously exclaimed, "Go on!" and so he continued to
speak in this manner for nearly two hours.
C. P. Montz, TRAVELS IN ENGLAND IN 1782

1 Mrs Crewe told me that on one occasion,
when it was remarked that Fox still retained
his early love for France, and everything
French, Burke said, "Yes, he is like a cat —
he is fond of the house though the family be
gone".
Samuel Rogers, TABLE TALK   1856

2 I have seen it stated somewhere that Fox
liked to talk about great people. Nothing
could be more untrue. He hardly ever
alluded to them — I remember indeed that
he once mentioned to me Queen Charlotte,
calling her "that bad woman".
Ibid.

3 Lady Holland announced the death of Fox
in her own odd manner to those relatives
and intimate friends of his who were sitting
in a room near his bedchamber and waiting
to hear that he had breathed his last — she
walked through the room with her apron
thrown over her head.
Ibid.

4 When he spoke he was sometimes very
eloquent. On Mr Hastings, trial he made
many people cry. There were all the peers
with their pocket handkerchiefs out — quite
a tragedy. But he made such a business of it,
he was worse than Punch.
Lady Hester Stanhope, MEMOIRS AS
RELATED TO HER PHYSICIAN,
DR MERYON   1846

JOHN FOXE (1516–1587)
English martyrologist

5 How learnedly he wrote, how constantly he
preached, how piously he lived and how
cheerfully he died, may be seen at large in
the life prefixed to this book.
Thomas Fuller

SAINT FRANCIS OF ASSISI (1182–1226)
Italian founder of the Franciscan Order

6 On a time he entered into the church of St.
Damian, for to make his prayers, and the
image of Jesus Christ spoke unto him and
said, "Francis, go and repair my house,
which is all destroyed as thou seest" and
from that hour the soul of him liquefied, and
the passion of Jesus Christ was marvellously
enfixed in his heart.
Jacobus de Voragine, THE GOLDEN LEGEND
(*translated by William Caxton*   1483)

BENJAMIN FRANKLIN (1706–1790)
American statesman and scientist

7 Benjamin Franklin, incarnation of the
peddling, tuppenny yankee.
Jefferson Davis. Quoted CAIRNS' HISTORY
OF AMERICAN LITERATURE

8 The body of / Benjamin Franklin, printer /
Like the cover of an old book / Its contents
worn out / And stript of its lettering and
guilding / Lies here food for the worms! /
Yet the work itself shall not be lost / For it
will, as he believed, appear once more / In a
new / And more beautiful edition /
Corrected and amended / By its Author.
Benjamin Franklin, epitaph for himself

9 I succeed him; no one could replace him.
*Thomas Jefferson, to the Comte de
Vergennes*

10 Antiquity would have raised altars to this
mighty genius, who, to the advantage of
mankind, compassing in his mind the
heavens and earth, was able to restrain alike
thunderbolts and tyrants.
*Mirabeau. Speech to the French National
Assembly on the death of Franklin*

FREDERICK II (THE GREAT) (1712–1786)
King of Prussia

11 When Frederick the Great would have his
secretary read history to him he would say
"Bring me my liar."
Edward Gibbon

12 He was one of the most rigid disciplinarians
ever to command an army. During the war
in Silesia he ordered that, under pain of
death, no candle should be burning in the
tents after a certain hour. As he passed
Captain Zietern's camp he perceived a light.
Entering he found the captain sealing a
letter which he had just written to his wife.
"Do you not know the orders?" asked the
king. "Add some words I shall dictate." The
officer obeyed and the king dictated,
"Tomorrow I shall perish on the scaffold."
Zietern wrote it, and was executed next
day.
PERCY ANECDOTES   1820

SIGMUND FREUD (1856–1939)
Austrian psychologist

13 What progress we are making. In the Middle Ages they would have burned me. Now
they are content to burn my books.
*Freud in a letter to Ernest Jones, on the
public burning of his books in Berlin*   1933

1   Freud and his three slaves, Inhibition, Complex and Libido.
    Sophie Kerr, Saturday Evening Post, The Age of Innocence   9 *Apr* 1932

2   Freud was a hero. He descended to the 'Underworld' and met there stark terrors. He carried with him his theory as a Medusa's head which turned these terrors to stone.
    R. D. Laing, THE DIVIDED SELF

3   Freud writes a highly perspicuous prose. He is an artist of thought, like Schopenhauer, and, like him, a European author.
    Thomas Mann, FREUD AND THE FUTURE

ROBERT FROST (1874–1963)
American poet

4   If it were thought that anything I wrote was influenced by Robert Frost I would take that particular work of mine, shred it, and flush it down the toilet, hoping not to clog the pipes.
    James Dickey, WRITERS AT WORK
    (*fifth series*)

5   When Frost was asked to explain one of his poems he replied, "What do you want me to do — say it in worser English?"
    H. E. F. Donohue

6   Although his blank verse is colloquial it is never loose, for it possesses the pithy, supercharged economy, indigenous to the New Englander.
    John D. Hart, OXFORD COMPANION TO AMERICAN LITERATURE

ELIZABETH FRY (1780–1845)
English prison reformer

7   I am glad you like what I said of Mrs Elizabeth Fry. She is very unpopular with the clergy; examples of living, active virtue disturb our repose and give one to distressing comparisons; we long to burn her alive.
    Sydney Smith

G

WILLIAM CLARK GABLE (1901–1960)
American film actor

1 When Clark Gable in *It Happened One Night* disclosed that he wore no undershirt, the knitwear manufacturers rocked from the shock to their sales.
Frederick Lewis Allen

2 I'm just a lucky slob from Ohio who happened to be in the right place at the right time.
Clark Gable

3 His ears made him look like a taxicab with both doors open.
Howard Hughes

4 Gable was as certain as the sunrise. He was consistently and stubbornly all man.
New York Times, obituary   1960

5 In Clark's copy of *The Misfits* Arthur Miller had written "To the man who did not know how to hate".
David Niven, BRING ON THE EMPTY HORSES   1975

6 Gable has enemies all right — but they all like him.
David O. Selznick. Quoted David Niven, Ibid.

THOMAS GAINSBOROUGH (1727–1788)
Painter

7 His subjects are softened and sentimentalised too much. It is not simple unaffected nature that we see, but nature sitting for her picture.
William Hazlitt, ON GAINSBOROUGH'S PICTURES

8 The landscape of Gainsborough is soothing, tender, and affecting. The stillness of noon, and the depths of twilight, and the dews and pearls of morning are all to be found on the canvases of this most benevolent and kind-hearted man. On looking at them we find tears in our eyes, and know not what brings them.
John Ruskin, lecture at the Royal Institution   16 Jun 1836

HUGH TODD NAYLOR GAITSKELL (1906–1963)
English politician

9 That desiccated calculating machine.
Aneurin Bevan. Quoted Philip M. Williams, HUGH GAITSKELL: A POLITICAL BIOGRAPHY

10 Gaitskell has a Wykehamistical voice and manner, and a thirteenth-century face.
Henry Channon, DIARY   10 Apr 1951

GALILEO (1564–1642)
Italian mathematician and astronomer

11 In my studies of astronomy and philosophy I hold this opinion about the universe, that the Sun remains fixed in the centre of the circle of heavenly bodies without changing its place, and the earth, turning upon itself, moves round the Sun.
Galileo, letter to Christina di Lorena, Grand Duchess of Tuscany   1615

JOHN GALSWORTHY (1867–1933)
English novelist and dramatist

12 He has the gift of becoming, as it were, a statesman of literature.
Robert Lynd, John o'London's weekly   8 Dec 1928

13 I first read the *Forsyte Saga* at the age of fifteen with great respect and pleasure. I re-read it in my late twenties with less respect, but still great pleasure. I re-read it last week with no respect and precious little pleasure.
Angus Wilson, DIVERSITY AND DEPTH IN FICTION   1983

INDIRA GANDHI (1917–1984)
First Indian woman Prime Minister

14 Her greatest flaw is that she has set too much store by loyalty, and in consequence has fostered too many rogues in her entourage, one of whom was her son Sanjay.
Trevor Fishlock, INDIAN FILE   1983

15 Extraordinarily imaginative, and self-centred or subjective, remarkably selfish, she lives in a world of dreams and vagaries and floats about on imaginary

clouds, full, probably, of all manner of brave fancies.
Pandit Nehru (her father). Quoted
Observer, Profile 21 *Mar* 1982

1 Mrs Gandhi never gives a performance less than the occasion demands.
Observer, Profile 21 *Mar* 1982

2 It is a measure of her iron will that private grief has never been allowed to mar her public appearances except, perhaps, when tears could be expected to yield a dividend.
Ibid.

MOHANDAS KARAMANCHAND (MAHATMA) GANDHI (1869–1948)
Indian social reformer

3 A dear old man with his bald pate and spectacles, beaky nose and birdlike lips and benign but somewhat toothless smile.
Rodney Bennett, Teacher's World
7 *May* 1930

4 It is nauseating to see Mr Gandhi, a seditious Middle Temple lawyer, now posing as a fakir of a type well known in the East, striding half naked up the steps of the Viceregal Palace, while he is still organising and conducting a defiant campaign of civil disobedience, to parley on equal terms with the representative of the King Emperor.
Winston Churchill. Speech at Epping
23 *Feb* 1931

5 I know of no other man in our time, or indeed in recent history, who so convincingly demonstrated the power of the spirit over material things.
Sir Stafford Cripps. Speech, Commonwealth Prime Ministers' Conference 1 *Oct* 1948

6 You've no idea what it costs to keep that old man in poverty.
Lord Mountbatten quoting a colleague,
BBC 1, *Lord Mountbatten Remembers*
12 *Nov* 1980

7 Gandhi was very keen on sex. He renounced it when he was 36, so thereafter it was never very far from his thoughts.
Woodrow Wyatt, Sunday Times, Homage to India's Strange Saint 27 *Nov* 1977

GRETA GARBO (1905–   )
Swedish-born film actress

8 People who know that we both appeared in *Grand Hotel* ask me "Is Garbo as strange a person as the newspapers say she is?" To which I answer, "I don't know. I've never seen her." Though I have been on the same lot with her for four years I have never met her. She goes between her dressing room and her set in a car, or closely guarded and in disguise. She never visits other actors or allows them to visit her.
Wallace Beery, MY UGLY MUG

9 She is every man's fantasy mistress. She gave you the impression that, if your imagination had to sin, it could at least congratulate itself on its impeccable taste.
Alistair Cooke

10 She could sniff an outsider a mile away and if anyone, no matter who, came on the set to get a peek at her she'd sense it even with a couple of hundred extras around and she'd just go and sit in her dressing room until they had been put out.
Bill Daniels, her cameraman. Quoted David Niven, BRING ON THE EMPTY HORSES 1975

11 Boiled down to essentials, she is a plain mortal girl with big feet.
Herbert Krezner

12 Making a film with Garbo does not constitute an introduction.
Robert Montgomery. Quoted David Niven,
BRING ON THE EMPTY HORSES 1975

13 Garbo had an icy look in her eyes when anyone sought to impose on her as Groucho Marx discovered one day. He saw a well-known figure approaching in slacks and a floppy hat, waylaid her, bent down in his famous crouch and peeked up under the brim. Two prisms of pure Baltic blue stared down at him, and he backed away muttering, "Pardon me, ma'am, I thought you were a guy I knew in Philadelphia".
David Niven, BRING ON THE EMPTY HORSES 1975

14 What, when drunk, one sees in other women, one sees in Garbo sober.
Kenneth Tynan, Sunday Times
25 *Aug* 1963

JAMES ABRAM GARFIELD (1831–1881)
Twentieth President of the United States

15 Every President who dies in office, whether from bacteria or bullets, is regarded as a martyr to the public weal, at least in some degree, James A. Garfield, whose troubled six months was marred by office mongering, was probably helped, as far as his reputation was concerned, by his assassination.
Thomas A. Bailey, PRESIDENTIAL GREATNESS

GIUSEPPE GARIBALDI (1807–1882)
Italian revolutionary

1 I offer neither pay, nor quarters, nor food; I offer only hunger, thirst, forced marches, battle and death. Let him who loves his country with his heart, and not merely with his lips, follow me.
Speech to the besieged Garibaldi Legion, Rome 2 *Jul* 1849

DAVID GARRICK (1717–1779)
English actor

2 Garrick was pure gold, beat out into thin leaf.
James Boswell

3 Talking one day to Mr Kemble, Johnson said, "Are you, sir, one of those enthusiasts who believe yourself transformed into the very character you represent?" Mr Kemble answering that he had never felt so strong a persuasion himself Johnson said "To be sure, sir, the thing is impossible. And if Garrick had really believed himself to be that monster, Richard III, he deserved to be hanged every time he performed it."
Boswell, THE LIFE OF JOHNSON 1797

4 Our Garrick's a salad; for in him we see / Oil, vinegar, sugar and saltness agree.
Oliver Goldsmith 1774

5 Here lies David Garrick, describe me who can / An abridgment of all that was pleasant in man.
Ibid.

6 As an actor, confess'd without rival to shine; / As wit, if not first, in the very first line; / Yet, with talents like these, and an excellent heart / The man had his failings — a dupe to his art / Like an ill-judging beauty, his colours he spread, / And he plastered with rouge his own natural red.
Ibid.

7 He cast off his friends as a huntsman his pack / For he knew when he pleased he could whistle them back. / Of praise a mere glutton, he swallowed what came / And the puff of a dunce he mistook it for fame.
Ibid.

8 Garrick, Madam was no disclaimer; there was not one of his own scene-shifters who could not have spoken "To be, or not to be" better than he did; yet he was the only actor I ever saw who I could call a master both in comedy and tragedy.
Samuel Johnson to Mrs Siddons. Quoted Boswell, THE LIFE OF JOHNSON 1797

9 . . . that stroke of death which has eclipsed the gaiety of nations, and impoverished the public stock of harmless pleasure.
Samuel Johnson, LIFE OF EDMUND SMITH

10 The wonderful actor loved the society of children, partly from good nature and partly from vanity. The ecstasy of mirth and terror which his gestures and play of countenance never failed to produce in the nursery flattered him quite as much as the praise of mature critics.
T. B. Macaulay, Edinburgh Review Jan 1843

11 He often displayed all his powers of mimicry for the amusement of the little Burneys, awed them by shuddering and crouching as if he saw a ghost, scared them by raving like a maniac in St. Luke's, and then at once became an auctioneer, a chimney-sweep, or an old woman, and made them laugh till the tears ran down their cheeks.
Ibid

12 A few nights before seeing Garrick in *Hamlet* I saw him in *Abel Drugger* and had I not seen both I should have thought it as possible for Milton to have written *Hudibras* and Butler *Paradise Lost* as for one man to have played *Hamlet* and *Drugger* with such excellence.
Hannah More, letter to Mrs Gwatkins 12 *May* 1776

13 On opening him a stone was found that measured five inches and a half round one way and four and a half the other, yet this was not the immediate cause of his death. His kidneys were quite gone.
Ibid., letter to her sister Jan 1779

14 Let the Muses shed tears, for Garrick has this day sold the patent of Drury Lane Theatre and will never act after this winter. He retires with all his blushing honours thick about him, his laurels as green as in their early spring. Who shall supply his loss to the stage? Who shall now hold the master key to the human heart? Who direct the passions with more than magic power? Who purify the stage; and who, in short, shall nurse and direct my dramatic muse?
Ibid., letter to her sisters 1776

15 Yesterday Mr Garrick called upon us. A volume of Pope lay on the table; we asked him to read, and he went through the latter part of the *Essay on Man.* He was exceedingly good humoured and expressed himself quite delighted with our eager desire for information. He read several lines we had been disputing about, with regard to

emphasis, in many different ways before he decided which was right.
Sarah More, letter to her sister Hannah 1775

1 That young man never had his equal and never will have a rival.
Alexander Pope

2 Jack Bannister told me he was behind the scenes one night when Garrick was playing Lear; and that the tones in which Garrick uttered the words "O fool! I shall go mad!" absolutely thrilled him.
Samuel Rogers, TABLE TALK 1856

3 Garrick used to pay an annual visit to Lord Spencer at Althrop, where, after tea, he generally entertained the company by reading scenes from Shakespeare. He would steal anxious glances at the faces of his audience to perceive what effect his reading produced. One night Garrick observed a lady listening to him very attentively, and yet never moved a muscle of her countenance. Speaking of her next day he said, "She seemed a very worthy person, but I hope she won't be at my reading tonight."
Ibid.

4 One evening at Althorp when Garrick was about to exhibit some particular stage-effect of which they had been talking, a young man got up and placed the candles on the floor, that the light be thrown on his face as from the lamps in the theatre. Garrick, displeased at this officiousness, immediately sat down again.
Ibid.

ELIZABETH CLEGHORN GASKELL
(1810–1865)
English novelist

5 Mrs Gaskell is a woman of whose conversation and company I should not tire. She seems to me kind, clever, animated and unaffected.
Charlotte Brontë, letter to George Smith 1 *Jul* 1851

6 A natural unassuming woman whom they have been doing their best to spoil by making a lioness of her.
Jane Carlyle, letter 17 *May* 1849

7 We have only to look at the portrait of Mrs Gaskell, soft-eyed beneath her charming veil, to see that she was a dove. In an age whose ideal of woman emphasised the feminine qualities at the expense of all others she was all a woman was expected to

be; gentle, domestic, tactful unintellectual, prone to tears, easily shocked.
David Cecil, EARLY VICTORIAN NOVELISTS

8 She is neither young nor beautiful; very retiring but quite capable of talking when she likes — a good deal of the clergyman's wife about her.
A. H. Clough, letter to Anne Clough 9 *Feb* 1849

JOHN GAY (1685–1732)
English dramatist and poet

9 Life is a jest and all things show it, / I thought so once and now I know it.
John Gay, MY OWN EPITAPH

10 He was a negligent and a bad manager. Latterly the Duke of Queensberry took his money into his keeping and let him have only what was necessary out of it; and as he lived with them he had not much occasion for much. He died worth £3000.
Alexander Pope. Quoted Rev. Joseph Spence, OBSERVATIONS, ANECDOTES AND CHARACTERS 1820

11 Dr Swift had been observing once to Mr Gay, what an odd pretty thing a Newgate pastoral might make. Gay was inclined to try at such a thing for some time; but afterwards thought it might be better to write a Comedy on the same plan. This was what gave rise to *The Beggars Opera*.
Ibid.

12 Secretary Craggs made Gay a present of stock in the South Sea year, and he was worth £20,000, but lost it all again.
Ibid.

13 *The Beggar's Opera* is a proof how strangely people will differ about a literary performance. Burke thinks it has no merit.
Sir Joshua Reynolds, DISCOURSES TO THE ROYAL ACADEMY

14 Gay was never designed by Providence to be more than two and twenty by his thoughtlessness and gullibility.
Jonathan Swift

GEORGE I (1660–1727)
King

15 "Vot?" asked George I courteously, "is the difference between a public nuisance and a public convenience?"
Caryl Brahms and S. J. Simon, NO NIGHTINGALES

16 George the First was an honest, dull, German gentleman, lazy and inactive even in his pleasures, which were therefore lowly

and sensual. He was diffident of his own parts, which made him speak little in public and prefer in his social, which were his favourite, hours the company of wags and buffoons.
Earl of Chesterfield

1   George I made so slight an impact on his subjects that after his death there was no clamour to perpetuate his memory in any public place; but during his lifetime one of the most strangely placed statues ever created was raised in his honour. This is the marble effigy which still surmounts Hawksmore's eccentric tower of St George's Church, Bloomsbury.
Ralph Dutton, ENGLISH COURT LIFE   1963

2   George I knew nothing and desired to know nothing, did nothing and desired to do nothing, and the only good thing that is told of him is that he wished to restore the crown to its hereditary successor.
Samuel Johnson. Quoted Boswell, THE LIFE OF JOHNSON   6 Apr 1775

3   The person of the king is as perfect in my memory as if I saw him but yesterday. It was that of an elderly man rather pale and exactly like his pictures and coins; not tall, of an aspect rather good than august, with a dark tie-wig, a plain coat, waistcoat and breeches of snuff-coloured cloth with stockings of the same colour, and a blue ribband over all.
Horace Walpole

GEORGE II (1683–1760)
King

4   Sir Robert Walpole advised the king to take Lady Deloraine till Madame Walmoden could be brought over. His Majesty said she stank of Spanish wine so abominably of late that he could not bear her.
Lord Hervey, MEMOIRS OF THE COURT OF GEORGE II   1848

5   Hanover so completed the conquest of his affections that there was nothing English that he did not always show was surpassed by something of the same kind in Germany. No English cook could dress a dinner, no English player could act, no English coachman could drive, or English jockey ride, nor were any English horses fit to drive or fit to be ridden; no Englishman knew how to come into a room, nor any Englishwoman know how to dress herself, whereas at Hanover all these things were the utmost perfection.
Ibid.

6   His Majesty stayed about five minutes in the gallery; snubbed the Queen, who was drinking chocolate, for being always stuffing; the Princess Emily, for not hearing him; the Princess Caroline for being grown fat; the Duke of Cumberland for standing awkwardly, Lord Hervey for not knowing what relation the Prince of Sultzbach was to the Elector Palatine, and then carried the Queen to walk, and be re-snubbed, in the garden.
Ibid.

7   He looked upon all men and women as creatures he might kick or kiss for his diversion.
Lady Mary Wortley Montagu

8   He was thought to reward his mistresses by giving them sweepstake tickets.
T. H. White, THE AGE OF SCANDAL   1950

9   George II was ruled by his wife Queen Caroline. He was a touchy, comic, obstinate, small man with a mania for being thought brave. He was charming because he was straightforward. Whether he was in a temper or not he spoke from his heart. He did not lie about his mistresses to his wife, whom he adored.
Ibid.

10   When the Queen was on her death-bed and urged him to marry again poor George was hardly able to sob out "Non, non, j'aurai des maitresses."
Ibid.

GEORGE III (1738–1820)
King

11   Throughout the greater part of his life George III was a kind of consecrated obstruction.
Walter Bagehot, THE ENGLISH CONSTITUTION   1867

12   George the Third / Ought never to have occurred / One can only wonder / At so grotesque a blunder.
E. C. Bentley, MORE BIOGRAPHIES

13   The King bathes, and with great success; a machine follows the royal one into the sea, filled with fiddlers who play 'God Save the King' as his Majesty takes his plunge.
Fanny Burney, writing from Weymouth to her father   8 Jul 1789

14   This morning, when I received my intelligence of the King from Dr John Willis, I begged to know where I might walk in safety? "In Kew Gardens," he said, "as the King would be in Richmond."

"Should any unfortunate circumstance," I cried, "at any time, occasion my being seen by his Majesty, do not mention my name, but let me run off without call or notice."

This he promised. Everybody, indeed, is ordered to keep out of sight.

Taking, therefore, the time I had most at command, I strolled into the gardens. I had proceeded, in my quick way, nearly half the round, when I suddenly perceived, through some trees, two or three figures. Relying on the instructions of Dr John, I concluded them to be workmen and gardeners; yet tried to look sharp, and in so doing, as they were less shaded, I thought I saw the person of his Majesty!

Alarmed past all possible expression, I waited not to know more, but turning back, ran off with all my might. But what was my terror to hear myself pursued — to hear the voice of the King himself loudly and hoarsely calling after me: "Miss Burney! Miss Burney!"

I protest I was ready to die. I knew not in what state he might be at the time; I only knew the orders to keep out of his way were universal; on I ran, too terrified to stop, and in search of some short passage, for the garden is full of little labyrinths, but which I might escape.

The steps still pursued me, and still the poor hoarse and altered voice rang in my ears — more and more footsteps resounded frightfully behind me — the attendants all running, to catch their eager master.

Heavens, how I ran! I do not think I should have felt the hot lava from Vesuvius — at least not the hot cinders — had I so run during its eruption. My feet were not sensible that they even touched the ground.

Soon after, I heard other voices, shriller, though less nervous, call out: "Stop! Stop! Stop!"

I could by no means consent; I knew not what was purposed, but I recollected fully my agreement with Dr John that very morning, that I should decamp if surprised, and not be named.

My own fears and repugnance, also, after a flight and disobedience like this, were doubled in the thought of not escaping: I knew not to what I might be exposed, should the malady be then high, and take the turn of resentment. Still, therefore, on I flew; and such was my speed, so almost incredible to relate or recollect, that I fairly believe no one of the whole party could have overtaken me, if these words, from one of the attendants, had not reached me:

"doctor Willis begs you to stop!"

"I cannot! I cannot!" I answered, still flying on, when he called out: "You must, ma'am; it hurts the King to run."

Then, indeed, I stopped — in a state of fear really amounting to agony. I turned round, I saw the two Doctors had got the King between them, and three attendants of Dr Willis's were hovering about.

As they approached, some little presence of mind happily came to my command: it occurred to me that, to appease the wrath of my flight, I must now show some confidence: I therefore faced them as undauntedly as I was able.

When they were within a few yards of me, the King called out: "Why did you run away?"

Shocked at the question impossible to answer, yet a little assured by the mild tone of his voice, I instantly forced myself forward, to meet him, though the internal sensation, which satisfied me this was a step the most proper to appease his suspicions and displeasure, was so violently combated by the tremor of my nerves, that I fairly think I may reckon it the greatest effort of personal courage I have ever made.

The effort answered: I looked up, and met all his unwonted benignity of countenance, though something still of wildness in his eyes. Think, however, of my surprise, to feel him put both his hands round my two shoulders, and then kiss my cheek!

He now spoke in such terms of his pleasure in seeing me, that I soon lost the whole of my terror; astonishment to find him so nearly well, and gratification to see him so pleased, removed every uneasy feeling, and the joy that succeeded, in my conviction of his recovery, made me ready to throw myself at his feet to express it.

What a conversation followed!

Fanny Burney, DIARY   *Feb* 1789

1 Just when some seabirds were hovering about, the king burst out (to an unfortunate young midshipman) "Young gentleman, what birds are those — pigeons?" "No your majesty, gulls.". "Gulls, gulls," continued the king "What do they feed upon? Where do they come from? Where do they roost?" All this was uttered with the greatest rapidity and without waiting for a reply to either question; indeed the poor mid was so confounded that he was saved only by His Majesty's attention being drawn to some other object.

Admiral Sir Thomas Byam Martin,
LETTERS AND PAPERS

1 An old, mad, blind, despised and dying
   king.
   Percy Bysshe Shelley, ENGLAND IN 1819,
   A SONNET

2 Dear Master Morgan,
   I think it's time now for you to write me
   another letter. Do you write every day? I
   can show you a big thick copy-book that
   when I was just your age I wrote for my
   father. And what do you think he did to
   reward me? Why, poor old George the
   Third was coming to summon Parliament.
   He was a good man and wanted to do right,
   but he was very obstinate and used to get
   very angry and at last very ill, and he quite
   lost his senses and kept calling the people
   about him peacocks.
       When the day came for him to meet his
   faithful commons, though very ill, he insisted on having his own way, so they gave it
   him, and he went, and I could see his
   carriage — all gold and glass, and I did so
   beg of papa to let me go across Palace Yard,
   and he carried me across and took me into
   the House of Commons. And there he was
   sitting on the Throne with his King's Crown
   on, his robes scarlet and ermine, and held
   his speech written out for him, just what he
   had to say. But, oh dear, he strode up and
   made a bow and began 'My Lords and
   Peacocks'.
       The people who were not fond of him
   laughed, the people who did love him cried,
   and he went back to be no longer a King,
   and his eldest son reigned in his stead, and
   Regent street was named after him.
   *Letter to E. M. Forster, as a boy, from his
   aunt Marianne Thornton*

GEORGE IV (1762–1830)
Prince Regent and King

3 The king behaved very indecently, he was
   continually nodding and winking at Lady
   Conyngham and sighing and making eyes at
   her. At one time in the Abbey he took a
   diamond brooch from his breast, and
   looking at her, kissed it, on which she took
   off her glove and kissed a ring she had on!!!
   Anybody who could have seen his disgusting figure, with a wig the curls of which
   hung down his back, and quite bending beneath the weight of his robes and his 60
   years, would have been quite sick.
   Lady Arbuthnot, JOURNAL 19 *Jul* 1821

4 He had a singular propensity, which was in
   fact a sort of madness, for conceiving that
   he had played a personal part in all the
   events which had passed in his reign.

Among other fancies of this sort he believed
he had been on the great battlefield which
had terminated the war in 1815; and I have
been told by a person present, that one day
at dinner, after relating his achievements on
this occasion, he turned to the Iron Duke
and said, "Was it not so, Duke?" "I have
often heard your Majesty say so," replied
the Duke drily.
Sir Henry Lytton Bulwer (Lord Dalling),
HISTORICAL CHARACTERS   1868

5 I was surprised to find him, amidst such
   constant dissipation, possessed of so much
   learning, wit, knowledge of books in general, discrimination of character as well as
   original humour. He quoted Homer in
   Greek to my son as readily as if the beauties
   of Dryden or Pope had been under discussion. And as to music, he is an excellent
   critic; has an enlarged taste, admiring whatever is good of its kind.
   Dr Burney, letter to his daughter Fanny
   12 *Jul* 1805

6 As a son, as a husband, as a father and
   especially as an adviser of young men, I
   deem it my duty to say that, on a review of
   his whole life, I can find no one good thing
   to speak of, in either the character or conduct of this king.
   William Cobbett

7 So poor Prinney is really dead — and on a
   Saturday, too.
   Thomas Creevey, letter to Elizabeth Ord
   26 *Oct* 1830

8 A more contemptible, cowardly, selfish, unfeeling dog does not exist than this king,
   with vices and weaknesses of the lowest and
   most contemptible order.
   Charles Greville, DIARIES

9 He sleeps very ill, and rings his bell forty
   times in the night; if he wants to know the
   hour, though a watch hangs close to him, he
   will have his valet de chambre down, rather
   than turn his head to look at it. The same
   thing if he wants a glass of water; he won't
   stretch out his hand to get it. His valets are
   nearly destroyed. Their labours are incessant, they cannot take off their clothes at
   night, and hardly lie down.
   Ibid.   17 *Mar* 1829

10 His attendants are quite worn out with
    being always about him and living in such
    hot rooms (which obliges them to drink)
    and seldom getting air and exercise. All
    about him are afraid of him.
    Ibid.

1 He leads a most extraordinary life, never gets up till six in the afternoon. They come to him and open the window curtains at six or seven o'clock in the morning; he breakfasts in bed, does whatever business he can be brought to transact in bed too, he reads every newspaper quite through, dozes three or four hours, gets up in time for dinner, and goes to bed between ten and eleven.
Ibid.

2 This delightful, blissful, wise, pleasurable, honourable, virtuous, true and immortal Prince was a violator of his word, a libertine over head and ears in debt and disgrace, a despiser of domestic ties, the companion of gamblers and demi-reps, a man who has just closed half a century without one single claim on the gratitude of his country or the respect of posterity.
Leigh Hunt, replying, in The Examiner 22 March 1812, to a flattering piece in the Morning Post. Hunt was subsequently imprisoned for two years.

3 I could not pray for George IV. I thought people very good who prayed for him and wondered if he could have been much worse if he had not been prayed for.
Florence Nightingale. Quoted Laurence Housman, GREAT VICTORIANS

4 He was a bad son, a bad husband, a bad father, a bad subject, a bad monarch and a bad friend.
Spencer Walpole

5 By God, you never saw such a figure in your life as he is. He speaks and swears so like old Falstaff that damn me if I wasn't ashamed to walk into a room with him.
Duke of Wellington, of George when he was Prince Regent

6 When he was dead they found in his wardrobe all the coats, boots, and pantaloons of fifty years. He had remembered them all and could call for any one of them at any moment. There were five hundred pocket books, containing forgotten sums of money amounting to £10,000 together with countless bundles of women's love letters and locks of hair.
T. H. White, THE AGE OF SCANDAL 1950

GEORGE V (1865–1936)
King

7 My dear old friend George V always told me that he would never have died but for that vile doctor [Dawson of Penn].
Margot Asquith, AUTOBIOGRAPHY 1936

8 Grandpa England.
Elizabeth II's *name for him when she was a child*

9 My father was frightened of his mother. I was frightened of my father, and I'm damned well going to make sure that my children are frightened of me.
George V. *Quoted Randolph Churchill,* LIFE OF THE EARL OF DERBY

10 He had a gruff, blue-water approach to all human problems.
Duke of Windsor, A KING'S STORY

GEORGE VI (1895–1952)
King

11 George VI prevented Churchill from taking an active part in the D-Day landings. He did this by threatening to take part himself.
A. J. P. Taylor, Observer, A Dutiful Monarch 24 *Oct* 1982

12 I am sure it will in no way detract from the prestige of my kingly brother when I say that when we were young I could always manage him.
Duke of Windsor. Quoted News Review 11 *Dec* 1947

EDWARD GIBBON (1737–1794)
English historian

13 The Prince (William Henry, Duke of Gloucester) received the author with much good nature and affability, saying to him as he laid the quarto on the table, "Another damned thick square book! Always scribble, scribble, scribble, eh Mr Gibbon?" We must suppose Mr Gibbon to be a very silly man, if he could be flattered by the leave given to lay his works before such an incompetent personage.
H. D. Best, PERSONAL AND LITERARY MEMORIALS 1829

14 Gibbon is an ugly, affected, disgusting fellow, and poisons our literary club for me. I class him among infidel wasps and venomous insects.
James Boswell, DIARY 1779

15 The other, deep and slow, exhausting thought / And hiving wisdom with each passing year, / In meditation dwelt, with learning wrought / And shaped his weapon with an edge severe, / Sapping a solemn creed with solemn sneer / The lord of irony, that master spell / Which stung his foes to wrath which grew from fear, / And doomed him to the zealot's ready Hell / Which answers to all doubts so eloquently well.
Lord Byron, CHILDE HAROLD 1818

1 Johnson's style was grand, Gibbon's elegant. Johnson marched to kettle-drums and trumpets. Gibbon moved to flutes and hautboys.
George Coleman the Younger, RANDOM RECORDS

2 At the conclusion of this first period of my life I am tempted to enter a protest against the trite and lavish praise of the happiness of our boyish years, which is echoed with so much affection in the world. That happiness I have never known.
Edward Gibbon, AUTOBIOGRAPHY 1792

3 At 16 I entered Oxford with a stock of erudition which might have puzzled a doctor, and a degree of ignorance for which a schoolboy would have been ashamed.
Ibid.

4 Before I was sixteen I had exhausted all that could be learned in English of the Arabs and Persians, the Tartars and the Turks; and the same ardour urged me to guess at the French of d'Herbelot, and to construe the barbarous Latin of Pocock's Abulpharagius. The maps of Cellarius and Wells imprinted in my mind the picture of ancient Geography; from Strauchius I imbibed the elements of Chronology; the tables of Helvicus and Anderson, the annals of Usher and Prideaux, distinguished the connection of events, and I engraved the multitude of names and dates in clear, indelible series.
Ibid.

5 It was at Rome, on the 16th October 1764, as I sat musing amid the ruins of the Capitol, that the idea of first writing the decline and fall of the city entered my mind. But my original plan was circumscribed to the decay of the city rather than of the empire and though my reading and reflections began to point towards the subject some years elapsed, and several avocations intervened, before I was seriously engaged in that laborious work.
Edward Gibbon, MEMOIRS 1796

6 It was on the day, or rather the night of the 27th of June 1787, between the hours of eleven and twelve that I wrote the last line of the last page of *Decline and Fall* in a summer house in my garden . . . a sober melancholy was spread over my mind by the idea that I had taken an everlasting leave of an old and agreeable companion and that whatsoever might be the future fate of my History, the life of the historian must be short and precarious.
Ibid.

7 His loaded and luxuriant style is disgusting to the last degree and his work is polluted everywhere by the most immoral as well as irreligious insinuations.
Bishop Richard Hurd

8 Gibbon might have been cut out of a corner of Burke's mind without his missing it.
Sir James Mackintosh

9 Gibbon is a malignant painter, and though he does give the likeness of a depraved Christianity he magnifies deformities and takes a profane delight in making the picture as hideous as he can . . . Whenever a Christian emperor or bishop of established reputation is brought forward his encomiums have so much coldness, and his praises so much sneer, that you cannot help discovering contempt where he professes panegyric.
Hannah More

10 Gibbon took very little exercise. He had been staying with Lord Sheffield in the country; and when he was about to go away the servants could not find his hat. "Bless me," said Gibbon, "I certainly left it in the hall on my arrival here." He had not stirred out of doors during the whole visit.
Samuel Rogers, TABLE TALK 1856

11 Sheridan observed Gibbon among his audience and took occasion to mention "the luminous author of *Decline and Fall*". After he had finished one of his friends reproached him with flattering Gibbon. "You called him the luminous author." "Luminous?" replied Sheridan. "Oh I meant — voluminous."
Ibid.

12 Gibbon talked a great deal, walking up and down the room, every now and then, too, casting a look of complacency on his own portrait by Sir Joshua Reynolds which hung over the chimneypiece — that wonderful portrait in which, while the oddness and vulgarity of the features are refined away, the likeness is perfectly preserved.
Ibid.

GIOTTO DI BONDONE (1267–1337)
Italian artist

13 When Pope Benedict XI asked for proof of Giotto's skill as a painter Giotto simply took his brush and with a free sweep drew for the pontiff's messenger a perfect circle. The

moral is that only the most assured skill can do the simple-seeming thing with ease.
Bergen Evans

1 While Giotto was still a boy, and with Cimabue, he once painted a fly on the nose of a figure which Cimabue had made, so naturally that when his master returned to go on with his work he more than once attempted to drive the fly away with his hand, believing it to be real, before he became aware of his mistake.
Giorgio Vasari, LIVES OF THE MOST EMINENT PAINTERS 1550

WILLIAM EWART GLADSTONE
(1809–1898)
British Prime Minister

2 The W. G. Grace of politics.
Clement Attlee. Quoted G. W. Lyttelton, THE LYTTELTON HART-DAVIS LETTERS 1982

3 Always there was this huge concentration of force; purpose at white heat roared like a furnace in every action of his life. When once he had convinced himself on any subject it ceased to be his opinion and became a cosmic truth which it was the duty of every right-minded person to uphold.
E. F. Benson, AS WE WERE 1930

4 It was with the most unfeigned pleasure that Queen Victoria saw the fall of Gladstone's last ministry. She commented on it privately to my father (the Archbishop of Canterbury). "Mr Gladstone has gone out, disappeared all in a moment," she gleefully observed.
Ibid.

5 He always paid Queen Victoria the most profound respect but his deference to her person did not include the least deference to her statecraft and nothing she said influenced him in the least when his mind was made up, for he knew he was right, whereas she, on those many occasions when their views differed, was equally certain he was wrong.
Ibid.

6 An almost spectral phantasm of a man — nothing in him but forms and ceremonies and outside wrappings.
Thomas Carlyle, letters 23 Mar 1873

7 They told me how Mr Gladstone read Homer for fun, which I thought served him right.
Winston Churchill, MY EARLY LIFE 1930

8 Someone said to Lord Morris that Gladstone was a heaven-born genius. "Then let us hope," remarked Lord Morris, a staunch old Tory, "that it is a long time before heaven is again in an interesting condition".
Sir James Crichton-Browne, WHAT THE DOCTOR ORDERED

9 Gladstone's jokes are no laughing matter.
Lord Derby. Quoted G. W. E. Russell, PORTRAITS OF THE SEVENTIES 1916

10 He has not a single redeeming defect.
Benjamin Disraeli

11 Gladstone, like Richelieu, can't write. Nothing can be more involved or more uncouth than all his scribblement.
Disraeli, in a letter 3 Oct 1877

12 My name may have buoyancy enough to float upon the sea of time.
Gladstone, ETON MISCELLANY Nov 1827

13 Without an effort he could always assume the attitude which most appealed to the sympathies of his audience, and his general pose was that of a very good man struggling with a wicked-minded opponent.
Lord George Hamilton, PARLIAMENTARY REMINISCENCES AND REFLECTIONS 1868–1885

14 If working men were today to vote by a majority that two and two make five Gladstone would believe it, and find them reasons for it that they had never dreamed of.
Thomas Henry Huxley

15 Gladstone with his untamable energy, his rich verbosity, his susceptibility to religious and moral influences rather amused Dizzy.
Henry Lucy, SIXTY YEARS IN THE WILDERNESS 1909

16 Everyone who ever met him at close quarters will recollect that the index finger of his left hand was only a stump which he protected by a black finger stall. This injury was the result of an accident in 1845; his gun burst as he was loading it, and his finger was shattered. When the surgeon saw it he pronounced that amputation was necessary. Gladstone laid his hand on the table and the finger was sawn off. This, be it remembered, was in the days before chloroform.
G. W. E. Russell, PORTRAITS OF THE SEVENTIES 1916

17 Archbishop Temple told me that Gladstone had been conspicuously abstemious during the Thirties; and yet in old age Gladstone told me that he would not trust himself to

write a paper or compose a speech with a bottle of port in the room. "I should drink it out to the last drop" he said, so conscious was he of the helpful stimulus.
Ibid.

1 There was one conspicuous gap in his intellectual range. He had not the slightest interest in physical science in any of its aspects or applications. Once under strong pressure he promised to go to Greenwich on a night when a particularly interesting eclipse of the moon was promised and his joy when a thick fog came on and forbade the attempt resembled that of a schoolboy who has got an unexpected half holiday.
Ibid.

2 Mr Gladstone tried, quite unsuccessfully, to please Her Majesty by chewing a milk pudding seventy-nine times every day.
W. C. Sellar and R. J. Yeatman, 1066 AND ALL THAT 1930

3 He can persuade himself that *everything* he takes up is right even though it be calling black white and wrong right.
Queen Victoria

4 He will not attend any suggestion but his own mind's. He does not care what you say, does not attend. I have told him two or three facts of which he was quite ignorant of foreign tone and temper. It makes no difference. He only says, "Is that so? Really?"
Queen Victoria to Edward Benson. Archbishop of Canterbury. Quoted E. F. Benson, AS WE WERE 1930

5 He speaks to me as if I were a public meeting.
Queen Victoria. Quoted G. W. E. Russell, COLLECTIONS AND RECOLLECTIONS 1903

6 Gladstone invariably filled his hot water bottle with tea, which he drank the next morning.
Lawrence Wright, WARM AND SNUG

ELINOR GLYN (1864–1943)
English novelist

7 Would you like to sin / With Elinor Glyn / On a tiger skin? / Or would you prefer / To err / With her / on some other fur?
Anon., after the publication of THREE WEEKS 1907

8 Mrs Glyn achieved the paradox of bringing not only "good taste" to Hollywood, but also "sex appeal". She coined the word "It" and taught Rudolf Valentino to kiss the palm of a lady's hand rather than its back.
Cecil Beaton, introduction to THREE WEEKS

9 When I think of all those hours I flung away reading Henry James and Santayana when I might have been reading life, throbbing, beating, perfumed life, I practically break down. Where, I ask you, have I been, that no true word of Madame Glyn's literary feats has come to me?
Dorothy Parker, New Yorker 26 *Nov* 1927

10 Elinor Glyn, fortified with coffee and brandy, took to her bed to write a 90,000 word novel in three weeks, and did it in 18 days.
Lawrence Wright, WARM AND SNUG

HERMANN GOERING (1893–1946)
German Air Marshal

11 He may be a blackguard, but he is not a dirty blackguard.
Sir Neville Henderson. Speech at Sleaford, Lancs

JOHANN WOLFGANG GOETHE (1749–1832)
German poet and man of letters

12 Goethe is the greatest genius who has lived for a century, and the greatest ass who has lived for three.
Thomas Carlyle on translating WILHELM MEISTER

13 If I were to say what I had really been to the Germans in general, and to the young German poets in particular I should say I had been their *liberator*.
Goethe. Quoted Matthew Arnold, ESSAYS IN CRITICISM: HEINRICH HEINE 1865

14 I cannot forgive Goethe for certain things in his *Faust* and *Wilhelm Meister*; the man who appeals to the worst side of my nature commits a great offence.
Samuel Rogers, TABLE TALK 1856

OLIVER GOLDSMITH (1728–1774)
Irish poet and dramatist

15 He hardly knew an ass from a mule, nor a turkey from a goose, but when he saw it on the table.
Richard Cumberland, MEMOIRS 1807

16 Her lies Nolly Goldsmith, for shortness called Noll / Who wrote like an angel and talked like poor Poll.
David Garrick, IMPROMPTU EPITAPH

17 No man was more foolish when he had not a pen in his hand, or more wise when he had.
Samuel Johnson. Quoted Boswell, THE LIFE OF JOHNSON 1797

1 Goldsmith was a plant that flowered late.
   Ibid.

2 Goldsmith was a man who, whatever he
   wrote, did it better than any other man
   could.
   Ibid.

3 The misfortune of Goldsmith in conversation is this; he goes on without knowing how he is to get off.
   Ibid.

4 Poet, Naturalist, Historian, who left
   scarcely any style of writing untouched, and
   touching nothing that he did not adorn.
   Samuel Johnson, EPITAPH ON GOLDSMITH

5 Was ever poet so trusted before.
   *Samuel Johnson, referring to the debts
   Goldsmith left at his death. Letter to Boswell
   4 Jul 1774*

6 There was in his character much to love but
   little to respect. His heart was soft even to
   weakness; he was so generous that he quite
   forgot to be just; he forgave injuries so
   readily that he might be said to invite them;
   and was so liberal to beggars that he had
   nothing left for his tailor and his butcher.
   He was vain, sensual, frivolous, profuse,
   improvident. One vice of a darker nature
   was imputed to him — envy.
   T. B. Macaulay

7 What play makes you laugh very much, and
   yet is a very wretched comedy? Dr
   Goldsmith's *She Stoops to Conquer.* Stoops
   indeed! — so she does. That is, the muse;
   she is draggled up to the knees and has
   trudged, I believe, from Southwark Fair.
   The whole view of the piece is low humour,
   and there is no humour in it. All the merit is
   in the situations, which are comic; the
   heroine has no more modesty than Lady
   Bridget, and the author's wit is as much
   manqué as the lady's, but some of the
   characters are well acted, and Woodward
   speaks a poor prologue, written by Garrick,
   admirably.
   Horace Walpole

8 An inspired idiot.
   Ibid.

CHARLES GEORGE GORDON (1833–1886)
British General

9 A man who habitually consults the prophet
   Isaiah when he is in difficulty is not apt to
   obey the orders of anyone.
   *Sir Evelyn Baring. Quoted Charles
   Chevenex Trench*, CHARLEY GORDON 1978

10 He spent much time pining for oysters,
   which he thought good for the brain.
   *Piers Brendon, Observer, God's eccentric
   12 Jun 1978*

11 In his famous essay on Gordon Lytton
   Strachey unaccountably failed to record the
   General's singular discovery of the Garden
   of Eden. That it had been located in the
   Seychelles became plain to Gordon when he
   noticed the remarkable similarity between
   the ripe fruits of the giant palms which grew
   there and Eve's pudenda, and the no less
   striking resemblance between the breadfruit
   and Adam's sexual organ. Clearly the trees
   were respectively the Tree of the Knowledge of Good and Evil, and the Tree of
   Life, and to clinch his case Gordon found a
   likely looking serpent.
   Ibid.

12 His reading was confined almost entirely to
   the Bible; but the Bible he read, and re-read
   with an untiring and and unending assiduity.
   There, he was convinced, all truth was to be
   found, and he was equally convinced that he
   could find it.
   Lytton Strachey, EMINENT
   VICTORIANS 1918

13 To *think* of your dear noble, heroic Brother,
   who served his Country and his Queen so
   truly, so heroically, with a self-sacrifice so
   edifying to the World not having been res-
   cued — is to me *grief inexpressible*! Indeed
   it has made me *ill*.
   Queen Victoria, letter to Gordon's sister

JOHN GOWER (1320–1402)
English poet

14 He is always polished, sensible, perspicuous, and not prosaic in the reproachful
   sense of the word.
   Henry Hallam, LITERATURE OF
   EUROPE 1839

15 The first of our authors who can properly be
   said to have written English was Sir John
   Gower who, in his *Confession of a Lover*,
   calls Chaucer his disciple and may therefore
   be considered as the father of our poetry.
   Samuel Johnson, LIVES OF THE
   POETS 1781

FRANCISCO GOYA Y LUCIENTES
(1746–1828)
Spanish painter

16 In his early life Goya made no concealment
   of his anarchistic propensities. He had many
   enemies and after being found one morning

lying in the grass with a dagger sticking in his back he decided to go to Rome for a time. He worked his way from Madrid as a bullfighter.
Julia de Wolf Addison, THE ART OF THE NATIONAL GALLERY 1905

WILLIAM GILBERT GRACE (1848–1915)
English cricketer

1 "Did the old man ever cheat?" I once asked an honest Gloucestershire cricketer who worshipped Grace. "Bless you sir, never in his life," was the indignant answer. "Cheat? No sir. Don't you ever believe it — he were too clever for that."
Neville Cardus, THE GREAT VICTORIANS: edited by *H.J. and Hugh Massingham*)

2 W.G. became an Institution in a day of Institutions, all of which, like the Albert Memorial, had to be impressive by sheer bulk. W.G. himself of course did not know what he stood for in the national consciousness; he was content to be a cricketer. He shared none of the contemporary habit of self-exposition.
Ibid.

3 He played as an amateur, and amateurs were not supposed to be paid. That did not prevent Grace making large sums of money out of the game. He was a cheat, on and off the cricket field.
C. P. Snow, Introduction to Arthur Conan Doyle's THE CASEBOOK OF SHERLOCK HOLMES

THOMAS GRAY (1716–1771)
English poet

4 Had Gray written nothing but his *Elegy*, high as he stands, I am not sure that he would not stand higher; without it, his *Odes* would be insufficient for his fame.
Lord Byron, JOURNALS

5 He was dull in company, dull in his closet, dull everywhere. He was dull in a new way, and that made many people think him GREAT.
Samuel Johnson. Quoted Boswell, THE LIFE OF JOHNSON 1791

6 He was a mechanical poet.
Ibid.

7 At Brighton, during my youth, I became acquainted with a lawyer who had known Gray. He said that Gray's pronunciation was very affected, e.g. "What *naise* (noise) is that?"
Samuel Rogers, TABLE TALK 1654

CHARLES CAVENDISH FULKE GREVILLE (1794–1865)
English diarist

8 The most conceited man I've ever met, though I have read Cicero and known Bulwer-Lytton.
Disraeli in 1875. Quoted G. W. E. Russell, COLLECTIONS AND RECOLLECTIONS 1903

9 He was not exactly a gossip, nor a busybody, he was an extremely inquisitive person in whom, somehow or other, it seemed natural for everybody to confide. Thus the broad current of London life flows through his ample pages and as one turns them over one glides swiftly into the curiously distant world of 80 years ago.
Lytton Strachey, QUEEN VICTORIA 1921

10 For fifty years he listened at the door, / He heard some secrets and invented more. / These he wrote down and women, statesmen, kings / Became degraded into common things.
Lord Winchilsea

GRIMALDI (1778–1837)
English clown

11 He was a sort of Shakespeare in his way. He exhausted natural monsters and then "imagined new", Frankenstein was nothing to him.
Anon. The Times 1828

12 I never saw anyone to equal him — there was so much mind in everything he did. It was said of Garrick that when he played a drunk he was "all over drunk". Grimaldi was "all over clown".
Charles Dibdin the Younger

ELEANOR (NELL) GWYNNE (1650–1687)
Actress. Mistress of Charles II

13 Let not poor Nelly starve.
Charles II, *on his deathbed, to his brother James* 5 Feb 1685

14 All matters of state from her soul she does haste, / And leave to the politic bitches. / The whore's in the right, for 'tis her delight / To be scratching just where it itches.
Contemporary rhyme, author unknown

15 Shall the dog lie where the deer once couched?
Nell Gwynne, refusing a lover after the death of Charles II

9 Good people, let me pass. I am the *Protestant* whore.
Nell Gwynne to an anti-Popish mob 1681

10 Pretty, witty Nell.
   Samuel Pepys, DIARY   3 *Apr* 1665

11 So great performance of a comical part was
   never, I believe, in the world before as Nell
   hath done this, both as mad girl and then,
   most and best of all, when she comes in like a young gallant, and hath the motions and
   carriage of a spark, the most that ever I saw
   any man have. It makes me, I confess,
   admire her.
   Samuel Pepys of Nell as Florimel in
   Dryden's MAYDEN QUEENE   2 *Mar* 1667

H

DOUGLAS HAIG (1861–1928)
(Earl of Bemersyde)
British Field Marshal

1 With the publication of his Private Papers in 1952 he committed suicide twenty-five years after his death.
Lord Beaverbrook, MEN AND POWER

2 He was devoid of the gift of intelligible and coherent expression.
David Lloyd George, WAR MEMOIRS 1936

EDMUND HALLEY (1656–1742)
English astronomer

3 He got leave of his father to go to the island of St. Helena purely on account of advancement of astronomy to make the globe of the Southern Hemisphere right, which before was very erroneous, as being done only after the observations of ignorant seamen . . . on his return he presented his Planisphere, with a short description to His Majesty who was very pleased with it, but received nothing but Prayse.
John Aubrey, BRIEF LIVES 1690

4 There went over with him to St. Helena, amongst others, a woman and her husband who had no child in several years; before he came from the Island she was brought to bed with Child.
Ibid.

5 Edmund Halley thought that Noah's Flood was caused by a comet. He was moved to suggest to the Royal Society in 1694 that the Deluge was due to "the casual shock of a comet". A comet strike might alter the Earth's axis of rotation and a mighty sloshing of the oceans could ensue, which would scour the sea bed. By drawing attenion to the possible consequences of a collision between a comet and the Earth, Halley triggered an unending succession of pseudo-scientific theories and prophecies of disaster that put publishers ever in his debt.
Nigel Calder, THE COMET IS COMING 1980

6 Halley, the astronomer, of whom it was remarked that "he could believe anything but the scriptures", talking against Christianity as wanting demonstration, was stopped by Newton, who said, "Man you had better hold your tongue; you have never sufficiently considered the matter."
M. Noble, A BIOGRAPHICAL HISTORY OF ENGLAND

GEORGE FREDERICK HANDEL (1685–1759)
German composer

7 He was the greatest composer that ever lived. I would uncover my head and kneel before his tomb.
Beethoven. Quoted Percy M. Young, HANDEL

8 Dr Maurice Greene, organist and composer to the Chapel Royal, had left a new solo anthem of his with Handel, who good-naturedly asked him to breakfast next morning. The great German was most affable, and discoursed on every possible subject, but all Greene's attempts to lead the conversation round to the anthem proved futile — at last, growing desperate, he interrupted his host's flow of talk with; "But my anthem, sir — how do you like my anthem?" "Oh, your anthem? Vell, sir, I did think it vanted air." "Wanted air, sir?" "Yes, sir, air — so I did hang it out of te vindow."
H. R. Haweis, MORALS AND MUSIC

9 Newton, hearing Handel play upon the harpsichord, could find nothing to remark but the elasticity of his fingers.
Joseph Warton, WORKS OF ALEXANDER POPE 1797

WARREN GAMALIEL HARDING (1865–1923)
Twenty-ninth President of the United States

10 Few deaths are unmingled tragedies. Harding's was not, he died in time.
Samuel Hopkins Adams, THE AMERICAN HERITAGE

11 Harding was not a bad man. He was just a slob.
Alice Roosevelt Longworth. Quoted Isabel Ross, GRACE COOLIDGE AND HER ERA

1   His speeches leave the impression of an
    army of pompous phrases moving over the
    landscape in search of an idea. Sometimes
    these meandering words would actually cap-
    ture a straggling thought and bear it
    triumphantly a prisoner in their midst until
    it died of servitude and overwork.
    Senator William McAdoo

2   He writes the worst English that I have ever
    encountered. It reminds me of a string of
    wet sponges; it reminds me of tattered
    washing on the line; it reminds me of stale
    bean soup, of college yells, of dogs barking
    idiotically through endless nights. It is so
    bad that a sort of grandeur creeps into it.
    H. L. Mencken

3   He has a bungalow mind.
    Woodrow Wilson. Quoted C. W.
    Thompson, PRESIDENTS I HAVE KNOWN

THOMAS HARDY (1840–1928)
English author

4   Hardy could scarcely look out of the
    window at twilight without seeing some-
    thing hitherto hidden from mortal eye.
    Sir James Barrie. Presidential address to the
    Society of Authors 28 Nov 1928

5   Hardy became a sort of village atheist
    brooding and blaspheming over the village
    idiot.
    G. K. Chesterton, THE VICTORIAN AGE
    IN LITERATURE 1913

6   He seems to me to have written as nearly for
    the sake of "Self-expression" as a man well
    can; and the self which he had to express
    does not strike me as a particularly whole-
    some or edifying matter of communication.
    T. S. Eliot, AFTER STRANGE GODS 1934

7   He was indifferent even to the postscripts of
    good writing; he wrote sometimes over-
    poweringly well, but always very carelessly;
    at times his style touches sublimity, without
    ever having passed through the stage of
    being good.
    Ibid.

8   By the side of George Eliot, Hardy, decent
    as he is, appears as a provincial manu-
    facturer of gauche and heavy fictions that
    sometimes have corresponding virtues.
    F. R. Leavis, THE GREAT TRADITION

9   There are passages in *Jude the Obscure*
    which will offend men in direct proportion
    to their manliness, and which all women,
    save the utterly abandoned, will hurry over
    with shuddering disgust.
    National Review 1895

GABRIEL HARVEY (1550–1630)
An obscure English poet who would
have been long forgotten, but for the
following

10 Thou arrant butter-whore, thou catquean
    and scrattop of scoldes, wilt thou never
    leave afflicting a dead Carcasse, you kitchin-
    stuff wrangler?
    Thomas Nashe, FOUR LETTERS
    CONFUSED 1593. (*See Nashe for Harvey*
    on Nashe)

WILLIAM HARVEY (1578–1657)
English anatomist

11 I have heard him say that after his *Booke of*
    the Circulation of the Blood came out (1628)
    that he fell mightily in his practise, and that
    'twas beleeved by the vulgar that he was
    crack-brained; and all the Physitians were
    against his Opinions, and envyed him. With
    much ado at last, in about 20 or 30 years
    time it was received in all the Universities in
    the World, and Mr Hobbes says in his book
    De Corpore "He is the only man that ever
    lived, perhaps, to see his own Doctrine
    established in his own lifetime."
    John Aubrey, BRIEF LIVES 1690

12 He did delight to be in the darke, and told
    me he could then best contemplate. He had
    a house heretofore at Combe in Surrey, a
    good aire and prospect, when he had Caves
    made in the Earth, in which in Summer time
    he delighted to meditate.
    Ibid.

13 He is the first Englishman of whom we
    know enough to say that he was definitely
    what we now mean by a 'scientific man'. He
    viewed the problems of life as we view
    them; he observed the facts as we observe
    them; he experimented as we experiment
    and he reasoned as we reason.
    Sir Wilmot Herrington, St Bartholomew's
    Hospital Journal, William Harvey at St
    Bartholomew's 1928

14 In merit, Harvey's rank must be compar-
    atively low indeed. So much had been dis-
    covered by others that little more was left
    for him to do than to dress it up into a
    system; and *that*, every judge in such
    matters will allow, requires no ex-
    traordinary talents. Yet, easy as it was, it
    made him *immortal*.
    William Hunter, ANATOMICAL LECTURES

NATHANIEL HAWTHORNE (1804–1864)
American author

1 How paltry, how shrivelled and shrunken does the swallow-tail culture appear of the literary snob in contrast with the provinciality which invests the works of Hawthorne with the swift passion of New England summers.
Joel Chandler Harris. Quoted Wiggins, LIFE OF HAWTHORNE

2 My father was two men, one sympathetic and intuitional, the other critical and logical; altogether they formed a combination that could not be thrown off its feet.
Julian Hawthorne, MEMOIR OF NATHANIEL HAWTHORNE 1883

JOSEPH HAYDN (1732–1809)
Austro-Hungarian composer

3 I recollect when it was still the fashion for gentlemen to wear swords. I have seen Haydn playing at a concert in a tie-wig, with a sword at his side.
Samuel Rogers, TABLE TALK 1856

BENJAMIN ROBERT HAYDON (1786–1846)
English painter of historical scenes

4 Haydon hardly contemplated a teaspoon without a desire to shout and hurl himself at it.
Edmund Blunden, Introduction to Haydon's AUTOBIOGRAPHY

WILLIAM HAZLITT (1778–1830)
English essayist

5 Under this stone does William Hazlitt lie / Thankless of all that God or man could give / He lived like one who never thought to die / He died like one who dared not hope to live.
Samuel Taylor Coleridge

6 At a card party at Charles Lamb's, Hazlitt and Lamb's brother got into a discussion as to whether Holbein's colouring was as good as Vandyke's. Hazlitt denied it, Lamb asserted the contrary; at length they both became so irritated they upset the card-table and seized each other by the throat. In the struggle that ensued Hazlitt got a black eye, but when the two combatants were parted Hazlitt turned to Talfourd, who was offering his aid, and said "You need not trouble yourself, Sir. I do not mind a blow, Sir. Nothing affects me but an abstract idea."
R. B. Haydon, JOURNAL 13 Oct 1828. (*The story is also told by Thomas Moore in his diary* 9 Sep 1820)

7 He is your only good damner, and if I am ever damned I should like to be damned by him.
John Keats

8 What is the reason we do not sympathise with pain short of some terrible surgical operation? Hazlitt, who boldly says all he feels, avows that not only does he not pity sick people, but he hates them.
Charles Lamb, letter to Bernard Barton 5 May 1826

9 A mere ulcer, a sore from head to foot, a poor devil so completely flayed that there is not a square inch of healthy flesh on his carcase; an overgrown pimple, sore to the touch.
Quarterly Review 1817

10 If this creature must make his way over the tombs of illustrious men, disfiguring the records of their greatness with the slime and filth that marks his track, it is right to point him out, so that he may be flung back to the situation in which nature designed that he should grovel.
Ibid.

11 Hazlitt, when at Keswick, narrowly escaped being ducked by the populace, and probably sent to prison, for some gross attacks on women. He even whipped one woman for not yielding to his wishes. The populace was incensed against him and pursued him, but he escaped to Wordsworth, who took him into his house at midnight, gave him clothes and money. Since that time Wordsworth, though he never refused to meet Hazlitt when by accident they came together, did not choose that with his knowledge he should be invited.
Crabb Robinson, DIARY 15 Jul 1815

12 Though we are mighty fine fellows these days we cannot write like Hazlitt.
R. L. Stevenson, VIRGINIBUS PUERISQUE, *Walking Tours* 1881

13 The miscreant Hazlitt continues, I have heard, his abuse of Southey, Coleridge and myself in the *Examiner*. I hope that you do not associate with the fellow; he is not a proper person to be admitted into respectable society, being the most perverse and malevolent creature that ill-luck has thrown in my way. Avoid him.
William Wordsworth, letter to B. R. Haydon Apr 1817

EDWARD RICHARD GEORGE HEATH
(1916–   )
British Prime Minister

1 If only he had lost his temper in public the way he does in private he would have become a more commanding and successful national leader.
William Davis. Quoted James Margach, THE ABUSE OF POWER 1981

2 Music means everything to me when I'm alone. And it's the best way of getting that bloody man Wilson out of my hair.
Edward Heath. Quoted ibid.

3 Edward Heath was once editor of the *Church Times*. It was a part of his career that he kept in the background. As Prime Minister he never expected a good Press, and was always wary of journalists.
James Margach, THE ABUSE OF POWER 1981

4 Heath was the first lower-middle-class grammar school boy to become Conservative leader. His misfortune was that he became leader too soon — not before *he* was ready, but before the party was ready for him.
Ibid.

5 We must kick Ted in the groin. We must be rough with him.
Harold Wilson. Quoted Richard Crossman, DIARIES 20 *Oct* 1969

HEINRICH HEINE (1797–1856)
German author

6 Heine's intense modernism, his absolute freedom, his utter rejection of stock classicism and stock romanticism, his bringing all things under the point of view of the nineteenth century were understood and laid to heart by Germany, through virtue of his immense, tolerant intellectualism, much as there was in all Heine said to affront and wound Germany.
Matthew Arnold, ESSAYS IN CRITICISM 1865

7 He wrote about love and food and drink and sometimes mixed them all together in the most lascivious of soufflés, and for further measure he had wisdom; breathtaking prophetic wisdom.
Michael Foot, Observer, reviewing Jeffrey L. Sammons' HEINRICH HEINE 28 *Mar* 1980

8 He was truly the wittiest German who ever lived, and if that compliment seems insufficiently glorious let us say he was the wittiest Jew, which is certainly saying something.
Ibid.

9 Heine, on the occasion of his meeting with Goethe, had time after time rehearsed appropriate speeches and telling points wherewith to charm the serene old man who was so accustomed to cleverness that he would all the more appreciate anything brilliant. Alas, when the long anticipated hour arrived, all the clever speeches, telling points and brilliant allusions vanished and left the mind a hopeless blank. A prolonged pause — a curious smile on the marble-like face of Goethe — and then at last the most brilliant and promising of the younger men of genius spoke. "The plums on the road between Jena and Weimar are perhaps the most excellent that I have ever tasted."
William Sharp, LIFE OF HEINE 1888

ERNEST MILLER HEMINGWAY
(1899–1961)
American writer

10 I want to run as a writer, not as a man who has been to the wars; not a bar-room fighter or a shooter; nor a horse-player; nor a drinker. I would like to be a straight writer and be judged as such.
Hemingway, SELECTED LETTERS 1917–1961

11 This is the prose I have been working for all my life that should read easily and simply and seem short and yet have all the dimensions of the visible world and the world of man's spirit. It is as good prose as I can write as of now.
Hemingway writing of THE OLD MAN AND THE SEA 1951

12 Cyril Connolly once said that Hemingway treated his own body like a Bentley "tested to destruction". Hemingway himself, with rare modesty, said it was like "a rebuilt jeep".
Richard Holmes, The Times, reviewing SELECTED LETTERS 23 *Apr* 1983

13 He's the original Limelight Kid, just you watch him for a few months. Wherever the limelight is, you'll find Ernest with his big, lovable boyish grin, making hay.
Robert McAlmon. Quoted Malcolm Cowley, A SECOND FLOWERING

14 I understand the hero kept getting in and out of bed with women, and the war wasn't fought that way.
Harold Ross, of FAREWELL TO ARMS. *Quoted James Thurber*, THE YEARS WITH ROSS 1957

1 Despite Hemingway's preoccupation with physical contests, his heroes are almost always defeated physically, nervously, practically; their victories are moral ones.
Edmund Wilson, THE WOUND AND THE BOW 1952

HENRY I (1068–1135)
King

2 He was very wanton as appeareth from his numerous natural issue, no fewer than fourteen, all by him publicly owned, the males highly advanced, the females richly married, which is justly reported to his praise, it being lust to beget, but love to bestow them.
Thomas Fuller, WORTHIES OF ENGLAND 1622

3 His sobriety otherwise was admirable, whose temperance was proof against any meat which objected to his appetite, Lampreys alone excepted, of a surfeit of which he died.
Ibid.

4 When therefore the King returned from hunting at St. Denis in the forest of Lyons he ate the flesh of lampreys, which always disagreed with him, and he always loved them. But when his doctor forbade this food the King did not acquiesce in this counsel of health.
Henry of Huntingdon, HISTORIA ANGLORUM 1154

HENRY II (1133–1189)
King

5 From the Devil he came, and to the Devil he shall return.
St. Bernard of Clairvaux, of Henry's boyhood behaviour 1140

6 His wife, Eleanor, brought a great portion (fair provinces in France) and a great stomach with her; so that it is questionable whether her froward spirit more drove her husband away from her chaste, or Rosamond's fair face more drew him to her wanton embraces.
Thomas Fuller, CHURCH HISTORY OF BRITAIN 1655

7 Henry II wants for nothing and has men, horses, gold, silk, jewels, fruit, game and everything else. We in France have nothing but bread and wine and gaiety.
Louis VII of France. Quoted Walter Map (twelfth-century traveller and chronicler), DE NUGIS CURIALIUM (*translated and edited by M. R. James* 1915)

8 Whenever in his dreams passion mocked him with vain shapes, he used to curse his body, because neither toil nor fasting was able to break or weaken it. I, however, ascribe his activities not to his incontinence, but to his fear of becoming too fat.
Walter Map, ibid.

HENRY III (1207–1272)
King

9 There is very great honour for me in the peace which I am making with the King of England, since he is now my vassal, which before he was not.
Louis IX of France, of the Treaty of Paris 1259

HENRY IV (1367–1413)
King

10 Henry the 4th ascended the throne of England much to his own satisfaction in the year 1399, after having prevailed on his cousin and predecessor Richard the 2nd, to resign it to him, and to retire for the rest of his life to Pomfret Castle, where he happened to be murdered. It is to be supposed that Henry was married, since he had certainly four sons, but it is not in my power to inform the Reader who was his wife. Be this as it may, he did not live for ever, but falling ill, his son the Prince of Wales came and took away the crown; whereupon the King made a long speech, for which I must refer the Reader to Shakespear's Plays, and the Prince made a still longer. This being thus settled between them the King died, and was succeeded by his son Henry.
Jane Austen, THE HISTORY OF ENGLAND BY A PARTIAL, PREJUDICED AND IGNORANT HISTORIAN

11 Henry IV's feet and armpits enjoyed an international reputation.
Aldous Huxley, THE DEVILS OF LOUDUN 1952

HENRY V (1387–1422)
King

12 The King dailie and nightlie in his own person visited and searched the watches, orders and stacions of everie part of his host, and whom he found diligent he praised and thanked, and the negligent he corrected and chastised.
Unknown contemporary writer, THE FIRST ENGLISH LIFE OF KING HENRY THE FIFTH

HENRY VI (1421–1471)
King

1 At three years of age he was brought to open Parliament and shryked and cryed and sprang; and he was then led upon his feet to the choir of St. Paul's by the Lord Protector and the Duke of Exeter, and afterwards set upon a fair courser and conveyed through Chepe.
John Blackman (Henry's chaplain),
MEMOIR OF HENRY VI

2 He visited Bath where are warm baths in which they say the men of that country customarily wash and refresh themselves. The king, looking into the baths, saw in them men wholly naked with every garment cast off. At which he was displeased, and went away quickly, abhorring such nudity as a great offence, and not unmindful of that sentence of Francis Petrarch, "the nakedness of a beast is in a man unpleasing; but the decency of raiment makes for modesty".
Ibid.

3 At Christmas time a certain great Lord had brought before him a show of young ladies with bared bosoms who were to dance in that guise before the king who very angrily averted his eyes, turned his back upon them, and went out of his chamber saying, "Fy, fy, for shame forsoothe yet be to blame."
Ibid.

4 The lord king himself complained heavily to me in his chamber at Eltham when I was alone there with him, employed together with him upon his holie booke and giving ear to his wholesome advice and the sighs of his most deep devotion. There came all at once a knock at the king's door from a certain mighty duke of the realm and the king said, "They do so interrupt me that by day and night I can hardly snatch a moment to be refreshed by reading of any holie reading without disturbance."
Ibid.

HENRY VII (1457–1509)
King

5 This Monarch soon after his accession married the Princess Elizabeth of York, by which alliance he plainly proved that he thought his own right inferior to hers, tho' he pretended to the contrary. By this Marriage he had two sons and two daughters, the elder of which Daughters was married to the King of Scotland and had

the happiness of being grandmother to one of the first Characters in the World. But of her, I shall have occasion to speak more at large in future. The youngest, Mary, married first the King of France and secondly the D. of Suffolk, by whom she had one daughter, afterwards the Mother of Lady Jane Grey, who tho' inferior to her lovely Cousin the Queen of Scots, was yet an amiable young woman famous for reading Greek while other people were hunting. It was in the reign of Henry the 7th that Perkin Warbeck and Lambert Simnel before mentioned made their appearance, the former of whom was set in the stocks, took shelter in Beaulieu Abbey, and was beheaded with the Earl of Warwick, and the latter was taken into the King's kitchen. His Majesty died and was succeeded by his son Henry whose only merit was his not being quite so bad as his daughter Elizabeth.
Jane Austen, THE HISTORY OF ENGLAND BY A PARTIAL, PREJUDICED AND IGNORANT HISTORIAN

6 He likes to be much spoken of and to be highly appreciated by the whole world. He fails in this because he is not a great man. Although he professes many virtues his love of money is too great. He spends all the time he is not in public or in the Council, in writing the accounts of his expenses with his own hand.
Ayala, Spanish ambassador, letter to King Ferdinand and Queen Isabella   25 Jul 1498

7 What he minded, he compassed
Francis Bacon, HISTORY OF HENRY VII   1622

8 He was sad, serious and thoughtful. In Triumphs and Jousts and Tourneys and Balls and Masks he was rather a Princely and Gentle Spectator than seeming to be much excited.
Ibid.

9 He was magnificent in his building; sparing in his rewards.
Ibid.

10 He dwelt more nobly Dead in his Tomb, then he did alive in Richmond or any of his palaces.
Ibid.

11 The people expected their king to live in splendour and he prudently, if reluctantly, fell in with the popular desire. But he early realised that this could not be achieved without unduly straining the national resources. His ingenious scheme was to impose heavy fines in place of imprisonment on the

richest transgressors, and by this means his treasury benefited and he himself gained a reputation for clemency.
Ralph Dutton, ENGLISH COURT LIFE

HENRY VIII (1491–1547)
King

1 Is there any foundation for the theory that Henry VIII's main reason for executing Anne Boleyn was her habit of eating biscuits in bed?
Cyril Asquith, LIFE OF LORD OXFORD AND ASQUITH

2 It would be an affront to my Readers were I to suppose that they were not as well acquainted with the particulars of this King's reign as I am myself. It will therefore be saving them the task of reading again what they have read before, and myself the trouble of writing what I do not perfectly recollect, by giving only a slight sketch of the principal Events which marked his reign. Among these may be ranked Cardinal Wolsey's telling the father Abbot of Leicester Abbey that "he was come to lay his bones among them", the reformation in Religion and the King's riding through the streets of London with Anna Bullen. It is however but Justice, and my Duty to declare that this amiable Woman was entirely innocent of the Crimes with which she was accused, and of which her Beauty, her Elegance, and her Sprightliness were sufficient proofs, not to mention her solemn protestations of Innocence, the weakness of the Charges against her, and the King's Character; all of which add some confirmation tho' perhaps but slight ones when in comparison with those before allegedly in her favour. Tho' I do not profess giving many dates, yet as I think it proper to give some and shall make choice of those which it is more necessary for the Reader to know, I think it right to inform him that her letter to the King was dated on the 6th of May. The Crimes and Cruelties of this Prince were too numerous to be mentioned (as this history I trust has fully shown;) and nothing can be said in his vindication, but that his abolishing Religious Houses and leaving them to the ruinous depredations of time has been of infinite use to the landscape of England in general, which probably was a principal motive for his doing it, since otherwise why should a Man who was of no Religion himself be at so much trouble to abolish one which had for ages been established in the Kingdom. His Majesty's 5th

Wife was the Duke of Norfolk's Neice who, tho' universally acquitted of the crimes for which she was beheaded, has been by many people supposed to have led an abandoned life before her Marriage — of this however I have many doubts, since she was a relation of that noble Duke of Norfolk who was so warm in the Queen of Scotland's cause, and who at last fell a victim to it. The King's last wife contrived to survive him, but with difficulty effected it. He was succeeded by his only son Edward.
Jane Austen, THE HISTORY OF ENGLAND BY A PARTIAL, PREJUDICED AND IGNORANT HISTORIAN

3 Henry the Eighth / Took a thuctheththion of mateth / He inthithted that the monkth / Were a lathy lot of skunkth.
E. C. Bentley, MORE BIOGRAPHY

4 A pig, an ass, a dunghill, the spawn of an adder, a basilisk, a lying buffoon, a mad fool with a frothy mouth, a lubberly ass, a frantic madman.
Martin Luther

5 The king put off our discussion until another time, as he was in a hurry to go and dine and dance afterwards. In this he does wonders and leaps like a stag.
The Milanese ambassador   1513

6 The king has a way of making every man feel that he is enjoying his special favour, just as the way the London wives pray before the images of Our Lady by the Tower till each of them believes it is smiling upon her.
Sir Thomas More, letter to Bishop John Fisher   1518

7 Henry never spared a man his anger, nor a woman in his lust.
Robert Nauton, FRAGMENTA REGALIA   1641

8 Dr Morris, addressing his annual diocesan conference at Monmouth, said it was wrong to think that Henry VIII set a royal example for divorce. He was never divorced; in the two cases where his wife was not killed, the marriages were annulled.
News Chronicle. Quoted Michael Bateman, THIS ENGLAND

9 The king no sooner heard that Anne of Cleves had landed at Rochester than he went thither incognito, to see his future comfort, and found her so different from her picture, which had been drawn by Holbein, that in the impatience of his dis-

appointment he swore they had brought him a Flanders mare.
Tobias Smollett, THE HISTORY OF ENGLAND 1757

1 He is the handsomest potentate I ever set eyes on; above the usual height, with an extremely fine calf to his leg, his complexion very fair and light, with auburn hair, and a round face so very beautiful that it would become a pretty woman, his throat being rather long and thick.
Report quoted in Venetian calendar 1515

2 The king is exceedingly fond of tennis at which game it is the prettiest sight in the world to see him playing, his fair skin glowing through a shirt of the finest texture.
Ibid.

3 That pig of a Henry VIII committed such sacrilege by profaning so many ecclesiastical benefices in order to give their goods to those who being so rewarded might stand firmly for the king in the Lower House.
Sir Francis Windebank to Panzani, *Papal Envoy* Apr 1635

4 He is a prince of royal courage and hath a princely heart; and rather than he will miss or want part of his appetite, he will hazard the loss of one half of his kingdom.
Thomas Wolsey to Sir William Kingston, *Constable of the Tower* Nov 1530

ROBERT HERRICK (1591–1674)
English poet

5 We have lately seen the whole of Herrick's poems published, a coarse-minded and beastly writer, whose dunghill, when the few flowers that grew there had been transplanted ought never to have been disturbed. Those flowers are indeed beautiful and perennial; but they should have been removed from the filth and ordure in which they are buried.
Robert Southey, COMMONPLACE BOOKS

SIR WILLIAM HERSCHEL (1738–1822)
German-born astronomer and musician, living in England

6 By the invitation of Mr Herschel I now took a walk which will sound to you rather strange; it was through his telescope and it held me upright and without the least inconvenience; so would it have done had I been dressed in feathers and a bell-hoop — such is its circumference.
Fanny Burney, DIARY 30 Dec 1787

7 While sublimely gauging the heavens with his instruments he continued patiently to earn his bread by piping to the frequenters of the Bath Pump-room. So eager was he in his astronomical observations that he would steal away from the room during an interval of the performance, give a little turn to his telescope, and contentedly return to his oboe.
Samuel Smiles, SELF HELP 1859

8 He has discovered that the Milky Way is not only a mob of stars, but that there is another dairy of them still further off, whence I conclude comets are nothing but pails returning from milking, instead of balloons filled with inflammable air.
Horace Walpole, *letter to the Countess of Upper Ossory* 4 Jul 1785

9 I must stop; I shall turn my own brain, which, while it is launching into an ocean of universe, is still admiring pismire Herschel. That he should not have a *wise* look does not surprise me. He may be stupified by his own discoveries.
Ibid. 6 Sep 1787

ALFRED HITCHCOCK (1899–1980)
British film producer

10 For me the cinema is not a slice of life, but a piece of cake.
Hitchcock. Quoted Sunday Times magazine 6 Mar 1977

11 As a boy he pinned a firecracker to a schoolmate's pants. As an adult he bet a property man that he wouldn't dare to spend a night alone in the studio, handcuffed to a camera, and offered the fellow a bottle of brandy to see him through. The brandy was spiked with laxative, and the man was found weeping in the morning, his clothes soiled, more exhausted by his humiliation than by his vigil . . . But some of Hitchcock's jokes are splendid, and have a sharp-edged justice to them. A friend tried the brandy-with-laxative trick on Hitchcock himself, offering a bottle as a thank-you gift. There were no visible effects, and Hitchcock did not mention the matter further. Finally, the friend could stand the uncertainty no longer, and asked Hitchcock if he had enjoyed the brandy. "O, yes," Hitchcock said, "I didn't want to mention it, but my mother is ill, and when the doctor prescribed brandy, we gave her some of yours." The guilt-stricken friend sent flowers and sympathy to Mrs. Hitchcock senior, only to discover she was

perfectly fit and knew nothing of any brandy.
Michael Wood, The New York Review of Books 26 Apr 1984

ADOLF HITLER (1880–1945)
Austrian-born dictator of Germany

1 It was impossible to converse with him in any normal way . . . he suddenly started shouting . . . I imagine that a man in a trance would behave in much the same way and while he was shouting I am convinced that I could have walked out of the room and he would not have noticed my departure.
Vernon Bartlett, THIS IS MY LIFE 1937

2 I, and many others who had interviews with him, were at first impressed by his sincerity, and later realised that he was sincere only in his belief that he was destined to rule the world.
Ibid.

3 Mind you, like Churchill he was a very bad artist. Neither of them were any bloody good at it.
Marquis of Bath, of Hitler paintings bought for Longleat, Daily Express 4 Apr 1978

4 The moustache of Hitler / Could hardly have been littler / Was the thought that kept recurring / To Field Marshal Goering
E. C. Bentley, CLERIHEWS

5 One evening Hitler went to a cinema where Kellermann's *Tunnel* was being shown. In this piece an agitator appears who arouses the masses by his speeches. Hitler almost went crazy. The impression it made on him was so strong that for days afterwards he spoke of nothing except the power of the spoken word.
Alan Bullock, HITLER: a Study in Tyranny

6 Hitler has missed the bus.
Neville Chamberlain, of the invasion of Norway, House of Commons 4 Apr 1940

7 That bloodthirsty guttersnipe.
Winston Churchill, House of Commons

8 I have only one purpose, the destruction of Hitler, and my life is much simplified thereby. If Hitler invaded Hell I would make at least a favourable reference to the Devil in the House of Commons.
Winston Churchill, THE GRAND ALLIANCE

9 To reject the world the most effective way is to act in such a manner as to force the world to spew one out — in which case Hitler

came "nearer to God" than St. Joan, St. Teresa or St. Vincent de Paul.
Richard Coe, THE VISION OF JEAN GENET

10 The most pathetic thing about Adolf Hitler was his passionate desire to be approved of by English gentlemen.
Daily Telegraph. Quoted Michael Bateman, THIS ENGLAND

11 I could not bear it if I ever had to despair of this man. This man has everything needed to be king.
Paul Joseph Goebbels, DIARIES

12 I go the way that Providence dictates with the assurance of a sleepwalker.
Hitler. Speech at Munich 26 Sep 1938

13 If Hitler had put his energies into promoting nuclear physics instead of persecuting the Jews the history of the world might have been very different. The first atomic bomb could well have exploded over London instead of Hiroshima.
David Irving, THE VIRUS HOUSE

14 I tell you, as one who has studied the whole situation, I don't think Hitler is a fool — he is not going to challenge the British Empire.
David Lloyd George. Speech in 1937

15 It was in Berchtesgaden that a miserable, undersized Viennese house painter with a diabolic inferiority complex showed up, and among the daydreams that infested his rickety mind was one in which he saw himself as the god of the fortress on top of the butte. Well — he achieved his goal as people do when they dream with overpowering intensity. But if it is violent enough to destroy the equilibrium of the whole world it would be better to take sleeping pills, *nicht wahr?*
Anita Loos, KISS HOLLYWOOD GOOD-BYE

16 I should be pleased, I suppose, that Hitler has carried out a revolution on our lines. But they are Germans. So they will end by ruining our idea.
Mussolini. Quoted Christopher Hibbert, BENITO MUSSOLINI

17 Herr Hitler has one of the endearing characteristics of Ferdinand the Bull. Just when the crowds expect him to be most violent he stops and smells the flowers.
Beverley Nichols, Sunday Graphic

18 A racing tipster who only reached Hitler's level of accuracy would not do well for his clients.
A. J. P. Taylor, ORIGINS OF THE SECOND WORLD WAR

1 The machine is running away with *him* as it ran away with *me*.
Ex-Kaiser Wilhelm II to Sir Robert Bruce Lockhart   27 *Aug* 1939

THOMAS HOBBES (1588–1679)
English philosopher

2 The day of Hobbes's birth was April 5th, Anno Domini 1588, on a Friday morning, which that year was Good Friday. His mother fell in labour with him upon the fright of the invasion of the Spaniards.
John Aubrey, BRIEF LIVES   1690

3 I have heard Mr Hobbes say that he was wont to draw lines on his thigh and on his sheets, abed, and also multiply and divide.
Ibid.

4 At night, when he was abed and the doors made fast and he was sure nobody heard him he sang loud (not that he had a very good voice) but for his health's sake; he did beleeve it did his lunges good, and conduced much to prolong his life.
Ibid.

5 He walked much and contemplated and he had in the head of his staff a pen and inkhorne; carried always a note-booke in his pocket and as soone as a thought darted he presently entered it in his booke, or otherwise he might perhaps have lost it.
Ibid.

6 His strong mind and body appear to have resisted all impressions but those which were derived from the downright blows of matter; all his ideas seemed to lie like substances in his brain; what was not a solid tangible, distinct, palpable object was to him nothing.
William Hazlitt, THE WRITINGS OF HOBBES

7 To my bookseller for Hobbes' *Leviathan* which is now mightily called for and what heretofore sold for 8s I now give 24s for at the second hand, and is sold for 30s, it being a book the bishops will not let be printed again.
Samuel Pepys, DIARY   1668

8 Where he is wrong, he is wrong from oversimplification, not because the basis of his thought is unreal or fantastic. For this reason, he is still worth refuting.
Bertrand Russell, HISTORY OF WESTERN PHILOSOPHY   1845

TOBIAS HOBSON (c 1544–1631)
English stable-keeper

9 **Hobson's choice,** the choice of a thing offered or nothing, from *Hobson*, a Cambridge horsekeeper, who lent out the horse nearest the stable door, or none at all.
CHAMBERS DICTIONARY   1977

10 It is one of fame's whimsies that this obscure man should have had a street named after him in Cambridge, a number of the *Spectator* devoted to him, been the subject of two poems by Milton, and had his name become a proverb. Few kings have gained as much fame.
Bergan Evans, DICTIONARY OF QUOTATIONS   1904

11 Where to elect there is but one / 'Tis Hobson's choice — take that or note
Thomas Ward, ENGLAND'S REFORMATION

ERNST THEODOR AMADEUS HOFFMAN (1776–1822)
German writer, composer and caricaturist

12 He was fantastic and odd in the greatest degree, much given to liquor and strange company, over which "he wasted faculties which might have seasoned the nectar of the gods" (Carlyle). He sang, composed, criticised, taught, conducted, managed theatres, wrote both poetry and prose, painted — all equally well; and in fact could, and did, turn his hand to anything.
Franz Gehring, GROVE'S DICTIONARY OF MUSIC AND MUSICIANS   1927

13 Though his *Tales of Hoffman* are now better known on the operatic stage than in literature he is in fact an extremely ingenious and quite original story-teller whose work deserves more attention than it has received, at least outside Germany.
J. B. Priestley, LITERATURE AND WESTERN MAN   1960

WILLIAM HOGARTH (1697–1764)
English painter and engraver

14 On one occasion, Hogarth, being present in some capacity at a tavern brawl, saw a man strike another with a pewter pot; the expression of the insulted person so impressed him that he took out his pencil and sketched him then and there.
Julia de Wolf Addison, THE ART OF THE NATIONAL GALLERY   1905

15 According to Murphy, Fielding had made many promises to sit to Hogarth, for whose genius he had a high esteem, but died with-

out fulfilling them; a lady accidentally cut a profile with her scissors, which recalled Fielding's face so completely to Hogarth's memory, that he took up the outline, corrected and finished it, and made a capital likeness.
Allan Cunningham, LIVES OF THE MOST EMINENT BRITISH PAINTERS   1833

1   Other prints we look at — his we read.
Charles Lamb, ON THE GENIUS AND CHARACTER OF HOGARTH

2   No man was ever less of a hero. You can see him before you and can fancy what he was — a jovial honest London citizen, stout and sturdy; a hearty plain-spoken man, loving his laugh, his friends, his glass, his roast beef of old England, and having a proper bourgeois scorn for French frogs, for mounseers, and wooden shoes in general, for foreign fiddlers, for foreign singers, and above all, for foreign painters, whom he held in the most amusing contempt.
William Makepeace Thackeray, THE ENGLISH HUMOURISTS   1851

FOURTEENTH EARL OF HOME
(1903–   )
(Sir Alexander Frederick Douglas-Home)
British Prime Minister

3   Your bleak, deathly smile is the smile not of the victor, but of the victim.
Christopher Booker, BBC TV, *That Was the Week That Was*   19 *Oct* 1963

4   I had to see that Master Alec didn't talk to the servants and that he didn't leave our part of the house.
Mrs Florence Hill, Lord Home's nurse. Quoted Evening Standard

5   Alec Douglas-Home, floating on the lethargic sea of his own simplicity, could not for a moment compete with Wilson.
Bernard Levin, THE PENDULUM YEARS   1976

6   A prime minister reputed to do his arithmetic with match sticks.
Leo Pliatsky, GETTING AND SPENDING   1982

7   The whole process of democracy has ground to a halt with the fourteenth Earl.
Harold Wilson, Labour Party Conference 1 *Aug* 1963. *To which Lord Home replied*, "*I suppose; if you come to think of it, Mr Wilson is the fourteenth Mr Wilson*", BBC TV 21 *Aug* 1963

HOMER (ca 800 BC)
Greek poet

8   O fortunate youth, who found a Homer to proclaim thy valour.
Alexander at the tomb of Achilles. Quoted Cicero

9   After your song the world could say it possessed eleven Pierian sisters.
Antiphilus of Byzantium, EPIGRAM

10   Homer himself must beg if he wants means as by report he sometimes did "go from door to door and sing ballads with a company of boys about him."
Robert Burton, ANATOMY OF MELANCHOLY   1621

11   If I read Homer today he seems different from what he did ten years ago. If one lived to be three hundred years old he would always seem different. To be convinced of this one need only glance into the past.
Goethe

12   I too am indignant when Homer nods but in a long work it is permitted to snatch a little sleep.
Horace, DE ARTE POETICA

13   Oft one wide expanse had I been told / That deep-browed Homer ruled as demesne / Yet never did I breathe its *pure serene* / Till I heard Chapman speak out loud and bold / Then felt I like some watcher of the skies / Where a new planet swims into his ken / Or like stout Cortez, when with eagle eyes / He stared at the Pacific — and all his men / Looked at each other with a wild surmise — Silent, upon a peak in Darien.
John Keats, ON FIRST LOOKING INTO CHAPMAN'S HOMER

14   Old Homer's theme was but a dream. Himself a fiction too.
Walter Scott, THE MONASTERY

15   As learned commentators view / In Homer more than Homer knew.
Jonathan Swift, ON POETRY

HERBERT CLARK HOOVER (1874–1964)
Thirty-first President of the United States

16   Facts to Hoover's brain are as water to a sponge; they are absorbed into every tiny interstice.
Bernard Baruch. Quoted D. Hinshaw, HERBERT HOOVER: *American Quaker*

QUINTUS HORATIUS FLACCUS
HORACE (65–8 BC)
Latin poet

1 Then farewell Horace, whom I hate so / Not for thy faults, but for my own.
Lord Byron, CHILDE HAROLD   1812

ALFRED EDWARD HOUSMAN (1859–1936)
English poet

2 The sad, compassionate, loving, romantic man.
Richard Graves, A. E. HOUSMAN; *The Scholar Poet*   1969

3 Housman is dry, shy, soft, prickly, smooth, conventional, silent, feminine, fussy, pernickety, sensitive, tidy, greedy, and a touch of a toper.
Harold Nicolson, DIARY   26 *Sep* 1931

4 A *bon bourgeois* who has seen more sensitive days. He does not talk much except about food. And at 10.30 he rises to take his leave. All his movements are best described in such Trollope expressions.
Ibid.

5 Housman was Masefield with a dash of Theocritus.
George Orwell, INSIDE THE WHALE   1940

VICTOR-MARIE HUGO (1802–1885)
French novelist, poet and playwright

6 In Victor Hugo we have the average sensual man impassioned and grandiloquent; in Zola we have the average sensual man going near the ground.
Matthew Arnold, DISCOURSES IN AMERICA   1885

7 *Les Misérables* is the greatest book ever written, not excepting Holy Writ. I have read it twenty times.
David Lloyd George. Quoted Thomas Jones, WHITEHALL DIARY   VOL I   1916–1925

8 He will be eighty-one in February and walked upright without a stick. His white hair is as thick as his dark eyebrows, and his eyes are as bright and clear as a little child's. After dinner, he drank my health with a little speech of which — though I sat just opposite him — my accursed deafness prevented me hearing a single word.
Algernon Swinburne, letter to his mother 26 *Nov* 1882

JAMES HENRY LEIGH HUNT (1784–1859)
English poet and essayist

9 Everything is pretence, affection, finery and gaudiness.
Blackwoods Magazine, anonymous reviewer

10 A great coxcomb and a very vulgar person in everything about him.
Lord Byron, JOURNALS

11 He improves upon acquaintance. The author translates admirably into the man. Indeed, the very faults of his style are virtues in the individual. His natural gaiety and sprightliness of manner, his high animal spirits, and the *vinous* quality of his mind, produce an immediate fascination and intoxication in those who come in contact with him, and carry off in society what in his writings may to some seem flat and impertinent.
William Hazlitt, THE SPIRIT OF THE AGE   1825

12 What though, for showing truth for flatter'd state / King Hunt was shut in prison, yet, as he / In his immortal spirit been as free / As the sky-searching lark, and as elate, / Minion of grandeur!
John Keats, SONNET WRITTEN ON THE DAY THAT MR LEIGH HUNT LEFT PRISON

13 This cockney-bred setter of rabbits.
Thomas Moore

14 One of those happy souls / Which are the salt of the earth and without whom / The world would smell like what it is — a tomb.
Percy Bysshe Shelley, letter to Maria Gladstone   1 *Jul* 1820

WILLIAM HOLMAN HUNT (1827–1910)
English painter

15 Hunt visited Palestine to paint *The Scapegoat* on the shores of the Dead Sea. The critics made fun of it. Hunt laughed over the wicked libel that he had starved a goat for his picture, though certainly four died in his service, probably feeling dull when separated from the flock. The one which was with them by the Dead Sea was better off for food than they were, as it could get at the little patches of grass in the clefts; still, it became ill, and they carried it so carefully on the picture-case ! But it died, and he was in despair about getting another white one. He aimed at giving it nothing beyond a goat's expression of countenance, but one in such utter desolation and solitude could not but be tragic.
Caroline Fox, JOURNAL   28 *Sep* 1860

ALDOUS LEONARD HUXLEY (1894–1963)
English novelist and essayist

1 He is at once the truly clever person, and the stupid person's idea of the clever person; he is expected to be relentless, to administer intellectual shocks.
Elizabeth Bowen, Spectator 11 *Dec* 1963

2 People will call Mr Huxley a pessimist; in the sense of one who makes the worst of it. To me he is that far more gloomy character; the man who makes the best of it.
G. K. Chesterton, THE COMMON MAN

3 Mr Huxley is perhaps one of those people who have to perpetrate thirty bad novels before producing a good one.
T. S. Eliot

4 Aldous Huxley sits there and emits streams of impersonal sound, like a sort of loudspeaker, about the habits of bees and ants, the excretions of elephants, and sexual intercourse among whales.
William Gerhardie, MEMOIRS OF A POLYGLOT 1925

5 I don't like his books; even if I admired a sort of desperate courage of repulsion and repudiation in them. But again, I feel as if only half a man writes the books — a sort of precocious adolescent.
D. H. Lawrence, letter to Lady Ottoline Morrell 5 *Feb* 1929

6 The more holy he gets, the more his books stink of sex. He cannot get off the subject of flagellating women.
George Orwell, letter to Richard Rees 3 *Mar* 1949

7 You could always tell by his conversation which volume of the *Encyclopedia Britanica* he'd been reading. One day it would be Alps, Andes and Apennines, and the next it would be Himalayas and the Hippocratic Oath.
Bertrand Russell, letter to R. W. Clark Jul 1965

THOMAS HENRY HUXLEY (1825–1895)
English scientist

8 Huxley's solicitude for Darwin's strength was characteristic of him. He often alluded to himself as "Darwin's bulldog".
H. F. Osborn, IMPRESSIONS OF GREAT NATURALISTS

9 As I knew Huxley he was a yellow-faced, square-faced old man with bright little brown eyes, lurking as it were in caves under the heavy grey eyebrows and a mane of grey hair brushed back from his wall of a forehead.
H. G. Wells, AN EXPERIMENT IN AUTOBIOGRAPHY 1934

10 He lectured in a clear, firm voice without hurry and without delay, turning to the blackboard behind him to sketch some diagram, and always dusting the chalk from his fingers rather fastidiously before he resumed.
Ibid.

I

HENRIK JOHAN IBSEN (1828–1906)
Norwegian dramatist and poet

1　What good is freedom if you've not got the money for it? It's all very fine to go on about Nora's escape at the end of *The Doll's House* but just how was she planning to eat that night?
Lillian Hellman. Quoted Sheridan Morley, Radio Times　9 Feb 1979

2　Ibsen's ideas are of little importance, and he owes everything to his superb technical mastery.
H. L. Mencken

SIR HENRY IRVING (1838–1905)
English actor

3　He had, in acting, a keen sense of humour — of sardonic, grotesque, fantastic humour. He had an incomparable power for eeriness, for stirring a dim sense of mystery, and no less masterly was he in stirring a dim sense of horror.
Max Beerbohm, Saturday Review 21 Oct 1905

4　It is by his picturesqueness that Mr Irving has made his place: by small ingenuities of "business" and subtleties of action by doing as a painter does who "goes in" for colour when he cannot depend on his drawing.
Henry James, Galaxy, The London Theatre　1877

5　His practice was to pare subsidiary rules down to the bone so that his leading role stood out strongly . . . He cut two thousand lines out of *Cymbeline*.
Frank Muir, THE FRANK MUIR BOOK　1975

6　Irving went down to one of our public schools to give some Shakespeare recitations. Talking over the arrangements he said "Each piece will take an hour and there must be a fifteen minute interval between the two." "Oh certainly," agreed the Head. "You couldn't expect the boys to stand two hours of it without a break."
G. W. E. Russell, COLLECTIONS AND RECOLLECTIONS　1903

7　As Romeo Irving reminded me of a pig who has been taught to play the fiddle. He did it cleverly, but would be better employed in squealing.
Ellen Terry, NOTES ON IRVING

8　His left leg was a poem.
Oscar Wilde

IVAN IV (The Terrible) (1530–1584)
First Russian monarch to style himself Tsar

9　Did I ascend the throne by robbery or armed bloodshed? I was born to rule by the grace of God; and I do not even remember my father bequeathing the kingdom to me and blessing me — I grew up upon the throne.
Ivan, letter to Prince Kurbsky　Sep 1577

10　He was merciless to the boyars, to Moscow, Tver, Novgorod and other towns. He died of sorrow for his son who three years before he had slain in a fit of rage.
D. Patrick and F. Hindes Groome, CHAMBERS BIOGRAPHICAL DICTIONARY 1897

J

THOMAS JONATHAN (STONEWALL) JACKSON (1824-1863)
American soldier

1 There is Jackson, standing like a stone wall.
Brigadier-General Barnard E. Bee, at the Battle of Bull Run   21 Jul 1861

2 Let us cross the river and rest in the shade.
Jackson's last words.

JAMES I (VI OF SCOTLAND) (1566-1625)
King

3 Though this King had some faults, on the whole I cannot help liking him.
 As I am myself partial to the roman catholic religion, it is with infinite regret that I am obliged to blame the Behaviour of any Member on it: yet Truth being I think very excusable in an Historian, I am necessitated to say that in this reign the roman catholics of England did not behave like Gentlemen to the protestants.
Jane Austen, THE HISTORY OF ENGLAND BY A PARTIAL, PREJUDICED AND IGNORANT HISTORIAN

4 Come tryumph, enter court, church, cittie, towne / Heere James the sixt, now James the first proclaymed, / See how all harts are heald that erst were mamed / The peere is pleased, the knight, the clark, the clowne.
Sir John Hannington, ODE OF WELCOME TO JAMES VI OF SCOTLAND ON HIS ACCESSION TO THE ENGLISH CROWN

5 The wisest fool in Christendom.
Henry IV of France, of James' foreign policy   1604

6 His sense of humour matched his personal habits; always coarse and anatomical, it rose sometimes to "a fluorescence of obscenity".
J. P. Kenyon, THE STUARTS   1958. *Quoting D. H. Wilson,* JAMES VI AND I

7 James I's reputation has taken a marked upward swing in the past 20 years; now that the economic and constitutional aspects of his reign are more perfectly understood he can no longer be dismissed as a drivelling, ineffectual, conceited old queer.
John Kenyon, Observer, reviewing Caroline Bingham's JAMES VI OF SCOTLAND   1 *Jul* 1979

8 He was the author of his line — / He wrote that witches should be burnt; / He wrote that monarchs are divine, / And left a son who proved they weren't.
Rudyard Kipling, JAMES I

9 A fly entering the eye of James I the king is reputed to have complained "Have I three kingdoms and thou must needs fly into my eye?"
John Selden, TABLE TALK, (*edited by Richard Milward*)   1680

10 James I slobbered at the mouth and had favourites; he was thus a Bad King.
W. C. Sellar and R. J. Yeatman 1066 AND ALL THAT

11 His skin was as soft as Taffeta sarsnet, which felt so because he never washed his hands, only rubbed his finger-ends slightly with the wet end of a napkin.
D. H. Wilson, JAMES VI AND I

JAMES II (1633-1701)
King

12 One of the strangest catastrophes that is in any history. A great king with strong armies and mighty fleets, a great treasure and powerful allies, fell all at once, and his whole strength, like a spider's web, was irrecoverably broken at a touch.
Gilbert Burnet, HISTORY OF HIS OWN TIMES   1734

13 He had no true judgement and was soon determined by those he trusted, but he was obstinate against all other advices. He was bred with high notions of kingly authority, and laid it down for a maxim that all who opposed the king were rebels in their hearts.
Ibid.

14 He was perpetually in one amour or another, without being very nice in his choice; upon which the King (i.e. Charles II) said once he believed his brother had mistresses given by Priests for penance.
Ibid.

1 The best that I can wish you is that we shall never see each other again.
Louis XIV *of France to James on his departure for Ireland   Mar* 1689

2 Our dear king James is good and honest, but the most incompetent man I have ever seen in my life. A child of seven years would not make such silly mistakes as he does.
Charlotte Elizabeth, Duchess of Orleans, letter to the Electress Sophia   6 Jun 1692

HENRY JAMES (1843–1916)
American novelist

3 Henry James has a mind so fine that no idea could violate it.
T. S. Eliot

4 Henry James was one of the nicest old ladies I ever met.
William Faulkner

5 Many readers cannot get interested in James. They cannot grant his premise, which is that most of human life has to disappear before he can do us a novel.
E. M. Forster, ASPECTS OF THE NOVEL   1927

6 Sargent's portrait of Henry James is nearly finished, and I hear is a masterpiece. There is a plaid waistcoat in it, like a sea in a storm, which is said to be prodigious.
Edmund Gosse, letter to Thomas Hardy   1913

7 The work of Henry James has always seemed divisible by a simple dynastic arrangement into three reigns. James I, James II, and the Old Pretender.
Philip Guedella, MEN OF LETTERS

8 He was a great American writer who came to Venice and looked out of the window and smoked his cigar and thought.
Ernest Hemingway, SELECTED LETTERS   1917–1961

9 Mr James' cosmopolitanism is, after all, limited; to be really cosmopolitan a man must be at home, even in his own country.
Thomas Wentworth Higginson, SHORT STUDIES OF AMERICAN WRITERS

10 I want in my short stories to leave a multitude of pictures of my time . . . going in for number as well as quality, so that the number may constitute a total having a certain value as observation and testimony.
James, letter to R. L. Stevenson, HENRY JAMES LETTERS VOL 3   1883–1895

11 He did not live, he observed life from a window, and too often was inclined to content himself with no more than what his

friends told him they saw when *they* looked out of the window.
W. Somerset Maugham, A WRITER'S NOTEBOOK   1949

12 Henry James fictions are like the cobwebs which a spider may spin in the attic of some old house, intricate, delicate and even beautiful, but which at any moment the housemaid's broom with brutal common sense may sweep away.
W. Somerset Maugham, THE VAGRANT MOOD

13 Leviathan retrieving pebbles a magnificent but painful hippopotamus resolved at any cost, even at the cost of its dignity, upon picking up a pea.
H. G. Wells, BOON

14 Henry James writes fiction as if it were a painful duty.
Oscar Wilde

WILLIAM JAMES (1842–1910)
American philosopher and psychologist

15 There was, in spite of his playfulness, a deep sadness about James. You felt that he had just stepped out of this sadness in order to meet you; and was to go back into it the moment he left you.
John Jay Chapman, MEMORIES AND MILESTONES

16 He could not help making the expression of his philosophy intelligible because to him a philosophy that was merely technical and professional missed the point of philosophy; the illumination and enlargement of the human mind on the things that are its vital concern.
John Dewey, CHARACTERS AND EVENTS

17 Philosophy to him was rather like a maze in which he happened to find himself wandering, and what he was looking for was the way out.
George Santayana. Quoted Bernard P. Brennan, WILLIAM JAMES

THOMAS JEFFERSON (1743–1826)
Third President of the United States

18 The moral character of Jefferson was repulsive. Continually puling about liberty, equality and the degrading curse of slavery, he brought his own children to the hammer, and made money of his debaucheries.
Alexander Hamilton

19 Murder, robbery, rape, adultery and incest will be openly taught and practised. The air

will be rent with the cries of distress, the soil soaked with blood and the nation black with crimes. Where is the heart that can contemplate such a scene without shivering with horror?
New England Courant editorial, on the election of Jefferson 1800

1 A gentleman of thirty-two who could calculate an eclipse, survey an estate, tie an artery, plan an edifice, try a cause, break a horse, dance a minuet and play the violin.
James Parton, LIFE OF THOMAS JEFFERSON

EARL JOHN RUSHWORTH JELLICOE
(1859–1953)
British admiral

2 Sailor with a flawed cutlass.
Corelli Barnett, THE SWORDBEARERS

3 Jellicoe was the only man on either side who could lose the war in an afternoon.
Winston Churchill, THE WORLD CRISIS

JOAN of ARC (1412–1431)
French patriot and martyr

4 I have come here to drive you man for man from France. If you will not believe the Maid's message from God wherever you happen to be we shall make such a great hahaye as has not been made in France these thousand years.
Joan, letter to the English besieging Orleans 22 *Mar* 1429

5 I saw her mount her horse, armed all in white except her head, a little battle-axe in her hand, on a great black courser which at the door of her lodging pranced boldly and would not at first suffer her to mount; and then she said "Lead him to the Cross." This cross was close to the church at the edge of the road. And then she mounted while he stood as quiet as though he had been bound.
Gui de Laval, letter to his mother. Quoted C. R. Sainte-Beuve, CAUSERIES DU LUNDI

6 Finally mounted on her courser the Maid turned towards the door of the church and said in a clear feminine voice, "You priests and churchfolk go in procession and make prayers to God." Then she took the road saying, "Forward, forward." Before her marched her folded standard borne by a gentle page, and she had her little battle-axe in her hand.
Ibid.

7 What is touching and truly sublime is that the first inspiration of this humble child, the source of her honest illusion, was the im-

mense pity that she felt for the land of France, and the Dauphin, its symbol . . . Pity was the inspiration of Jeanne, not the pity of a woman who weeps and groans, but the magnanimous pity of a heroine who feels called to a mission and takes the sword to succour others.
C. A. Sainte-Beuve, CAUSERIES DU LUNDI

JOSEPH JACQUES CÉSAIRE JOFFRE
(1852–1931)
French Commander-in-Chief

8 The only time he ever put up a fight was when we asked him to resign.
Georges Clemenceau. Quoted A. M. Thomson, HERE I LIE 1937

JOHN (1167–1216)
King of England

9 Our war-work style of history in which King John is always pulling out Jews' teeth with the celerity and industry of an American dentist, and Alfred is always spoiling cakes.
G. K. Chesterton, A MISCELLANY OF MEN: *The Medieval Village* 1912

10 King John was not a good man / He had his little ways / And sometimes no one spoke to him / For days and days and days.
A. A. Milne, NOW WE ARE SIX 1927

11 A very great grief troubled him, for he had lost his chapel with his relics and some of his pack-horses with different kinds of household effects at the Willstream during the course of that journey. Many of his household also, were drowned in the waters of the sea, and sucked into the quicksands there.
Ralph, Abbot of Coggeshall, CHRONICAN ANGLICANUM *Oct* 1216

12 He passed the next night at a convent called Swineshead where he surfeited himself with peaches and new cider. He rode to Newark. There his sickness increased, and he confessed himself and received the sacrament from the abbot of Croxton.
Roger of Wendover, FLORES HISTORIARUM 1235

AUGUSTUS EDWIN JOHN (1878–1961)
English artist

13 He seemed to be of the opinion that men are attracted to women through a subconscious wish to get their own back by causing them to become pregnant. I have it on good authority that he was disappointed with the

whole business and considered it something of a joke.
Romilly John, SEVENTH CHILD   1975

1   We may not always have estimated him at his true worth. One of my brothers complained that a certain person had stolen a number of his drawings. His reaction, unexpected as so often, was to remark that at least this showed they were appreciated by someone. "A pity none of you ever stole any."
Ibid.

LYNDON BAINES JOHNSON (1908–1973)
Thirty-Sixth President of the United States

2   Let's face it, Mr President, you're not a very likeable man.
Dean Acheson, when Johnson asked why he wasn't popular. Quoted Robert A. Caro; THE YEARS OF LYNDON JOHNSON: *The Path to Power*   1983

3   We now have a president who tries to save money by turning off the lights on the White House even as he heads towards a staggering addition to the national debt. L. B. J. should stand for Light Bulb Johnson.
Barry Goldwater. Speech, Chicago 10 *Apr* 1964

4   You never can tell what you'll find in Lyndon's bedroom. I walked in this morning for coffee and who should I find sitting there but Richard Nixon.
Lady Bird Johnson, A WHITE HOUSE DIARY   1970

5   Kennedy promised, Johnson delivered.
Arthur Schlesinger Jnr, Observer, The Kennedy Legend   20 *Nov* 1983

6   A great raw man of immense girth, wandering as a stranger in the Pepsi generation. Coarse, earthy / — a brutal intrusion into the misty Kennedy renaissance that still clung to the land.
Hugh Sidey, A VERY PERSONAL PRESIDENCY

SAMUEL JOHNSON (1709–1784)
English author and lexicographer

7   He never knew the natural joy of a free and vigorous use of his limbs; when he walked it was like the struggling gait of one in fetters; when he rode he had no command or direction of his horse, but was carried as if in a balloon.
Boswell, THE LIFE OF JOHNSON   1791

8   I shall never forget the indulgence with which Dr Johnson treated Hodge, his cat, for whom he himself used to go out and buy oysters, lest the servants having that trouble should take a dislike to the poor creature.
Ibid.

9   Thomas Gray was strolling with his friend Bonstetten about the year 1760 when he exclaimed with great bitterness, "Look! look! Bonstetten! The great bear! There goes *Ursa Major!*" This was Johnson. Gray could not abide him.
Sir Samuel Egerton Bridges, AUTOBIOGRAPHY   1834

10 The dictionary is a supreme monument of industry, skill and perseverance. It is as though Raffles raised Singapore single-handed or Brunel scooped out the Thames tunnel with his own shovel.
Anthony Burgess, Observer, The Book of Samuel   28 *Feb* 1982

11 Indeed the freedom with which Dr Johnson condemns whatever he disapproves is astonishing.
Fanny Burney, DIARY   23 *Aug* 1778

12 Rough Johnson, the great moralist.
Lord Byron, DON JUAN   1824

13 He has the aspect of an idiot without the faintest ray of sense gleaming from any one feature, with the most awkward garb and unpowdered grey wig on one side of his head; he is for ever dancing the devil's jig, and sometimes he makes the most drivelling effort to whistle some thought in his absent paroxysms.
Dr John Campbell

14 Would that every Johnson in the world had his veridical Boswell, or leash of Boswells.
Thomas Carlyle, ESSAYS; VOLTAIRE

15 Dr Johnson called on Mrs Digby and Mrs Brooke one day shortly after the production of his immortal dictionary. The two ladies paid him due compliments on the occasion. Among other topics of praise they very much approved the omission of all naughty words. "What my dears! Then you have been looking for them?" said the moralist. The ladies, confused at being caught, dropped the subject of the dictionary.
Henry Digby Beste, PERSONAL AND LITERARY MEMORIALS   1829

1 Of music in general he has been heard to say "It exerts in my mind no ideas, and hinders me from contemplating my own."
Sir John Hawkins, LIFE OF SAMUEL JOHNSON 1787

2 Here lies Samuel Johnson — Reader have a care / Tread lightly lest you wake the sleeping bear, / Religious, moral, generous and humane / He was; but self-sufficient, proud and vain, / Fond of, and overbearing in, dispute / A Christian and a scholar — but a brute.
Soame Jenyns, EPITAPH FOR SAMUEL JOHNSON

3 What a singular destiny has been that of this remarkable man! To be regarded in his own age as a classic, and in ours as a companion! To receive from his contemporaries that full homage which men of genius have in general only received from posterity; to be known more intimately in posterity than other men are known to their contemporaries.
T. B. Macaulay, Edinburgh Review
Sep 1831

4 Not finding Johnson in his little parlour when we came in Hannah seated herself in his great chair, hoping to catch a little ray of his genius; when he heard it he laughed heartily and told her it was a chair on which he never sat.
One of Hannah More's sisters, in a letter home 1774

5 The conversation of Johnson is strong and clear, and may be compared to an antique statue where every vein and muscle is distinct and bold. Ordinary conversation resembles an inferior cast.
Thomas Percy, Bishop of Dromore. Quoted Boswell, LIFE OF JOHNSON 1791

6 His notions rose up like the dragon's teeth sown by Cadmus, all ready clothed, and in bright armour, ready for battle.
Mrs Hester Piozzi, ANECDOTES OF DR JOHNSON 1786

7 Of Mr Johnson's erudition the world has been the judge, and we who produce each a score of his sayings, as proofs of that wit which in him was inexhaustible, resemble travellers who having visited Delhi or Golconda bring home each a handful of oriental pearls, to evince the riches of the Great Mogul.
Ibid.

8 Lady Spencer recollected Johnson well, as she used to see him often in her girlhood. Her mother, Lady Lucan, would say

"Nobody dines with us today, therefore, child, we'll go down and get Dr Johnson." So they would drive to Bolt Court and bring the doctor home with them.
Samuel Rogers, TABLE TALK 1856

9 This last and long enduring passion for Mrs Thrale was, however, composed of cupboard love, Platonic love, and vanity tickled and gratified.
Anna Seward, LETTERS 1811

10 I have not wasted my life trifling with literary fools in taverns, as Johnson did, when he should have been shaking England with the thunder of his spirit.
George Bernard Shaw, PREFACE TO PLAYS, PLEASANT AND UNPLEASANT 1898

11 Garrick, had he called Dr Johnson Punch, would have spoken profoundly and wittily, whereas Dr Johnson, in hurling this epithet at him, was but picking up the cheapest sneer an actor is subject to.
Ibid.

12 That Great Cham of Literature.
Tobias Smollett, in a letter to Wilkes
16 *Mar* 1750

13 Of those who have thus survived themselves most completely, left a sort of personal seduction behind them in the world and retained, after death, the art of making friends, Montaigne and Samuel Johnson certainly stand first.
R. L. Stevenson, FAMILIAR STUDIES OF MEN AND BOOKS: CHARLES OF ORLEANS 1882

14 Johnson made the most brutal speeches to living persons; for though he was good-natured at bottom he was ill-natured at top. He loved to dispute to show his superiority. If his opponents were weak he told them they were fools; if they vanquished him he was scurrilous.
Horace Walpole, LETTERS 1859

BENJAMIN JONSON (1572–1637)
English actor, poet, dramatist and critic

15 Too nicely Jonson knew the critic's part; / Nature in him was almost lost in art.
William Collins, AN EPISTLE TO SIR THOMAS HAMMER

16 Let Hebron, nay, let Hell produce a Man / So made for Mischief as Ben Jochanan / A Jew of Humble parentage was He / By trade a Levite, though of low degree, / His pride no higher than the Desk aspired.
John Dryden, ABSALOM AND ACHITOPHEL 1681

1 Ah Ben! Say how or when / Shall we thy
   guests meet at those Lyric Feasts / Made at
   the Sun, the Dog, the Triple Tun? / Where
   we such clusters had / As made us nobly
   wild, not mad; / And yet each verse of thine /
   Out-did the meat, out-did the frolic wine.
   Robert Herrick, AN ODE FOR BEN JONSON

2 Here lies Jonson with the rest / Of the
   Poets; but the Best. / Reader, wouldn't thou
   more have known? Ask his Story, not this
   Stone. / That will speak what this can't tell /
   Of his glory. So farewell.
   Ibid.

3 Then Jonson came, instructed from the
   school / To please in method and invent by
   rule.
   *Samuel Johnson, on the opening of Drury
   Lane Theatre*

4 Ben Jonson, his best piece of poetry.
   Ben Jonson's epitaph on his son

5 O Rare Ben Jonson!
   *Epitaph by Sir John Young, on Jonson's
   gravestone in Westminster Abbey. Aubrey in
   his Brief Lives says: "This was done at the
   charge of Jack Young who, walking there
   when the grave was covering, gave the fellow
   18 pence to cut it."*

JAMES AUGUSTINE JOYCE (1882–1941)
Irish author

6 It would be silly to pretend that *Ulysses* is
   not a difficult book, but over the years a
   web of criticism, exegesis and explication
   has been woven around it that can have the
   effect of making it seem more inaccessible
   than it really is. At times it seems like one of
   those cathedrals that cannot be viewed properly because of the network of scaffolding
   that seems permanently to surround them.
   *Walter Allen, Daily Telegraph, Dublin
   16 Jun 1904   24 Apr 1969*

7 We cannot, I suppose, finally judge *Ulysses*
   as a work of fiction at all. It is a kind of
   magical codex of the same order as Dante's
   Divine Comedy in which Hell, Heaven and
   Purgatory go on for ever and nothing
   changes.
   *Anthony Burgess, Observer Magazine
   20 May 1979*

8 Joyce, in effect, was saying that the de-
   piction of life as it is really lived cannot be
   achieved in neat, periodic sentences and the
   puppetry of an author (like Thackeray)
   smugly in control.
   Ibid.

9 *Ulysses* is a dogged attempt to cover the
   universe with mud.
   E. M. Forster, ASPECTS OF THE
   NOVEL 1927

10 He is a sort of M. de Sade, but does not
   write so well.
   Edmund Gosse

11 He is a literary charlatan of the extremist
   order. His principal book, *Ulysses*, is an
   anarchical production infamous in taste, in
   style, in everything.
   Ibid.

12 Joyce imagined an ideal reader "suffering
   from ideal insomnia" and was not altogether
   joking.
   John Gross, JOYCE   1971

13 My God, what a clumsy *olla putrida* James
   Joyce is! Nothing but old fags and cabbage
   stumps of quotations from the Bible and the
   rest, stewed in the juice of deliberate, jour-
   nalistic dirty-mindedness.
   *D. H. Lawrence in a letter to Aldous
   Huxley   1928*

14 There are passages of *Ulysses* that can be
   read only in the toilet if one wants to extract
   the full flavour from them.
   Henry Miller, BLACK SPRING   1936

15 He started to study medicine three times.
   No two occupations are closer than that of
   doctor and novelist. Both are trying to
   arrive at a truth of some kind and hence are
   both purgative and balm to the living. Had
   he qualified he would have been bound to
   have gone on and been a gynaecologist, he
   with his obsession with womb and ovary and
   Holles Street hospital.
   Edna O'Brien, A BASH IN THE TUNNEL:;
   *James Joyce by the Irish (edited by John
   Ryan)   1970*

16 He was prone to betting. He wagered a pound
   of dried apricots with his friend Ezra Pound
   that his play *Exiles* would not be produced.
   Ibid.

17 He must often have longed to have his brain
   dry-cleaned or exposed to the gales of the
   Atlantic Ocean.
   Ibid.

18 Wasn't ould Jimmy Joyce the quare bloody
   man.
   John Ryan, ibid.

19 Joyce has freed us from the superstition of
   syntax.
   Dorothy L. Sayers, CLOUD OF
   WITNESSES   1926

20 The latest acquisition to her library is
   Ulysses. "It cost me thirty-five shillings and

I got stuck in the first page. I think that's disgusting, don't you? No, not the content. I mean writing a book so that people can't understand it."
Russell Twisk quoting Cilla Black, Radio Times 25 Jan 1968

1 *Ulysses* is the work of a queasy undergraduate, scratching his pimples.
Virginia Woolf

JULIUS CAESAR (101 bc–43 bc)
Roman general and member of the Triumvirate

2 Julius Caesar, being hard put to it near Alexandria, leaped into the sea and laying some books on his head made shift to swim a good way with one hand.
Sir Thomas Browne, NOTES FROM COMMONPLACE BOOKS

3 What millions died that Caesar might be great.
Thomas Campbell, THE PLEASURES OF HOPE 1799

4 O, I don't repent my heavyweight quest! For it went very pleasantly. But when he arrived at Philippus' on the second evening of the Saturnalia, the villa was so full of soldiers that there was scarcely a dining room empty for Caesar himself to sup in. On the third day of the Saturnalia he stayed with Phillipus till one o'clock and admitted no one; doing accounts, I think, with Balbus. Then he walked on the shore. After two, the bath. He was anointed, and took his place at the table. He was taking emetics, so he ate and drank freely and boldly. Now you have the tale of my hospitality, or billeting you might call it; troublesome but not annoying.
Cicero, letter to Atticus 45 BC

5 Every woman's man and every man's woman.
Curio. Quoted Suetonius, LIVES OF THE CAESARS.

6 Nothing is worthier the study of a statesman than that part of the republic which we call the advancement of letters. Witness the case of Julius Caesar who in the heat of the civil war writ his books of Analogy, and dedicated them to Tully.
Ben Jonson, DISCOVERIES

7 Caesar however, when summoned as witness, gave no testimony against Clodius, and denied that he had condemned his wife for adultery, but said he had put her away because Caesar's wife must be free not only

from shameful conduct, but even from shameful report.
Plutarch, LIVES

8 Caesar with three legions fought a great battle with King Pharnaces by the city of Zela where he slew his army and drove him out of all the realm of Pont. And because he would advise one of his friends of the suddenness of his victory he wrote only these three words unto Anicius at Rome, "Veni, Vidi, Vici."
Ibid.

9 Caesar was held great because of his benefactions and great generosity. Caesar gained glory by giving, helping and forgiving. Finally, Caesar had schooled himself to work hard and sleep little, to devote himself to the welfare of his friends and neglect his own, to refuse nothing that was worth giving. He longed for great power, for an army, a new war to give scope to his merit.
Sallust, CATILINA

10 Imperious Caesar, dead and turned to clay / Might stop a hole to keep the wind away.
Shakespeare, HAMLET, *Act* v *Scene* i

11 Upon what meat does this our Caesar feed / That he is grown so great?
Shakespeare, JULIUS CAESAR, *Act* i *Scene* ii

JUSTINIAN I (483–565)
(Flavius Anicius)
Byzantine emperor Justianianus

12 The original manuscript of the Justinian Code was discovered by the Pisans, accidentally, when they took a city in Calabria; that vast code of laws had been in a manner unknown from the time of that emperor.
Isaac D'Israeli, CURIOSITIES OF LITERATURE 1824

13 The emperor was easy of access, patient of hearing, courteous and affable in all discourse, and a master of the angry passions which rage with such destructive violence in the breast of a despot.
Edward Gibbon, DECLINE AND FALL OF THE ROMAN EMPIRE 1788

14 The emperor professed himself a musician and architect, a poet and philosopher, and a lawyer and theologian, and if he failed in the enterprise of reconciling the Christian sects, the review of the Roman jurisprudence is a noble monument of his spirit and industry.
Ibid.

K

FRANZ KAFKA (1883-1924)
German novelist

1 Kafka could not attribute his pervasive guilt to any notion of a Fall, nor purge it through a 'conversion experience'. An unjustified sinner who did not recognise original sin, he sought instead to escape his own humanity through transformation — man into cockroach, or into some androidal form built of flesh and metal — and, of course, through death.
Neal Ascherton, Observer, Twisting Away From Life   13 Nov 1982

2 Kafka's greatness in his life and art arises from his joy in the world, despite the weakness in body and character that often made living in that world such agony.
Roy Fuller, THE WORLD OF FRANZ KAFKA   1981

3 Kafka changed human consciousness. Walking up the emergency stairway, driving into a cul-de-sac, arriving too early or too late, we get that Kafka feeling.
Barbara Hardy, Daily Telegraph, Kafka brought into daylight   1 Mar 1973

EDMUND KEAN (1787-1833)
English actor

4 To see Kean act was like reading Shakespeare by flashes of lightning.
Samuel Taylor Coleridge, TABLE TALK

5 I went to see Mr Kean and was thoroughly disgusted. This monarch of the stage is a little insignificant man, slightly deformed, strongly ungraceful, seldom pleasing to the eye, still seldomer satisfying to the ear — with a voice between grunting and croaking, a perpetual hoarseness which suffocates his words and a vulgarity of manner which his admirers are pleased to call mature.
Mary Russell Mitford, LETTERS   3 Jul 1814

6 Kean! Ah Kean! I saw him once. He was a splendid Gipsy.
Arthur Pinero, TRELAWNEY OF THE WELLS   1898

JOHN KEATS (1795-1821)
English poet

7 Keats' art turns what might appear embarrassing into what is rich and disconcerting; for at his most characteristic Keats always disconcerts.
John Bayley. Quoted Christopher Ricks, Sunday Times, The poet beneath the skin   9 Nov 1969

8 It is a better and a wiser thing to be a starved apothecary than a starved poet; so back to the shop, Mr John, back to plasters, pills and ointment boxes.
Blackwoods Magazine, review of ENDYMION, *usually attributed to John Lockhart*

9 Mr Keats is only a boy of pretty abilities which he has done everything in his power to spoil. We venture to make one small prophecy, that his bookseller will not a second time venture £50 on anything he may write.
Blackwoods Magazine   1818

10 A Mr John Keats, a young man who had left a decent calling for the melancholy trade of Cockney-poetry, has lately died of a consumption after having written two or three little books of verse, much neglected by the public.
Blackwoods Magazine, reviewing ADONIS, *Shelley's elegy for Keats*   1821

11 Here is Johnny Keats' piss-a-bed poetry. No more Keats, I entreat; flay him alive; if some of you don't I must skin him myself; there is no bearing the idiotism of the Mankin.
Lord Byron, letter to the publisher John Murray   12 Oct 1821

12 Fricassée of dead dog.
Thomas Carlyle reviewing Monckton Milnes' LIFE OF KEATS

13 He can conceive of a billiard ball that it may have some sense of delight from its own roundness, smoothness, volubility, and the rapidity of its motion.
John Jones, JOHN KEATS' DREAM OF TRUTH   1969

14 I know nothing. I have read nothing; I mean to follow Solomon's directions, "Get

learning, get understanding." There is but one way for me. The road lies through application, study, thought. I will pursue it.
Keats. Quoted Matthew Arnold, ESSAYS IN CRITICISM (second series) 1880

1 This grave contains all that was mortal of a young English poet who, on his deathbed, in the bitterness of his heart at the malicious power of his enemies, desires these words to be graven on his tombstone, "Here lies one whose name was writ in water."
Keats' epitaph on himself, engraved on his tomb in Rome

2 The savage criticism of his *Endymion*, which appeared in the Quarterly Review, produced the most violent agitation in his susceptible mind; the agitation thus originated ended in the rupture of a blood vessel in the lungs; a rapid consumption ensued.
Percy Bysshe Shelley, preface to ADONIS 1821

3 But now the youngest, dearest one has perished / The nursling of thy widowhood, who grew / Like a pale flower by some sad maiden cherished / And fed with true love tears instead of dew / Most musical of mourners, weep anew.
Percy Bysshe Shelley, ADONIS

4 He has outsoared the shadow of our night; / Envy and calumny and hate and pain. / And that unrest which men miscall delight / Can touch him not and torture not again.
Ibid.

5 I am borne darkly, fearfully afar, / Whilst, burning through the inmost veil of Heaven / The soul of Adonis like a star / Beacons from the abode where the eternal are.
Ibid.

6 I see a schoolboy when I think of him / With face and nose pressed to a sweetshop window.
W. B. Yeats

BARON KELVIN (1824–1907)
(William Thomson)
Irish scientist

7 An undergraduate of Peterhouse, named William Thomson, better known to fame as Lord Kelvin, was so certain that he would be top of the examinations list that he sent his servant to find out who was second. (It was William Thomson.)
B. V. Bowden, FASTER THAN THOUGHT

8 At lunch one day I remember when his mind had apparently been pondering some

abstruse scientific question, and Lady Thomson had been discussing plans for an afternoon excursion, Sir William suddenly looked up and said "At what times does the dissipation of energy begin?"
Sir Ambrose Fleming, MEMORIES OF A SCIENTIFIC LIFE

9 Kelvin, with all his immense achievements, had certain failings in temperament. His fault as a scientist lay in an independence which led him to disregard the views of others, and perhaps to underrate their work. Thus he rejected Clerk Maxwell's theory of light and Rutherford's theory of the divisibility of the atom, and refused to alter in the least his theory as to the age of the earth.
J. A. Hammerton (editor) CONCISE UNIVERSAL BIOGRAPHY

10 His mind was extraordinarily fertile in ideas. Even in a lecture, if a new idea occurred to him he would start off on a new tack. He has been known to lecture for the hour before reaching the subject of his lecture.
J. J. Thomson, RECOLLECTIONS AND REFLECTIONS

JOHN PHILIP KEMBLE (1757–1823)
English actor

00 Frogs in a marsh, flies in a bottle, wind in a crevice, a preacher in a field, the drone of a bagpipe, all added to the soporific monotony of Kemble.
George Coleman the Younger, RANDOM RECORDS OF MY LIFE 1830

12 Kemble turned his head so slowly that people might have imagined he had a stiff neck, while his words followed so slowly that he might have been reckoning how many words he had got by heart.
Leigh Hunt, CRITICAL ESSAYS ON PERFORMERS IN THE LONDON THEATRE 1807

13 He never pulls out his handkerchief without a design upon the audience.
Ibid.

14 One night when John Kemble was performing, at some country theatre, one of his favourite parts, he was much interrupted, from time to time, by the squalling of a young child in the gallery. At length, angered by the rival performance, Kemble walked with solemn step to the front of the stage and, addressing the audience in his most tragic tones, said, "Ladies and gentlemen, unless the play is stopped the

child cannot possibly go on." The effect on the audience of his earnest in favour of the child, can be easily conceived.
Thomas Moore, JOURNAL   *Aug* 1845

JOHN FITZGERALD KENNEDY
(1917–1963)
Thirty-fifth President of the United States

1   The most dangerous and megalomaniac of presidents.
Eric Hobshawm

2   I am an idealist without illusions.
Kennedy. Quoted Harris Wolford, OF KENNEDYS AND KINGS   1981

3   I had no cause for regret once Kennedy became president.
N. Khrushchev, MEMOIRS

4   There is something very eighteenth century about this young man. He is always on his toes during our discussion. But in the evening there will be music and wine and pretty women.
Harold Macmillan, New York Journal — American   21 *Jan* 1962

5   The Cuban missile crisis enabled the United States to pull defeat out of the jaws of victory.
Richard M. Nixon

6   Contrary to revisionist myth, Kennedy did not relish confrontation. Prudence was one of his favourite words.
Ibid.

7   Kennedy loved his wife; but Kennedy the politician exuded that musk odour which acts as an aphrodisiac to many women.
Theodore H. White, IN SEARCH OF HISTORY   1979

JOHANN KEPLER (1571–1630)
German astronomer

8   Kepler, the German exile who became royal mathematician, magician and musician of the planets of Prague, inaugurated modern planetary astronomy by discovering that the orbit of a planet round the sun was always an ellipse, the somewhat squashed circle you get if you slice obliquely through a cone.
Nigel Calder, THE COMET IS COMING   1980

9   In one respect Kepler as a man stands out from every other scientist. He was the victim, not of religious prejudice or vested interests, but of almost unbelievable misfortune. His father was a worthless adventurer, his mother wild and ignorant; prematurely born, he was by constitution feeble. An

attack of smallpox at the age of four ruined his sight and left his hands crippled.
J. A. Hammerton (editor), CONCISE UNIVERSAL BIOGRAPHY

10   He was persecuted for religious beliefs he did not hold, was forced to leave Graz for being a protestant, and Linz because it was in a continual stage of siege; and spent the whole of 1621–22 in freeing his mother from prison where* she had been flung on a trumped-up charge of witchcraft.
Ibid.

11   God provides for every animal his means of sustenance. For the astronomer he has provided astrology.
Kepler

12   My aim is to show that the celestial machine is to be likened not to a divine organism but rather to a clockwork, insofar as nearly all the manifold movements are carried out by means of a single, quite simple magnetic force, as in the case of a clockwork where all motions are caused by a simple weight.
Ibid.

JOHN MAYNARD BARON KEYNES
(1883–1946)
British economist

13   His wit was shattering and his capacity for rudeness unequalled. But he was completely disinterested, bore no malice however fierce the controversy, and was so charming that even those wounded could not bear a grudge.
New Statesman, obituary   27 *Apr* 1946

14   How sad it is that a man by nature so brilliant should have been so badly educated and should have passed the errors of his education on to a wider world.
William Rees-Mogg, The Times, Confessions of a justified monetarist   10 *Nov* 1983

15   It is hard to think of any economist who has achieved so much practical good.
Robert Skidelsky, JOHN MAYNARD KEYNES VOL I   1983

16   The history of the Keynesian revolution is largely a story of Keynes' escape from the quantity theory of money.
Ibid.

NIKITA SERGEYEVICH
KHRUSHCHEV (1894–1972)
Russian First Secretary

17   Khrushchev's greatest work, outweighing all his idiocies and major howlers, was his

destruction of the Stalin legend and the emptying of the labour camps, returning to their homes millions of survivors and formally rehabilitating millions who were dead.
Edward Crankshaw, Observer, reviewing Roy Medvedev's KHRUSHCHEV
9 Jan 1983

1 A bullying, driving peasant politician, an illiterate determined to learn, who taught himself as he worked, a party chieftain almost unique in not minding getting mud on his boots, a sycophant who bayed as loudly as any with the pack during the blood purge, yet somehow managed to preserve a deep vein of decent humanity which could only begin to show itself when he was supreme, an intriguer afflicted with a strain of almost childlike candour, a philistine who knew he was a philistine and was saddened by the knowledge.
Ibid.

2 Khrushchev kissed me when we met / Bending o'er the pram I sat in; / I was sticky, weeping, wet — / But, reporters, don't put that in / Say that I'm a sturdy lad, / Say that no one could resist me / Say that I'd be happier had / Khrushchev missed me.
E. V. Milner, Punch, Brief Encounter
20 Jul 1960

CHARLES KINGSLEY (1810–1875)
English author and churchman

3 I have seen Mr Kingsley, Christian socialist and author of *Alton Locke* etc. Was much struck by his originality and intenseness. Few men have pleased me more. With every tendency to wildness and exaggerated colouring, he never can speak or write otherwise than according to a noble character, I am sure.
Elizabeth Barrett Browning, letter to Mrs David Ogilvy   8 Sep 1852

4 Hast thou read Kingsley's *Westward Ho*? A fine foe-exterminating book of Elizabeth's time, done and written in the religious spirit of Joshua and David.
Caroline Fox, letter to Elizabeth Carne
Jun 1855

5 We sat out the service in Chester Cathedral and heard Canon Kingsley preach. Poor Kingsley is, in the pulpit, a decidedly weak brother. His discourse, on the Athanasian Creed was, intellectually, flat, and, sentimentally, boyish.
Henry James, letter to his father
29 May 1872

6 Nothing roused him so much as cant. Once a scoundrel, on being refused, and thinking at a parsonage it would be a successful trick, fell on his knees on the doorstep, turned up the whites of his eyes, and began the disgusting counterfeit of a prayer. In an instant the man found himself, to his astonishment, seized by the collar and wrist and being thrust towards the gate with a firm grip and a shake that deprived him of all his inclination to resist or, till he found himself safely outside, even to remonstrate.
John Martineau, CHARLES KINGSLEY: *His Letters and Memories of his Life   1877*

RUDYARD KIPLING (1865–1936)
Anglo-Indian author

7 What I like about Mr Kipling is that his pomes are right off th' bat. No cold storage pothry f'r Kipling. All lays laid this morning.
Mr Dooley (Finlay Peter Dunne). Quoted Michael Green, COMPANION TO ENGLISH AND AMERICAN LITERATURE *(edited by Bergen Evans)*

8 One of the greatest literary geniuses of the Anglo-Saxon race, and when time has winnowed away all the vulgarity, lack of taste, jingoism and cocksure brassiness, the residue will be read and enjoyed without end.
Rupert Hart-Davis, THE LYTTELTON HART-DAVIS LETTERS   *13 Jan 1956*

9 I doubt that the infant monster has any more to give.
Henry James in 1898, LETTERS, VOL 3

HENRY KISSINGER (1923–   )
American Secretary of State

10 Henry's idea of sex is to slow the car down to thirty miles an hour when he drops you off at the door.
Barbara Hower

11 I do not believe in doing something just for the sake of action.
Kissinger, THE WHITE HOUSE YEARS   1979

12 Machiavellian, deceitful, egotistical, arrogant and insulting.
William Rogers, US Secretary of State. Quoted ibid.

HORATIO HERBERT KITCHENER
(1850–1916)
(Earl of Khartoum and Broome)
British Field Marshal

1 If he was not a great man, at least he was a great poster.
Margot Asquith, AUTOBIOGRAPHY 1936

2 Lord K. is playing Hell with its lid off at the War Office — What the papers call "standing no nonsense" but which often means "listening to no nonsense".
Lady Jean Hamilton, DIARY 12 *Aug* 1914

3 He is rather like one of those revolving lighthouses which radiate momentary gleams of revealing light far out into the surrounding gloom and then relapse into complete darkness.
David Lloyd George. Quoted John Grieg,
Sunday Times 4 *Sep* 1977

4 When in 1898 Kitchener came to Balmoral after the battle of Omdurman to see the Queen he had related how he had been rather inconvenienced after the battle was over by having two thousand women on his hands. Princess Beatrice asked what the women were like and he replied, "Very like all women. They talked a great deal."
Sir Frederick Ponsonby, RECOLLECTIONS OF THREE REIGNS

5 On 5 June the *Hampshire*, with Kitchener on board, struck a mine within two hours of leaving Scapa Flow. Kitchener and most of the crew were drowned. Next morning Northcliffe burst into his sister's drawing-room with the words, "Providence is on the side of the British Empire after all."
A. J. P. Taylor, ENGLISH HISTORY
1914–1945

PAUL KLEE (1879–1940)
Swiss painter

6 Klee's pictures seem to me to resemble, not pictures, but a sample book of patterns for linoleum.
The Hon. Sir Cyril Asquith, letter to Sir Alfred Munnings

7 Klee went to the insane asylums for his inspirations.
George A. Dondero. Speech 16 *Aug* 1949

SIR GODFREY KNELLER (1646–1723)
(Gottfried Kniller)
German-born artist who settled in England and became court painter

8 The portraits of Kneller seem all to have been turned in a machine; the eyebrows are arched as if by a compass; the mouth curled, the chin dimpled, the head turned on one side and the hands placed in the same affected position.
William Hazlitt

9 Kneller, by Heav'n and not a master, taught, / Whose Art was Nature, and whose pictures Thought.
Alexander Pope, EPITAPH ON SIR GODFREY KNELLER

10 I paid Sir Godfrey Kneller a visit but two days before he died and I think I never saw a scene of so much vanity in my life. He was lying in his bed, contemplating the plan he had made for his own monument. He said many gross things in relation to himself and the memory he should leave behind him. He said he should not like to lie among the rascals at Westminster. A memorial there would be sufficient; and desired me to write an epitaph for it. I did so afterwards and I think it the worst thing I ever wrote in my life.
Alexander Pope. Quoted Rev. Joseph Spence, OBSERVATIONS, ANECDOTES AND CHARACTERS 1826

11 The downright shoddiness of much of his enormous output is a mirror of the cynicism of the age, but he had a wonderfully sharp eye for character, could draw and paint a face with admirable economy, and maintains, even in his inferior work, a certain virility and down-to-earth quality which is refreshing after the languishments of the age of Lely.
Ellis Waterhouse, PAINTING IN BRITAIN
1530–1790

12 He was one of the first to concentrate on the portrait as a document concerned with the likeness of a historical personality rather than as a work of art.
Ibid.

JOHN KNOX (1505–1572)
Scottish reformer

13 One is tempted almost to say that there is more of Jesus in St. Theresa's little finger than in John Knox's whole body.
Matthew Arnold, LITERATURE AND DOGMA 1872

14 The light of Scotland, the comfort of the Church within the same, the mirror of godliness and pattern and example to all true ministers in purity of life, soundness of

doctrine and boldness in reproving of wickedness.
George Bannatyne (Knox's secretary),
MEMORIAL OF TRANSACTIONS IN
SCOTLAND 1573

1 They go far wrong who think that Knox was a gloomy, spasmodic, shrieking fanatic. Not at all; he is one of the solidest of men. Practical, cautious-hopeful, patient; a most shrewd, observing, quietly discerning man.
Thomas Carlyle, HEROES AND
HEROWORSHIP 1841

2 The ringleader of all these insults on the Majesty was John Knox, who possessed an uncontrolled authority in the Church, and even triumphed in the contumelious usage of his sovereign. The political principles of the man, which he communicated to his brethren, were as full of sedition as his theological were full of rage and bigotry.
David Hume, HISTORY OF GREAT
BRITAIN 1761

3 His maxims were often too severe and the impetuosity of his temper excessive. Rigid and uncomplying himself, he showed no indulgence to the infirmities of others. Regardless of the distinction of rank and character, he uttered his admonitions with an acrimony and vehemence more to irritate than to reclaim. This often betrayed him into indecent and undutiful expressions with respect to the Queen's person and conduct. Those very qualities, however, which now render his character less amiable, fitted him to be the instrument of Providence for advancing the Reformation among a fierce people and enabled him to face dangers, and surmount opposition from which a person of more gentle disposition would have been apt to shrink back.
W. Robertson, HISTORY OF SCOTLAND
DURING THE REIGNS OF QUEEN MARY AND
JAMES VI 1759

4 He had a grim reliance in himself, or rather, in his mission; if he were not sure he was a great man, he was at least sure that he was one set apart to do great things.
R. L. Stevenson, STUDIES OF MEN AND
BOOKS 1882

5 In Knox we see foreshadowed the whole Puritan Revolution and the scaffold of Charles I.
Ibid.

KUBLAI KHAN (1216–1294)
Chinese emperor, founder of the Mongol dynasty

6 Kublai, as the Chinese historians describe him, was a very different character from his half-savage predecessors. He had absorbed many of the best elements of Chinese culture, including some of the humanitarian spirit of Buddhism, while retaining much of the simplicity and vigour of the nomad. In the courtyard of his palace at Khan-balik (Peking) he sowed seeds of prairie grass to remind him of the freer world from which he had come.
R. E. Latham, Introduction to his translation of Marco Polo's TRAVELS 1958

7 By his four wives the Great Khan had twenty-two male children. By his mistresses he had a further twenty-five sons, all good men and brave soldiers. And each of them is a great baron. Of his sons by his four wives seven are kings of great provinces and kingdoms.
Marco Polo, TRAVELS 1298

8 I shall tell you now of the great and wonderful magnificence of the Great Khan now reigning, by name Cublay Khan. All men know of certain truth that he is the most potent man, as regards forces and lands and treasure, that exists in the world.
Ibid.

9 His whole city is arranged in squares just like a chessboard, and disposed in a manner so perfect and masterly that it is impossible to give a description that should do it justice.
Ibid.

10 He sends emissaries and inspectors throughout his dominions and kingdoms and provinces to learn whether any of his people have suffered a failure of their crops either through the weather or through locusts or other pests, and if he finds they have lost their harvest he exempts them that year from their tribute — and even gives them some of his own grain to sow and eat — a magnificent act of royal bounty. This he does in the summer. And in winter he does likewise in the matter of cattle. If he finds a man whose cattle have been killed by an outbreak of plague, he gives him some of his own.
Ibid.

L

CHARLES LAMB (1775–1834)
English essayist

1 He is now a confirmed, shameless drunkard, *asks* vehemently for gin and water in strangers' houses . . . Poor Lamb! Poor England, when such a despicable abortion is named genius.
Thomas Carlyle

2 Charles Lamb I sincerely believe to be in some considerable degree insane. A more pitiful, rickety, gasping, staggering, stammering Tomfool I do not know.
Ibid.

3 On a ramble he once delivered to me orally the subject of the *Essay on the Defect of Imagination in Modern Artists* subsequently printed in the *Atheneum*. But besides the criticism there were snatches of old poems, golden lines, and sentences culled from old books, and anecdotes of men of note. Marry, it was like going a ramble with gentle Isaak Walton, without the fishing.
Thomas Hood, HOOD'S OWN   1827

4 His sensibility to strong contrasts was the foundation of his humour, which was that of a wit at once melancholy and willing to please.
Leigh Hunt

5 He would beard a superstition and shudder at the old phantasm while he did it. One could have imagined him cracking a joke in the teeth of a ghost, and then melting into thin air himself out of sympathy with the aweful.
Ibid.

6 My poor, dear, dearest sister, in a fit of insanity, has been the death of her own mother. I was at hand only in time enough to snatch the knife from her hand. She is at present in a madhouse.
Lamb, letter to Coleridge   27 Sep 1796

7 C. Lamb told me he had got £170 for his two years' contributions to the *London Magazine* (*Letters of Elia*). Should have thought it more.
Tom Moore, DIARY 4 Apr 1823

8 On Robinson's receiving his first brief he called upon Lamb to tell him of it. "I

suppose," said Lamb, "you addressed that line of Pope's to it, 'Thou great *first cause*, least understood'."
Ibid.

9 Charles Lamb, a clever fellow certainly, but full of villainous and abortive puns when he miscarries of every minute.
Ibid.

10 I looked over Lamb's library in part. He has the finest collection of shabby books I ever saw; such a number of first-rate works in very bad condition is, I think, nowhere to be found.
Henry Crabb Robinson, DIARY 10 Jan 1824

11 Lamb was the slave of quip and whimsy; he stuttered out puns to the detriment of all serious conversation and twice or so in the year he was overtaken in liquor. Well, in spite of these things, perhaps because of these things, I love his memory.
Alexander Smith

SIR EDWIN HENRY LANDSEER (1802–1873)
English artist

12 Landseer is said to have asked Sydney Smith to sit to him for a portrait and to have received the Biblical reply, 2 Kings viii 13 — is thy servant a dog that he should do this thing?
Daniel George, A BOOK OF ANECDOTES   1957

13 His paintings of sad, coy, comical, noble and bleeding animals were so popular that at the peak of his career he kept 126 engravers busy turning out copies of such works as *Dignity and Impudence, Fighting Dogs Getting Wind, The Stag at Bay*. When he died he left over £200,000.
Frank Muir, THE FRANK MUIR BOOK   1975

WILLIAM LANGLAND (fourteenth century)
English poet

14 The first English writer who can be read with approbation is William Langland, the author of *Piers Plowman's Vision*, a severe satire upon the clergy. Though his measure is more uncouth than that of his predecessors there is a real energy in his conception

which he caught, not from the chimeras of knight-errantry, but the actual manners and opinions of his times.

Henry Hallam, INTRODUCTION TO THE LITERATURE OF EUROPE 1839

1 In his hands an alliterative line becomes capable of an astonishing range of effects from the terse, dramatic conversational to those of great rhetorical splendour.

E. Salter, AN INTRODUCTION TO PIERS PLOWMAN 1962

2 His education was at a Benedictine school in Malvern, which prepared him for the Church. He took minor orders but his marriage barred him from advancement. Some time before 1362 he went to London where he earned a meagre living as a copyist and psalm singer. He began the composition of *Piers the Plowman* in 1362 and the expansion and revision of the poem occupied him until his death.

Michael Stapleton, CAMBRIDGE GUIDE TO ENGLISH LITERATURE 1982

GEORGE LANSBURY (1859–1940)
English socialist politician

3 Lansbury has been going about dressed in saint's clothes for years, waiting for martyrdom; I set fire to the faggots.

Ernest Bevin. Quoted Alan Bullock, THE LIFE AND TIMES OF ERNEST BEVIN

4 Commissioner of Works in the second Labour government of 1929–1931, he was responsible for the institution of bathing facilities at the Serpentine, Hyde Park — known popularly as the Lansbury Lido.

A. J. Hammerton (editor), CONCISE UNIVERSAL BIOGRAPHY

5 Not a very clear head but with a heart that reached beyond the stars.

Harold Laski, letter to Maurice Firuski Aug 1920

6 The most loveable figure in modern politics.

A. J. P. Taylor, ENGLISH HISTORY 1914–1945

WILLIAM LAUD (1573–1645)
Archbishop of Canterbury

7 He applied the brains of a college pedant to the spacious life of England.

John Buchan, OLIVER CROMWELL 1934

8 Laud conceived of government as the expression and expansion of Christian civilisation and saw in that belief the surest

pledge that man would find his true freedom and his highest wealth. The Church to his mind was the great instrument of this Christian civilisation.

A. S. Duncan-Jones, LIFE OF LAUD 1927

9 His zeal was unrelenting in the cause of religion; that is, in imposing by rigorous measures his own tenets and pious ceremonies on the obstinate puritans who had profanely dared to oppose him. In the prosecutions of his holy purposes he overlooked every human consideration; or, in other words, the heat and indiscretion of his temper made him neglect the views of prudence and rules of good manners.

David Hume, HISTORY OF THE STUARTS 1754

10 A poor creature, who never did, said or wrote anything more than indicating the ordinary capacity of an old woman.

T. B. Macaulay, HISTORY OF ENGLAND 1861

11 What single definition can embrace his comprehensive social ideal and his narrow-minded application of it; his tolerant theology and his intolerant methods; his huge efforts and their tenuous results; the social justice he advocated and the savage punishments which he inflicted?

Hugh Trevor-Roper, ARCHBISHOP LAUD

ANTOINE LAURENT LAVOISIER (1743–1794)
French physicist

12 On 13th September 1765 people in fields near Luce, in France, saw a stone-mass drop from the sky after a violent thunderclap. The great physicist, Lavoisier, who knew better than any peasant that this was impossible, reported to the Academy of Science that the witnesses were mistaken or lying. The Academy would not accept the reality of meteorites until 1803.

Fortean Times

13 His work in both chemistry and physics ranks with the leading names in history in both sciences. He destroyed the phlogiston theory and established the true notions of the process of combustion; he gave the name oxygen (acid producer) to that gas. He showed that water was a composition of oxygen and hydrogen, and founded the modern theory of chemical elements.

J. A. Hammerton (editor), CONCISE UNIVERSAL BIOGRAPHY

ANDREW BONAR LAW (1858–1923)
Canadian-born British Prime Minister

1 He had the mind of a Glasgow baillee.
*H. H. Asquith to Lloyd George. Quoted
Robert Blake,* THE UNKNOWN PRIME
MINISTER

2 It is fitting that we should have buried the
Unknown Prime Minister by the side of the
Unknown Warrior.
*H. H. Asquith, after Bonar Law's funeral at
Westminster Abbey* 5 *Nov* 1923

3 Bonar would never make up his mind on
anything. Once a question had been decided, Bonar would stick to it and fight for it
to a finish, but he would never help in the
taking of a decision.
*David Lloyd George. Quoted
A. J. Sylvester,* LIFE WITH LLOYD GEORGE

4 The public has never realised the creative
common sense of Bonar Law — he was the
most creative objector I have ever known.
*David Lloyd George. Quoted Harold
Nicolson,* DIARY 6 *Jul* 1936

5 Bonar always jibs a good deal before taking
a long jump.
Frances Stevenson, DIARY 16 *Mar* 1920

DAVID HERBERT LAWRENCE (1885–1930)
Novelist and poet

6 He is one of the great denouncers, the great
missionaries the English send to themselves
to tell them they are crass, gross, lost, dead,
mad and addicted to unnatural vices.
Kingsley Amis, WHAT BECAME OF JANE
AUSTEN?

7 Lawrence seemed to me sometimes to suffer
from a delusion similar to the delusion of a
sick man who thinks that if a given quantity
of medicine will do him good, twice the
quantity will do him twice as much good.
Arnold Bennett, Evening Standard
12 *Apr* 1930

8 The picture of D. H. Lawrence suggested by
the obituary notice, of competent critics is
of a man morose, frustrated, tortured —
Lawrence was as little morose as any open
clematis flower, as little tortured, or sinister
or hysterical as a humming bird.
Catherine Carswell, letter to Time and Tide
14 *Mar* 1934

9 *The Rainbow,* a novel by Mr D. H. Lawrence is more hideous than any imaginable
reality. The thing is done so coldly, so
pompously, so gravely that it is like a savage
rite. There is not a gleam of humour in the
fog of eloquent lubricity. The thud, thud,
thud of hectic phrases is intolerably weari-
some.
James Douglas, Star (London)
22 *Oct* 1915

10 This pictorial account of the day-to-day life
of an English gamekeeper is full of considerable interest to outdoor-minded
readers . . . Unfortunately one is obliged to
wade through many pages of extraneous
material, and in this reviewer's opinion the
book cannot take the place of J. R. Miller's
*Practical Gamekeeping. Field and Stream
(review of* LADY CHATTERLEY'S LOVER)

11 Interesting, but a type I could not get on
with. Obsessed with self. Dead eyes and a
red beard, long narrow face. A strange bird.
John Galsworthy, LIFE AND LETTERS
(edited by H. V. Marriot) 1935

12 A bum poet and a bum person.
Robert Graves, LETTERS

13 Is *Lady Chatterley's Lover* a book you
would leave lying around your own house?
Is it a book you would wish your wife, or
even your servant to read?
*Mervyn Griffith-Jones prosecuting at
obscenity trial* 1961

14 For Lawrence, existence was one long con-
valescence, it was as though he were newly
reborn from a mortal illness every day of his
life.
Aldous Huxley, THE OLIVE TREE

15 To be solemn about the organs of
generation is only possible to someone who,
like Lawrence, has deified the will and denied the spirit.
*Hugh Kingsmill. Quoted Malcolm
Muggeridge,* TREAD SOFTLY FOR YOU
TREAD ON MY JOKES 1966

16 You mustn't think I advocate perpetual sex.
Far from it. Nothing nauseates me more
than promiscuous sex in and out of season.
*D. H. Lawrence, letter to Lady Ottoline
Morrell* 20 *Dec* 1928

17 A book should be either a bandit, or rebel,
or a man in the crowd . . . whoever reads
me will be in the thick of the scrimmage,
and if he doesn't like it – if he wants a safe
seat in the audience – let him read someone
else.
D. H. Lawrence, letter to Carlo Linati
22 *Jan* 1923

18 I sincerely believe in restoring the phallic
consciousness into our lives because it is the
source of all real beauty and all real
gentleness. And these are the two things,

tenderness and beauty, which will save us from the horrors.
D. H. Lawrence, letter to Harriet Munroe 15 *Mar* 1928

1 *Lady Chatterley's Lover* is an extremely dull and portentously silly and pretentious book.
G. W. Lyttelton, THE LYTTELTON HART-DAVIS LETTERS 22 *Dec* 1955

2 I do not claim to be a literary critic but I know dirt when I smell it and here it is in heaps — festering, putrid heaps which smell to high heaven.
W. Charles Pilley, John Bull, reviewing WOMEN IN LOVE 17 *Sep* 1921

3 Capable of an occasional joke in his letters, he is consistently without humour in his books; a failure rarely, if ever, to be found in novelists of the highest class, from Petronius to Proust.
Anthony Powell, THE STRANGERS ARE ALL GONE

4 I have seen Osbert Sitwell kick a copy of *Sons and Lovers* across Duckworth's office to express his feelings on the subject — though he did add "but that is a good book".
Anthony Powell, Daily Telegraph, The Sitwell panorama 23 *Nov* 1978

5 No other writer in the twentieth century, except Freud, has been subject to so much abuse from otherwise intelligent people.
Philip Rieff, THE TRIUMPH OF THE THERAPEUTIC

6 *Lady Chatterley's Lover* is a book that all Christians might read with profit.
John Robinson (Bishop of Woolwich) for the defence, in the obscenity trial 1961

7 Lawrence was his wife's mouthpiece. He had the eloquence, but she had the ideas. Lawrence was essentially a timid man who tried to conceal his timidity by bluster. His wife was not timid and her denunciations have the character of thunder, not bluster. Under her wing he felt comparatively safe.
Bertrand Russell, AUTOBIOGRAPHY 1967

8 His excessive emphasis on sex was due to the fact that in sex alone he was compelled to admit that he was not the only human being in the universe. It was so painful that he conceived of sex relations as a perpetual fight in which each is attempting to destroy the other.
Ibid.

9 His descriptive powers were remarkable, but his ideas cannot too soon be forgotten.
Ibid.

10 Mr Lawrence looked like a plaster gnome on a stone toadstool in some suburban garden. At the same time he bore some resemblance to a bad self-portrait by Van Gogh. He had a rather matted, dank appearance. He looked as if he had just returned from spending an uncomfortable night in a very dark cave, hiding, perhaps, in the darkness from something which, at the same time, he on his side was hunting.
Edith Sitwell, TAKEN CARE OF

11 It seems to us now that his system, for all its fervour, was largely negative, a mere denial of the system of his upbringing. His God, for instance, must be the exact opposite of the 'gentle Jesus' of his childhood.
Rex Warner, THE CULT OF POWER

12 Had I married you, dear, when I was nineteen / I had been little since but a printing machine, / For before my fortieth year had run / I well had produced you a twenty-first son.
Anna Wickham, MULTIPLICATION, FOR D.H.L.

SIR THOMAS LAWRENCE (1769–1830)
English painter

13 The family anecdotes of his own precocity had always entertained him; on an early drawing which he sent to an admiring friend, he wrote; "Done when three weeks old, I believe".
Julia de Wolf Addison, THE ART OF THE NATIONAL GALLERY 1905

14 There is a mild scandal, that Lawrence made love to Mrs Siddons's eldest daughter, and then wantonly transferred his attentions to the youngest; that this fickleness caused the death of both — one from the chagrin of being jilted, and the other from dissatisfaction at discovering she was only second fiddle! But such legends sound rather fanciful and must be taken with a grain of salt.
Ibid.

15 A lady, in alluding to him, writes, "He could not write a common answer to an invitation to dinner without it assuming the tone of a *billet-doux*; the very commonest conversation was held in that soft, low whisper, and with that tone of deference and interest which are so unusual, and so calculated to please."
Ibid.

16 His manner was elegant, but not high bred. He had too much that air of always sub-

mitting. He had smiled so often and so long, that at last his smile wore the appearance of having been set in enamel.
B. R. Haydon, DIARY   9 *Jan* 1830

1   Lawrence made coxcombs of his sitters, and his sitters made a coxcomb of Lawrence.
John Opie

2   This young man has begun at the point of excellence where I left off.
Sir Joshua Reynolds

3   Sir Thomas Lawrence has painted several very pleasing pictures of people, but generally his men are effeminate and his women meretricious.
Samuel Rogers, TABLE TALK   1856

THOMAS EDWARD LAWRENCE OF ARABIA (1888–1935)
Soldier and author

4   He made so many mysteries; told one person one set of facts, another, another. If all compared notes most would be known, but not all.
Robert Graves, letter to Liddell Hart May 1931

5   There are those who have tried to dismiss his story with a flourish of the Union Jack, a psycho-analytical catchword, or a sneer. It should move our deepest admiration and pity. Like Shelley and like Baudelaire it may be said of him that he suffered, in his own person, the neurotic ills of an entire generation.
Christopher Isherwood, EXHUMATIONS

6   If he hides in a quarry he puts red flags all round.
George Bernard Shaw. Quoted Guardian 22 *Jan* 1963

7   He had a genius for backing into the limelight.
Lowell Thomas, LAWRENCE OF ARABIA

8   They only got two things right, the camels and the sand.
Lowell Thomas, of the film, LAWRENCE OF ARABIA. *Quoted The Times, obituary* 29 *Aug* 1981

SIR PETER LELY (1618–1680)
(Pieter Van Der Faes)
Anglo-Dutch portrait painter

9   Th' amazed world shall henceforth find / None but my Lely ever drew a mind.
Richard Lovelace, TO MY WORTHY FRIEND MR PETER LELY

10   Lely an animated canvas stole / The sleepy eye, that spoke the melting soul.
Alexander Pope, IMITATION OF HORACE

11   Lely supplied the want of taste with *clinquant*; his nymphs trail fringes and embroidery through purling streams. Add, that Vandyck's habits are those of the times; Lely's a sort of fantastic nightgown fastened with a single pin. The latter was in truth the ladies' painter.
Horace Walpole, ANECODOTES OF PAINTERS IN ENGLAND   1771

VLADIMIR ILYICH ULYANOV LENIN (1870–1924)
Russian revolutionary leader

12   The Germans turned upon Russia the most grisly of all weapons. They transported Lenin in a sealed truck, like a plague bacillus, from Switzerland into Russia.
Winston Churchill, THE WORLD CRISIS   1929

13   The Russian people's worst misfortune was his birth, their next worst — his death.
Ibid.

LEONARDO DA VINCI (1452–1519)
Italian painter, sculptor, architect and scientist

14   He was the most relentlessly curious man in history. Everything he saw made him ask how and why. Why does one find sea-shells in the mountains? How do they build locks in Flanders? How does a bird fly? What accounts for cracks in walls? What is the origin of winds and clouds? Find out; write it down; if you can see it, draw it.
Sir Kenneth Clark, CIVILISATION   1969

15   Of all these questions the one he asks most insistently is about man. How does he walk? How does the heart pump blood? What happens when he yawns and sneezes? How does a child live in the womb? Why does he die of old age? Leonardo discovered a centenarian in a hospital in Florence and waited gleefully for his demise so that he could examine his veins.
Ibid.

16   Curiosity and the desire for beauty — these are the two elementary forces in Leonardo's genius; curiosity often in conflict with the desire for beauty, but generating, in union with it, a type of subtle and curious grace.
Walter Pater, STUDIES IN THE HISTORY OF THE RENAISSANCE   1873

1   He bores me. He ought to have stuck to his flying machines.
Auguste Renoir

2   Leonardo painted *The Last Supper* for the Dominicans at St. Maria delle Grazie in Milan, endowing the heads of the Apostles with such majesty and beauty that he left that of Christ unfinished, feeling that he could not give it that celestial divinity which it demanded.
Giorgio Vasari, LIVES OF PAINTERS, ARCHITECTS AND SCULPTORS   1550

3   The other head which caused him thought was that of Judas. The prior incessantly importuned him to finish the work. He was willing in this case to seek no further, and for lack of a better he would do the head of the importunate and tactless prior. The poor prior, covered with confusion, went back to his garden and left Leonardo in peace to finish his Judas, making him a veritable likeness of treason and cruelty.
Ibid.

4   Leonardo undertook for Francesco Zanobi del Giocondo the portrait of his wife Mona Lisa. She was very beautiful and while he was drawing her portrait he engaged people to play and sing, and jesters to keep her merry, and remove that melancholy which painting usually gives to portraits. This figure of Leonardo's has such a pleasant smile that it seems rather divine than human, and was considered marvellous, an exact copy of Nature.
Ibid.

LEOPOLD I (1790–1865)
King of the Belgians

5   Dear Uncle is given to believing that he must rule the roost everywhere. However, that is not necessary.
Queen Victoria, letter to Prince Albert 8 Dec 1839

CLIVE STAPLES LEWIS (1898–1963)
Irish novelist, essayist and critic

6   His appearance was scarcely that of a crusader. He looked like a high-living pugnacious butcher or grocer; his manner was bluff and no-nonsense.
Rachel Trickett, Daily Telegraph, A Warfaring Christian   19 Nov 1983

7   There is a story that Lewis returned three days after his death to an old disciple perplexed by moral problems. He appeared as in life — red-faced, loud-voiced, robust — and said simply, "It's all right, you know. It's all right." To anyone who knew Lewis it has the ring of authenticity.
Ibid.

PERCY WYNDHAM LEWIS (1884–1957)
English novelist, essayist and artist

8   One of his minor purposes is to disembowel his enemies, who are numerous, for the simple reason that he wants them to be numerous. He would be less tiresome if he were more urbane.
Arnold Bennett, Evening Standard 28 Apr 1927

9   I do not think I have ever seen a nastier-looking man. Under the black hat, when I had first seen them, the eyes were those of an unsuccessful rapist.
Ernest Hemingway, A MOVEABLE FEAST   1964

10 Mr Lewis's pictures appeared, as a very great painter said to me, to have been painted by a mailed fist in a cotton glove.
Edith Sitwell, TAKEN CARE OF

11 He brought a painter's technique to his novels and there is a remarkable precision about his word-pictures. He rejected the stream-of-consciousness technique, verbal antics transferred to paper, and the idea of sex as the prime mover of the universe; he had no patience with the contrived artlessness of some American writers, nor with what he saw as selective Christian piety.
Michael Stapleton, CAMBRIDGE GUIDE TO ENGLISH LITERATURE   1982

SINCLAIR LEWIS (1885–1951)
American novelist

12 Lewis is the historian of America's catastrophic going-to-pieces — or at least the going-to-pieces of her middle class — with no remedy to offer for the decline he records.
Malcolm Cowley, AFTER THE GENTEEL TRADITION   1937

13 He was one of the worst writers in modern American literature, but without his writing one cannot imagine modern American literature. This is because, without his writing, we can hardly imagine ourselves.
Mark Schorer, SINCLAIR LEWIS; *An American Life*   1961

ABRAHAM LINCOLN (1809–1865)
Sixteenth President of the United States

1 In the character of the victim [Lincoln] and even in the accessories of his last moments, there is something so homely and innocent that it takes the question, as it were, out of all the pomp of history and the ceremonial of diplomacy — it touches the heart of nations and appeals to the domestic sentiment of mankind.
Benjamin Disraeli, House of Commons
1 May 1865

2 My heart burned within me with indignation and grief; we could think of nothing else. All night long we had but little sleep, waking up perpetually to the sense of a great shock and grief. Everyone is feeling the same. I never knew such a universal feeling.
Mrs Gaskell, letter to C. E. Norton when the news of Lincoln's assassination reached England   28 Apr 1865

3 I have now come to the conclusion never again to think of marrying and for this reason: I could never be satisfied with anyone who would be blockhead to have me.
Lincoln in a letter to Mrs Browning of Mary Owen's refusal   1 Apr 1838

4 If the good people in their wisdom should see fit to keep me in the background I have been too familiar with disappointment to be much chagrined.
Lincoln, letter to the Sangamon Journal

5 Nobody ever expected me to be President. In my poor, lean, lank face nobody has ever seen any cabbages sprouting.
Lincoln. Campaign speech   1860

6 Mr Lincoln's soul seems made of leather, and incapable of any grand or noble emotion. Compared with the mass of men he is a line of flat prose in a beautiful and spirited lyric. He lowers, he never elevates you.
New York Post, editorial   1863

7 When he hits upon a policy, substantially good in itself, he contrives to belittle it, smear it in some way to render it mean, contemptible and useless. Even wisdom from him seems but folly.
Ibid.

8 Mr Lincoln is deficient in those little links which make up the path of a woman's happiness.
Mary Owen, giving her reason for refusing Lincoln's offer of marriage   1838

JENNY LIND (1820–1887)
(Madame Goldschmidt)
Swedish soprano

9 She went on a tour of the USA under contract to Phineas P. Barnum, from which she returned with a profit in excess of £20,000. This she spent on founding art scholarships, and on extending hospitals in Liverpool and London.
Frank Muir, THE FRANK MUIR BOOK   1978

10 Then we went to Jenny Lind's concert, for which a gentleman gave us tickets, and at the end of the first act we agreed to come away. It struck me as atrociously stupid. I was thinking of something else the whole time she was jugulating away.
William Makepeace Thackeray, letter to Mrs Brookfield   1850

JOSEPH, LORD LISTER (1827–1912)
British surgeon, pioneer in antiseptics

11 Speaking of the importance of draining abscesses he referred to the time when he was called to Balmoral to operate upon Queen Victoria for an axillary abscess and playfully said, "Gentlemen, I am the only man who has ever stuck a knife in the Queen."
J. R. Leeson, LISTER AS I KNEW HIM   1927

12 The methodical life of Lord Lister is one on which a neat pattern is carefully imprinted, everything he did conforming to the one overriding motif of his work. Subtract his professional and scientific activities from his life and literally there is nothing of any moment to record.
Kenneth Walker, JOSEPH LISTER

FRANZ LISZT (1811–1886)
Hungarian pianist and composer

13 Liszt is a mere commonplace person, with his hair on end — a snob out of Bedlam. He writes the ugliest music extant.
Dramatic and Musical Review   7 Jan 1843

14 Turn your eyes to any one composition that bears the name of Liszt, if you are unlucky enough to have such a thing on your pianoforte, and answer frankly if it contains one bar of genuine music. Composition indeed! — decomposition is the proper word for such hateful fungi, which choke up and poison the fertile plains of harmony, threatening the world with drought.
Musical World   30 Jun 1855

DAVID LIVINGSTONE (1813–1873)
Scottish missionary and explorer

1   I never met a man who fulfilled more completely my idea of a Christian gentleman.
Sir Bartle Frire, PROCEEDINGS OF THE ROYAL GEOGRAPHICAL SOCIETY   1874

2   When Mr Stanley entered Ujiji pm Nov 3 1871 with the procession of his servants he found a crowd of people in the street attracted by his approach. In the centre of a group of Arabs, to the left hand, he perceived a pale, grey-bearded white man, dressed in a shirt or jacket of red serge, with trousers, and wearing on his head a naval cap with a gold band. "Dr Livingstone, I presume," said Mr Stanley in accosting him with the calmness of an ordinary greeting at first sight, as he might have done in New York or London.
Illustrated London News   9 Nov 1872

3   When I got to the lowest verge, vague rumours of an English visitor reached me. I thought of myself as the man who went down from Jerusalem to Jericho; but neither Levite nor Samaritan could pass my way. Yet the good Samaritan was close at hand and one of my people rushed up at the top of his speed and in great excitement gasped out "An Englishman coming. I see him" and off he dashed to meet him. The American flag, the first ever seen in these parts, told me the nationality of the stranger. I am as cold and non-demonstrative as we islanders are usually reported to be, but your kindness made my frame thrill.
Livingstone, letter to James Gordon Bennett, owner of the New York Herald, which financed Stanley's expedition   Nov 1871

4   There is a group of respectable Arabs, and as I come nearer I see the white face of an old man among them. I am shaking hands with him. We raise our hats, and I say "Dr Livingstone I presume?" and he says "Yes".
H. M. Stanley, HOW I FOUND LIVINGSTONE   1872

5   His religion is not of the theoretical kind, but is a constant, earnest, sincere practice. It is neither demonstrative nor loud, but manifests itself in a quiet practical way, and is always at work.
Ibid.

DAVID LLOYD GEORGE (1863–1945)
(Earl Lloyd George of Dwyfor)
British Prime Minister

6   Lloyd George could not see a belt without hitting below it.
Margot Asquith, AUTOBIOGRAPHY   1936

7   The little man has been so surrounded for years with adulation that he thinks he is the only one fit to be Prime Minister.
Stanley Baldwin. Quoted Thomas Jones, WHITEHALL DIARY   1916–1925

8   Mr Lloyd George spoke for a hundred and seventeen minutes, in which period he was detected only once in the use of an argument.
Arnold Bennett, THINGS THAT HAVE INTERESTED ME

9   The vehement, contriving, resourceful, nimble-leaping Lloyd George.
Winston Churchill, GREAT CONTEMPORARIES   1937

10   He is without malice of any kind; without prejudices, without morals. He has many enemies and no friends. He does not understand what friendship means . . . and yet he is the best man we have got.
F. S. Oliver, THE ANVIL OF WAR

11   Of the three parties I find Labour least painful. My objection to the Tories is temperamental, and my objection to the Liberals is Lloyd George.
Bertrand Russell, letter to Maurice Amos MP 16 Jun 1930

12   He is incapable of *achieving* anything without reducing all around him to nervous wrecks. In this way he *distributes* his own nerves in a crisis and, I believe, saves himself
in the process . . . it is necessary for him to produce this state of enervation in everyone else in order that he himself may derive some sort of nervous energy which fortifies him.
Frances Stevenson, DIARY   29 Mar 1934

13   A master of improvised speech and improvised policies.
A. J. P. Taylor, ENGLISH HISTORY 1914–1945

JOHN LOCKE (1632–1704)
English philosopher

14   Locke, we feel, is not so much cleverer than ourselves as to be capable of playing tricks with us, even if he wanted to. He is the Mr Baldwin of philosophy, and he derives from his literary style some of the advantages which that statesman derived from his pipe and pigs.
C. D. Broad, ETHICS AND THE HISTORY OF PHILOSOPHY

1 Mr Locke spent a good part of his first years at the university in reading romances from his aversion to the disputatious way then in fashion there.
Dr Cocchi. Quoted Rev. Joseph Spence,
OBSERVATIONS, ANECDOTES AND CHARACTERS 1820

2 Locke approaches the most awful speculation with the same indifference as if he were about to handle the properties of the triangle.
James Hogg

3 The affectation of passing for an original thinker glares strongly and ridiculously in Mr Locke who sees not that a great part of his *Essay On Man* is taken from Hobbes and almost everything in his *Letters on Toleration* from Bayle. Yet he nowhere makes acknowledgement of his obligations to either of these writers. They were both of them, indeed, writers of ill-fame, but was that a reason for his taking no notice of them? He might have distinguished between their ill and good deserts.
Richard Hurd, DIALOGUES IN SINCERITY 1759

4 Some of Locke's opinions are so odd that I cannot see how to make them sound sensible. He says that a man must not have so many plums that they are bound to go bad before he and his family can eat them; but he may have as much gold and as many diamonds as he can lawfully get, because gold and diamonds do not go bad. It does not occur to him that the man who has the plums might sell them before they go bad.
Bertrand Russell, HISTORY OF WESTERN PHILOSOPHY 1945

5 This great Man could never subject himself to the tedious Fatigue of Calculations, nor to the Dry Pursuit of Mathematical Truths, which do not at first present any sensible Objects to the Mind; and no one has given better Proofs than he, that 'tis possible for a man to have a Geometrical Head without the assistance of Geometry.
Voltaire, LETTERS CONCERNING THE ENGLISH NATION 1734

6 This John Locke was a man of turbulent spirit, clamorous and never contented. The club wrote and took notes from the mouth of their master, Peter Stahl, who sat at the upper end of the table, but the said John Locke scorned to do it, so that while every man besides of the club were writing, he would be prating and troublesome.
Anthony à Wood, ATHENAE OXONIENSES 1674

HENRY WADSWORTH LONGFELLOW
(1807–1882)
American poet

7 Longfellow is to poetry what the barrel-organ is to music.
Van Wyck Brooks, THE FLOWERING OF NEW ENGLAND 1936

8 The gentleman was a sweet, beautiful soul, but I have entirely forgotten his name.
Attributed to R. W. Emerson, attending Longfellow's funeral

LOUIS XIV (1638–1715)
King of France

9 I have often seen the King consume four plates of different soups, a whole pheasant, a partridge, a large plate of salad, two big slices of ham, a dish of mutton in garlic sauce, a plateful of pastries followed by fruit and hard-boiled eggs.
Charlotte Elizabeth, Duchess of Orleans, letter to her stepsister Louisa 1682

10 The dominating feature of his long reign was the almost complete tranquillity which existed in the interior of the country, the end of those civil wars hitherto almost incessant. Hence industry and commerce flourished to an amazing degree and the arts in France arrived at their period of greatest glory.
J. A. Hammerton (editor), CONCISE UNIVERSAL BIOGRAPHY

11 I see no point in reading.
Louis XIV. *Quoted Louis, duc de Saint-Simon,* MEMOIRS

12 Louis XIV was more interested in dancing than in singing — his nickname of the Sun King originated from the 'sun' costume he wore when he danced in the *Ballet de la Nuit* at court when he was fifteen (it lasted thirteen hours).
Frank Muir, THE FRANK MUIR BOOK 1978

LOUIS XVI (1754–1793)
King of France

13 I hear daily more and more affecting accounts of the saint-like end of the martyred Louis. When the king left the Temple to go to the sacrifice the cries of his wretched family were heard loud and shrill through the courts without.
Fanny Burney, letter to her father
4 Feb 1793

1   The path to the scaffold was extremely
     rough and difficult to pass; the King was
     obliged to lean on my arm; I feared for a
     moment that his courage might fail; but
     what was my astonishment, when we
     arrived at the last step, I felt that he
     suddenly let go of my arm, and I saw him
     cross with a firm foot the breadth of the
     whole scaffold. I heard him pronounce dis-
     tinctly these memorable words "I die in-
     nocent of all the crimes laid to my charge; I
     pardon those who have occasioned my
     death; and I pray to God that the blood you
     are going to shed may never be visited on
     France."
     Abbé Edgworth. Quoted J. M. Thomson,
     ENGLISH WITNESSES OF THE FRENCH
     REVOLUTION   1938

2   Seizing with violence the most virtuous of
     kings they dragged him under the axe of the
     guillotine which with one stroke severed his
     head from his body. All this passed in a
     moment. The youngest of the guards, who
     seemed about eighteen, immediately seized
     the head and showed it to the people as he
     walked round the scaffold; he accompanied
     this monstrous ceremony with the most
     atrocious and indecent gestures. At first an
     awful silence prevailed. At length some
     cries of "Vive la Republique!" were heard.
     By degrees the voices multiplied, and be-
     came the universal shout of the multitude.
     Ibid.

3   Citizens, we are talking of a republic yet
     Louis lives. We are talking of a republic and
     the person of the king still stands between
     us and liberty. Because the country must
     live, Louis must die.
     *Maximilien Robespierre. Speech to the
     Convention*   3 Dec 1792

LICINICUS LUCULLUS (c.110–57 BC)
Roman general

4   Lucullus has been admired for many
     accomplishments, but censured for severity
     and extravagance; the expenses of his meals
     were immoderate; his halls were distin-
     guished by the different names of the Gods,
     and when Cicero and Pompey endeavoured
     to surprise him, they were astonished at the
     costliness of a supper prepared on the word
     of Lucullus, who had merely said to a
     servant that he would sup in the hall of
     Apollo.
     John Lempriere, BIBLIOTHECA
     CLASSICA   1788

5   He was a vain man in his ordinary service at
     his board, not only that his beds whereon he

fed were covered with rich carpets of purple, and himself served in rich gold and
silver vessels set with precious stones, and
that there was dancing, music, plays and
other such ordinary pastimes, but also that
he was continually served with all sorts of
fine dainty dishes, with works of pastry and
fruit curiously wrought and prepared, which
only made him to be wondered at by men of
simple understanding and mean condition.
In such things therefore did Lucullus
lavishly and riotously spend his goods, like
spoils indeed gotten of slaves and barbarous
people.
PLUTARCH'S LIVES

MARTIN LUTHER (1483–1546)
German religious reformer

6   The Diet of Worms. Luther's appearing
     there on 17th April 1521 may be considered
     as the greatest scene in Modern European
     history, the point, indeed, from which the
     whole subsequent history of civilisation
     takes its rise.
     Thomas Carlyle, HEROES AND
     HEROWORSHIP   1841

7   A single friar who goes counter to all Chris-
     tianity for a thousand years must be wrong.
     *Charles V, Holy Roman Emperor and King
     of Spain, at Diet of Worms*   19 Apr 1521

8   Luther was guilty of two great crimes — he
     struck the Pope in his crown and the monks
     in their bellies.
     Erasmus, COLLOQUIES   1519

9   I shall never be a heretic, I may err in dis-
     pute; but I do not wish to decide anything
     finally; on the other hand, I am not bound
     by the opinions of men!
     *Luther, letter to George Spaltin, chaplain to
     the Elector of Saxony*   28 Aug 1518

10   I can do no other *(Ich kann nicht anders).*
     *Luther. Closing words of his speech at the
     Diet of Worms. Inscription on his
     monument.*   18 Apr 1521

SIR EDWIN LANDSEER LUTYENS
(1869–1944)
English architect

11   He had been commissioned by Lloyd
     George, only two weeks before it was
     needed, to design a catafalque past which
     the troops could march in the victory parade
     of 1919. He quickly sketched the design for
     his temporary monument. It was built in
     wood and plaster and was an instant suc-
     cess. Next day *The Times* in a leading article

demanded that it be rebuilt in stone and by November 11 1920 the body of the Unknown Warrior was carried past Lutyens' new stone cenotaph.
Roderick Gradidge, The Times, The human face of genius 14 *Nov* 1981

1 That most delightful, good-natured, irresponsible, imaginative jester of genius.
Vita Sackville-West, PEPITA

EDWARD GEORGE BULWER-LYTTON, LORD LYTTON (1804–1873)
English author and politician

2 He never wrote an invitation to dinner without an eye to posterity.
Benjamin Disraeli, REMINISCENCES

3 Bulwer-Lytton I detest. He is the very pimple of the age's humbug.
Nathaniel Hawthorne

4 If he would but leave off scents for his handkerchief, and oil for his hair; if he would confine himself to three clean shirts a week, a couple of coats a year, a beef steak and onions for dinner, his beaker a pewter pot, his carpet a sanded floor, how much might be made of him, even yet.
William Makepeace Thackeray, reviewing, ERNEST MALTRAVERS   1837

M

THOMAS BABINGTON,
LORD MACAULAY (1800–1859)
English historian, essayist and politician

1 An honest, good sort of fellow, made out of oatmeal.
Thomas Carlyle

2 At bottom this Macaulay is but a poor creature with his dictionary literature and erudition, his saloon arrogance. He has no vision in him. He will neither say nor do any great thing.
Ibid.

3 Macaulay was well for a while, but one wouldn't *live* under *Niagara*
Thomas Carlyle. Quoted R. M. Milne,
NOTEBOOK

4 I settled that he was some obscure man of letters or of medicine, perhaps a cholera doctor, when Auckland, who was sitting opposite me, addressed my neighbour, "Mr Macaulay, will you drink a glass of wine?" I thought I should have dropped off my chair . . . here I had been sitting next to him, hearing him talk, and setting him down for a dull fellow.
Charles Greville, DIARY 6 *Feb* 1832

5 It is impossible to mention any book, in any language, with which he is not familiar; to touch upon any subject, whether relating to a person or thing, on which he does not know everything there is to be known.
Ibid. *Jan* 1841

6 His conversation was a procession of one.
Florence Nightingale. Quoted Cecil Woodham-Smith, FLORENCE NIGHTINGALE 1950

7 Macaulay is laying waste society with his waterspouts of talk; people in his company burst for want of an opportunity of dropping in a word.
Henry Reeve

8 Macaulay is like a book in breeches.
Sydney Smith. Quoted Lady Holland,
MEMOIRS

9 He not only overflowed with learning, but stood in the slop.
Ibid.

10 He is certainly more agreeable since his return from India. His enemies might perhaps have said before (though I never did so) that he talked rather too much; but now he has occasional flashes of silence that make his conversation perfectly delightful.
Sydney Smith. Quoted G. O. Trevelyan,
LORD MACAULAY: LIFE AND
LETTERS 1879

11 He could repeat the whole History of the Virtuous Blue-Coat Boy in 3 volumes, post octavo, without a slip. He should take two spoonfuls of the waters of Lethe every morning.
Ibid.

JAMES RAMSAY MACDONALD
(1866–1937)
British Prime Minister

12 He is the greatest living master of falling without hurting himself.
Winston Churchill, House of Commons
21 *Jan* 1921

13 He, more than any other man, has the gift of compressing the largest amount of words into the smallest amount of thought.
Ibid. 23 *Mar* 1933

14 MacDonald was conscientious almost to a fault and he never acquired the art of delegating responsibility; it was said of him that he had been known, when Prime Minister, to look up trains for one of his secretaries.
Lord Elton, DICTIONARY OF NATIONAL BIOGRAPHY

15 He dramatizes his position, as always. Always there is something histrionic and therefore fraudulent about him. I respect and admire him in many ways. But I do now see why many people regard him as a complete humbug.
Harold Nicolson, DIARIES 28 *Apr* 1935

16 We travelled up in the train with Ramsay MacDonald, who spent the time telling long stories of pawky Scots humour so dull that it was almost impossible to tell when the point had been reached.
Bertrand Russell, AUTOBIOGRAPHY 1967

17 Mr MacDonald had become the type of actor which the cruel French call "M'as tu

vu?" "Have you seen me as the Prime Minister? The greatest role, I assure you," Mr MacDonald is anxiously asking the nation. Yes, we have seen him.
John Strachey, THE COMING STRUGGLE FOR POWER 1932

NICCOLO DI BERNARDO DEI MACHIAVELLI (1469–1527)
Florentine author, philosopher and statesman

1 As cunning as Old Nick, and as wicked as Old Nick, were originally meant for our Nicholas Machiavelli, and so came afterwards to be perverted for the devil.
Dr Cocchi. Quoted Rev. Joseph Spence, CHARACTERS, ANECDOTES AND OBSERVATIONS 1820

2 Machiavelli is not an evil genius, nor a cowardly and miserable writer, he is nothing but the fact. And he is not merely the Italian fact, he is the European fact, the fact of the sixteenth century. He seems hideous, and is so, in presence of the moral idea of the nineteenth.
Victor Hugo, LES MISERABLES 1862

WILLIAM McKINLEY (1843–1901)
Twenty-fifth President of the United States

3 He had about as much backbone as a chocolate éclair.
Theodore Roosevelt. Quoted D. H. Elletson, ROOSEVELT AND WILSON; *A comparative study*

4 In his photographs he is always the same. He would never consent to be photographed in a negligent pose and always took the most meticulous care about every detail of his appearance and his posture. He embalmed himself, so far as posterity is concerned.
C. W. Thomson, PRESIDENTS I HAVE KNOWN

HAROLD MACMILLAN (1894–   )
(Lord Stockton)
British Prime Minister

5 By far the most radical man I've known in politics wasn't on the labour side at all — Harold Macmillan. If it hadn't been for the war he'd have joined the Labour party. If that had happened Macmillan would have been Labour Prime Minister, and not me.
Clement Attlee. Quoted James Margach, THE ABUSE OF POWER 1981

6 Harold Macmillan was, and is, a highly complex character. He is an actor to a greater extent than most politicians. Sometimes he is the great aristocrat, sometimes the cultured publisher, sometimes the Edwardian dandy and man-about-town.
John Boyd-Carpenter, WAY OF LIFE

7 One can never escape the suspicion, with Mr Macmillan, that all his life was a preparation for elder statesmanship.
Frank Johnson, The Times 30 Mar 1981

8 I am Macwonder one moment, and Macblunder the next.
Macmillan. Quoted Colin R. Coote, Daily Telegraph 15 Nov 1973

9 Macmillan's no Walpole. "You've never had it so good" is hollow and unconvincing stuff compared with "They now ring the bells, they will soon wring their hands."
Leslie Marsh, Punch, What is history coming to? 1 Aug 1962

10 H. M. always struck me as a parody of a Conservative politician in a novel by Trollope.
Malcolm Muggeridge, CHRONICLE OF WASTED TIME: *The Infernal Grove* 1972

EDOUARD MANET (1832–1883)
French painter, founder of Impressionism

11 Is this drawing? Is this painting? I see garments without seeing the anatomical structure that supports them and explains their movements. I see boneless fingers and heads without skulls. I see sidewhiskers made of two strips of black cloth that could have been glued to the cheeks.
Jules Castagnary, Salons, of Déjeuner sur l'herbe

12 This is a young man's practical joke, and is not worth exhibiting in this way.
Louis Etienne, of Déjeuner sur l'herbe

13 Giorgione had conceived the happy idea of a *fête champêtre* in which although the gentlemen were dressed, the ladies were not. Now some wretched Frenchman has translated this into modern French realism, on a much larger scale, and with the horrible modern French costume instead of the graceful old Venetian one.
Philip Gilbert Hamerton, Fine Arts Quarterly Review, Déjeuner sur l'herbe Oct 1863

14 Unfortunately the nude hasn't a decent figure and one can't think of anything uglier

than the man stretched out next to her, who hasn't even thought of taking off, out of doors, his horrid padded cap. It is the contrast of a creature so inappropriate in a pastoral scene with this undraped bather that is so shocking.
Thoré, L'Indépendance Belge, of Déjeuner sur l'herbe

KATHERINE MANSFIELD (1886–1923)
(Katherine Mansfield Beauchamp)
New Zealand born short story writer

1 Trying to read her after Chekhov was like hearing the carefully artificial tales of a young old-maid compared to those of an articulate and knowing physician who was a good and simple writer.
Ernest Hemingway, A MOVEABLE FEAST 1964

2 Let us hope the insects will bite K. to death.
D. H. Lawrence, in a letter, when Katherine Mansfield was dying.

3 Whenever I prepare for a journey I prepare as though for death. Should I never return, all is in order. That is what life has taught me.
Katherine Mansfield, JOURNALS *(edited by her husband John Middleton Murry)* 1954

4 We could both wish that our first impression of Katherine Mansfield was not that she stinks like — well, a civet cat that had taken to street walking. In truth I am a little shocked by her commonness at first sight; lines so hard and cheap. However, when this diminishes she is so intelligent and inscrutable that she repays friendship.
Virginia Woolf, A WRITER'S DIARY 11 *Oct* 1917

GUGLIELMO MARCHESE MARCONI (1874–1937)
Italian inventor of wireless telegraphy

5 The recently discovered marvel of the electric telegraph without a wire conductor has earned speedy renown for a young Italian student, Guglielmo Marconi of Bologna, whose mother is an English lady. He is but twenty-two years of age, of formidable promise, or threat, of increasing the means of naval warfare is supplied by the notion that a gunpowder magazine on board ship might be fired by electrical agency from a long distance. But we shall see what we shall be.
Illustrated London News, 31 July 1897

MARIE ANTOINETTE (1755–1793)
Wife of King Louis XVI of France

6 It is now sixteen or seventeen years since I saw the Queen of France at Versailles, and surely never lighted on this orb a more delightful vision, glittering like the morning star full of life and splendour and joy.
Edmund Burke, Reflections on the Revolution in France 1790

7 Little did I dream that I should have lived to see disasters fallen upon her in a nation of gallant men, in a nation of men of honour, and of cavaliers. I thought ten thousand swords must have leapt from their scabbards to avenge even a look that threatened her with insult. But the age of chivalry is gone.
Ibid.

JOHN CHURCHILL, FIRST DUKE OF MARLBOROUGH (1652–1722)
British military leader

8 In 1716 he had a paralytic stroke which was followed by senile decay. The story is famous of the broken man, hobbling to gaze at Kneller's portrait which showed him in the full splendour of manhood and murmuring, "That was once a man."
T. Charles Edwards and Brian Richardson, THEY SAW IT HAPPEN 1958

9 The Duke of Marlborough, talking over some point of English history with Bishop Burnet, and advancing some strange anachronisms and matters of fact, his Lordship, in great astonishment at this new history, inquired where he had met with it. The Duke, equally surprised to be asked that question by so knowing a man in history, replied, "Why, don't you remember? It is the only history of those times I have ever read, in Shakespeare's plays."
Gentleman's Magazine 1771

10 He was playing Dean Jones at picquet for sixpence a game, and left off when winning by one game. He desired the Dean to pay him his sixpence. The Dean said he had no silver. The Duke desired he should change a guinea to pay it him because he should want it to pay the chair that would carry him home. The Dean, after so much pressing, did at last get change and paid the Duke his sixpence. After all the bustle that had been made for his sixpence the Duke actually walked home to save that little expense a chair would have put him to.
Alexander Pope. Quoted Rev. Joseph Spence, OBSERVATIONS, ANECDOTES AND CHARACTERS 1820

1 The Duke is a profound dissembler, all the more dangerous that his manner and his words give the impression of frankness itself. His ambition knows no bounds, and an avarice which I can only call sordid guides his entire conduct.
Sicco van Goslinga, MEMOIRS

CHRISTOPHER MARLOWE (1564–1593)
English dramatist

2 There is a lust for power in his writings, a hunger and thirst after unrighteousness, a glow of the imagination unhallowed by any thing except its own energies. His thoughts burn within him like a furnace with bickering flames; or throwing out black smoke and mists, that hide the dawn of genius, or like a poisonous mineral, corrode the heart.
William Hazlitt, DRAMATIC LITERATURE OF THE AGE OF ELIZABETH 1821

3 It so happened that at Deptford, a little village about three miles distant from London, as he went to stab with his poynard one named Ingram, that had invited him thither to a feast, and was then playing at tables, he quickly perceyving it, so avoyded the thrust, that withal drawing out his dagger for his defence, he stabbed this Marlowe in the eye, in such sort, that his braines comming out at the daggers point, hee shortly after dyed.
William Vaughan, GOLDEN GROVE 1600

HARRIET MARTINEAU (1802–1876)
English author

4 Broken into utter wearisomeness, a mind reduced to these three elements; Imbecility, Dogmatism and Unlimited Hope.
Thomas Carlyle

5 Driven to the peak of inspiration by duty, Harriet, in her 53rd year, diagnosed as a dying woman, decided that life as she had known it and intellectualised about, should be set down for posterity. Posterity's duty, in her view, was to read her. So in three months she completed, with the immaculate facility of a born journalist, this self-imposed task, which, clearly, turned out to be a therapeutic exercise, since she then immediately recovered from the menace of impending death, and lived a further robust and productive 21 years.
Kay Dick, The Times, Daunting memoirs of a harridan of virtue 9 Jul 1983

6 My scholars are welcome to read as much Voltaire as they like. His voice is mighty among the ages. Whereas they are entirely forbidden Miss Martineau — not because she is an infidel, but because she is a vulgar and foolish one.
John Ruskin, FORS CLAVIGERA 1887

KARL MARX (1818–1883)
German founder of international socialism, author of Das Kapital

7 Karl Marx wasn't a Marxist all the time. He got drunk in the Tottenham Court Road.
Michael Foot. Quoted Susan Barnes, BEHIND THE IMAGE

8 Much of the world's work is done by men who do not feel quite well. Marx is a case in point.
J. K. Galbraith, THE AGE OF UNCERTAINTY 1977

9 Marx sought to replace natural antagonisms by class antagonisms.
H. G. Wells, SHORT HISTORY OF THE WORLD 1922

MARY I (1516–1558)
Queen of England

10 This woman had the good luck of being advanced to the throne of England, in spite of the superior pretensions, Merit and Beauty of her Cousins Mary Queen of Scotland and Jane Grey. Nor can I pity the Kingdom for the misfortunes they experienced during her Reign, since they fully deserved them, for having allowed her to succeed her Brother — which was a double piece of folly, since they might have foreseen that as she died without children, she would be succeeded by that disgrace to humanity, that pest of society, Elizabeth. Many were the people who fell martyrs to the protestant Religion during her reign; I suppose not fewer than a dozen. She married Philip King of Spain who in her sister's reign was famous for building Armadas. She died without issue, and then the dreadful moment came in which the destroyer of all comfort, the deceitful Betrayer of trust reposed in her, and the Murderess of her Cousin succeeded to the Throne.
Jane Austen, THE HISTORY OF ENGLAND BY A PARTIAL, PREJUDICED AND IGNORANT HISTORIAN

11 Under no other reign in English history during peacetime was so much Christian blood, so many Englishmen's lives been spilled, as under the said Queen Mary.
John Foxe, BOOK OF MARTYRS 1563

1   She makes a great use of jewels in which she delights greatly, and although she has plenty of them left by her predecessors, yet were she better supplied with money than she is, she would doubtless buy many more.
Venetian ambassador

2   She is of very spare diet and never eats until 1 or 2 p.m. although she rises at daybreak when, after saying her prayers and hearing Mass in private, she transacts business incessantly until after midnight, when she returns to rest, for she chooses to give audience, not only to all the members of her Privy Council, and to hear from them every detail of public business, but to all other persons who ask it of her.
Ibid.

MARY (1867–1953)

(Victoria Mary Augusta Louise Olga Pauline Claudine Agnes)
Queen Consort to King George V

3   Queen Mary looked like the Jungfrau, white and sparkling in the sun.
Henry Channon, DIARY   22 *Jun* 1937

4   Queen Mary would never, in any circumstances, use the telephone.
Roger Fulford, HANOVER TO WINDSOR   1960

MARY STUART (1542–1587)

Queen of Scots

5   If I ever really love it will be like Mary Queen of Scots, who said of her Bothwell that she could follow him round the world in her nightie.
J. M. Barrie, WHAT EVERY WOMAN KNOWS *Act* ii   1908

6   Greater abomination was never in the nature of any woman than is in her, whereof we have seen but the bud.
John Knox, HISTORY OF THE REFORMATION IN SCOTLAND

7   This may be truly said, that if a life of exile and misery, endured with almost saintly patience from the 15th June 1567 to the day of her death on the 8th February 1587 could atone for crimes and errors of the class attributed to her, no such penalty was ever more fully discharged than by Mary Stuart.
Walter Scott, HISTORY OF SCOTLAND

JOHN MASEFIELD (1878–1967)

English poet, novelist and dramatist

8   Masefield's sonnet? Ah yes, very nice. Pure Shakespeare. Masefield's *Reynard the Fox*? Very nice too. Pure Chaucer. Masefield's *Everlasting Mercy*? H'm. Yes. Pure Masefield.
Robert Bridges. Quoted Beverley Nichols, TWENTY-FIVE

9   He wrote in a hut in his garden, surrounded by tall gorse bushes, and only appeared at meal times. In the evening he used to read his day's work over to Mrs Masefield, and they corrected it together.
Robert Graves, GOODBYE TO ALL THAT   1929

10 He's a cheap sentimentalist — the cheap Byron of his day.
D. H. Lawrence, letter to Edward Garnett 3 *Mar* 1913

11 One never forgets Masefield's face. It is not the face of a young man, for it is lined and grave. And yet it is not the face of an old man, for youth is still in the bright eyes. Its dominant quality is humility. There were moments when he seemed almost to abase himself before his fellow creatures. And this humility was echoed in everything he did or said, in the quiet, timid tone of his voice, in the way in which he always shrank from exerting himself.
Beverley Nichols, TWENTY-FIVE

HENRI MATISSE (1869–1954)

French painter

12 It is comparatively easy to achieve a certain unity in a picture by allowing one colour to dominate, or by muting all the colours. Matisse did neither. He clashed his colours together like cymbals and the effect was like a lullaby.
John Berger, TOWARD REALITY

13 The goitrous, torpid and squinting husks provided by Matisse in his sculpture are worthless except as tactful decorations for a mental home.
Percy Wyndham Lewis, THE ART OF BEING RULED

WILLIAM SOMERSET MAUGHAM (1874–1965)

English novelist and playwright

14 Willie Maugham has a stopwatch by his side and, on completion of the day's quota, goes to the terrace and prepares for the elaborate ritual of the dry martini.
Cecil Beaton, THE STRENUOUS YEARS

1 One day recently Willie was walking in the garden with his companion Alan Searle, when they stopped in their tracks to watch the progress of a snail. Alan picked up a small bit of gravel and tossed it at the snail. Willie shouted "Don't do that!" Alan threw another little pebble. The next thing Alan knew he was lying with an unrecognisable face in a nearby hospital.
Ibid.

2 Two fundamental failings rob him of greatness. His works do not suggest those "mysteries" which, as Proust puts it "have their explanation probably only in other worlds and a presentiment of which is precisely what moves us most in life and art". His other fault is the fear of appearing old-fashioned.
William Gerhardie, MEMOIRS OF A POLYGLOT 1925

3 My world popularity is the most interesting thing about me.
W. Somerset Maugham. Quoted Ted Morgan, SOMERSET MAUGHAM 1980

4 He combined an Edwardian sense of propriety about the details of his own life with a pirate's instinct towards his literary material. He had a low opinion of the human species, but a high tolerance of human frailties.
Ibid.

WILLIAM LAMB, VISCOUNT MELBOURNE (1779–1848)
British Prime Minister

5 Lord Melbourne was thus in Queen Victoria's journals preserved for posterity. What other man has had his sovereign for a Boswell?
Louis Auchincloss, PERSONS OF CONSEQUENCE: *Queen Victoria and her circle* 1979

6 Of all the men who had held supreme office none was ever so thoroughly a man of the world. He never dined at home, talked with a rollicking laugh and refused to take anything — even his own loss of office — too seriously. It was his creed that it was best to try to do no good, and then one could do no harm; his favourite remark, "Why not leave it alone?"
Arthur Bryant, ENGLISH SAGA

7 Lord Melbourne sees the Queen every day for a couple of hours, and his situation is certainly the most dictatorial, the most despotic, that the world has seen. Wolsey and Walpole were in strait waistcoats compared to him.
John Wilson Croker, letter to Sir Robert Peel 17 Aug 1837

8 I have no doubt that Melbourne is as passionately fond of the Queen as he might be of his daughter if he had one; and the more because he has a capacity for loving without anything to love. It is become his province to educate, instruct and form the most interesting mind and character in the world.
Charles Greville, MEMOIRS

9 Now is it to lower the price of corn, or isn't it? It is not much to matter what we say, but we must all say *the same*.
Melbourne at a cabinet meeting Mar 1841

10 I am sorry to hurt any man's feelings and to brush away the magnificent fabric of gaiety and levity that he has reared, but I accuse our minister of honesty and diligence.
Sydney Smith

11 He is nothing more than a sensible, honest man who means to do his duty to his Sovereign and his country, instead of the ignorant man he pretends to be.
Ibid.

12 He is the person who makes us feel safe and comfortable.
Queen Victoria, JOURNAL 4 Jul 1838

GEORGE MEREDITH (1828–1909)
English novelist and poet

13 His obscurity, like that of Carlyle and Browning, is due less to extreme subtlety than to the plethoric abundance of his ideas. He cannot stop to express himself. If he could he might be more popular.
Max Beerbohm, OUIDA

14 At best, a sort of daintily dressed Walt Whitman.
G. K. Chesterton, THE VICTORIAN AGE IN LITERATURE 1913

15 What with the faking, what with the preaching, which was never agreeable and is now said to be hollow, and what with the home counties posing as the universe, it is no wonder Meredith now lies in a trough.
E. M. Forster, ASPECTS OF THE NOVEL 1927

16 He is much the wittiest Englishman, and the most famed for conversation, that I have ever known — for playing with intellectual fire. His main fault is that he thinks he is French, which he is not.
Henry James, LETTERS, VOL 3 1883–1895

1 Meredith is, to me, chiefly a stink. I should never write of him as I detest him too much ever to trust myself to criticise him.
Ezra Pound, letter to John Quinn
4 Jun 1918

2 To read Meredith to our greatest advantage we must make certain allowances and relax certain standards. We must not expect the perfect quietude of a traditional style, nor the triumphs of a patient and pedestrian psychology.
Virginia Woolf, SECOND COMMON READER 1932

MICHELANGELO BUONARROTI
(1475–1564)
Florentine painter and sculptor

3 He was a good sort of man, but didn't know how to paint.
El Greco

4 The whole is a scene of enormous, ghastly confusion, in which you can only make out quantity and number, and vast uncouth masses of bone and muscle.
William Hazlitt, of THE LAST JUDGEMENT

5 Lump the whole thing! Say the Creator made Italy from designs by Michelangelo.
Mark Twain, INNOCENTS ABROAD 1869

6 None will marvel that Michelangelo should be a lover of solitude, devoted as he is to Art, which demands the whole man, with all his thoughts, for herself.
Giorgio Vasari, LIVES OF THE PRINCIPAL PAINTERS, ARCHITECTS AND SCULPTURES 1550

SIR JOHN EVERETT MILLAIS (1829–1896)
English painter

7 In the foreground of the carpenter's shop is a hideous, wry-necked, blubbering red-headed boy in a nightgown, who appears to have received a poke playing in a neighbouring gutter and to be holding it up for the contemplation of a kneeling woman so horrible in her ugliness that (supposing it were possible for any human creature to exist for a moment with that dislocated throat) she would stand out from the rest of the company as a monster in the vilest cabaret in France or the lowest gin-shop in Europe.
Charles Dickens, Household Words, of Millais' Christ in the House of his Parents

8 This strangely unequal painter — a painter whose imperfectly great powers always suggest to me the legend of the spiteful fairy

at the christening feast. The name of Mr Millias' spiteful fairy is vulgarity.
Henry James, Nation, The Grosvenor Gallery 23 *May* 1878

9 Millais' was a complex and multiple career. He had a keen sense of the touching mystery of a child's facial expression. His *Blind Girl* is a miracle by which he will survive . . . That was his scale . . . His interest was in faces.
W. R. Sickert, Manchester Guardian 2 *Mar* 1926

HENRY MILLER (1891–   )
American author

10 Miller is not really a writer, but a non-stop talker to whom someone has given a typewriter.
Gerald Brennan, THOUGHTS IN A DRY SEASON 1981

11 I went back to intuition when I turned to Henry, who represents the non-rational. The very fact that he is all paradox and contraries, unresolved and without care, is like life itself.
Anaïs Nin, DIARIES, VOL II 1967

12 I don't think he has read a pornographic book in his life. Pornography puts him to sleep, he has told me time and again.
Alfred Perles, MY FRIEND HENRY MILLER 1955

13 At least, an unprintable book that's readable.
Ezra Pound, of TROPIC OF CANCER

14 Last week I went up to London to meet Henry Miller who is a dear, mad, mild man, bald and fifty, with great enthusiasm for commonplaces.
Dylan Thomas, letter to Vernon Watkins

JOHN MILTON (1608–1674)
English poet

15 He was mightily importuned to go into France and Italie. Foreigners came much to see him and offered him great preferments to come over to them, and the only inducement of several foreigners that came over into England was chiefly to see O. Protector and Mr J. Milton, and would see the house and chamber where he was born; he was much more admired abroad than at home.
John Aubrey, BRIEF LIVES 1680

16 Milton the prince of poets — so we say / A little heavy but no less divine / An inde-

pendent being in his day — / Learn'd, pious, temperate in love and wine.
Lord Byron, DON JUAN, *canto* iii   1824

1   The words of Milton were true in all things, and were never truer than in this: "He who would write heroic poems must make his whole life a heroic poem."
Thomas Carlyle, ESSAYS: BURNS

2   The whole of Milton's poem, *Paradise Lost*, is such barbarous trash, so outrageously offensive to reason and to common sense that one is naturally led to wonder how it can have been tolerated by a people amongst whom astronomy, navigation and chemistry are understood.
William Cobbett, A YEAR'S RESIDENCE IN THE UNITED STATES

3   As a poet, Milton seems to me the greatest of eccentrics. His work illustrates no general principles of good writing; the only principles of writing that it illustrates are such as are valid only for Milton himself to observe.
T. S. Eliot, ESSAYS: MILTON

4   The peculiar feeling, almost a physical sensation of a breathless leap, communicated by Milton's long periods, and by his alone, is impossible to procure from rhymed verse.
Ibid.

5   After I had, with the best Attention read it [*Paradise Lost*] through he asked me how I liked it and what I thought of it; I pleasantly said to him, Thou hast said much here of *Paradise Lost*, but what hast thou to say of *Paradise Found*? He made me no answer but sate some time in a Muse; then broke off that Discourse and fell upon another subject. Afterwards he shewed me his Second Poem called *Paradise Regained* and in a pleasant tone said to me, "This is owing to you! For you put it into my head by the question you put to me which, before, I had not thought of."
Thomas Ellwood, HISTORY OF HIS LIFE   1714

6   The poems of Milton betray a narrowness of education and a degeneracy of habit. His theological quibbles and perplexed speculations are daily equalled and excelled by the most abject enthusiasts, and if we consider him as a prose writer, he has neither the learning of a scholar nor the manners of a gentleman. There is no force in his reasonings, no eloquence in his style, and no taste in his composition.
Oliver Goldsmith

7   He that rode sublime / Upon the seraph wings of Ecstasy / The secrets of th' Abyss to spy / He pass'd the flaming bounds of Place and Time / The living Throne, the sapphire blaze / Where Angels tremble while they gaze. He saw, but blasted with excess of light / Closed his eyes in endless night.
Thomas Gray, PROGRESS OF POETRY

8   "I never read *Paradise Lost*," said a celebrated Cambridge mathematician. "But you must read it, everybody has read Milton's great epic," said his friend. "Well, as it is absolutely necessary, I shall read it." After a short respite the mathematician said to his friend, "I have read your famous poem; I have read it attentively; but what does it prove? There is more instruction in half a page of Euclid! A man might read Milton's poem a hundred, aye a thousand times, and he would never learn that the angles at the base of an isoceles triangle are equal."
Jefferson Hogg, LIFE OF SHELLEY   1858

9   And malt does more than Milton can / To justify God's way to man.
A. E. Housman, A SHROPSHIRE LAD, LXII   1896

10   *Paradise Lost* is a book that, once put down, is very hard to pick up again.
Samuel Johnson. Quoted Boswell, THE LIFE OF JOHNSON   1791

11   He was a Phidias that could cut a Colossus out of rock, but could not cut heads out of cherry stones.
Samuel Johnson. Quoted Hannah More, MEMOIRS AND LETTERS

12   Milton seems to the colleges profound because he wrote of hell, a great place, and is dead.
Stephen Leacock, CHARLES DICKENS

13   Reading *Paradise Lost* is a matter of resisting, of standing up against the verse-movement, of subduing it into something tolerably like sensitiveness, and in the end our resistance is worn down; we surrender at last to the monotony of ritual.
F. R. Leavis, REVALUATION

14   The agreement between "John Milton, gent, of the one part, and Samuel Symons, printer, of the other part" is among the curiosities of our literary history. The curiosity consists in the contrast between the present fame of the book and the waste-paper price at which the copyright was valued. The author received £5 down, was to receive a second £5 when the first edition

should be sold, a third £5 when the second, and so on. Milton lived to receive the second £5 and no more. £10 in all for *Paradise Lost*.
Mark Pattison, MILTON   1879

1   There was a period in his life when Fox used to say that he could not forgive Milton for having occasioned him the trouble of reading through a poem — *Paradise Lost*, three parts of which was not worth reading. He afterwards, however, estimated it more justly.
Samuel Rogers, TABLE TALK   1856

2   This obscure, eccentric and disgusting poem.
Voltaire, of PARADISE LOST

3   The old blind schoolmaster hath published a tedious poem on the Fall of Man. If its length be not considered its merit, it hath no other.
Edmund Waller

4   That mighty orb of song, the divine Milton.
William Wordsworth, THE EXCURSION

5   The sightless Milton, with his hair / Around his placid temples curled.
William Wordsworth, THE ITALIAN ITINERANT

6   Milton! Thou shouldst be living at this hour / England hath need of thee.
William Wordsworth, LONDON   1802

MOLIÈRE (1622–1673)
(Jean-Baptiste Poquelin)
French dramatist

7   Molière had cruel enemies, especially among the inferior writers of the day and their cliques. He also aroused the opposition of the pious, who accused him of writing scandalous books. He was charged with having exposed the characters of powerful persons in the characters of his plays, whereas he had done nothing but hold up views in general for the reprobation of mankind. He would have suffered punishment as a result of these accusations had not Louis XIV, who had encouraged and supported Racine and Despreaux, likewise protected him.
Voltaire, LIFE OF MOLIÈRE

8   From 1658 to 1673 Molière wrote and produced all his plays, to the number of thirty. He had ambitions to play tragedy, but in this field was not successful. He was exceedingly voluble in speech and had a sort of hiccough which was quite unsuitable to serious roles. This, however, only served to make his acting in comedy more enjoyable.
Ibid.

JAMES FITZROY SCOTT, DUKE OF MONMOUTH
(1649–1685)
English pretender

9   Young Monmouth was a liability to anyone who espoused his cause. He had inherited his father's sexual prowess and his mother's brains.
J. P. Kenyon, THE STUARTS   1958

MARILYN MONROE (1926–1962)
(Norma Jeane Baker)
American film actress

10   If she was a victim of any kind, she was a victim of her friends.
George Cukor. Quoted Gavin Lambert, ON CUKOR

11   She was never permitted to mature into a warm, vibrant woman, or fully use her gifts for comedy, despite the signals and flares she kept sending up. Instead she was turned into a figure of mockery in the parts she played and to the men she played with.
Molly Haskell, FROM REVERENCE TO RAPE

12   She was good at being inarticulately abstracted for the same reason that midgets are good at being short.
Clive James, AT THE PILLARS OF HERCULES

13   A very Stradivarius of sex, so gorgeous, forgiving, humorous, compliant and tender that even the most mediocre musician would relax his lack of art in the dissolving magic of her violin.
Norman Mailer, MARILYN

14   Of course, as a sex symbol she was stunning, but sadly, she must be one of the silliest women I ever met.
Donald Sinden, A TOUCH OF THE MEMOIRS

ELIZABETH MONTAGU (1728–1800)
English author and blue stocking hostess

15   Mrs Montagu does not make a trade of her wit; but Mrs Montagu is a very extraordinary woman; she has a constant stream of conversation; and it is always impregnated; it always has meaning.
Samuel Johnson. Quoted Boswell, THE LIFE OF JOHNSON   1791

16   Mrs Montagu received me with the most encouraging kindness; she is not only the

finest genius, but the finest lady I ever saw; she lives in the highest style of magnificence; her apartments and table are in the most splendid taste; but what baubles are these when speaking of a Montagu? Her form (for she has no *body*) is delicate even to fragility; her countenance the most animated in the world; the sprightly vivacity of fifteen, with the judgement and experience of a Nestor. But I fear she is hastening to decay very fast; her spirits are so active that they must soon wear out the little frail receptacle that holds them.
Hannah More, letter to her sister 1775

1 Mrs Montagu was extremely rich, a happy circumstance which she did nothing to hide. She built a mansion in Portman Square, one room of which she herself covered with feathers from almost every known bird. It was in that room she later gave a breakfast party for seven hundred guests. Her best known literary work was an essay (of 288 pages) defending Shakespeare against the opinions of Voltaire.
Frank Muir, THE FRANK MUIR BOOK 1975

2 She deserved the respect of contemporary society because she was as fine a justification for the capitalist system as the time provided, and not to remember her as that today is to withhold justice.
Rebecca West, ELIZABETH MONTAGU

LADY MARY WORTLEY MONTAGU
(1689–1762)
English author

3 Lady Mary lived before the age in which people wasted half their lives washing the whole of their bodies.
Walter Bagehot, ESTIMATIONS IN CRITICISM

4 I have got fifty or sixty of Mr Pope's letters by me. You shall see what a goddess he made of me in them, though he makes such a devil of me afterwards in his writings, without any reason that I know of.
Lady Mary Wortley Montagu. Quoted Rev. Joseph Spence, OBSERVATIONS, ANECDOTES AND CHARACTERS 1820

5 When I was very young I was a vast admirer of Ovid's *Metamorphoses* and that was one of the chief reasons that set me upon the thoughts of studying the Latin language. Mr Wortley was the only person to whom I communicated my design and he encouraged me in it. I used to study for five or six hours a day for two years in my father's library and so got that language whilst everybody

else thought I was reading nothing but novels and romances.
Ibid.

6 A dilapidated macaw, with a hard, piercing laugh, mirthless and joyless, with a few unimaginative phrases, with a parrot's powers of observation and a parrot's hard and poisonous bite.
Edith Sitwell, ALEXANDER POPE 1930

7 Her dress, her avarice and her independence must amaze anyone that never heard her name. She wears a foul mob that does not cover her greasy black locks, that hang loose, never combed or curled, an old mazarine blue wrapper, that gapes open and discovers a canvas petticoat.
Horace Walpole, letter to Hon. H. S. Conway 25 Sep 1740

8 With regard to the indelicacy of Lady Mary's letters, no thinking person can exonerate her from having had a corrupted mind, whatever her conduct may, or may not, have been. Neither do we accept the late Lord Wharncliffe's excuse, that it was in accordance with the times that Lady Mary indulged in *double entendre* and in expressions neither to be written nor uttered by a modest woman.
Brace Whatron, QUEENS OF SOCIETY 1860

MONTGOLFIER BROTHERS
(Joseph Michel (1740–1810) and
Jacques Etienne (1745–1799)
French experimental balloonists

9 Joseph Montgolfier was a dreamer, and a maverick, the very type of the inventor, imaginative with objects and processes, impractical in business and affairs. Etienne was a complete contrast, a sharp administrator with an eye for cost and detail, the man who kept the family business going while his brother was gadding round the houses of the aristocracy, giving flying demonstrations.
Charles Coulston Gillespie, THE MONTGOLFIER BROTHERS 1983

10 The Montgolfiers were unlikely aviators. They were scions of a prosperous provincial paper-making family. They had 17 brothers and sisters, which may explain why they were so keen to get aloft and stay there.
John Naughton, Observer, Enterprising Gasbags 21 Aug 1983

11 The family paper-making connection is important. Paper was an essential element in the fabric of the early balloons, which were made of taffeta with a paper skin, which explains why their early balloons were so

gorgeously decorated, for essentially they appear to have been clad in eighteenth century wallpaper.
Ibid.

BERNARD LAW, VISCOUNT MONTGOMERY OF ALAMEIN (1887–1976)
British Field Marshal

1 He was almost insanely jealous. Nobody must share the credit and the glory. He and he alone had gained it and, although the sun of his glory could shine down on those who had served under him, there must be no other source of light.
Field Marshal Lord Carver, The Times, Monty; the toughest battle 8 Jun 1981

2 In defeat he is unbeatable, in victory, unbearable.
Winston Churchill. Quoted Edward Marsh, AMBROSIA AND SMALL BEER

3 If he is to do himself full justice he must cultivate tact, tolerance, and discretion.
Comment of his commanding officer when he was a colonel in 1932. Quoted Nigel Hamilton, MONTY: THE MAKING OF A GENERAL 1981

GEORGE AUGUSTUS MOORE (1852–1935)
Irish novelist

4 That old pink, petulant walrus.
Henry Channon, DIARY 20 May 1941

5 George Moore unexpectedly pinched my behind; I felt rather honoured that my behind should have drawn the attention of the great master of English prose.
Ilka Chase

6 Susan Mitchell sensed something lacking. Women are like that. She wrote "Some men kiss and do not tell. Some men kiss and tell; but George Moore tells and does not kiss."
Oliver St. John Gogarty, AS I WAS WALKING DOWN SACKVILLE STREET 1937

7 The technical perfection of the novels of Mr George Moore does not prevent them from being faultlessly dead.
Q. D. Leavis, FICTION AND THE READING PUBLIC

8 An inveterate romancer whose crimson inventions suggested that he had been brought into the world by a union of Victor Hugo and Ouida.
George Bernard Shaw, PEN PORTRAITS AND REVIEWS

9 George Moore is always conducting his education in public.
Oscar Wilde. Quoted Hesketh Pearson, LIFE OF OSCAR WILDE 1946

10 George Moore wrote brilliant English until he discovered grammar.
Ibid.

11 He leads his readers to the latrine and locks them in.
Ibid.

SIR JOHN MOORE (1761–1809)
Scottish General

12 I wish Sir John had united something of the Christian with the hero in his death.
Jane Austen, LETTERS 1809 (*published 1932*)

13 Not a drum was heard, not a funeral note / As his corpse to the rampart we hurried / Not a soldier discharged his farewell shot / O'er the grave where our hero was buried / . . . Slowly and sadly we laid him down / From the field of fame fresh and gory; / We carved not a line and we raised not a stone — / But we left him alone with his glory.
William Cowper, BURIAL OF SIR JOHN MOORE AT CORUNNA

HANNAH MORE (1745–1833)
English novelist, dramatist, pamphleteer and social reformer

14 She was born with a birch-broom in her hand, and worst of all was a shameless flatterer and insatiable of flattery. Her acceptance of a pension in compensation for a husband is a vile blot, never to be expunged from her character.
Caroline Bowles, letter to Robert Southey 21 Dec 1834

15 She led a happier life than anyone I ever heard of. All that elegant luxury afforded, she enjoyed, without the care, anxiety and expense that their owners find unavoidable; she luxuriated in the highest intellectual pleasures and drank them from the purest sources, living as she did with the wise, the worthy, the witty and the elegant, the learned, the pious, philosophers and saints. Of the praise that flows from the heart no queen or princess ever received more to the last day of her protracted, though not painless, existence.
Mrs Ann Grant, LETTERS

16 With all her might Hannah, and her sisters, acted as missionaries throughout these Somersetshire wolds, where the country was

so beautiful and the people so degraded. Her dramas and poems, stories and essays, important as they are, pale in interest before the records which tell of ten schools she established, and of the simple stories and verses she wrote, at a loss to herself, to be sold cheaply by hawkers among the poor of the district.
W. R. Richmond, HISTORY OF SOMERSET

SIR THOMAS MORE (1478–1535)
English statesman

1   My Lord Ambassador, we understand that the king your master hath put his faithful servant and grave wise councillor, Sir Thomas More, to death. This will we say, that if we had been master of such a servant of whose doings we ourselves have had these many years no small experience, we would rather have lost the best city of our dominions than have lost such a worthy councillor.
Charles V, Holy Roman Emperor and King of Spain to Sir Thomas Eliott, on hearing of More's execution   July 1535

2   He diligently cultivates true piety while being remote from all superstitious observance. He has set hours in which he offers to God not the customary prayers, but prayers from the heart. With his friends he talks of the life of the world to come so that one sees he speaks sincerely and not without firm hope.
Erasmus, letter to Ulrich Von Hutten 25 Jul 1519

3   In human relations he looks for pleasure in everything he comes across, even in the gravest matters. If he has to do with intelligent and educated men he takes pleasure in their brilliance; if with the ignorant and foolish men he enjoys their foolery. He is not put out by perfect fools, and suits himself with marvellous dexterity to all men's feelings. For women generally, even for his wife, he has nothing but jests and merriment.
Ibid.

4   In social intercourse he is of so rare a courtesy and charm of manners that there is no man so melancholy that he does not gladden, no subject so forbidding that he does not dispel the tedium of it. From his boyhood he has loved joking, so that he might seem born for this, but in his jokes he has never descended to buffoonery, and has never loved the biting jest.
Ibid.

5   When did Nature mould a temper more gentle, endearing and happy than the temper of Thomas More?
Erasmus. Quoted Jasper Ridley, THE STATESMAN AND THE FANATIC

6   When we reflect that Sir Thomas More was ready to die for the doctrine of Transubstantiation we cannot but feel some doubt whether the doctrine may not triumph over all opposition. More was a man of excellent talents. He had all the information of the subject that we have, or that while the world lasts any human being will have. The text "This is my body" was in his New Testament as it is in ours. The absurdity of the literal interpretation was as great and as obvious in the sixteenth century as it is now. No progress that science has made, or will make, can add to what seems to us the overwhelming force of argument against the Real Presence. We are therefore unable to understand why what Sir Thomas believed respecting Transubstantiation may not be believed to the end of time by men equal in abilities and honesty to Sir Thomas More. But Sir Thomas More is one of the choice specimens of wisdom and virtue; and the doctrine of Transubstantiation is kind of proof charge. A faith that stands that test will stand any test.
T. B. Macaulay, Edinburgh Review, Von Ranke's history of the popes   Oct 1840

7   Sir Thomas More is a man of angel's wit and singular learning. I know not his fellow. For where is the man of that gentleness, lowliness and affability? And as time requireth, a man of marvellous mirth and pastimes, and sometimes as sad a gravity. A man for all seasons.
Robert Whittinton, passage composed for schoolboys to put into Latin

8   The day appointed for his execution being come, about nine of the clock he was brought out of the Tower, ascending the scaffold, he seemed so weak that he was ready to fall; whereupon he said merrily to the Lieutenant, "I pray you, Mr Lieutenant, see me safely up, and for my coming down let me shift for myself."
Winstanley, ENGLAND'S WORTHIES

JOHN PIERPONT MORGAN (1837–1913)
American financier

9   J. P. Morgan, it is worth remembering, spent millions on manuscripts and artifacts brought over from the lands of precisely

those immigrants who could be bought in job lots for eight cents an hour.
Alistair Cooke, AMERICA

1 Morgan's ruby nose added to his personal fame and with some humour he once said "It would be impossible for me to appear on the streets without it." His nose, he remarked on another occasion, was "part of the American business structure".
Stewart Holbrook, THE AGE OF THE MOGULS

2 It is commonly supposed that J. P. was a self-made man and that the Almighty was thereby relieved of an awful responsibility. Not true; he inherited money, power, and a fine start in life from his Pa, old Junius Morgan, though he was nearly fifty before the old man finally gave up the ghost.
John Naughton, Observer, reviewing Andrew Sinclair's CORSAIR: *The Life of J. P. Morgan* 21 Jun 1982

3 Pierpont would collect everything, from a pyramid to Mary Magdalene's tooth.
Mary Anderson de Navarro. Quoted Andrew Sinclair, CORSAIR 1981

GEORGE MORLAND (1763–1804)
English painter

4 His proud father ruined his life by only allowing him to leave his drawing and painting for an hour at twilight. His pals would assemble under his window in the afternoon, and George would let down to them by a string some drawings of improper subjects which they would go off and sell; so that by sunset they had a sum of money ready to enjoy with the young artist.
Julia de Wolf Addison, THE ART OF THE NATIONAL GALLERY 1905

5 He died in delirium tremens in a sponging house, when he was not yet forty-two years old; and yet, in spite of his neglect, his wife was so much overcome with grief at his death that she went into convulsions and died herself. They were buried in one grave. He had composed his own epitaph "Here lies a drunken dog". Poor Morland, it was appallingly simple and true.
Ibid.

WILLIAM MORRIS (1834–1896)
English poet, painter and designer

6 He is unquestionably an all-round man, but the act of walking round him has always tired me.
Max Beerbohm. Quoted S. N. Behrman, CONVERSATIONS WITH MAX 1960

7 With a grey beard like the foam of the sea, with grey hair through which he continually ran his hands, erect and curly on his forehead, with a hooked nose, a florid complexion and clean, clear eyes, dressed in a blue serge coat and carrying, as a rule, a satchel, to meet him was always, as it were, to meet a sailor ashore.
Ford Madox Ford, ANCIENT LIGHTS 1911

8 The dream-world of Morris was as much the antithesis of daily life as with other men of genius, but he was never conscious of the antithesis and so knew nothing of intellectual suffering.
W. B. Yeats, AUTOBIOGRAPHIES 1955

WOLFGANG AMADEUS MOZART
(1756–1791)
Austrian musician and composer

9 Whether the angels play only Bach praising God I am not quite sure, I am sure however that *en famille* they play Mozart.
Karl Barth. Quoted New York Times 11 Dec 1968

10 If I were a dictator I should make it compulsory for every member of the population between the ages of four and eighty to listen to Mozart for at least a quarter of an hour daily for the coming five years.
Sir Thomas Beecham. Quoted Harold Atkins and Archie Newman, BEECHAM STORIES

11 Play Mozart in memory of me — and I will hear you.
Chopin

12 Dined with Goethe. We talked of Mozart. "I saw him," said Goethe, "when he was seven and gave a concert while travelling our way. I myself was about fourteen, and I remember perfectly the little man with his frisure and sword."
J. P. Eckermann, CONVERSATIONS WITH GOETHE 1837

13 For Mozart each work was a task to be performed. It is thus fruitless to search his music for the emotion he experienced while composing it.
Wolfgang Hildesheimer, MOZART 1983

14 It is sobering to consider that when Mozart was my age he had been dead a year.
Tom Lehrer. Quoted Nat Shapiro, ENCYCLOPEDIA OF QUOTATIONS ABOUT MUSIC

1 You ask my opinion about taking the young Salzburg musician into your service. I do not know where you can place him, since you do not need a composer, or other useless people . . . It gives one's service a bad name when such people run about like beggars.
Empress Maria Theresa, letter to the Archduke Ferdinand 1771

2 I was introduced to the people of Mannheim. Some who knew me by repute were very polite and fearfully respectful; others, however, who had never heard of me, stared at me wide-eyed, and certainly in a rather sneering manner. They probably think because I am little and young nothing great or mature can come out of me; but they will soon see.
Mozart, letter to his father 31 *Oct* 1777

3 The sonatas of Mozart are unique; they are too easy for children and too difficult for adults.
Arthur Schnabel, MY LIFE AND MUSIC

4 Mozart, asked for an explanation of his works, said frankly, "How do I know?"
George Bernard Shaw, THE PERFECT WAGNERITE

5 From Mozart I learned to say important things in a conversational way.
George Bernard Shaw in conversation with Ferruccio Busoni

6 There is no shadow of death anywhere in Mozart's music. Even his funeral was a failure. It was dispersed by a shower of rain, and to this day nobody knows where he was buried.
George Bernard Shaw, MUSIC IN LONDON

7 The finale of Mozart's Jupiter Symphony is like the Cathedral of Cologne.
Dmitri Shostakovich, TESTIMONY

8 No composer had ever understood the qualities of individual instruments as did Mozart; neither has anyone, except Mozart, had such power in imparting a quality of ephemeral beauty, so that, in a Serenade or Cassation, the impression is given that this is the most beautiful little thing ever heard, and that it was only meant for a single performance and no more than that.
Sacheverell Sitwell, MOZART 1932

9 What Mozart did, that is, composed up to his thirty-sixth year, no copyist could write down in the same amount of time.
Franz Strauss. Quoted by his son Richard Strauss, MELODIC INSPIRATION 1940

10 I remember being handed a score composed by Mozart at the age of eleven. What could I say? I felt like de Kooning, who was asked to comment on a certain abstract painting and answered in the negative. He was then told it was the work of a celebrated monkey. "That's different. For a monkey, it's terrific."
Igor Stravinsky. Quoted Robert Craft, CONVERSATIONS WITH STRAVINSKY 1958

MALCOLM MUGGERIDGE (1903–)
English writer

11 The most wonderful deceitful character, saved by his sense of humour.
Osbert Lancaster. Quoted Duncan Fallowell, The Times 11 *Oct* 1982

12 He thinks he was knocked off his horse by God, like St Paul on the road to Damascus. His critics think he simply fell off from old age.
Katherine Whitehorn, Observer 20 *May* 1979

IRISH MURDOCH (1919–)
English novelist

13 She is like a character out of Hieronymus Bosch — the very nicest character.
Rachel Billington, The Times, Profile, Iris Murdoch 25 *Apr* 1983

14 A tousled heel-less, ladder-stockinged little lady — crackling with intelligence, but nothing at all of a prig.
The Hon. George Lyttelton, THE LYTTELTON HART-DAVIS LETTERS 1959

BARTOLOMÉ ESTABAN MURILLO (1618–1682)
Spanish artist

15 In Spain I did not think much of Murillo.
Lord Byron, letter to John Murray 14 *Apr* 1817

16 Lord Godolphin bought the pictures of the boys by Murillo the Spaniard, for 80 guineas. Dear enough!
John Evelyn, DIARY 1906

17 . . . the brown gleams of gipsy Madonna-hood from Murillo.
John Ruskin

BENITO MUSSOLINI (1883–1945)
Italian dictator

1 He was a splendid actor with a good sense of
stage management. The visitor shown into
the huge study in the Palazzo Venezia was
embarrassed to see the Duce at his desk in
the diagonally opposite corner and the
embarrassment was increased, at least in my
case, by the way in which he went on working as if he was alone.
Vernon Bartlett, I KNOW WHAT I LIKE

2 The crafty, cold-blooded, black-hearted
Italian.
*Winston Churchill, radio broadcast
9 Feb 1941*

3 Italy's pinchbeck Caesar.
*Winston Churchill. Speech, London
Guildhall   30 Jun 1943*

4 This whipped jackal is frisking by the side of
the German tiger.
*Winston Churchill, House of Commons
Apr 1941*

5 The bloody beast is dead.
*Winston Churchill announcing the death of
Mussolini*

6 Kipling cherished an unworthy admiration
for Mussolini — the only journalist, so far as
I know, to become a dictator.
*Jan Morris, Daily Telegraph,
The Marvel of Kipling   20 Oct 1978*

7 I have a tremendous admiration for Caesar,
but I myself belong rather to the class of
Bismarck.
Mussolini to Emil Ludwig

8 My ambition is this; I want to make the
people of Italy strong, prosperous and free.
*Mussolini. Speech to the Italian senate
8 Jun 1923*

9 Asked by his ex-son-in-law, the comedian
Vic Oliver, to name the greatest name of
World War II, Winston Churchill retorted
peremptorily, "Mussolini. He, at least, had
the courage to kill his son-in-law."
*Samedi Soir (Paris). Quoted News Review
28 Nov 1946*

10 I have great personal admiration for
Mussolini, who has welded a nation out of a
collection of touts, blackmailers, ice-cream
vendors and gangsters.
*Letter to Saturday Review. Quoted Michael
Bateman*, THIS ENGLAND

11 Sawdust Caesar.
George Seldes, book title

N

NAPOLEON I (1769–1821)
(Napoleon Bonaparte)
Emperor of France

1 That infernal creature who is the curse of all the human race becomes every day more and more abominable.
Tsar Alexander I, in a letter to his sister Catherine 5 Jan 1812

2 He is an ordinary human being after all! Now he will trample under foot the Rights of Man, being a slave to his own ambition; now he will push himself above everyone else and become a tyrant.
Beethoven, on hearing that Napoleon had proclaimed himself Emperor 1804

3 Napoleon is a dangerous man in a free country. He seems to me to have the makings of a tyrant, and I believe that were he to be king he would be fully capable of playing such a part, and his name would become an object of detestation to posterity and every right-minded patriot.
Lucien Bonaparte in a letter to his brother Joseph 1790

4 Crushed was Napoleon by the northern Thor / Who knocked his army down with an icy hammer.
Lord Byron, BEPPO

5 Napoleon has not been conquered by men. He was greater than any of us. God punished him because he relied solely on his own intelligence until that incredible instrument was so strained that it broke.
Charles XIV of Sweden of Napoleon's death 1821

6 Only after I had taken part in the government of men did I learn to be just to Napoleon.
François Guizet, French Prime Minister, MEMOIRS 1858

7 Napoleon — mighty somnambulist of a vanished dream.
Victor Hugo, LES MISERABLES 1862

8 God was bored by him.
Victor Hugo, LES CHATIMENTS

9 Napoleon is a torrent which as yet we are unable to stem. Moscow will be the sponge that will suck him dry.
Marshal Mikhail Kutnzov. Address to Russian troops 13 Sep 1812

10 Napoleon gets very sulky if he is not treated with that deference and respect he has been accustomed to, and sometimes appears quite peevish and sullen. His followers the Generals pay him just the same respect as if he was still emperor.
Letter from an unknown officer aboard HMS Northumberland taking Napoleon to St. Helena. Quoted Rachel Leighton, Cornhill Magazine Mar 1933

11 I am the successor, not of Louis XVI, but of Charlemagne.
Napoleon to Pope Pius VII, on his coronation 1 Dec 1804

12 Napoleon ought never to be confused with Nelson, in spite of their hats being so alike.
W. C. Sellar and R. J. Yeatman, 1066 AND ALL THAT 1930

13 Napoleon's armies always used to march on their stomachs shouting "Vive l'Intèrier", and so moved about very slowly (ventre-à-terre, as the French say) thus enabling Wellington to catch them up and beat them.
Ibid.

14 Gentlemen, we have a master; this young man does everything, can do everything, and will do everything.
Count Emmanuel Joseph Sievès. Address to the National Assembly

15 I attended Napoleon at Strasburg, at the home of the Préfet and no one in the room but ourselves, when Napoleon was suddenly seized with a fit, foaming at the mouth; he cried, "Fermez la porte!" and then lay senseless on the floor. I bolted the door. He recovered in about half an hour. Next morning, by daybreak, he was in his carriage, and within sixty hours the Austrian army had capitulated.
Talleyrand. Quoted Samuel Rogers, TABLE TALK 1856

16 The great Napoleon did not plan his wars. He merely marched against his enemies and took his chance.
A. J. P. Taylor, Observer, The games generals play 7 Sep 1979

1 There I stood at the arm of Napoleon III, his nephew, before the coffin of our bitterest foe! I, the grand-daughter of that king who hated him most and most vigorously opposed him, and this very nephew, who bears his name, being my nearest and dearest ally.
Queen Victoria, JOURNAL 24 *Aug* 1855

2 Bonaparte's whole life, civil, political and military, was a fraud. There was not a transaction, great or small, in which lying and fraud were not introduced.
Duke of Wellington in a letter 29 *Dec* 1835

3 I used to say of him that his presence on the field made the difference of forty thousand men.
Duke of Wellington to Lord Stanhope
2
Nov 1831

4 Napoleon was a little guy / They used to call him Shorty / He only stood about so high / His chest was under forty / But when folks started talking mean / His pride it didn't injure / "My queen," he said to Josephine / "The thing that counts is ginger."
P. G. Wodehouse, HAVE A HEART *(musical)* 1916

CHARLES LOUIS NAPOLEON BONAPARTE (1808–1873)
(Napoleon III)
Emperor of France

5 A great unrecognised incapacity.
Bismarck, in a letter while minister in France 1862

6 His mind was a kind of extinct sulphur pit.
Thomas Carlyle

7 She [Queen Victoria] had never been on such a social footing with anybody, and he [Napoleon III] has approached her with the familiarity of equal positions, and with all the experience and knowledge of womankind he has acquired during his long life, passed in the world and in mixing with every sort of society. She seems to have played her part throughout with great propriety and success.
Greville, DIARY 5 *Sep* 1855

8 Because we have had Napoleon the Great must we have Napoleon the Little?
Victor Hugo. Speech, French Chamber of Deputies 17 *Jul* 1851

9 At eleven o'clock this morning Napoleon III passed away at Campden House, Chislehurst. It has been a life of marvellous vicissitudes and the most wonderful romance since that of Charles Edward.
Francis Kilvert, DIARY 6 *Jan* 1873

10 Copies never succeed.
Kossuth, in conversation

RICHARD NASH (1674–1762)
(Beau Nash)
English man of fashion

11 He became an arbiter of fashion in London, supporting himself on the proceeds of gambling. Grasping the possibilities of a summer centre of fashionable life he went to Bath in 1705 and set on foot a revolution which changed the face of English life. He established the Assembly Rooms, forbade duelling, and promulgated a code of behaviour and dress which he rigidly and successfully enforced. From Bath his code of polite manners spread quickly among the upper classes and largely contributed to make the society of 18th century England remarkable for good sense and civilisation.
T. Charles Edwards and Brian Richardson, THEY SAW IT HAPPEN 1958

THOMAS NASHE (1567–1601)
English satirist and dramatist

12 Vaine Nashe, railing Nashe, cracking Nashe, bibbing Nashe, baggage Nashe, swaddish Nashe, roguish Nashe, the swish-swash of the press, the bum of impudency, the shambles of beastliness, the toadstool of the realm.
Gabriel Harvey

HORATIO, VISCOUNT NELSON (1758–1805)
English Admiral

13 His Lordship used a great deal of exercise, generally walking on the quarter deck six or seven hours a day. He always rose early, for the most part shortly after daybreak. He breakfasted in summer about six, and at seven in winter; and if not occupied in reading or writing despatches, or examining into details of the Fleet, he walked on the quarter deck the greater part of the forenoon, going down to his cabin occasionally to commit to paper such incidents or reflections as occurred to him during that time and as hereafter might be useful to the service of his country.
Dr Beatty, surgeon on the Victory.
Narrative, included in DESPATCHES AND LETTERS OF LORD NELSON *(edited Nicholas)* 1846

1 At dinner he was alike attentive and affable to everyone; he ate very sparingly himself; the liver and wing of a fowl; a small plate of macaroni, in general composed his meal during which he occasionally took a glass of champagne. He never exceeded four glasses of wine after dinner and seldom drank three, and even those were diluted with Bristol or common water.
Ibid.

2 He seldom wore boots and was consequently very liable to have his feet wet. When this occurred he has often been known to go down to his cabin, throw off his shoes and walk on the carpet in his stockings for the purpose of drying the feet of them. He chose rather to adopt this uncomfortable expedient than to give his servants the trouble of assisting him to put on fresh stockings, which, from his having only one hand, he could not himself conveniently effect.
Ibid.

3 It was about fifteen minutes past one o'clock which was in the heat of the engagement, when the fatal ball was fired from the enemy's mizzentop. The ball struck the epaulette on his left shoulder and penetrated his chest. He fell with his face on the deck. Captain Hardy expressed a hope that he was not severely wounded, to which the gallant Chief replied, "They have done for me at last, Hardy. My backbone is shot through."
Ibid.

4 Captain Hardy now came to the cockpit to see his Lordship a second time. He then told Captain Hardy that he felt that in a few minutes he should be no more, adding in a low tone, "Don't throw me overboard, Hardy." The Captain answered, "Oh no, certainly not." Then replied his Lordship, "You know what to do. Take care of my dear Lady Hamilton. Kiss me, Hardy." The Captain now knelt and kissed his cheek, when his Lordship said, "Now I am satisfied. Thank God I have done my duty."
Ibid.

5 I was walking with him on the poop when he said, "I'll now amuse the fleet with a signal." The words were scarcely uttered when his last well known signal was made: "England expects every man will do his duty." The shout with which it was received throughout the fleet was truly sublime. "Now," said Lord Nelson, "I can do no more. We must trust to the Great Disposer of All Events, and the justice of our cause".
Captain Blackwood, despatch from Trafalgar 21 Oct 1805

6 The trouble with Lady Hamilton is that Nelson left her to the nation when he might have left her to Sir William Hamilton.
Philip Guedella, MEN OF AFFAIRS, MEN OF WAR, STILL LIFE

7 Our dear Admiral Nelson is killed. All the men in our ship who have seen him are such soft toads, they have done nothing but blast their eyes and cry, ever since he was killed. God bless you! Chaps that fought like the devil sit down and cry like a wench.
Letter home after Trafalgar from one of the crew of the Royal Sovereign. Quoted LETTERS OF ENGLISH SEAMEN *(Edited Moorhouse)* 1910

8 I was riding a blackguard horse that ran away with me at Common, carried me round all the works into Portsmouth, by the London gates, through the town, out of the gate that leads to Common, where there was a wagon on the road which is so narrow that a horse could hardly pass. To save my legs and perhaps my life I was obliged to throw myself from the horse, which I did with great agility but unluckily upon hard stones, which has hurt my back and my leg, but done no other mischief.
Nelson in a letter 22 Apr 1784

9 Lord Nelson was a remarkably kind-hearted man. I have seen him spinning a teetotum with his *one* hand a whole evening, for the amusement of some children.
Samuel Rogers, TABLE TALK 1856

10 I heard him once at dinner utter many bitter complaints (which Lady Hamilton vainly attempted to check) of the way he had been treated at court that forenoon; the Queen had not condescended to take the slightest notice of him. In truth, Nelson was hated at court, they were jealous of his fame.
Ibid.

11 Lady Hamilton showed us the neckcloth which Nelson had on when he died. Of course I could not help looking at it with extreme interest; and she threw her arms round my neck and kissed me.
Ibid.

12 It is a pity that the Bank of England forgot Nelson and put the Duke of Wellington on the back of £5 notes. Without Trafalgar there would have been no Waterloo.
James Saunder, founder of the Nelson Society, The Times 9 Dec 1981

13 Lord Nelson was at this time, as he had been during the whole action, walking the starboard side of the quarterdeck. After a

turn or two he said to me in a quick manner, "Do you know what signal's shown on board the Commander-in-Chief: No 39." On asking him what they meant he replied, "Leave off action" and then added with a shrug, "Now damn me if I do." He also observed, I believe to Captain Foley, "You know, Foley, I have only one eye. I have a right to be blind sometimes" and then with an archness peculiar to his character, putting the glass to his blind eye exclaimed, "I really do not see the signal."
Colonel Stewart, narrative of the Battle of Copenhagen, 2 Apr 1801

NERO (AD 37–68)
Roman emperor

1   Pretending to be offended with the deformity of the ancient buildings and the narrow passages and turnings of the streets he set it on fire so publicly that many persons of consular dignity, having apprehended several of the Gentlemen of his Chamber in their house with fire and wisps of tow in their hands, durst not meddle with them but were forced to let them go again.
Suetonius, LIVES OF THE FIRST TWELVE CAESARS

2   While he, beholding the dreadful conflagration from Maecenas's Tower, and rejoicing, as he said, at the Beauty of the Flames, in his actor's habit sang the Tragedy of the Destruction of Troy, or the Taking and Sacking of Ilium.
Ibid.

3   He ordered a grave to be made in his presence, exactly according to the dimensions of his body, and that what pieces of marble could be found should be laid together, and that water and wood should be got ready for the washing and burning of his body; weeping every time he cast his eye upon these funeral preparations, and often crying out "What an Artist will the world lose."
Ibid.

4   He clapped the dagger to his throat, Epaphroditus, the Master of his Requests, assisting his fainting hand to thrust it home . . . He was burnt at the expense of five thousand crowns, his body being wrapped up in white silk coverlets interwoven with gold. His ashes were gathered up by his nurses Ecloge and Alexandria, and his concubine Acte, and deposited in the monument of the Domitii.
Ibid.

JOHN HENRY, CARDINAL NEWMAN (1801–1890)
English theologian

5   His appearance was striking. He was above the middle height, slight and spare. His head was large, his face remarkably like that of Julius Caesar. The forehead, the ears and the shape of the nose were almost the same.
J. A. Froude, SHORT STUDIES ON GREAT SUBJECTS   1905

6   When Cardinal Newman was a child "he wished he might believe that the *Arabian Nights* was true". When he came to be a man his wish seems to have been granted.
Lytton Strachey, EMINENT VICTORIANS   1918

SIR ISAAC NEWTON (1642–1727)
English mathematician, physicist and astronomer

7   Or Newton leaning in Woodsthorpe against the garden wall / forgot his indigestion and all such trivialities / but gaped up to heaven and with / true gravity witnessed the vertical apple fall. / O what a marvellous observation, who would have reckoned / that such a pedestrian miracle would have altered history / that henceforward everyone must fall, whatever / their rank at thirty-two feet per second per second.
Dannie Abse, WALKING UNDER WATER; letter to Alex Comfort

8   When Newton saw an apple fall he found / A mode of proving that the earth turn'd round / In a most natural whirl called gravitation / And this is the sole mortal who could grapple / Since Adam with a fall or with an apple.
Lord Byron, DON JUAN   1824

9   Sir Isaac Newton himself has owned that he began with studying judicial astrology and that it was his pursuit of that idle and vain study which led him into the beauties and love of astronomy.
Dr Cocchi. Quoted Rev. Joseph Spence, OBSERVATIONS, ANECDOTES AND CHARACTERS   1820

10 He lived the life of a solitary, and like all men who are occupied with profound meditation, he acted strangely. Sometimes, in getting out of bed, an idea would come to him, and he would sit on the edge of the bed, half dressed, for hours at a time.
Louis Figuier, VIES DES SAVANTS (translated by B. H. Clark)   1870

1 To myself I seem to have been only like a boy playing on the seashore, and diverting myself in now and then finding a smoother pebble or a prettier seashell than ordinary, while the great ocean of truth lay all undiscovered before me.
Newton. Quoted Sir David Brewster, MEMOIRS OF NEWTON 1875

2 As Sir Isaac was reading one day under an apple tree one day that species of fruit fell and struck him a smart blow on the head. When he observed the smallness of the apple he was surprised at the force of the blow. This led him to consider the accelerating motion of falling bodies and laid the foundations of that philosophy for which his name is so justly famous.
PERCY ANECDOTES 1823

3 Nature and nature's laws. / Lay hid in night / God said "Let Newton be" / and all was light.
Alexander Pope, epitaph intended for Westminster Abbey 1730

4 Sir Isaac Newton, though so deep in algebra and fluxions, could not readily make up a common account; and whilst he was Master of the Mint, used to get someone to make up the accounts for him.
Alexander Pope. Quoted Rev. Joseph Spence, OBSERVATIONS, ANECDOTES AND CHARACTERS 1820

5 He was a highly neurotic young don at Trinity College, Cambridge, who became the most revolutionary mathematician in Europe at the age of 24. He also transformed the science of optics, was immersed in dangerous theology and secret alchemical studies. There was nothing cosy about Isaac Newton.
Michael Ratcliffe, The Times, The lust for knowledge 26 Mar 1981

6 He was a Christian who deplored the Trinity and demoted Christ, and argued that if you could mathematicise philosophy and nature, then you could quantify God.
Ibid.

7 How very English that Queen Anne should have knighted him, not for his work on the mathematics of motion, nor even for his painstaking supervision of the recoinage at the Mint, to which he was appointed in 1696, but for his genuine, though modest, services to the Whigs.
Ibid.

8 He said he never was at more than one opera. The first act he heard with pleasure, the second stretched his patience, at the third he ran away.
Rev. William Stukeley, DIARY 18 *Apr* 1720

9 The antechapel where the statue stood / Of Newton with his prism and silent face, / The marble index of a life for ever / Voyaging through strange seas of thought, alone.
William Wordsworth, of Newton's statue in Trinity College, Cambridge, THE PRELUDE 1850

FRIEDRICH WILHELM NIETZSCHE (1844–1910)
German philosopher and poet

10 Rightly construed, this surging anarchism of his is a revolt against the doctrine which the supermen have imposed upon the world, and a call to the holy and the meek to assert their manhood against their oppressors, and it is a singular perversion which makes it the gospel and justification of the oppressors.
J. A. Spender, THE COMMENTS OF BAGSHOT

FLORENCE NIGHTINGALE (1820–1910)
English nursing reformer

11 What a comfort it was to see her pass. She would speak to one, and nod and smile to as many more, but she could not do it to all, you know. We lay there by the hundreds, but we could kiss her shadow as it fell and lay our heads on the pillow again content.
Anonymous soldier in the Crimean War. Quoted Cecil Woodham-Smith, FLORENCE NIGHTINGALE

12 Miss Nightingale did inspire awe, not because one felt afraid of her *per se* but because the very essence of *Truth* seemed to emanate from her, and because of her perfect fearlessness in telling it.
William Richmond, THE RICHMOND PAPERS

13 She cured the troops of their sufferings every night with doses of deadly lampshade.
W. C. Sellar and R. J. Yeatman, 1066 AND ALL THAT 1930

14 Her conception of God was certainly not orthodox. She felt towards Him as she might have felt towards some glorified sanitary engineer; and in some of her speculations she seems hardly to have distinguished between the Deity and the Drains.
Lytton Strachey, EMINENT VICTORIANS 1918

1 You are well aware of the high sense I entertain of the Christian devotion which you have displayed during this great and bloody war, and I need hardly repeat to you how warm my admiration is for your services, which are fully equal to those of my dear and brave soldiers, whose sufferings you have had the *privilege* of alleviating in so merciful a manner . . . I send you with this letter a brooch, the form and emblems of which commemorate your blessed work.
Queen Victoria, letter to Florence Nightingale Jan 1856

RICHARD MILHOUS NIXON (1913–)
Thirty-seventh President of the United States

2 President Nixon's motto was, if two wrongs don't make a right, try three.
Norman Cousins. Quoted Christie Davies, Daily Telegraph 17 Jul 1979

3 I'll speak for the man or against him, whichever will do him most good.
Nixon, in a TV interview with David Frost

4 For years politicians have promised the moon. I'm the first one to be able to deliver it.
Nixon 20 July 1969

FREDERICK NORTH (1732–1792)
(Earl of Guildford)
British Prime Minister

5 Heber told me a capital jest of Frederick North at Algiers. North asked the Dey permission to see his women. After some parley the Dey said; "He is so ugly, let him see them all."
Lord Broughton, RECOLLECTIONS OF A LONG LIFE

6 A statesman who, in a long, stirring, and at length unfortunate administration, had many political opponents, almost without a personal enemy; who has retained, in his fall from power, many faithful and disinterested friends; and who, under the pressure of severe infirmity, enjoys the lively vigour of his mind and the felicity of his incomparable temper.
Edward Gibbon, Dedication to DECLINE AND FALL OF THE ROMAN EMPIRE 1788

7 Thomas Grenville told me that he was present in the House when Lord North, suddenly rising from his seat and going out, carried off on the hilt of his sword the wig of Welbore Ellis, who was stooping to pick up some papers.
Samuel Rogers, TABLE TALK 1836

8 I have myself often seen Lord North in the House. While sitting there he would often hold a handkerchief to his face; and once after a long debate, when somebody said to him, "My Lord, I fear you have been asleep," he replied, "I wish I had".
Ibid.

9 Lord North was a coarse and heavy man, with a wide mouth, thick lips and puffy cheeks, which seemed typical of his policy.
J. H. Rose. Quoted Sir Charles Petrie, THE FOUR GEORGES

10 He had neither system nor principles nor shame; sought neither the favour of the Crown nor of the people, but enjoyed the good luck of fortune with a gluttonous Epicurism that was equally careless of glory or disgrace.
Horace Walpole, MEMOIRS 1746–1791

ALFRED CHARLES WILLIAM HARMSWORTH, VISCOUNT NORTHCLIFFE (1865-1922)
Newspaper proprietor

11 Have you heard? The Prime Minister has resigned, and Northcliffe has sent for the king.
Anonymous member of the Daily Mail staff. Quoted Hamilton Fyfe, NORTHCLIFFE; An Intimate Biography

12 The late Lord Northcliffe would not print anything in criticism of himself. He would always print the words of praise. Even from the publicity point of view, he was wrong.
Lord Beaverbrook, letter to Tom Driberg 3 Dec 1952

13 He is an extraordinarily commonplace man, with a very good brain for business. He is rather dull to talk to, very vain, but kind-hearted I should say. Nothing original. Those are the men that get on.
Frances Stevenson, DIARY 19 May 1917

14 He aspired to power instead of influence, and as a result forfeited both.
A. J. P. Taylor, ENGLISH HISTORY 1914–1945

15 Alfred was born in 1865, a little more than a year before me and he seems to have entered Henley House School when he was nine or ten years old. He made a very poor impression on his teachers and became one of those unsatisfactory, rather heavy, good-tempered boys who in the usual course of

things drift ineffectually through school to some second rate employment. It was J. V. Milne's ability that saved him from that. Somewhere about the age of twelve Master Harmsworth became possessed of a jelly-graph for the reproduction of a mock news-paper. J. V., with the soundest pedagogic instinct, seized upon the educational pos-sibilities of this display of interest and en-couraged young Harmsworth, violet with copying ink and not quite sure whether he had done well or ill, to persist with the Henley House Magazine, even at the ex-pense of his school work.

H. G. Wells, AN EXPERIMENT IN AUTOBIOGRAPHY 1934

1 The second success of the Harmsworth brothers was a publication called *Comic Cuts.* Some rare spasm of decency seemed to have prevented them calling this enormously profitable, nasty, taste-destroying appeal for the ha'pence of small boys *Komic Kuts.* They sailed into this busi-ness of producing saleable letterpress for the coppers of the new public, with an entire disregard of good taste, good value, educational influence, social consequences or political responsibility. They were as blind as young kittens to all those aspects of life. This is the most remarkable fact about them from my present point of view, and I think posterity will find it even more astonishing.

Ibid.

O

CAPTAIN LAWRENCE EDWARD GRACE OATES (1880–1912)
Antarctic explorer

1 Captain Oates did just what we all expected of him, sir. He was a fine man that, sir. Not much talk about him, but chock full of grit.
Anonymous seaman. Quoted Sue Limb and Patrick Gordingley, CAPTAIN OATES 1983

2 He was sardonic, taciturn, scornful of women and anybody with brains. Someone said his thought processes were like snails crawling up a cabbage stalk.
Nicholas Wollaston, Observer, Popping out for a breather, reviewing Sue Lamb and Patrick Gordingley's CAPTAIN OATES 9 Jan 1983

TITUS OATES (1649–1705)
Religious conspirator

3 In this year [1685] I saw Dr Oates whipped at the cart's tail the second time, while his back, miserably swelled from his first whipping, looked as if it had been flayed. Dr Oates was a man of invincible courage and resolution, and endured what would have killed a great many others. He occasioned a strange turn in the nation, after a general lethargy that had been of some years, continuance. By awakening us out of sleep he was instrumental in the hand of God for our salvation. Yet after all he was but a sorry, foul-mouthed wretch as I can testify from what I once heard from him in company.
Edmund Calamy, AN HISTORICAL ACCOUNT OF MY LIFE

4 He seemed to be a bold man, and in my thoughts furiously indiscreet; but everyone believed what he said, and it quite changed the genius and motions of Parliament, growing now corrupt with long sitting and court practices; but withal this popery would not go down.
John Evelyn, DIARY 1 Oct 1678

5 The fact that Oates was an active and practising homosexual has always been known, but historians have evaded one obvious conclusion; that this explains the astonishing ease with which he was admitted to certain Catholic circles which one would have supposed barred a disreputable Anglican clergyman with heterodox leanings.
J. P. Kenyon, THE POPISH PLOT

6 By birth he was an Anabaptist, by prudence a clergyman, and by profession a perjurer.
John Pollock, THE POPISH PLOT

7 Mr Reading being new come from London was at my father's. I heard him say that he saw Oates, that discovered the Popish Plot, whipped according to his condemnation most miserably; and as he was hauled up the streets the multitude would much pity him, and would cry to the hangman or he whose office was to whip him, "Enough! Strike easy!" To whom Mr Oates replied, turning his head cheerfully behind him, "Not enough! good people, for truth, not enough."
Abraham de la Prynne, DIARY 1686

EUGENE GLADSTONE O'NEILL (1888–1953)
American dramatist

8 Eugene O'Neill died as he (largely) had lived, in frustration and anguish. For all his delving he had not solved the mystery of man's eternal struggle with himself and an overwhelming universe. The closest he came to a solution was his belief, so forcibly stated in *The Iceman Cometh*, that man must cling to his illusions or perish.
Jean Gould, MODERN AMERICAN PLAYWRIGHTS

9 Mr Eugene O'Neill has done nothing much in American drama save to transform it utterly, in ten or twelve years, from a false world of neat and competent trickery to a world of splendour and fear and greatness.
Sinclair Lewis. Quoted John Mason Brown, DRAMATIS PERSONAE

10 He hates the idea of publicity, and the searching impertinences of interviewers with the same enthusiasm as the devil hates baptismal fonts.
Burns Mantle, AMERICAN PLAYWRIGHTS OF TODAY

1 There is something relatively distinguished about even his failures; they sink, not trivially, but with a certain air of majesty, like a great ship, its flags flying, full of holes.
George Jean Nathan, AMERICAN DRAMA AND ITS CRITICS *(edited by Alan S. Downs)*

2 Though not without certain obvious limitations he must be considered the best all-round dramatist America has produced so far.
J. B. Priestley, LITERATURE AND WESTERN MAN 1960

JOHN OPIE (1761–1807)
English painter

3 He began his artistic career early; an amusing incident of his childhood is related. Opie wished to draw a picture of his father in a rage; and deliberately teased him, running in and disturbing him at his reading until the mood had reached such a climax as he wished to portray.
Julia de Wolf Addison, THE ART OF THE NATIONAL GALLERY 1905

4 The fellow can paint nothing but thieves and murderers, and when he paints thieves and murderers he looks in the glass.
Henry Fuseli

GEORGE ORWELL (1903–1950)
(Eric Arthur Blair)
English author

5 I often feel that I will never pick up a book by Orwell again until I have read a frank discussion of the dishonesty and hysteria that mar some of his best work.
Kingsley Amis, WHAT BECAME OF JANE AUSTEN?

6 He would not blow his nose without moralising on the state of the handkerchief industry.
Cyril Connolly, THE EVENING COLONNADE

7 Mr Orwell is a silly billy. He is full of political tittle-tattle — but he gets it all wrong. He thinks people are always falling in love with political Stars. I am so glad that emotional schoolboy has transferred his excitable loyalties to the Partisans.
Percy Wyndham Lewis, Letter to Dwight MacDonald 26 Jan 1947

8 He was a kind of saint, and in that character, more likely in politics to chastise his own side than the enemy.
V. S. Pritchett, New Statesman, obituary 1950

OVID (43 BC–AD 17)
(Publius Ovidius Naso)
Latin poet

9 Ovid had nothing in common with the older Roman poets; their dignity, virility and piety were entirely lacking in him. But he possessed an exquisite sensitiveness to beauty, and abounding imaginative power, which they lacked.
J. A. Hammerton (editor), CONCISE UNIVERSAL BIOGRAPHY

10 The true cause of Ovid's sudden exile is not known; some attribute it to a shameful amour with Livia, wife of Augustus; others support that it arose from the knowledge which Ovid had of the unpardonable incest of the emperor with his daughter Julia; these reasons are indeed merely conjectural; the cause was of a private and secret nature of which Ovid himself was afraid to speak.
John Lemprière, CLASSICAL DICTIONARY 1788

11 In his exile Ovid showed nothing of the philosopher, but in hopes of pardon was continually praising the emperor with such extravagance as bordered even upon idolatry; and what was more singular, he made an idol of him literally, as soon as he heard of his death, by consecrating a chapel to him.
PERCY ANECDOTES 1820

P

THOMAS PAINE (1737–1809)
English radical author

1 What a poor, ignorant, malicious, short-sighted, crapulous mass is Tom Paine's *Common Sense*.
John Adams, letter to Thomas Jefferson 22 *Jun* 1819

2 In digging up your bones, Tom Paine / Will Cobbett has done well; / You visit him on earth again / He'll visit you in Hell.
Lord Byron, EPIGRAM

3 Tom Paine invented the name of the Age of Reason; and he was one of those sincere but curiously simple men who really did think that the age of reason was beginning, at about the time when it was really ending.
G. K. Chesterton, WILLIAM COBBETT

4 Paine was a Quaker by birth and a friend by nature. The world was his home, mankind were his friends, to do good was his religion.
Alice Hubbard, Introduction to an American Bible

VISCOUNT PALMERSTON (1784–1865)
(Henry John Temple)
British Prime Minister

5 "Sentences", he wrote on one occasion, "should begin with the nominative, go on with the verb, and end with the accusative." Such men were accustomed to leave no doubt as to what they meant in the minds of those they ruled.
Arthur Bryant, ENGLISH SAGA

6 Palmerston comes to any conference so fully and completely master of the subject of it in all the minutest details that this capacity is a peculiar talent with him; it is so great that he is apt, sometimes, to lose himself in the details.
M. Dedel, Dutch foreign minister. Quoted Charles Greville, MEMOIRS 23 *Sep* 1839

7 Lounging, voluble and pert. At best ginger beer, not champagne.
Disraeli

8 I met some clerks in the Foreign Office to whom the very name of Palmerston is hateful, but I was surprised to hear them give ample testimony to his abilities. They said that he wrote admirably, and could express himself perfectly in French, very sufficiently in Italian, and understood in German; that his diligence and attention were unwearied — he read everything and wrote an immense quantity; that the foreign ministers (who detest him) did him justice as an excellent man of business.
Charles Greville, MEMOIRS 17 *Feb* 1835

9 His great fault is want of punctuality, and never keeping an engagement if it did not suit him, keeping everybody waiting for hours on his pleasure or caprice.
Ibid.

10 It is surprising to hear how Palmerston is spoken of by those who know him well officially — the Granvilles, for example. Lady Granville, a woman expert in judging, thinks his capacity first rate; that it approaches to greatness from his enlarged views, disdain of trivialities, resolution, decision, confidence and above all his contempt of clamour and abuse.
Ibid. 7 *Aug* 1836

11 Queen Victoria's dislike of Palmerston is of very long standing, partly on moral, partly on political grounds. Palmerston always enterprising and audacious with women, took a fancy to Mrs Brande (now Lady Dacre) and at Windsor Castle when she was in waiting and he was a guest, he marched into her room one night. His tender temerity met with an invincible resistance. The lady did not conceal the attempt and it came to the Queen's ears. Her indignation was somehow pacified by Lord Melbourne, his brother-in-law. Palmerston got out of the scrape with his usual luck; but the Queen has not forgotten and will never forgive it.
Ibid. 28 *Aug* 1853

12 Europe depended on which leg — the left or the right — he put out of bed first.
Princess Lieven. Quoted GREAT VICTORIANS *(edited by H. J. and Hugh Massingham)*

13 Palmerston is Mama England's spoilt child and the more mischief he does the more she admires him. "What spirit he has!" cries Mama — and smash goes the crockery.
Lord Lytton. Quoted ibid.

1 He will be a source of mischief to this country as long as he lives.
Queen Victoria. Quoted ibid.

2 He had many valuable qualities, though many bad ones, and we had, God knows, terrible trouble with him about foreign affairs. Still, as Prime Minister, he managed affairs at home well, and behaved to me well, but I *never* liked him.
Ibid.

DOROTHY ROTHSCHILD PARKER
(1893–1967)
American writer

3 Discussing a job with a prospective employer Mrs Parker explained "Salary is no object. I only want enough to keep body and soul apart."
Robert E. Brennan, WITS END

4 She had the imagination of disaster, and she cultivated this imagination and made it flourish. Her knack for making things end badly amounted, in her friends' eyes, to genius.
Brendon Gill, Introduction to THE COLLECTED DOROTHY PARKER

5 Ducking for apples — change a letter and it's the story of my life.
Dorothy Parker

6 Thirty-nine years old and a very toothsome dish, she immediately made every other woman in the assemblage feel dowdy, and for a moment the sound of their teeth gnashing drowned out the buzz of chit-chat.
S. J. Perelman, THE LAST LAUGH

7 She is a combination of Little Nell and Lady Macbeth.
Alexander Woollcott, WHILE ROME BURNS 1934

8 I found her in hospital typing away lugubriously. She had given her address as Bedpan Alley and represented herself as writing her way out. There was a hospital bill to pay before she dared get well.
Ibid.

CHARLES STEWART PARNELL
(1846–1891)
Irish politician

9 To me, watching him closely, it appeared that the humiliation of England, and of everything English, was the master-passion of his life.
G. W. E. Russell, PORTRAITS OF THE SEVENTIES 1916

10 He hated England, he condemned the House of Commons, he despised the Liberals much more profoundly than the Tories, and he regarded his followers as merely voters, or at best as fit for work too dirty for a gentleman to undertake.
Ibid.

11 He had a mass of lightish brown hair, beard, moustache and whiskers, all worn long and tangled; insomuch that when his toadies called him the Uncrowned King of Ireland his critics substituted 'uncombed'.
Ibid.

12 The fall of Parnell left Ireland with a dead god instead of a leader.
G. M. Young, VICTORIAN ENGLAND: *Portrait of an Age*

LOUIS PASTEUR (1822–1895)
French bacteriologist

13 Some years after his death it was decided by a popular vote conducted in his country that Louis Pasteur was the greatest Frenchman of all time. The success of his method might be explained as being due to the exercise of three fundamental rules, keen observation, precise tests, and the drawing of irrefutable conclusions from critical premises.
Piers Compton, THE GENIUS OF LOUIS PASTEUR 1932

14 The victory over rabies, that most dreaded of diseases, lifted Pasteur into indisputable fame. He had risen by progressive steps, by studies which were all, despite their diversity, connected and supported by one another.
L. Descour, PASTEUR AND HIS WORK 1922

15 We can well understand the feeling of happiness and the nervous excitement by which Pasteur was overcome on making his discovery. Rushing from his laboratory and meeting a curator he embraced him exclaiming, "I have just made a great discovery. I have separated the sodium ammonium protartrate with two salts of opposite action on the plane of polarisation of light. The dextro-salt is in all respects identical with the dextroptartrate. I am so happy and so overcome by such nervous excitement that I am unable again to place my eye to the polarisation instrument."
Alexander Findlay, CHEMISTRY IN THE SERVICE OF MAN 1916

WALTER HORATIO PATER (1839–1894)
English essayist and critic

16 Mr Walter Pater's style is to me like the face of some old woman who has been to Madame Rachel and had herself enamelled.

The bloom is nothing but powder and paint, and the odour is cherry-blossom.
Samuel Butler, NOTEBOOKS 1912

1 Faint, pale, embarrassed, exquisite Pater! He reminds me, in the disturbed midnight of our actual literature, of one of those lucent match boxes which you place, on going to bed, near the candle, to show you, in the darkness, where you can strike a light; he shines in the uneasy gloom — vaguely, and has a phosphorescence, not a flame.
Henry James, letter to Edmund Gosse
13 Dec 1894

2 You must not expect him to talk like his prose. Of course, no true artist ever does that. But, besides that, he never talks about anything that interests him. He will not breathe one golden word about the Renaissance. No! He will probably say something like this; "So you wear cork soles to your shoes? Is that really true? And do you find them comfortable? . . . How extremely interesting."
Oscar Wilde. Quoted Richard Le Gallienne,
THE ROMANTIC NINETIES

SIR ROBERT PEEL (1788–1850)
British Prime Minister

3 He smashed his party, and no man has the right to destroy the property of which he is trustee.
Lord Balfour. Quoted by his niece,
Blanche Dugdale, LIFE OF LORD BALFOUR

4 The Right Honourable gentleman's smile is like the silver fittings on a coffin.
Disraeli

5 The Right Honourable gentleman caught the Whigs bathing and walked away with their clothes.
Disraeli, House of Commons 28 Feb 1845

6 The Right Honourable gentleman is reminiscent of a poker. The only difference is that a poker gives off occasional signs of warmth.
Disraeli

7 In the higher efforts of oratory he was not successful. His vocabulary was ample and never mean; but it was neither rich nor rare. His speeches will afford no sentiment of surpassing grandeur or beauty that will linger in the ears of coming generations.
Disraeli, LIFE OF GEORGE BENTINCK 1851

8 In pathos he was quite deficient; when he attempted to touch the tender passions it was painful. His face became distorted, like

that of a woman who wants to cry but cannot succeed.
Ibid.

9 He is so vain that he wants to figure in history as the settler of all great questions; but a Parliamentary constitution is not favourable to such ambitions; things must be done by parties, not by persons using parties as tools.
Disraeli, letter to Lord John Manners
17 Dec 1846

10 "A constitutional statesman", wrote Bagehot, "is in general a man of common opinions and uncommon abilities". It would be difficult to find a better description of Sir Robert Peel.
H. J. Laski, THE GREAT VICTORIANS:
Robert Peel *(edited by H. J. and Hugh Massingham)*

11 Sir Robert Peel, in one of his communicative moods, told me that, when he was a boy, his father used to say to him, "Bob, you dog, if you are not Prime Minister one day I shall disinherit you." I mentioned this to Sir Robert's sister, Mrs Dawson, who assured me she had often heard her father use those very words.
Samuel Rogers, TABLE TALK 1856

12 All Peel's affinities are towards wealth and capital. His heart is manifestly towards the mill-owners; his lips occasionally for the operatives. *What* has he ever done or proposed for the working classes? His speech of last night was a signal instance of his tendencies. He suppressed all the delinquencies of the manufacturers, bepraised machinery and treated the distress as severe but temporary. His speech was a transcript of his mind. Cotton is everything, man nothing.
Lord Shaftesbury, DIARY 24 Feb 1842

WILLIAM PENN (1644–1718)
Founder of Pennsylvania

13 The first sense he had of God was when he was eleven years old at Chigwell being retired into a chamber alone; he was so suddenly surprised with a sense of inward comfort and (as he thought) an external glory in the room that he has many times said that from thence he had the Seal of Divinity and Immortality, that there was a God and that the Soul of man was capable of enjoying his divine communications.
John Aubrey, BRIEF LIVES 1690

14 He had such an opinion of his own faculty of persuading, that he thought none could

stand before it; tho' he was singular in that opinion; for he had a tedious luscious way, that was not apt to overcome a man's reason, though it might tire his patience.
Gilbert Burnet, HISTORY OF HIS OWN TIMES 1734

1 He will always be mentioned with honour as the founder of a colony, who did not in his dealings with a savage people, abuse the strength derived from civilisation, and as a lawgiver who, in the age of persecution, made religious liberty the corner stone of a polity.
T. B. Macaulay, HISTORY OF ENGLAND 1848

2 Mrs Turner tells me that Mr Will Pen, who has lately come over from Ireland is a Quaker again, or some very melancholy thing; that he cares for no company, nor comes to any — which is a pleasant thing, after his being abroad so long — and his father such a hypocritical rogue, and at this time an atheist.
Samuel Pepys, DIARY 29 *Dec* 1667

3 I took a trip once with Penn to his colony of Pennsylvania. The laws there are contained in a small volume and are so extremely good that there has been no alteration in them ever since Sir William made them. 'Tis a fine country, and the people are neither oppressed by poor rates, tithes nor taxes.
Lord Peterborough. Quoted Rev. Joseph Spence, OBSERVATIONS, ANECDOTES AND CHARACTERS 1830

SAMUEL PEPYS (1633–1703)
English diarist

4 His journal contains the most unquestionable evidence of veracity; and as the writer made no scruple of committing his most secret thought to paper, encouraged no doubt by the confidence which he derived from the use of shorthand, perhaps there never was a publication more implicitly to be relied on for authenticity of its statements and the exactness with which every fact is detailed.
Lord Braybrooke, editor of the diaries 1825

5 A vain, silly, transparent coxcomb without either solid talents or a solid nature.
J. G. Lockhart

6 Matter-of-fact, like the screech of a sash window being thrown open, begins one of the greatest texts in our history and our literature. The subject of this biography turns his head to us across the centuries and

addresses us as though we were across the room. Not to be moved is to be deficient in humanity.
Richard Ollard, PEPYS

7 The variety of Pepys' tastes and pursuits led him into almost every department of life. He was a man of business, a man of information, if not of learning; a man of taste, a man of whim, and to a certain degree, a man of pleasure. He was a statesman, a *bel-esprit*; a virtuoso and a connoisseur. His curiosity made him an unwearied as well as a universal learner, and whatever he said found its way into his tablets. Thus his Diary absolutely resembles the genial cauldrons at the wedding of Camacho, a souse into which was sure to bring forth at once abundance and variety of whatever could gratify the most eccentric appetite.
Walter Scott, Quarterly Review Jan 1826

8 Obliged to give up writing today — read Pepys instead.
Walter Scott, JOURNAL 5 *Jan* 1826

9 He was a man known to his contemporaries in a halo of almost historical pomp, and to his remote descendants with an indecent familiarity, like a tap-room companion.
R. L. Stevenson, FAMILIAR STUDIES OF MEN AND BOOKS: *Samuel Pepys* 1882

10 He was loved and respected by some of the best and wisest men in England. He was President of the Royal Society; and when he came to die, people said of his conduct in that solemn hour — thinking it needless to say more — that it was answerable to the greatness of his life.
Ibid.

11 It seems he had no design except to appear respectable, and here he keeps a private book to prove that he was not.
Ibid.

12 Pepys was a young man for his age, came slowly to himself in the world, sowed his wild oats late, took late to industry, and preserved till nearly forty the headlong gusto of a boy.
Ibid.

13 Equally pleased with a watch, a coach, a piece of meat, a tune on the fiddle, or a fact in hydrostatics, Pepys was pleased yet more by the beauty, the worth, the mirth, or the mere scenic attitude in life of his fellow creatures. He shows himself throughout a sterling humanist. Indeed, he who loves himself, not in idle vanity, but with a

plenitude of knowledge, is the best equipped of all to love his neighbours.
Ibid.

1 'Tis never a drudgery to wait on Mr Pepys, whose conversation, I think, is more nearly akin to what we are taught to hope for in heaven, than that of anybody else I know.
Humphrey Wanly. Quoted Richard Ollard,
PEPYS

PERICLES (d. 429 BC)
Athenian governor

2 Greek architecture and sculpture under Pericles reached perfection. To him Athens owes the Parthenon, the Erechtheum, the Propylea, the Odeum, and numberless other public and sacred edifices.
David Patrick and E. Hindes Groome,
CHAMBERS BIOGRAPHICAL
DICTIONARY 1897

3 What a value above all is that in the whole exercise of my authority in turbulent times, and when I had many great enemies, yet I never gave any of my fellow citizens to put on mourning either for themselves or any of their relatives.
Pericles, on his deathbed

PETER THE GREAT (1672–1725)
Russian Tsar

4 I went to Deptford to view how miserably the Tsar of Muscovy had left my house after 3 months making it his court. Having gotten Sir Christopher Wren, his Majesty's surveyor, and Mr Loudon, his gardener to go down and make an estimate of the repairs, they allowed a hundred and fifty pounds.
John Evelyn, DIARY 9 *Jun* 1689

5 Unpopularity neither increased nor decreased the ferocity of the Tsar. His will did not waver, neither did his personality alter. He throve in an atmosphere of fear, cruelty and burlesque mirth. Screams mingled with his dance orchestra. He could feast while the air was heavy with the odour of death. He had no evil conscience. On the contrary he had a sense of virtue and God-serviceableness which nothing could shake.
Stephen Graham, PETER THE GREAT 1920

6 The soldiers of Peter the Great, the Czar of Muscovy, were no sooner masters of the town of Narva than they fell to plundering and committing the most enormous barbarities. The Czar ran from place to place to put an end to the disorder and massacre . . . He actually killed with his own

hands several Muscovites who did not obey his orders.
PERCY ANECDOTES 1820

7 Peter the Great made a law in 1722 that if any nobleman beat or ill-treat his slaves he should be looked upon as insane, and a guardian should be appointed to take care of his person and estate. This great monarch once struck his gardener, who being a man of great sensibility, took to his bed and died in a few days. Peter, hearing of this, exclaimed with tears in his eyes, "Alas! I have civilised my own subjects; I have conquered other nations; yet I have not been able to civilise or to conquer myself."
Ibid.

HRH PRINCE PHILIP (1921–)
(Duke of Edinburgh)
Consort of Queen Elizabeth II

8 Whatever happens to him in his present capacity as royal poor relation can't do him much good in the long run. My advice to him would be to give up being a royal personage, stick to the sea, learn a trade, and find an anchorage with an average good wife.
Daily Worker 12 *Dec* 1946

9 He seemed to me completely English in manner and outlook — intelligent and broadminded, fair and good-looking. He cannot, in fact, even speak Greek.
Tom Driberg, Reynolds News 8 *Dec* 1946

10 A man attractive to women, envied by men, a bit vicious on the polo field, autocratic, a bit of a ham actor — and in the red. He lives a good life but he has to pay for it. He has never been rich.
Andrew Duncan. Quoted Philip Howard,
The Times, Profile of the Duke of
Edinburgh 26 *Apr* 1982

11 With his great (and carefully calculated) talent for putting his foot in it, we might consider Prince Philip to be the most eloquent, literate and classless member of the Royal Family.
Willie Hamilton. Quoted ibid.

12 No one has a kinder heart, or takes more trouble to conceal it.
Michael Parker. Quoted Basil Boothroyd,
PRINCE PHILIP 1971

13 Why do you think I am getting married: It's because I've never had a home. From the time I was eight I've always been away at school, or in the Navy.
Prince Philip on the eve of his wedding

1 I am referred to in that splendid language,
  pidgin English, as Feller-belong-Queen.
  Prince Philip. Speech, Ottawa 29 *Oct* 1958

PHILIP II (1527–1598)
King of Spain

2 Philip was meagre in stature, with a large,
  oddly shaped head, thinly covered with
  sandy hair; his face was pale and his small
  eyes were blue and weak. He was in no way
  a heroic figure, even in his sumptuous
  clothes.
  Ralph Dutton, ENGLISH COURT LIFE

PABLO RUIZ PICASSO (1881–1973)
Spanish painter

3 A Catalan wizard who fools with shapes.
  Bernard Berenson. Quoted Sylvia Sprigge,
  BERENSON: *a biography*

4 His sickness has created atrocities that are
  repellent. Every one of his paintings de-
  forms man, his body and his face.
  V. Kemenov (Soviet art critic)

5 Nothing unites the English like war.
  Nothing divides them like Picasso.
  Hugh Mills, PRUDENCE AND THE PILL

6 Many painters and writers have made
  beautiful works out of repulsive subjects.
  Picasso enjoys making repulsive works out
  of beautiful subjects.
  Raymond Mortimer, TRY ANYTHING ONCE

7 I remember Winston Churchill saying to me,
  "Alfred, if you met Picasso coming down
  the street would you help me in kicking his
  backside?" I said, "Yes, sir, I would."
  *Alfred Munnings. Speech, Royal Academy
  dinner* 28 *Apr* 1949

8 If my husband would ever meet a woman on
  the street who looked like the women in his
  paintings he would fall over in a dead faint.
  Mme Picasso

9 "How can you remember which paintings
  are yours?" "If I like it I say it's mine. If I
  don't I say it's a fake."
  Picasso. Quoted Sunday Times
  10 *Oct* 1965

10 I paint objects as I think them, not as I see
   them.
   Picasso. Quoted John Golding, CUBISM

11 Picasso had a whim of iron.
   John Richardson, PICASSO IN PRIVATE

12 Picasso painted in the head of Gertrude
   Stein before seeing her and presented her
   with the portrait. Nobody liked the picture

except the painter and the painted. Picasso's
answer, when somebody said Gertrude did
not look like the painting, was, "Never
mind. She will."
Elizabeth Sprigge, GERTRUDE STEIN: *Her Life
and Work*

13 I was accused of trying to smuggle a plan of
   fortifications — in fact my portrait by
   Picasso — out of Germany.
   *Igor Stravinsky, detained by Italian border
   guards in* 1917

MARY PICKFORD (1893–1979)
(Gladys Smith)
American film actress

14 She was the girl every young man wanted to
   have — as a sister.
   Alistair Cooke

15 On one of our tours there was a girl called
   Gladys Smith and a few months later we
   heard that a terrible misfortune had befallen
   her, which was that unable to get work in
   the theatre she'd been forced to go out to
   California and change her name to Mary
   Pickford and seek jobs in motion pictures
   which in those days was considered
   thoroughly disreputable.
   *Lillian Gish, to Sheridan Morley, The
   Times* 10 *Nov* 1980

16 Mary Pickford spent the last 15 years of her
   life in bed and eventually it killed her, as I
   always told her it would
   Ibid.

17 You're too little and too fat, but I might
   give you a job.
   D. W. Griffith, at their first meeting

THE PILGRIM FATHERS
*Puritans who settled in Massachusetts
in* 1620

18 The Pilgrim Fathers landed on Plymouth
   Rock, but in the opinion of this house it
   would have been better for Plymouth Rock
   to have landed on the Pilgrim Fathers.
   *Motion debated by Cambridge Union
   Jan* 1948

19 They fell upon an uncongenial climate that
   called out the best energies in the men, and
   the women too, to get a mere subsistence
   out of the soil. In their efforts to do that
   they cultivated industry and frugality at the
   same time — which is the real foundation of
   the greatness of the Pilgrims.
   U. S. Grant. Speech, New England Society
   22 *Dec* 1880

LUIGI PIRANDELLO (1867–1936)
*Italian dramatist, novelist and
short-story writer*

1   The relentless pessimism that pervades his
work is best articulated by a character in
the short story *The Deathwatch*: "I'm not
suffering on my account, or on your
account, I'm suffering because life is what it
is."
William Rose Benét, READER'S
ENCYCLOPAEDIA   1948

WILLIAM PITT THE ELDER (1708–1778)
(First Earl of Chatham)
British statesman

2   Lord Chatham is a greater paradox than
ever; — is seen at home by no human creature; — absolutely by none; rides twenty
miles a day, — is seen on the road and
appears to be in perfect good health; but
will now speak to no creature he meets. I
am much persuaded all is quackery; — he is
not mad; that is, no madder than usual.
*David Hume, letter to Sir Gilbert Elliot
Jul* 1768

3   Lord Chatham with his sword undrawn / Is
waiting for Sir Richard Strachan / Sir
Richard, longing to be at 'em / Is waiting for
the Earl of Chatham.
Morning Chronicle in 1809, *referring to
recriminations over the failure of the
Walcheren expedition, in which Strachan
had referred to "the late Earl of Chatham"
because of his dilatoriness*

4   "We must muzzle" Walpole said, "this terrible cornet of horse." As well might he
attempt to stop a hurricane with a hairnet.
J. H. Plumb, CHATHAM

5   This immaculate man has accepted the
Barony of Chatham for his wife, with a
pension of three thousand pounds a year for
three lives. The pension he has left *us* is a
war for three thousand lives! Perhaps for
twenty times three thousand lives.
*Horace Walpole, letter to the Countess of
Ailesbury*   10 *Oct* 1761

6   The doors opened and at the head of a large
acclaiming concourse was seen Mr Pitt,
borne by the arms of his servants, who,
setting him down within the bar, he crawled
by the help of a crutch and with the
assistance of some few friends to his seat . . .
In truth there was a mixture of the very
solemn and the theatric in this apparition.
His health or his choice had led him to present himself as a subject of affliction to his
country, and his ungrateful country was not
afflicted.
*Horace Walpole, referring to Pitt's
denunciation of the Peace of Paris, Dec* 1762,
MEMOIRS OF THE REIGN OF GEORGE III

WILLIAM PITT THE YOUNGER
(1759–1806)
British Prime Minister

7   Not merely a chip off the old block, but the
block itself.
*Edmund Burke, of Pitt's maiden speech
Feb* 1781

8   With death doomed to grapple / Beneath
this cold slab, he / who lied in the Chapel /
Now lies in the Abbey.
Lord Byron, EPITAPH ON PITT

9   His eloquence was so great he could explain
even ev'ry disaster into almost the contrary.
His choice of words was perfect, his voice
beautiful, and his way of putting aside the
question when he chose, and fascinating the
minds of men, extraordinary.
*Georgiana, Duchess of Devonshire, letter to
the Marquis of Hartington*   23 *Jan* 1806

10 Pitt's voice sounded as if he had worsted in
his mouth.
Samuel Rogers, TABLE TALK   1856

11 No one suspected his honesty, no one
doubted his capacity; no one impeached his
aims. He had, as Canning said, qualities
rare in their separate excellence, and
wonderful in their combination.
Lord Rosebery, LIFE OF WILLIAM
PITT   1914

12 He had a sort of slovenly or negligent look;
and the same when he was in a passion. His
passion did not show itself by knitting his
brows or pouting his mouth, nor were his
words very sharp; but his eyes lighted up in
a manner quite surprising. It was something
that seemed to dart from within his head,
and you might see sparks coming from
them. At another time his eyes had no colour at all.
Lady Hester Stanhope (Pitt's niece),
MEMOIRS AS RELATED TO DR
MERYON   1846

13 Pitt little knew what he had to do. Up at
eight o'clock with people enough to see for
a week, obliged to talk all the time he was at
breakfast, and receiving first one, and then
another, until four o'clock, then eating a
mutton chop, hurrying off to the House,
and then badgered and compelled to speak

and waste his lungs until two or three in the
morning.
Ibid.

PLATO (c. 427–347 BC)
Greek philosopher

1 O Plato! Plato! You have paved the way /
With your confounded fantasies, to more /
Immoral conduct by the fancied sway / Your
system feigns o'er the controlless core / Of
human hearts, than all the long array / Of
poets and romancers.
Byron, DON JUAN   1824

2 I know nothing about platonic love except
that it is not to be found in the works of
Plato.
Edgar Jepson. Quoted James Agate, EGO 5
24 *Aug* 1940

3 From a wedding banquet he has passed to
that city he founded for himself and planted
in the sky.
Diogenes Laertius, epitaph on Plato

4 An attachment *à la* Plato / For a bashful young
potato / Or a not-too-French French bean.
W. S. Gilbert, PATIENCE, ACT I   1881

5 Take from him his sophisms, futilities and
incomprehensibilities, and what remains?
His foggy mind.
Thomas Jefferson

6 See there the olive groves of Academe /
Plato's retirement where the Attic bird / Trills
her thick-warbl'd notes the summer long.
Milton, PARADISE REGAINED   1671

7 Who could fathom Plato's mind? Unless
one is a genius philosophy is a mug's game.
Iris Murdoch, THE PHILOSOPHER'S PUPIL
1983

8 Plato is a bore.
Friedrich Nietzsche

9 Come hither, O fire-god. Plato has need of
thee.
*Plato, after listening to Socrates, throwing
into the fire the manuscript of a tragedy he
had written for a competition*

10 Some of Plato's and Cicero's reasonings on
the immortality of the soul are very foolish;
but the latter's are less so than the former's.
*Alexander Pope. Quoted Rev. Joseph
Spence*, OBSERVATIONS, ANECDOTES AND
CHARACTERS   1820

11 Philosophy did not find Plato already a
nobleman. It made him one.
Seneca, EPISTULAE AD LUCILIUM

12 The safest general characterisation of the
European philosophical tradition is that it
consists of a series of footnotes to Plato.
A. N. Whitehead, PROCESS AND
REALITY   1929

EDGAR ALLEN POE (1809–1849)
American poet, author and critic

13 I've an idea that if Poe had been an
exemplary, conventional, tax-oppressed
citizen, like Longfellow, his few poems, as
striking as they are, would not have made so
great a stir.
*Thomas Bailey Aldrich, letter to
E. C. Stedman*   15 *Nov* 1900

14 Edgar Allen Poe / Was passionately fond of
roe. / He always liked to chew some / When
writing anything gruesome.
E. C. Bentley, CLERIHEWS

15 That Poe had a powerful intellect is undeniable, but it seems to me the intellect of a
highly gifted young person before puberty.
The forms which his lively curiosity takes
are those in which a pre-adolescent delights;
wonders of nature and mechanics and the
supernatural, cryptograms and cyphers,
puzzles and labyrinths, mechanical chess-
players and wild flights of speculation.
T. S. Eliot, COLLECTED ESSAYS

16 The substance of Poe is refined; it is the
form that is vulgar. He is, as it were, one of
Nature's gentlemen, unhappily cursed with
incorrigible bad taste.
Aldous Huxley, VULGARITY IN LITERATURE,
*A Collection of Critical Essays (edited by
Robert Regan)*

17 He was an adventurer into the vaults and
cellars and horrible underground passages
of the human soul. He sounded the horror
and the warning of his own doom.
D. H. Lawrence, STUDIES IN CLASSICAL
AMERICAN LITERATURE   1926

18 There comes Poe, with his raven like
Barnaby Rudge / Three fifths of him genius
and two fifths sheer fudge.
James Russell Lowell, A FABLE FOR CRITICS

19 Poe is a kind of Hawthorne with delirium
tremens.
Leslie Stephen, HOURS IN A LIBRARY   1879

MARQUISE DE POMPADOUR (1721–1764)
(Jeanne Antoinette Poisson)
Mistress of Louis XV, *King of France*

20 Madam has a wet day for her journey.
Louis XV, *watching from a window
Pompadour's coffin on a handcart, being
wheeled through the rain to its burial*

1 She assumed the entire control of public affairs, for twenty years swayed the whole policy of the state, and lavished its treasures on her own ambitions. She reversed the policy of France because Frederick the Great lampooned her, filled all public offices with her nominees, and made her own creatures ministers of France. Her policy was disastrous.
David Patrick and F. Hindes Groome, CHAMBERS BIOGRAPHICAL DICTIONARY 1897

2 Après nous le déluge.
Pompadour to Louis XV after Frederick the Great's victory at Rossbach 3 Nov 1757

ALEXANDER POPE (1688–1744)
English poet

3 We are to regard Dryden as the puissant and glorious founder, Pope as the splendid high priest, of our age of prose and reason, of our excellent and indispensable eighteenth century.
Matthew Arnold, ESSAYS IN CRITICISM 1888

4 I told Dr Johnson that Voltaire had distinguished Pope and Dryden thus — "Pope drives a handsome chariot, with a couple of neat, trim nags; Dryden a coach and six stately horses." Johnson said, "Why sir the truth is they both drive coaches and six; but Dryden's horses are either galloping or stumbling. Pope's go at a steady even trot."
James Boswell, THE LIFE OF JOHNSON *Feb 1766*

5 O Pope had I thy satire's darts / to gi'e the rascals their deserts / I'd rip their rotten yellow hearts / An' tell aloud / Their jugglin' hocus-pocus hearts / To cheat the crowd.
Robert Burns, TO THE REV. JOHN M'MATH

6 Those miserable mountebanks of the day disgrace themselves and deny God in running down Pope. The most faultless of poets, and almost of men.
Lord Byron, letter to John Murray 4 Nov 1820

7 The manuscripts of Pope's version of the *Iliad* and the *Odyssey* are written chiefly on the backs of letters.
Isaac D'Israeli, CURIOSITIES OF LITERATURE 1823

8 We owe to the deformities of Pope's person the inimitable beauties of his elaborate verse.
Ibid.

9 When Pope wrote in his Epilogue to the Satires, "Yes, I am proud; I must be proud to see / Men, not afraid of God, afraid of me." / This provoked the famous retort, "The great honour of that boast is such / That hornets and mad dogs may boast as much."
T. K. Hervey, THE DIFFERENCE BETWEEN VERBAL AND PRACTICAL VIRTUE

10 He hardly drank tea without a stratagem.
Samuel Johnson, LIVES OF THE POETS 1781

11 Pope's frame of body did not promise long life, but he certainly hastened his death by feeding much on high-seasoned dishes, and drinking spirits.
Dr William King, ANECDOTES

12 Where sense with sound and ease with weight combine / In the pure silver of Pope's ringing line.
Lord Lytton, THE NEW TIMON

13 The wicked asp of Twickenham.
Lady Mary Wortley Montagu

14 You are very wrong in thinking that Mr Pope could write blank verse well; he has got a knack indeed of writing the other, but was he to attempt to write blank verse I dare say he would appear quite contemptible in it.
Lady Mary Wortley Montagu. Quoted Rev. Joseph Spence, OBSERVATIONS, ANECDOTES AND CHARACTERS 1820

15 I admired Mr Pope's essay in Criticism very much at first because I had not read any of the ancient critics, and did not know that it was all stolen.
Ibid.

16 In his last moments, not being able to carry a glass of jelly to his mouth, he was in such a passion, feeling his own weakness, that he threw jelly, glass and all, into Lady Chatham's face, and expired.
Hannah More, letter to her sister 1750

17 I believe no one ever studied so hard as my brother did in his youth. He did nothing but write and read.
Mrs Racket (Pope's sister-in-law). Quoted Rev. Joseph Spence, OBSERVATIONS, ANECDOTES AND CHARACTERS 1820

18 He was about four feet six inches high, very hump-backed and deformed. He wore a black coat and according to the fashion of that time had a little sword. He had a large and very fine eye, and a long handsome nose; his mouth had those peculiar marks which are always found in the mouths of

crooked persons and the muscles which run across the cheek were so strongly marked that they seemed like small cords.
Sir Joshua Reynolds, MEMOIRS   1818

1   I have several times talked to a very aged boatman on the Thames who recollected "Mr Alexander Pope". This boatman, when a lad, had frequently assisted his father in rowing Pope up and down the river. On such occasions Pope usually sat in a sedan chair.
Samuel Rogers, TABLE TALK   1856

2   Lawless told me that he was once walking through Twickenham accompanied by a friend, and a little boy, the son of that friend. On the approach of a very diminutive, misshapen and shabbily dressed person the child drew back, half afraid. "Don't be alarmed," said Lawless, "it is only a poor man." "A poor man!" cried his friend, "Why, that is Mr Alexander Pope."
Ibid.

3   His verses resembled nothing so much as a spoonful of boiling oil ladled out by a fiendish monkey at an upstairs window upon such of the passers-by as the wretch had a grudge against.
Lytton Strachey, Spectator   20 Nov 1909

4   In Pope I cannot read a line / But with a sigh I wish it mine. / When he can in one couplet fix / More sense than I can do in six / It gives me such a jealous fit / I cry "Pox take him and his wit".
Jonathan Swift

5   His wit is as thick as Tewkesbury mustard.
Lewis Theobald, PREFACE TO THE WORKS OF SHAKESPEARE   1733

GREGORY ALEXANDROVICH, PRINCE POTEMKIN (1739–1791)
Polish-born Russian statesman, favourite of Catherine the Great

6   Potemkin shows himself to his army with the air of an Agamemnon amidst the kings of Greece. What is his magic? Genius, and then genius and again genius; natural intelligence, an excellent memory, elevation of the soul, malice without malignity, craft without cunning, a happy mixture of caprices of which the good when they are uppermost win him all hearts.
Charles-Joseph, Prince de Ligne, letter to Count de Segur   10 Aug 1788

7   When, in 1787 Catherine paid a visit to his government in the South, he caused an immense number of wooden houses to be grouped into towns and villages along the czarina's route, and hired people to act the part of villagers. The czarina, gratified at the seeming improvement of the country, covered Potemkin with honours.
David Patrick and F. Hindes Groome,
CHAMBERS BIOGRAPHICAL
DICTIONARY   1897

EZRA WESTON LOOMIS POUND (1885–1972)
American poet and critic

8   His costume — the velvet jacket and the open-road shirt, was that of the English aesthete of the period. There was a touch of Whistler about him. His language, on the other hand, was pure Huckleberry Finn.
Sylvia Beach, SHAKESPEARE AND COMPANY

9   I remember only one thing about Pound. He had a beard, and it looked false.
Anthony Burgess, quoting an anonymous contributor to the Times Literary Supplement, Observer, Mad about Writing   13 Mar 1983

10   I have never known a man, of any nationality, to live so long out of his native country without seeming to settle anywhere else.
T. S. Eliot, EZRA POUND: *A Collection of Critical Essays (edited by Walter Sutton)*

11   To me Pound remains the exquisite showman minus the show.
Ben Hecht, POUNDING EZRA

12   Pound has spent his life trying to live down a family scandal — he is Longfellow's grand-nephew.
D. H. Lawrence, letter to Robert Graves

13   Ezra Pound, I feel, is probably a poet of higher and rarer order than it is easy at times to realise, because of much irrelevant dust kicked up by his personality as it rushes, strides or charges across the temporal scene.
Percy Wyndham Lewis. Quoted William Van O'Connor, EZRA POUND

ELVIS ARON PRESLEY (1935–1977)
American singer

14   . . . that half-melted vanilla face.
Brad Barrach, Life magazine   1974

15   Mr Presley has no discernible singing ability. His speciality is rhythm songs which he renders in an undistinguished whine; his phrasing,

phrasing, if it can be called that, consists of
the stereotyped variations that go with a
beginner's arias in a bath tub. For the ear he
is an unutterable bore.
Jack Gould, New York Times 7 *Jun* 1956

JOSEPH PRIESTLEY (1733–1804)
English chemist and writer on theology

1 From his discoveries we are assured that no
vegetable grows in vain; but that from the
oak in the forest to the grass in the field
every individual plant is serviceable to mankind; if not always distinguished by some
private virtue, yet making a part of the
whole which cleanses and purifies our
atmosphere. In this the fragrant rose and
the deadly nightshade co-operate. Nor is the
herbage nor the woods that flourish in the most
remote and unpopulated regions of the
world unprofitable to us, nor we to them,
considering how constantly the winds convey to them our vitiated air, for our relief
and for their nourishment.
*Sir John Pringle. Speech at the Royal
Society* 30 *Nov* 1733

2 I was intimately acquainted with Dr
Priestley, and a more amiable man never
lived; he was all gentleness, kindness and
humility. He was once dining with me when
someone asked him, rather rudely, how
many books he had published. He replied,
"Many more, sir, than I should care to
read."
Samuel Rogers 1856

3 The attention of Dr Priestley, the founder
of a new branch of science and the dis-
coverer of many gasses, was accidentally
drawn to the subject by the circumstance of
his residing in the neighbourhood of a large
brewery. Being an attentive observer he
noted, in visiting the brewery, the peculiar
appearances attending the extinction of
lighted chips in the gas floating over the
fermented liquor.
Samuel Smiles, SELF HELP 1859

SERGE SERGEYEVICH PROKOFIEV (1891–1953)
Russian composer

4 Prokofiev might well be described as a
cubist in music. His thematic material is
generally square-cut and clearly defined, his
idiom hard and dry, his texture free from
half-tones and haziness, and his forms are
angular and symmetrical. The continuous,
unflagging rhythmic motion of many of his

movements gives an impression of physical
energy and sureness of purpose.
Eric Blom, GROVE'S DICTIONARY OF MUSIC
AND MUSICIANS (*third edition*) 1928

5 The music of *The Love of Three Oranges*, I
fear, is too much for this generation . . . Mr
Prokofiev might well have loaded up a
shotgun with several thousand notes of
various lengths and discharged them against
the side of a blank wall.
Edward Moore, Chicago Tribune
31 *Dec* 1921

HENRY PURCELL (1658–1695)
English composer

6 He was so superior to all his predecessors
that his compositions seem to speak a new
language; yet, however, different from that
to which the public had been accustomed, it
was universally understood. His songs seem
to contain whatever the ear could wish, or
the heart could feel.
Dr Charles Burney, A GENERAL HISTORY
OF MUSIC 1798

7 The heavenly choir, who heard his notes
from high / Let down the scale of Music
from the sky / They handed him along / And
all the way he taught, and all the way they
sang. / Ye brethren of the lyre, and tuneful
voice, / Lament his loss, but at your own
rejoice. / Now live secure and linger out
your days, / The gods are pleas'd alone with
Purcell's lays / Nor know to mend their
choice.
John Dryden, ODE ON THE DEATH OF MR
HENRY PURCELL

8 The Orfeus Britannicus, Mr H. Purcell, who
unhappily began to show his great skill before the reform of musick *al'Italliana*, and
while he was warm to the pursuit of it dyed;
but a greater musicall genius England never
had.
Roger North, THE MUSICALL GRAMMARIAN

9 What no one will fail to find in Purcell at his
best is a spring of life, a vitality that glows
with the whole man. To listen to is to share an
experience, to catch some of his glancing
fire, and to have a part in his aching regret.
Sir Jack Westrup, PURCELL

PYTHAGORAS (sixth century BC)
Greek philosopher

10 Pythagoras might have had more calmer
sleepes if he totally abstained from beanes.
Sir Thomas Browne, ON DREAMS

1 The which Pythagoras said to his scholars of old may be for ever applied to melancholy men, *A fabis abstinete*, eat no beans.
Robert Burton, ANATOMY OF MELANCHOLY, *Democritus to the Reader* 1621

2 I am not disposed to approve the practice traditionally ascribed to the Pythagoreans who, when questioned as to the grounds of any assertion that they advanced in debate, are said to have been accustomed to reply "The Master says so", the master being Pythagoras. So potent was an opinion already decided, making authority prevail unsupported by reason.
Cicero

3 The greatest asceticism was required from his followers, who were compelled to undergo rigorous training not only in gymnastics, but also in mathematics and music. Pythagoras held that number was the fundamental thing in the universe. Not simply that things had numerical attributes, but that they were number.
J. A. Hammerton (editor), CONCISE UNIVERSAL BIOGRAPHY

4 The principle of the clavichord had been worked out by Pythagoras in the sixth century BC. On pressing a key a tongue of brass at the other end of the key rose up and struck a string. The piece of brass, known as the "tangent", not only produced a note, but measured out the right amount of string to give that note, and stayed put until the key was released.
Frank Muir, THE FRANK MUIR BOOK 1975

5 Pythagoras founded a religion, of which the main tenets were the transmigration of souls and the sinfulness of eating beans. His religion was embodied in a religious order which, here and there, acquired control of the state and established a rule of the saints. But the unregenerate still hankered after beans, and sooner or later rebelled.
Bertrand Russell

R

FRANÇOIS RABELAIS (1483–1553)
French author

1 Pantagruel is a kind of comic Christ. Wherever he appears he promotes ecstasy. He wishes to redeem the world through wine, which is Christ's blood.
Anthony Burgess, Observer, reviewing M. A. Screech's RABELAIS 20 *Jan* 1980

2 Rabelais was a genuine reformer in that he wanted not merely to clean up the Church but to reinfuse it with that primitive joy which had once made men willing to die for it.
Ibid.

3 Rabelais has touched English literature — Sterne, Burns, Joyce, even Shakespeare — more than French.
Ibid.

4 Rabelais is the wondrous mask of ancient comedy detached from the Greek proscenium, from bronze made flesh, henceforth a human living face, remaining enormous and coming among us to laugh at us and with us.
Victor Hugo

5 Rabelais must be read among the rich lands of the Chionnais in Touraine, on the edge of a white road with cornfields and vineyards on either side. But let there be a farmyard near, with a ripe and aromatic muck-heap in it, the scent of which must be borne to you on the wind; and let there also be loud bursts of rustic laughter, and a bottle of Chinon.
D. B. Wyndham Lewis, ON STRAW AND OTHER CONCEITS 1927

6 Dr Swift was a great reader and admirer of Rabelais and used sometimes to scold me for not liking him enough. Indeed there were so many things in his works in which I could not see any manner of meaning driven at, that I never could read him over with any patience.
Alexander Pope. Quoted Rev. Joseph Spence, OBSERVATIONS, ANECDOTES AND CHARACTERS 1820

7 Rabelais has writ some sensible pieces which the world did not regard at all. "I will write something", says he, "which they shall take notice of" and so sat down to write nonsense.
Ibid.

SERGEI VASILYEVICH RACHMANINOV (1873–1943)
Russian composer and pianist

8 Rachmaninov was the only pianist I have ever seen who did not grimace. That is a great deal.
Igor Stravinsky. Quoted Robert Craft, CONVERSATIONS WITH IGOR STRAVINSKY 1958

ANN RADCLIFFE (1764–1823)
English novelist

9 Charming as were all Mrs Radcliffe's works, charming as were the works of all her imitators, it was not in them, perhaps, that human nature, at least in the midland counties of England, was to be looked for.
Jane Austen, NORTHANGER ABBEY 1818

10 In harrowing up the soul with imaginary horrors, and making the flesh creep and the nerves thrill, she is unrivalled among her fair country-women. She makes her readers twice children.
William Hazlitt, ENGLISH COMIC WRITERS 1819

11 Mrs Radcliffe makes an appeal, less to the nerves than to the imagination, using as we have seen the desiccated idiom of the age, like Scott and she does achieve a total effect.
Q. D. Leavis, FICTION AND THE READING PUBLIC

12 The most influential novelist of the eighteenth century, only very incidentally a writer of absurdities.
Michael Sadleir, THINGS PAST 1944

SIR WALTER RALEGH (1552–1618)
English courtier, explorer, statesman and historian

13 He was a tall, handsome and bold man but his failing was that he was damnably proud. He had a most remarkable aspect, an

exceeding high forehead, long-faced and sour eie-lidded, a kind of pigge-eie.
John Aubrey, BRIEF LIVES 1680

1 He took a pipe of tobacco, a little before he went to the scaffold, which some formal persons were scandalised at, but I think 'twas well and properly done, to settle his spirits.
Ibid.

2 Thou art a monster; thou has an English face but a Spanish heart. Thou art the most vile and execrable Traitor that ever lived . . . There never lived a viler viper upon the face of the earth than thou.
Sir Edward Coke to Ralegh during his trial

3 The events of his life are interesting; but his character is ambiguous, his actions are obscure, his writings are English, and his fame is confined to the narrow limits of our language and our island.
Edward Gibbon, MEMOIRS AND MISCELLANEOUS WRITINGS (*edited by Lord Sheffield*) 1796

4 The tobacco business is a conspiracy against womanhood and manhood. It owes its origin to that scoundrel Sir Walter Ralegh, who was likewise the founder of American slavery.
Dr John Harvey Kellogg, TOBACCO

5 The soldier, the sailor, the scholar, the courtier, the orator, the poet, the historian, the philosopher whom we picture to ourselves sometimes reviewing the Queen's guard, sometimes giving chase to a Spanish galleon, then answering to the chiefs of the country party in the House of Commons, then again murmuring one of his sweet love-songs too near the ears of Her Majesty's maids of honour, and soon after poring over the Talmud, or collating Polybius with Livy.
T. B. Macaulay, Edinburgh Review, Burleigh and His Times Apr 1832

6 The origin of Ralegh's advancement in the Queen's graces was by an act of gallantry. Ralegh spoiled a new plush cloak, while the Queen, stepping cautiously on it, shot forth a smile in which he read promotion. Captain Ralegh soon became Sir Walter, and rapidly advanced in the Queen's favour.
Vigneul Marville

7 In talking over the design for a dictionary that might be authoritative for our English writers Mr Alexander Pope rejected Sir Walter Ralegh twice, as too affected.
Rev. Joseph Spence, OBSERVATIONS, ANECDOTES AND CHARACTERS 1820

8 Some few days before suffering, he sent for Master Walter Burre, who formerly printed his first volume of *The History of the World* whom he asked how that work had sold. Mr Burre returned this answer that it had sold so slowly that it had undone him. At which words Sir Walter, stepping to his desk, took the other unprinted part of the work in his hand, with a sigh, saying, "Ah my friend, hath the first part undone thee, the second part shall undo no more; this ungrateful world is unworthy of it." Immediately going to the fireside he threw it in, and set his foot on it until it was consumed, as great a loss to Learning as Christendom could have, or owned, for his first volume after his death sold thousands.
Winstanley, ENGLAND'S WORTHIES

9 He was one that fortune had pickt up out of purpose, of whom to make an example, or to use as her Tennis Ball, thereby to show what she could do; for she tost him up nothing, and to and fro to greatness, and from thence down to little more than to that wherein she had found him (a bare Gentleman).
Anthony à Wood, ATHENAE OXONIENSES 1692

RAPHAEL (1488–1520)
(Raffaello Santi)
Italian artist

10 The mediaeval principles lead up to Raphael, and the modern principles lead down from him.
John Ruskin

11 The ideal of florid, passionless human beauty, benign, sweet, serenely rhythmical, that made Raphael the most classical artist of modern times is the favourite ideal of Italian painters from those days to our own times.
Adolfo Venturi

GREGORY EFIMOVICH RASPUTIN (1871–1916)
Russian religious fanatic

12 To follow our Friend's (Rasputin's) counsels, lovey — I assure you is right — He prays *so* hard day and night for you, only one must listen, trust and ask advice — not think. He does not know. God opens everything to him. He will be less mistaken in people than we — experience in life blessed by God.
Empress Alexandra to Tsar Nicholas II
18 *Dec* 1916

RONALD REAGAN (1911–)
Fortieth president of the United States

1   The words that come out of his mouth don't
    always start in his heart: his heart and his
    mouth don't work together.
    An 87-year-old great-great-grandmother.
    Quoted Robert Chesshyre, Observer, Agony
    of America   26 Jun 1983

2   It looks very much as if he is going to stand
    again for president; but you never know.
    He's an actor. He loves happy endings. So
    maybe he won't.
    J. K. Galbraith. Quoted Peter Hillmore,
    Observer   29 Jan 1984

3   I once started a trade union with Ronald
    Reagan. He was quite a lot to the left of me
    then. A real firebrand.
    Ibid.

4   That youthful sparkle in his eyes is caused
    by his contact lenses, which he keeps highly
    polished.
    Sheilah Graham, The Times   22 Aug 1981

5   He is the first man for twenty years to make
    the presidency a part-time job, a means of
    filling up a few of the otherwise blank days
    of retirement.
    Simon Hoggart, Observer   21 Jun 1981

6   In a disastrous fire in President Reagan's
    library both books were destroyed. And the
    real tragedy was that he hadn't finished col-
    ouring one.
    Jonathan Hunt, Observer, Public Eye
    30 Aug 1981

7   As the age of television progresses the
    Reagans will be the rule, not the exception.
    To be perfect for television is all a President
    has to be these days.
    Gore Vidal. Quoted Martin Amis, Observer
    7 Feb 1981

8   A triumph of the embalmer's art.
    Gore Vidal. Quoted John Heilpern,
    Observer   26 Apr 1981

9   Ask him the time, and he'll tell you how the
    watch was made.
    Jane Wyman (Reagan's first wife). Quoted
    Sheilah Graham, The Times   22 Aug 1981

REMBRANDT VAN RIJN (1606–1669)
Dutch painter

10 Shadow in a Rembrandt is a means of con-
    centrating on the parts that are felt most
    intensely.
    Sir Kenneth Clark, CIVILISATION   1969

11 He was of a dual nature; one, an adept,
    facile workman, a Dutch realist; the other,

an idealist, a romancer, a seer of visions,
whose principle and whose ideal was light.
Eugene Fromentin, LIFE OF REMBRANDT

12 Rembrandt is not to be compared in the
    painting of character with our extra-
    ordinarily gifted artist Mr Rippingale.
    John Hunt, The Examiner

13 Rembrandt was one day employed in taking
    the portraits of a family who were all to be
    included in a large picture. A servant
    acquainted him that his favourite ape was
    dead. The artist, forgetful of his own inter-
    est, ordered the dead animal to be brought
    in and began gravely to sketch out its res-
    emblance on the canvas among the figures
    already painted. The representations which
    the family made were all fruitless; Rem-
    brandt persisted, and chose rather to lose
    the price of the picture, already half
    painted, than to submit to deprive himself
    of so singular a whim.
    PERCY ANECDOTES   1823

SIR JOSHUA REYNOLDS (1723–1792)
English painter

14 The complexions of the figures, too, are
    most cadaverously insulted. It is well known
    that the two principals were always troubled
    with the gripes, but nevertheless it was cruel
    of Sir Joshua to physic them to that un-
    merciful degree to bring them down to the
    deadly tone of his palette.
    Rev. H. Bate, of Reynolds portrait of the
    Marlborough family, Morning Post   1778

15 When Sir Joshua Reynolds died / All nature
    was degraded; / The King drop't a tear into
    the Queen's ear / And all his Pictures
    Faded.
    William Blake, ANNOTATION TO SIR JOSHUA
    REYNOLDS' DISCOURSE   1783

16 Reynolds is all right. He's got no ideas, but
    he can paint.
    Sir Edward Burne-Jones. Quoted Mary
    Jago, BURNE-JONES TALKING   1982

17 I have been informed by Sir Thomas Law-
    rence, his admirer and rival, that in 1787 Sir
    Joshua's prices were two hundred guineas
    for the whole length, one hundred for the
    half; seventy for the kit-kat, and fifty for
    what is called the three-quarters. But even
    on these prices some increase must have
    been made, as Horace Walpole said, "Sir
    Joshua in his old age became avaricious. He
    had three thousand guineas for my picture
    of the three Ladies Walgrave."
    J. W. Croker, Quarterly Review   c.1810

18 I remember a picture by Sir Joshua
    Reynolds with a very poor tiger in it. It was

explained that he had not got a live tiger at hand when he painted the picture.
Mr Justice Darling, Edward Huntingdon v. Lewis and Simmons   May 1917

1   His pencil was striking, restless and grand; / His manners were gentle, compelling and bland; / Still born to improve us in every part, / His pencil our faces, his manner our heart.
Oliver Goldsmith, RETALIATION   1774

2   A flattering painter who made it his care, / To draw men as they ought to be, not as they are.
Ibid.

3   Here Reynolds is laid, and to tell you my mind / He has not left a wiser or better behind.
Ibid.

4   He found English portraiture stiff and monotonous; he made it gracious and infinitely varied.
Sir Charles Holmes

5   I wish you could see a picture Sir Joshua has just finished, of the prophet Samuel, on his being called. The gaze of young astonishment was never so beautifully expressed. Sir Joshua tells me he is exceedingly mortified when he shows this picture to some of the great — they ask him who Samuel was?
Hannah More, letter to her family   1776

6   Reynolds damaged his hearing in Rome when trying to copy a Raphael in a particularly draughty corner of the Vatican.
Frank Muir, THE FRANK MUIR BOOK   1975

7   Curiously, because Reynolds employed a number of assistants who should have been able to correct the fault, he never mastered the technique of preparing his colours, consequently the carmine in the cheeks of his portraits began to fade almost before the paint was dry. Horace Walpole suggested that the portraits should be paid for by annuities so long as they lasted.
Ibid.

8   Of Reynolds all good should be said and no harm; / Tho' the heart is too frigid the pencil too warm / Yet each fault from his converse we still must disclaim / As his temper 'tis peaceful, and pure as his fame / Nothing in it o'erflows, nothing ever is wanting; / It nor chills like his kindness, nor glows like his painting / When Johnson by strength overpowers our mind / When Montagu dazzles and Burke strikes us blind / To Reynolds well pleas'd for relief we may run / Rejoice in his shadow and shrink from the sun.
Mrs Hester Piozzi

9   When Sir Joshua's *Puck* was put up for auction it excited such admiration that there was a general clapping of hands; yet it was knocked down to me at a comparatively trifling price. I walked home from the sale, a man carrying *Puck* before me and so well was the picture known that more than one person as they passed us in the street, called out "There it is!"
Samuel Rogers, TABLE TALK   1856

10 Count d'Adhemar was the original purchaser of Sir Joshua's *Muscupila*. Sir Joshua, who fancied that he was bargaining for a different and less important picture, told him the price was fifty guineas; and on discovering his mistake allowed him to have it for that sum. It is now at St Anne's Hill. It would fetch, at the present day, a thousand guineas.
Ibid.

11 What a quantity of snuff Sir Joshua took! I once saw him at an academy dinner when his waistcoat was absolutely powdered with it.
Ibid.

12 I can hardly believe what was told me long ago by a gentleman living in the Temple, who, however, assures me it is a fact. He happened to be passing by Sir Joshua's house in Leicester Square when he saw a poor girl seated on the steps and crying bitterly. He asked what was the matter and she replied that she was crying" because the *one shilling* which she had received from Sir Joshua for sitting to him as a model had proved to be a bad one and he would not give her another".
Ibid.

13 Sir Joshua was always thinking of his art. He was one day walking with Dr Lawrence near Beaconsfield when they met a beautiful little peasant boy. Sir Joshua, after looking earnestly at the child, exclaimed, "I must go home and deepen the colouring of my *Infant Hercules*." The boy was a good deal sunburnt.
Ibid.

14 That wonderful portrait of Gibbon, in which while the ugliness and vulgarity of the features are refined away, the likeness is perfectly preserved.
Ibid.

15 Sir Joshua Reynolds used great quantities of snuff and he would take it so freely when he was painting that it greatly inconvenienced those sitters who were not addicted to it; so

that by sneezing they much deranged their positions, and often totally destroyed expressions which might never return.
J. T. Smith, NOLLEKENS AND HIS TIMES 1828

1 All his own geese are swans, and the swans of others are geese.
Horace Walpole, letter to Henry Walpole
1 *Dec* 1786

CECIL JOHN RHODES (1853–1902)
English-born South African financier and politician

2 He had grey curly hair and a face like a jubilee bonfire.
Lionel Curtis, WITH MILNER IN SOUTH AFRICA

3 The Duchess of Buccleuch once told me that she had met Cecil Rhodes at a party, but she had not asked to be introduced to him as she had heard that he disliked all women and that at times he could be very rude. She had told the Queen (Victoria) about this, but the Queen replied, "Oh dear, I don't think that can be true because he was very civil to me when he came here."
Sir Frederick Ponsonby, RECOLLECTIONS OF THREE REIGNS

4 Too big to get through the gates of Hell.
Olive Schreiner. Quoted Elizabeth Longford, THE JAMESON RAID

5 I admire him. I frankly confess it; and when his time comes I shall buy a piece of rope as a keepsake.
Mark Twain, FOLLOWING THE EQUATOR 1897

RICHARD I (1157–1199)
(The Lionheart)
King

6 The sun has set. No night has followed.
Giralus de Barri, of the accession of Richard on the death of Henry II 1189

7 Six months were all he devoted to his kingdom in ten years' reign.
A. J. Poole, FROM DOMESDAY BOOK TO MAGNA CARTA

8 He used England as a bank on which to draw and overdraw to finance his ambitious exploits abroad. Twice in four years England was called upon to furnish money on a wholly unprecedented scale; first for the crusade, and secondly for the king's ransom when he fell into the hands of the Emperor on his return.
Ibid.

9 As the earth darkens when the sun departs, so the face of this kingdom was changed by the absence of the king. All the barons were restless, castles were strengthened, towns fortified, moats dug.
Richard of Devizes, CHRONICLES 1192

10 I have long heard that your king is a man of greatest honour and bravery, but he is imprudent, and shows too great recklessness of his own life. I would rather have abundance of wealth with wisdom and moderation than display immoderate valour and rashness
Saladin to the Bishop of Salisbury, during Crusade truce 2 *Sep* 1192

11 O Richard! Oh my king, the universe forsakes thee / On earth there is none but I who cares for thy welfare.
Michael Jean Sedaine, BLONDEL'S SONG

RICHARD II (1367–1400)
King

12 A weak, vain, frivolous and inconstant prince; without weight to balance the scales of government; without discernment to choose a good ministry; without virtue to oppose the measures and advice of evil counsellors, even when they happened to clash with his own principles and opinions. He was a dupe to flattery, a slave to ostentation.
Tobias Smollett, HISTORY OF ENGLAND 1757

13 He was idle, profuse and profligate, and although brave by starts, naturally pusillanimous and irresolute. His pride and resentment prompted him to cruelty and breach of faith; while his necessities obliged him to fleece his people, and degrade the dignity of his character and station.
V. H. Galbraith, A NEW LIFE OF RICHARD II

14 If for no other reason, he should go down in history as the inventor of the handkerchief, the *chef d'oeuvre* of a dilettante of genius. The clerk who recorded his personal expenses specified that the cloths supplied were "little pieces made for giving to the lord king for carrying in his hand to wipe and cleanse his nose".
Anthony Steel. Quoted John Harvey, THE PLANTAGENETS 1948

RICHARD III (1452–1485)
King

15 The Character of this Prince has been in general very severely treated by Historians,

but as he was a York, I am rather inclined to suppose him a very respectable Man. It has indeed been confidently asserted that he killed his two Nephews and his Wife, but it has also been declared that he did not kill his two Nephews, which I am inclined to believe true; and if this is the case, it may also be affirmed that he did not kill his Wife, for if Perkin Warbeck was really the Duke of York, why might not Lambert Simnel be the Widow of Richard. Whether innocent or guilty, he did not reign long in peace, for Henry Tudor E. of Richmond as great a villain as ever lived, made a great fuss about getting the Crown and having killed the King at the battle of Bosworth, he succeeded to it.

Jane Austen, HISTORY OF ENGLAND BY A PARTIAL, PREJUDICED AND IGNORANT HISTORIAN

1   He contents the people wherever he goes, best that ever did prince. For many a poor man that hath suffered wrong many days has been relieved and helped by him. On my troth, I liked never the condition of any prince so well as him. God hath sent him to us for the weal of us all.

Thomas Langton, Bishop of St. Davids   1484

2   Friend and foe was much what indifferent, where his advantage grew, he spared no man's death, whose life withstood his purpose.

Sir Thomas More, THE HISTORY OF RICHARD III   1513

SAMUEL RICHARDSON (1689–1761)
English novelist

3   His mind is so very vile a mind, so cosy, so hypocritical, praise-mad canting, envious, concupiscent.

Samuel Taylor Coleridge, ANIMAE POETAE

4   Oh Richardson! Remarkable genius, thou shalt always form my reading. If compelled by bitter necessity — if my means are insufficient to educate my children I will sell my books, but thou shalt remain! Yes, thou shalt rest in the same class with Moses, Homer, Euripides and Sophocles, to be read in turn.

Denis Diderot

5   Blessed be the shade of Richardson, who bequeathed to us the divine *Clarissa*, shining through sufferings, glorious in her fall, and almost visible in her ascent to the regions of immortality. Matchless creation of the only mind that ever conceived and drew truly a Christian heroine.

Mrs Ann Grant, LETTERS

6   What are his numerous blemishes but dust in the balance when compared to his endless beauties? But then, his faults are obvious to every common mind, and no common mind takes in his merits.

Ibid.

7   I read seventeen hours a day at *Clarissa* and held the book so long up, leaning on my elbows in an armchair, that I stopped the circulation and could not move. When Lovelace writes "Dear Belton, it is all over and Clarissa lives" I got up in a fury and wept like an infant, and cursed and d—d Lovelace till exhausted. This is the triumph of genius over the imagination and hearts of his readers.

B. R. Haydon, MEMOIRS

8   In *Pamela* Richardson produced an essay in vulgarity, of sentiment and morality alike, which has not been surpassed.

W. E. Henley, COLLECTED WORKS   1908

9   He could not be contented to sail quietly down the stream of reputation, without lingering to taste the froth from every stroke of the oar.

Samuel Johnson. Quoted Hester Piozzi, ANECDOTES OF THE LATE SAMUEL JOHNSON   1786

10   Richardson is the first of our novelists who set the fashion of concentrating all the interest of human life upon the war between men and women.

Lord Lytton

11   When his story *Pamela* first came out some extracts got into the public papers and used by that means to find their ways as far as Preston in Lancashire where my aunt who told me the story then resided. One morning as she rose the bells were set ringing and the flag was observed flying from the great steeple. She rang her bell and enquired the reason for these rejoicings when her maid came in bursting with joy and said, "Why, madam, poor Pamela's wed at last. The news came down to us in the morning papers."

A. D. McKillup, SAMUEL RICHARDSON, PRINTER AND NOVELIST

12   In my youth *Clarissa* and *Sir Charles Grandison* were the reigning entertainment. Whatever objections may be made to them in certain respects they contain more maxims of virtue and sound moral principle than half the books called moral. A large

volume of valuable aphorisms has been collected from them, abounding in practical lessons for conduct.
Hannah More

1 I suppose a novel cannot well succeed without contrasted characters and I am afraid that of Lovelace has been more admired than Clarissa's, and the last words of Lovelace, when he throws up a handful of blood towards heaven, "Let this expiate" are to me full proof that Richardson was no more competent to teach divinity than Fielding. I have heard likewise that Mr Richardson, when asked if he knew an original answerable to his portrait of Sir Charles Grandison, said he might apply it to Lord Dartmouth if he was not a Methodist.
Rev. J. Newton, letter to Hannah More 7 Apr 1799

CARDINAL RICHELIEU (1585–1642)
(Armand-Jean Duplessis)
French statesman

2 The cardinal was one of those ambitious men who foolishly attempt to rival every kind of genius; and seeing himself constantly disappointed he envied, with all the venom of rancour, those talents which are so frequently the *all* of men of genius. He was jealous of Balzac's splendid reputation, and offered the elder Heinsius ten thousand crowns to write a criticism which should ridicule his elaborate compositions. This Heinsius refused.
Isaac D'Israeli, CURIOSITIIES OF LITERATURE 1824

3 Richelieu leaned to the good whenever his interests did not draw him towards evil.
Cardinal de Retz, MEMOIRS 1717

MAXIMILIAN FRANÇOIS ISADORE DE ROBESPIERRE (1758–1794)
President of the Committee of Public Safety during the French Revolution

4 "A republic?" said the Seagreen with one of his dry, husky, unsportful laughs. "What is that?" O Seagreen Incorruptible, thou shalt see!
Thomas Carlyle, THE FRENCH REVOLUTION 1837

5 There is something paradoxical in the fact that a precise, cultivated, theory-ridden young dandy wielded such power over a collection of men, passionate, brutal, unbalanced and for the most part incapable of understanding the theories he held.
J. A. Hammerton (editor), CONCISE UNIVERSAL BIOGRAPHY

JOHN DAVISON ROCKEFELLER (1839–1937)
American financier and philanthropist

6 Rockefeller made his money in oil, which he discovered at the bottom of wells. Oil was crude in those days, but so was Rockefeller. Now both are considered quite refined.
Richard Armour, IT STARTED WITH COLUMBUS

7 A sort of lone wolf with whom aloofness has been second nature.
Richard Gilbert Collier, FAMOUS LIVING AMERICANS

8 John D. Rockefeller can be fully described as a man made in the image of the ideal money-maker. An ideal money-maker is a machine the details of which are diagrammed on the asbestos blueprints which paper the walls of Hell.
Thomas Lawson. Quoted Jules Abels, THE ROCKEFELLER MILLIONS

9 I believe the power to make money is a gift of God.
Rockefeller. Quoted Matthew Josephson, THE ROBBER BARONS

ANNA ELEANOR ROOSEVELT (1884–1962)
Wife of the thirty-second president of the United States, chairman of the UN Human Rights Commission, newspaper columnist

10 Eleanor Roosevelt's hats had the look of having been found under the bed.
Joseph Alsop, THE LIFE AND TIMES OF FRANKLIN D. ROOSEVELT

11 No woman has ever so comforted the distressed or so distressed the comfortable.
Clare Boothe Luce, ANNA ELEANOR ROOSEVELT

12 She would rather light candles than curse the darkness, and her glow has warmed the world.
Adlai Stevenson. Speech, United Nations Assembly 9 Nov 1962

FRANKLIN DELANO ROOSEVELT (1882–1945)
Thirty-second president of the United States

13 It is a mystery to me how each morning he selects the things he *can* do from the thousands he *should* do.
W. E. Binkley, THE MAN IN THE WHITE HOUSE

1 Roosevelt has exploded one of the most popular myths in America — he has dissociated the concept of wealth from the concept of virtue.
J. M. Burns, ROOSEVELT; THE LION AND THE FOX

2 Restless and mercurial in his thinking, a connoisseur of theories but impatient with people who took theories seriously, he trusted no system except the system of endless experimentation.
Earl Goldman, RENDEZVOUS WITH DESTINY

3 A chameleon on plaid.
Herbert Hoover. Quoted J. M. Burns, ROOSEVELT, THE LION AND THE FOX

4 The man who started more creations since Genesis — and finished none.
Hugh Johnson

5 I am advocating making him king in order that we may behead him if he goes too far beyond the limits of the endurable. A president, it appears, cannot be beheaded, but kings have been subject to the operation since ancient times.
H. L. Mencken. Quoted G. Wolfskill and J. A. Hudson, ALL BUT THE PEOPLE: F. D. ROOSEVELT AND HIS CRITICS

6 If he became convinced tomorrow that coming out for cannibalism would get him the votes he so sorely needs he would begin fattening a missionary on the White House backyard come Wednesday.
H. L. Mencken, FRANKLIN D. ROOSEVELT: A PROFILE *(edited by W. F. Leuchtenberg)*

7 His inaugural speech, beamed directly to the people, so roused the country that 400,000 persons sat down to write the new President a congratulatory letter. Ever since that historic day the postman has been a vital link in the decision-making process of a President-centred democracy.
Robert and Leona Rienow, THE LONELY QUEST

THEODORE ROOSEVELT (1858–1919)
Twenty-sixth president of the United States

8 He was the first influential man of his time to see clearly that the United States was no longer a rural nation but an industrial giant running amok.
Alistair Cooke, AMERICA

9 Theodore Roosevelt is affectionately recalled today as a half-heroic, half-comic figure, a bespectacled barrel of a man, choking with teeth and jingoism.
Ibid.

10 I told William McKinley it was a mistake to nominate that wild man as Vice-President. Now look, that damned cowboy is President of the United States.
Marcus Hanna to H. H. Kohlsaat at President McKinley's funeral Sep 1901

11 I wish to preach, not the doctrine of ignoble ease, but the doctrine of the strenuous life.
Roosevelt. Speech, Chicago 10 Apr 1899

12 His idea of getting hold of the right end of the stick is to snatch it from the hands of someone who is using it effectively and to hit him over the head with it.
George Bernard Shaw

13 Roosevelt bit me and I went mad.
William Allen White. Quoted Richard Hofstader, THE AMERICAN POLITICAL DECISION

EARL OF ROSEBERY (1847–1929)
(Archibald Philip Primrose)
British Prime Minister

14 I always admired the glib way Rosebery spoke, when he knew little or nothing of the subject of which he was speaking.
A. J. Balfour. Quoted Frederick Ponsonby, RECOLLECTIONS OF THREE REIGNS

15 By marrying a young Rothschild, being Prime Minister and winning the Derby he demonstrated that it was possible to improve one's financial status and run the Empire without neglecting the study of form.
Claud Cockburn, ASPECTS OF ENGLISH HISTORY

16 He sought the palm without the dust.
His tutor at Eton. Quoted Winston Churchill, GREAT CONTEMPORARIES 1937

CHRISTINA GEORGINA ROSSETTI (1830–1894)
English poet

17 Miss Christina was exactly the pure and docile-hearted damsel that her brother portrayed God's Virgin pre-elect to be be.
William Holman-Hunt, PRERAPHAELITISM

1 She wrote enough poems about lilies, briar
roses, pomegranates and fiery singing birds
to keep Morris and Co in wallpaper and
fabric orders through many a prosperous
season.
*Michael Ratcliffe, The Times, reviewing
Georgina Battiscombe's,* CHRISTINA
ROSSETTI: *A divided life* 21 *May* 1981

DANTE GABRIEL ROSSETTI (1828–1882)
English painter and poet

2 I should say that Rossetti was a man without
principles at all, who earnestly desired to
find salvation along the lines of least resistance
Ford Maddox Ford, ANCIENT LIGHTS

3 There was what one critic has well called the
"re-birth of wonder" in his work. To him
the world was an enchanted place and his
women were all heroines of the spirit.
Frank Harris, MY LIFE AND LOVES 1927

4 Personally he struck me as an unattractive,
poor man. I suppose he was horribly bored.
But his pictures, as I saw them in his room, I
thought decidedly strong. They were all
large, fanciful portraits of women of the
type *que vous savez*, narrow, special,
monotonous, but with lots of beauty and
power.
Henry James, letter to John le Farge
20 *Jun* 1869

5 Rossetti is not a painter. Rossetti is a ladies'
maid.
J. M. Whistler. Quoted R. Emmons, LIFE
AND OPINIONS OF WALTER SICKERT

JEAN-JACQUES ROUSSEAU (1712–1778)
French philosopher and writer

6 Rousseau was the first militant lowbrow.
*Sir Isaac Berlin, Observer, Sayings of the
Week* 9 *Nov* 1952

7 Without one natural pang he casts away, as
a sort of offal or excrement, the spawn of his
disgustful amours, and sends his children to
the hospital for foundlings.
Edmund Burke. Quoted Matthew Arnold,
ESSAYS IN CRITICISM; *Literary Influence of
Academics* 1865

8 Wild Rousseau / The apostle of affliction,
he who threw / Enchantment over passion,
and from woe / Wrung overwhelming
eloquence.
Lord Byron, CHILDE
HAROLD, III lxxvii 1816

9 Rousseau, sir, is a very bad man. I would
sooner sign a sentence for his transportation

than that of any felon who has gone from
the Old Bailey these many years. Yes, I
would like to have him work in the
plantations.
Samuel Johnson. Quoted Boswell, THE
LIFE OF JOHNSON 1791

10 It was not Napoleon who made the French
Revolution; but Rousseau, a crazy Swiss
who took to knitting and dressing up in
Armenian costume, had a lot to do with it.
Malcolm Muggeridge, TREAD SOFTLY FOR
YOU TREAD ON MY JOKES 1966

11 As a child I had the faults common to my
age, was talkative, a glutton and sometimes
a liar; made no scruple of stealing
sweetmeats, fruits, or indeed any kind of
eatables; but never took delight in mischievous waste, in accusing others, or in
tormenting harmless animals. I recollect indeed that one day, while Madame Clot, a
neighbour of ours, was gone to church, I
made water in her kettle; the remembrance,
even now, makes me smile, for Mme Clot
was one of the most tedious, grumbling old
women I ever knew. Thus have I given a
brief, but faithful history of my childish
transgressions.
Rousseau, CONFESSIONS 1781

12 The *Social Contract* became the Bible of
most of the leaders in the French Revolution, but no doubt, as is the fate of
Bibles, it was not carefully read and was still
less understood by many of its disciples.
Bertrand Russell, HISTORY OF WESTERN
PHILOSOPHY 1946

PETER PAUL RUBENS (1577–1640)
Flemish painter

13 To my eye Rubens' colouring is most contemptible. His shadows are a filthy brown
somewhat of the colour of excrement.
*William Blake, annotation to Sir Joshua
Reynolds'* DISCOURSES

14 I never was so disgusted in my life as with
Rubens and his eternal wives and infernal
glare of colours, as they appear to me.
Lord Byron, letter to John Murray
14 *Apr* 1817

15 His force, vehemence and *éclat* with him
take the place of grace and charm.,
Eugène Delacroix, JOURNAL 1893

16 A chemist tendered him a share of his
laboratory, and of his hopes for the
philosopher's stone. Rubens took the
visionary into his painting room, and told
him his offer was dated twenty years too late
"for so long it is," said he "that I found the

art of making gold with my pencil and pallet".
PERCY ANECDOTES   1823

1   Rubens was sent by the Court of Spain on a secret embassy to King Charles I, and while in England painted the ceiling of the Banqueting House at Whitehall for which he received three thousand pounds.
Ibid.

2   He never hesitated on his triumphal progress. However much we may regret his lack of self-criticism, it is to that he owed his surety. He was quite simply a man of action, and he painted as other men fenced, or fought, or made business. Quite frankly, art was his business.
Herbert Read

3   The fellow mixes blood with his colours.
Guido Reni

4   Indeed the facility with which he invented, the richness of his composition, the luxuriant harmony and brilliancy of his colouring, so dazzle the eye, that whilst his works continue before us we cannot help thinking that all his deficiencies are fully supplied.
Sir Joshua Reynolds, DISCOURSES

RUDOLF I (1218–1291)
Founder of the Hapsburg dynasty

5   By God, let any man who will come to me. I have not become king to live hidden in a closet.
After his coronation   1273

JOHN RUSKIN (1819–1900)
English author

6   We should read Ruskin for the very quality of his mind which, when abused, makes him unreadable; his refusal to consider any human faculty in isolation. This characteristic, which produced the intellectual chaos of his later works, also allowed him to make his original and important discoveries.
Sir Kenneth Clark, RUSKIN TODAY

7   He is a chartered libertine — he has possessed himself by prescription of the function of a general scold.
Henry James, The Nation, On Whistler and Ruskin   19 *Dec* 1878

8   Leave to squeamish Ruskin / Popish Apennines / Dirty stones of Venice / And his gas-lamps seven / We've the stones of Snowdon / And the lamps of heaven.
Charles Kingsley

9   Went to the Working Men's Club to hear Ruskin's talk about Switzerland. The room was full, many of the teachers there. Ruskin had brought one or two of his best Turners, and photographs and maps. He spoke well and in his normal free pleasant way; with as usual a little too much *infant school* humour — like the funny papa telling stories to good boys. His lecture was historical and geographical chiefly — without book, he standing before the fire with hands under coat tails, and whisking about in his airy way.
A. J. Munby, JOURNAL   2 *May* 1849

10 Ruskin is one of the most turbid and fallacious minds of the century. To the service of the most wildly eccentric thoughts he brings the ascerbity of a bigot.
Max Nordau

11 His mental temperament is that of the first Spanish Grand Inquisitor. He is a Torquemada of aesthetics. He would burn alive the critic who disagrees with him. Since stakes do not stand within his reach he can at last rage and rave in word, and annihilate the heretic figuratively by abuse and cursing.
Ibid.

12 It is as a social philosopher, not as an art critic, that he has had the wildest influence during the last seventy-five years. His remarkable style, with its long and elaborate sentences, fascinated Marcel Proust, who imitated it.
J. B. Priestley, LITERATURE AND WESTERN MAN   1960

13 A certain girlish petulance of style that distinguishes Ruskin was not altogether a defect. It served to irritate and fix attention where a more evenly judicial writer might have remained unread.
W. R. Sickert, New Age, The Spirit of the Hive   26 *May* 1910

14 I doubt that art needed Ruskin any more than a moving train needs one of its passengers to shove it.
Tom Stoppard, Times Literary Supplement   3 *Jun* 1977

15 Because he approached every aspect of Victorian life — aesthetic, scientific, moral, social and spiritual — as part of his own search for himself Ruskin's life and work seem to embody all the conflicts that we have inherited from that time.
Angus Wilson, Observer, reviewing John Dixon Hunt's THE WILDER SEA: *A Life of Ruskin*   14 *Feb* 1982

BERTRAND ARTHUR WILLIAM, THIRD EARL RUSSELL (1872–1970)
Philosopher and writer

1 I told D. H. Lawrence how enchanted I had been by the lucidity, the suppleness and pliability of Bertrand Russell's mind. He sniffed. "Have you ever seen him in a bathing dress?" he asked. "Poor Bertie Russell. His is all Disembodied Mind."
William Gerhardie, MEMOIRS OF A POLYGLOT

2 If I were the Prince of Peace I would choose a less provocative Ambassador.
A. E. Housman. Quoted Alan Wood, BERTRAND RUSSELL: *The Passionate Sceptic*

3 He is much too inexperienced in personal contact and conflict for a man of his age and calibre. It isn't that life has been too much for him, but too little.
D. H. Lawrence, letter to Lady Ottoline Morrell 1915

4 Lord Russell explained that he had two models for his own style — Milton's prose and Baedeker's guide books. The Puritan never wrote without passion, he said, and the cicerone used only a few words in recommending sights, hotels, and restaurants. Passion was the voice of reason, economy the signature of brilliance.
Ved Mehta, THE FLY AND THE FLY-BOTTLE

5 In one of his books he speaks very favourably of adultery, but he does so in the scientific way in which one might say a word for the method of least squares, the hookworm, or a respectable volcano.
H. L. Mencken, Baltimore Sun May 1940

6 He felt that excellence came from the special nurturing of individual talent and that mediocrity or cultural decline would follow from the overthrow of privilege. He desired its overthrow, but he mourned in advance some of the consequences as he saw them.
Ralph Schoenmann, BERTRAND RUSSELL AND THE PEACE MOVEMENT

S

VICTORIA (VITA) MARY SACKVILLE-WEST (1892–1962)
English writer

1 She looked like Lady Chatterley above the waist, and the gamekeeper below.
Cyril Connolly

2 She would wish life to be conducted on a series of *grandes passions*. Or she thinks she would. In practice, had I been a passionate man I should have suffered tortures of jealousy on her behalf, have made endless scenes, and we should now have separated, I living in Montevideo as H. M. minister, and she breeding Samoyeds in the Gobi Desert.
Harold Nicolson, DIARY 24 Dec 1933

3 Working always in her garden, caring for her friends, her flowers and her poetry, modest and never interesting herself in literary disputes, her friendship had the freedom of silence and watchfulness about it.
Stephen Spender, WORLD WITHIN WORLD

CHARLES CAMILLE SAINT-SAENS (1835–1921)
French composer

4 I am told that Saint-Saens has informed a delighted public that since the war began he has composed music for the stage, melodies, an elegy, and a piece for the trombone. If he'd been making shell-cases instead it might have been all the better for music.
Maurice Ravel, letter to Jean Marnold 5 Oct 1916

5 It is one's duty to hate, with all possible fervour, the empty and ugly in art; and I hate Saint-Saens the composer with a hate that is perfect.
J. F. Runciman, Saturday Review 12 Dec 1896

SALADIN (1137–1193)
Sultan of Damascus, Saracen commander

6 When Allah has given into my hands all the Christian towns I shall divide them among my children. I shall leave them my final in-structions and then embark on the sea and subdue the lands of the West. I do not intend to lay down my arms until there is not a single infidel left alive on earth.
Saladin declaring his intentions at Ascalon 1188

FIRST EARL OF SALISBURY (1563–1612)
(Robert Cecil)
English statesman

7 He was no fit counsellor to make affairs better, yet he was fit to stop them from getting worse.
Francis Bacon

8 The Queen was wont to call Sir Robert Cecil her register of remembrances.
Sir Henry Wootton, CHARACTER OF ROBERT CECIL

9 His making ready to die was the greatest blessing of his life to him; for he never went to bed without cares till then, but had alarums everywhere to wake him, save in his conscience; when death came to be his business, he was in peace, and so died.
Ibid.

THIRD MARQUIS SALISBURY (1830–1903)
(Robert Arthur Talbot Gascoyne Cecil)
British Prime Minister

10 Not a man who measures his words, but a great master of jibes and flouts and jeers.
Disraeli, House of Commons 5 Aug 1874

11 I am always very glad when Lord Salisbury makes a great speech. It is sure to include at least one blazing indiscretion which it is a delight to remember.
Earl of Morley. Speech, Hull 29 Nov 1887

12 Of Lord Salisbury I can only observe that the combination of such genuine amiability in private with such calculated brutality in public utterance is a psychological phenom-enon which might profitably be made the subject of a Romanes Lecture at Oxford.
G. W. E. Russell, SIXTY YEARS OF EMPIRE

GEORGE SAND (1804–1876)
(Amantine Lucile Aurore Dupin)
French writer

1 As to Papa, why he knows nothing of
Madame Dudevant and I don't feel inclined
to explain her to him. If I were to say "She is
a great genius, and no better than she
should be, and I have read her books and I
want to write to her" he would think I was
mad and required his parental restraint.
*Elizabeth Barrett (Browning), letter
7 Oct 1844*

2 George Sand is as famous for her love
affairs with such prominent artistic figures
as Alfred de Musset and Frederic Chopin as
she is for her writings.
*William Rose Benét, THE READER'S
ENCYCLOPEDIA 1948*

3 How the devil did George Sand manage?
That sturdy woman of letters found it possible to finish one novel and start another in
the same hour. And she did not thereby lose
either a lover or a puff of the narghile, not
to mention a *Story of My Life* in 20
volumes, and I am overcome by
astonishment.
Colette, in 1946

4 A great cow full of ink.
Gustav Flaubert

ARTHUR SCHOPENHAUER (1788–1860)
German philosopher

5 He proclaimed that the world was his idea,
but meant only (what is undeniable) that his
idea of the world was his idea.
George Santayana

FRANZ PETER SCHUBERT (1797–1828)
Austrian composer

6 I lost myself in a Schubert quartet at the end
of a Crowndale Road concert, partly by
ceasing all striving to understand the music,
partly by driving off intruding thoughts,
partly by feeling the music coming up inside
me, myself a hollow vessel filled with sound.
Joanna Field, A LIFE OF ONE'S OWN

7 It was his privations, his absolute poverty
and the distress which he naturally felt at
finding that no exertions could improve his
circumstances, or raise him in the scale of
existence, that in the end dragged him
down. Within a year of his death we catch a
glimpse of him putting up with coffee and
biscuits because he has not 8½d to buy his
dinner with, selling his great trio for 17s
10d, and his songs at 10d each, and dying

the possessor of effects which were valued
at little more than two pounds.
*Sir W. H. Hadow, GROVE'S DICTIONARY
OF MUSIC AND MUSICIANS (THIRD
EDITION) 1928*

8 On their first meeting Beethoven treated
Schubert kindly, but without much
appreciation, and contented himself with
pointing out to him one or two mistakes in
harmony. Being quite deaf, he requested
Schubert to write his answers; but the young
man's hand shook so from nervousness that
he could do and say nothing, and left in the
greatest vexation and disappointment. It
was only during his last illness that
Beethoven learned that Schubert had composed more than five hundred songs, and
from that time till his death he passed many
hours over them.
H. R. Haweis, MUSIC AND MORALS

9 Franz Schubert, a lesser artist perhaps than
some other great masters, but of them all
endowed with the most abounding heritage
of music.
Friedrich Nietzsche

ROBERT FALCON SCOTT (1868–1912)
British Antarctic explorer

10 A topper — a better leader or tent-
companion one could not have. I can say
unhesitatingly that he is one of the best —
an absolute 'sahib'.
*Lieutenant Bowers. Quoted Roland
Huntford, SCOTT AND AMUNDSEN 1979*

11 Scott is presented as a middle-class social
climber, a back-stairs intriguer, and string-
puller; a Polar explorer primarily because
he thought that success in that field would
compensate for failure in a more orthodox
career, an incompetent planner, abully and
a manipulator of the written word.
*Bernard Fergusson, Daily Telegraph,
reviewing Roland Huntford's SCOTT AND
AMUNDSEN 1 Oct 1979*

12 I dislike Scott intensely — he is not straight,
it is himself first and the rest nowhere, and
when he has got what he can from you it is
shift for yourself.
*Captain L. E. G. Oates, in a letter to his
mother*

SIR WALTER SCOTT (1771–1832)
Scottish novelist and poet

13 The Ariosto of the North.
*Lord Byron, CHILDE HAROLD,
Canto iv 1818*

1 It can be said of him, when he departed he took a Man's life with him. No sounder piece of British manhood was put together in that eighteenth century of time.
Carlyle, ESSAYS: *Lockhart's Life of Scott*

2 What I felt in *Marmion* I feel still more in *The Lady of the Lake* — viz — that a man accustomed to use words in metre, and familiar with descriptive Poets and Tourists, himself a Picturesque Tourist, must be troubled with a mental strangury, if he could not lift up his leg six different times in six different corners, and each time piss a canto.
Samuel Taylor Coleridge, letter to Wordsworth 1810

3 He is seen to have a heavy mind and a trivial style. He cannot construct. He has neither artistic detachment nor passion . . . He only has a temperate heart and gentlemanly feelings, and an intelligent affection for the countryside; and this is not basis enough for great novels.
E. M. Forster, ASPECTS OF THE NOVEL 1927

4 Sir Walter Scott one day in spring was walking round Abbotsford with Lady Scott. Passing a field where there were a number of ewes and frolicking lambs Sir Walter said "'Tis no wonder that poets from the earliest ages have made lambs an emblem of peace and innocence." "Delightful animals indeed," rejoined Lady Scott, "especially with mint sauce.".
Daniel George, A BOOK OF ANECDOTES 1957

5 Mr Scott always seems to me like a glass through which the rays of admiration pass without sensibly affecting it.
Mrs Ann Grant, LETTERS

6 Sir Walter Scott, when all is said and done, is an inspired butler.
William Hazlitt, MRS SIDDONS

7 The second and third volumes of a strange book entitled *Tales of My Landlord* are very fine in their way. People say 'tis like reading Shakespeare! I say 'tis as like Shakespeare as a bottle of peppermint water is to a bottle of the finest French brandy.
Mrs Hester Piozzi

8 The last series of those half novels, half romantic things called *Tales of My Landlord* are dying off apace; but if their author gets money he will not care about the rest. Having never owned his work, no celebrity can be lost, nor no venture can injure him.
Ibid.

9 During Scott's first visit to Paris I walked with him through the Louvre and pointed out for his particular notice the St. Jerome of Domenichino and some other *chefs d'oeuvre*. Scott merely glanced at them and passed on, saying, "I really have no time to examine them."
Samuel Rogers, TABLE TALK 1856

10 I introduced Sir Walter Scott to Madame D'Arblay having taken him with me to her home. She had not heard that he was lame; and when he limped towards a chair she said, "Dear me, Sir Walter, I hope you have not met with an accident." He answered, "An accident, madame, nearly as old as my birth."
Ibid.

11 Sir Walter (then Mr) Scott accompanied me to a party given by Lady Jersey. We met Sheridan there, who put the question to Scott in express terms, "Pray, Mr Scott, did you, or did you not, write *Waverley?*" Scott replied, "On my honour I did not." Now, though Scott may perhaps be justified for returning an answer in the negative, I cannot think he is to be excused for strengthening it with "on my honour".
Ibid.

12 I feel very unwell, and think it is the bile that hangs about me. I strive to amuse myself by reading novels and have finished that of the *Black Dwarf* by Sir Walter Scott. I must be reduced to a sad state when I feel obliged to read such nonsense for a pastime.
John Skinner, DIARY 17 Feb 1830

13 I passed three days with Walter Scott, an amusing and highly estimable man. You see the whole extent of his powers in the *Minstrel's Lay,* of which your opinion seems to accord with mine — a very amusing poem; it excites a novel-like interest, but you discover nothing on after-perusal. Scott bears a great part in the *Edinburgh Review,* but does not review well.
Southey to W. Taylor, of Norwich (the learned German translator of whom Sydney Smith once said "It takes nine men to make a Taylor.")

14 Then comes Sir Walter Scott with his enchantments. He sets the world in love with dreams and phantoms, with decayed and swinish forms of religion, with decayed and degraded forms of government; with silliness and emptiness, sham grandeurs, sham gauds, and sham chivalries of a brainless and worthless long-vanished society. He did measureless harm, more

real and lasting harm, perhaps, than any other man who ever wrote.
Mark Twain

1 Either Scott the novelist is swallowed whole, and becomes part of the body and brain, or he is rejected entirely. There is no middle party in existence, no busybodies run from camp to camp with offers of mediation. For there is no war.
Virginia Woolf, THE MOMENT

2 Part of the *Lay of the Last Minstrel* was recited to me by Scott while it was yet in manuscript and I did not expect that it would make much sensation; but I was mistaken, for it went up like a balloon.
William Wordsworth. Quoted Samuel Rogers, TABLE TALK 1856

ANNAEUS SENECA (4BC–65AD)
Roman philosopher. Tutor to Nero

3 Seneca writes as a Boare doth pisse — by jerks.
Dr Ralph Kettle. Quoted John Aubrey,
BRIEF LIVES

THOMAS SHADWELL (1642–1692)
English dramatist

4 Drink, Swear and Roar, forebear no lewd Delight / Fit for thy Bulk, do anything but write, / Thou art of lasting Make, like thoughtless men / A strong Nativity — but for the pen; Eat Opium, mingle Arsenic in thy Drink / Still thou mayst live, avoiding Pen and Ink.
John Dryden, ABSALOM AND
ACHITOPHEL 1681

5 The Virtuoso of Shadwell does not maintain his character with equal strength to the end; and this was the writer's general fault. Wycherley used to say of him that he knew how to start a fool very well, but that he was never able to run him down.
Alexander Pope. Quoted Rev. Joseph Spence, OBSERVATIONS, ANECDOTES AND
CHARACTERS 1820

SEVENTH EARL OF SHAFTESBURY
(1801–1885)
(Anthony Ashley Cooper)
English politician, philanthropist and reformer

6 You have given me the privilege of seeing one of the most impressive of all spectacles — a great English nobleman living in patriarchal state in his own hereditary halls.
Benjamin Disraeli

7 Lord Shaftesbury would have been in a lunatic asylum if he had not devoted himself to reforming lunatic asylums.
Florence Nightingale

WILLIAM SHAKESPEARE (1564–1616)
English dramatist and poet

8 Shakespeare, Madam, is obscene, and, thank God, we are sufficiently advanced to have found that out.
An American. Quoted Mrs Frances Trollope

9 Good friend for Jesus sake forebeare / To dig the dust enclosed here / Blest be ye man yt spares these stones / And curst be he yt moves my bones.
Anonymous. Inscription on Shakespeare's tombstone in Stratford church

10 Others abide our question, thou art free; / We ask and ask. Thou smilest and art still / Out-topping knowledge.
Matthew Arnold, SHAKESPEARE

11 Mr William Shakespeare was borne at Stratford-on-Avon in the county of Warwick. His father was a Butcher, and I have been told heretofor by some of the neighbours, that when he was a boy he exercised his father's Trade, but when he killed a Calfe he would do it in high style, and make a speech.
John Aubrey, BRIEF LIVES

12 I have heard Sir William Davenant and Thomas Shadwell (who is the best comedian we have now) say that he is a most prodigious wit.
Ibid.

13 Shakespeare is in the singularly fortunate position of being, to all intents and purposes, anonymous.
W. H. Auden, FOREWORDS AND
AFTERWORDS

14 The only tribute a French translator can pay Shakespeare is not to translate him — even to please Sarah Bernhardt.
Max Beerbohm, AROUND THEATRES 1930

15 Shakespeare, coming upon me unawares, struck me like a thunderbolt. The lightning flash of that discovery revealed to me at a stroke the whole heaven of art, illuminating its darkest corners.
Hector Berlioz, on first seeing a performance of Hamlet 1827

16 If I say that Shakespeare is the greatest of intellects I have said all concerning him. But

there is more in Shakespeare's intellect than we have yet seen. It is what I call an unconscious intellect; there is more virtue in it than he himself is aware of.
Thomas Carlyle, CHARACTERISTICS OF SHAKESPEARE

1 Shakespeare, who (taught by none) did first impart / To Fletcher wit, to labouring Jonson art; / He, Monarch-like, gave those his subjects law, / And is that Nature which they paint and draw.
John Dryden, Prologue to his version of THE TEMPEST

2 But Shakespeare's magic could not copy'd be, / Within that circle none durst walk but he.
Ibid.

3 He was the man who of all modern, and perhaps ancient, poets had the largest and most comprehensive soul.
John Dryden, ESSAY ON DRAMATIC POETRY

4 Heaven that but once was prodigal before / To Shakespeare gave as much; she could not give him more.
John Dryden, TO MR CONGREVE

5 We can say of Shakespeare that never has a man turned so little knowledge to so great account.
T. S. Eliot, THE CLASSICS AND THE MAN OF LETTERS 1942

6 If the only way to prove that Shakespeare did not feel and think exactly as people felt in 1815 or in 1860 or in 1880 is to show that he felt and thought as we felt and thought in 1927 then we must accept gratefully the alternative.
T. S. Eliot, SHAKESPEARE AND THE STOICISM OF SENECA

7 I saw Hamlet, Prince of Denmark played; but now the old plays begin to disgust this refined age, since his majesty has been so long abroad.
John Evelyn, DIARY 26 *Oct* 1661

8 Many were the wit combats between Shakespeare and Ben Jonson, which two I behold like a Spanish great galleon and an English man-o-war. Master Jonson like the former, was built far higher in learning; solid, but slow in his performance. Shakespeare, with the English man-o-war lesser in bulk, but lighter in sailing, could turn with all the tides, and take advantage of all winds by the quickness of his wits and invention.
Thomas Fuller, WORTHIES OF ENGLAND 1662

9 Was there ever such stuff as the greater part of Shakespeare? Only one must not say so. But what do you think? What? Is there not sad stuff? What? What?
George III. *Quoted Fanny Burney,* DIARY

10 Among the many reasons which make me glad to have been born in England, one of the first is that I read Shakespeare in my mother tongue.
George Gissing, THE PRIVATE PAPERS OF HENRY RYECROFT 1903

11 To him the mighty mother did unveil / Her awful face.
Thomas Gray, THE PROGRESS OF POESY

12 An upstart crow, beautiful with our feathers.
Robert Greene, A GROATSWORTH OF WIT BOUGHT WITH A MILLION OF REPENTANCE. (*Greene claimed that Shakespeare had stolen Henry* VI *from him.*)

13 His mind and hand went together and what he thought he uttered with that easiness that we have scarce received from him a blot [i.e. correction] in his papers.
John Heminge and Henry Cordell. Preface to the First Folio 1623

14 Playing Shakespeare is very tiring. You never get to sit down unless you're a king.
Josephine Hull. Quoted THE FRANK MUIR BOOK 1976

15 Shakespeare never had six lines without a fault.
Samuel Johnson. Quoted Boswell, THE LIFE OF JOHNSON 19 *Oct* 1769

16 The stream of Time, which is continually washing the dissoluable fabrics of other poets, passes without injury by the adamant of Shakespeare.
Samuel Johnson, PREFACE TO SHAKESPEARE

17 It must be at last confessed that, as we owe everything to him, he owes something to us; that, if much of our praise is paid by perception and judgement, much is likewise given by custom and veneration. We fix our eyes upon his graces, and turn them from his deformities and endure in him what we should in others loathe or despise.
Ibid.

18 Each change of many-coloured life he drew; / Exhausted worlds and then imagined new; / Existence saw him spur her bounded reign; / And, panting, toiled after him in vain.
Samuel Johnson, PROLOGUE AT THE OPENING OF DRURY LANE THEATRE

1 Corneille is to Shakespeare as a clipped hedge is to a forest.
Samuel Johnson, Rambler No. 160

2 Reader, look not at his picture, but his book.
Ben Jonson, on the portrait of Shakespeare in the First Folio

3 Sweet swan of Avon.
Ben Jonson, TO THE MEMORY OF MY BELOVED, THE AUTHOR, WILLIAM SHAKESPEARE 1628

4 He was not of an age, but for all time.
Ibid.

5 Thou hast little Latin and less Greek.
Ibid.

6 Thou art a monument without a tomb / And art alive still, while thy book doth live / And we have wits to read, and praise to give.
Ibid.

7 I loved the man and do honour his memory, on this side idolatry, as much as any.
Ben Jonson, TIMBER, OR DISCOVERIES MADE ON MEN AND MATTER

8 The players have often mentioned it as an honour to Shakespeare that in his writing (whatsoever he penned) he never blotted out a line. My answer hath been "Would that he had blotted out a thousand."
Ibid.

9 If Shakespeare led a life of Allegory his works are comments on it.
John Keats, letter to Georgina Keats 14 *Feb* 1819

10 When I read Shakespeare I am struck with wonder / That such trivial people should muse and thunder / In such lovely language.
D. H. Lawrence, WHEN I READ SHAKESPEARE

11 And so sepulchr'd in such pomp dost lie / That kings for such a tomb would wish to die.
John Milton, ON SHAKESPEARE 1630

12 Or sweetest Shakespeare, fancy's child / Warble his native wood-notes wild.
John Milton, L'ALLEGRO 1632

13 What needs my Shakespeare for his honoured bones / The labour of an age in piled stones, / Or that his hallowed relics should be hid / Under a starry-pointed pyramid? / Dear son of memory, great heir to fame / What needest thou such weak witness to thy Name? / Thou in our wonder and astonishment / Hast build thyself a live-long monument.
John Milton, AN EPITAPH ON THE ADMIRABLE DRAMATIC POET W. SHAKESPEARE

14 This evening I am engaged to spend with a foreigner. He is a Dane, unjustly deprived of his father's fortune by his mother's marrying a second time. I have never yet seen him, but I hear that all the world will be there, which I think is a little unfeeling, as he is a little low-spirited sometimes almost to madness. For my part, from what I have heard, I do not think the poor young man will live out the night.
Hannah More, letter to her family 1776

15 I know of no more heart-rending reading than Shakespeare. How a man must have suffered to be in such need of playing the clown.
Friedrich Nietzsche, ECCE HOMO

16 To the King's Theatre, where we saw *Midsummer Night's Dream*, which I had never seen before, nor shall ever see again, for it is the most insipid, ridiculous play that ever I saw in my life.
Samuel Pepys, DIARY

17 Shakespeare generally used to stiffen his style with high words and metaphors for the speeches of kings and great men; he mistook it for a mark of greatness. This is strongest in his early plays, but in his very last, his *Othello*, what a forced language he has put into his Duke of Venice!
Alexander Pope. Quoted Rev. Joseph Spence, OBSERVATIONS, ANECDOTES AND CHARACTERS 1820

18 Shakespeare (whom you and every playhouse bill / Style the divine! the matchless! What you will) / For gain, not glory, wing'd his roving flight / And grew immortal in his own despite.
Alexander Pope, IMITATIONS OF HORACE 1733

19 Or damn all Shakespeare, like the afflicted fool / At court, who hates whate'er he read at school.
Ibid.

20 He seems to have known the world by intuition, to have looked through nature at one glance.
Alexander Pope, PREFACE TO THE WORKS OF SHAKESPEARE

21 I lay an eternal curse on anyone who shall now or at any time hereafter make schoolbooks of my work and make me hated as Shakespeare is hated. My plays were not designed as instruments of torture.
George Bernard Shaw

22 Literature has no place in Henry Irving's death as it had no place in his life. Irving would turn in his coffin if I came, just as

Shakespeare will turn in his coffin when Irving comes.
George Bernard Shaw, letter to George Alexander, declining to attend Irving's funeral

1 There is no getting round the fact that Shakespeare was an aristocrat and what we should term nowadays a bit of a snob.
George Bernard Shaw, Public Opinion 29 Dec 1905

2 With the single exception of Homer there is no eminent writer, not even Sir Walter Scott, whom I can despise so entirely as I can despise Shakespeare when I measure my mind against his.
George Bernard Shaw, Saturday Review

3 It would positively be a relief to me to dig Shakespeare up and throw stones at him.
Ibid.

4 It is our misfortune that the sordid misery and hopeless horror of Shakespeare's view of man's destiny is still so appropriate to English society that we even today regard him as not for an age, but for all time.
George Bernard Shaw, THE UNSOCIAL SOCIALIST

5 Hamlet's experience simply could not have happened to a plumber.
George Bernard Shaw

6 Our Prime Minister carries a pocket Shakespeare with him wherever he travels. He put Shakespeare on the map with a quotation from *Henry IV* when he set out for the Munich conference.
Sheffield Star. Quoted Michael Bateman, THIS ENGLAND

7 And he the man whom Nature self had made / To mock her self, and truth to imitate / With kindly counter under Mimic shade. / Our pleasant Willy, ah! is dead of late; / With whom all joy and jolly merriment / Is also deaded and in dolour drent.
Sir Philip Sidney, TEARS OF THE MUSES

8 To Shakespeare even the meanest thing that lives is worthy of the light of the sun.
Edith Sitwell, RHYME AND REASON

9 No man ever spake as he that bade our England be but true / Keep but faith England fast and firm; and none shall bid her rue; / None may speak as he; / but all may know the sign that Shakespeare knew.
Algernon Swinburne, ENGLAND: AN ODE

10 The undisputed fame enjoyed by Shakespeare as a writer is, like every other lie, a great evil.
Leo Tolstoy

11 Shakespeare is a savage with sparks of genius which shine in a dreadful darkness of night.
Voltaire, IRENE, PRELIMINARY LETTER

12 I have heard that Mr Shakespeare was a natural wit, without any art at all; he frequented the plaies all his younger time, but in his elder days lived at Stratford and supplied the stage with two plaies every yeare and for itt had an allowance so large that he spent att the rate of 1000 a year, as I have heard.
Rev. J. Ward 1648

13 He had read Shakespeare and found him weak in chemistry.
H. G. Wells, LORD OF THE DYNAMOS

14 The central problem in Hamlet is whether the critics are mad, or only pretending to be mad.
Oscar Wilde

15 If the copyright had not expired the royalties from Shakespeare's works would have paid off the National Debt.
Lord Willis, House of Lords 22 Nov 1978

16 Scholars should have kept watch beside the graves of Shakespeare and Bacon to see which one of them turned over.
Alexander Woollcott, WHILE ROME BURNS, of a bad actor's performance of Hamlet 1934

GEORGE BERNARD SHAW (1856–1950)
Irish dramatist and critic

17 You invite Shaw down to your place because you think he will entertain your friends with brilliant conversation. But before you know where you are he has chosen a school for your son, made your will for you, regulated your diet and assumed all the privileges of your family solicitor, your housekeeper, your clergyman, your doctor and your dressmaker. When he has finished with everyone else he incites the children to rebellion. And when he can find nothing more to do he goes away and forgets all about you.
Anonymous hostess. Quoted Bennet Cerf, SHAKE WELL BEFORE USING 1948

18 Shaw was charming with one person, fidgetty with two, and stood on his head with four.
Stanley Baldwin. Quoted G. W. Lyttelton, THE LYTTELTON HART-DAVIS LETTERS 18 Jul 1956

1 Shaw cannot see beyond his own nose. Even the fingers he outstretches from it to the world are often invisible to him.
Max Beerbohm AROUND THEATRES

2 I really only enjoy his stage directions; the dialogue is vortical and, I find, fatiguing. It is like being harangued. He uses the English language like a truncheon.
Max Beerbohm. Quoted S. N. Behrens, CONVERSATIONS WITH MAX 1960

3 Wells was a cad who didn't pretend to be anything but a cad. Bennett was a cad pretending to be a gentleman. Shaw was a gentleman pretending to be a cad.
Hilaire Belloc. Quoted J. B. Priestley, THOUGHTS IN THE WILDERNESS

4 Shaw, one day you will eat a pork chop, and then God help all women.
Mrs Pat Campbell

5 Mr Shaw is cruelly hampered by the fact that he cannot tell any lie unless he thinks it is the truth
G. K. Chesterton, ORTHODOXY 1908

6 Mr Shaw is — I suspect — the only man on earth who has never written any poetry.
Ibid.

7 Bernard Shaw is never frivolous. He never gives his opinions a holiday, he is never irresponsible even for an instant. He has no nonsensical second self which he can get into as one gets into a dressing gown; that ridiculous disguise which is yet more real than the real person.
G. K. Chesterton, SHAW THE PURITAN

8 The world has long watched with tolerance and amusement the nimble antics and gyrations of the unique, double-headed chameleon while all the time the creature was anxious to be taken seriously
Winston Churchill, GREAT CONTEMPORARIES 1937

9 His brain is a half-inch layer of champagne poured over a bucket of Methodist near-beer.
Benjamin de Casseres

10 He is a freakish homunculus germinated outside lawful procreation.
Henry Arthur Jones, MY DEAR WELLS

11 Shaw's works make me admire the magnificent tolerance and broadmindedness of the English.
James Joyce. Quoted Gerald Griffin, THE WILD GEESE

12 He has a curious blank in his make-up. To him all sex is infidelity, and only infidelity is sex. Marriage is sexless, null. Sex is only manifested in infidelity . . . if sex crops up in marriage it is because one party falls in love with somebody else and wants to be unfaithful.
D. H. Lawrence, A PROPOS OF LADY CHATTERLEY'S LOVER 1930

13 He is a good man fallen among Fabians.
Lenin

14 He writes like a Pakistani who has learned English when twelve years old in order to become a chartered accountant.
John Osborne

15 I remember coming across him at the Grand Canyon and finding him peevish and refusing to admire it or even look at it properly. He was jealous of it.
J. B. Priestley, THOUGHTS IN THE WILDERNESS

16 He would pretend to be through with sex, as if it were fretwork or stamp collecting, when really he had hurriedly by-passed it.
Ibid.

17 Bernard Shaw has discovered himself and given ungrudgingly of his discovery to the world.
Saki (H. H. Munro)

18 I am a disciple of Bernard Shaw
George Bernard Shaw, THE DOCTOR'S DILEMMA 1906

19 I told my father that I had just read a new book by Bernard Shaw. My father stopped dead in the path where we were walking and said "I have heard of other people having children like that, but I have always prayed God I might be spared."
Stephen Spender, THE OLD SCHOOL

20 At 83 Shaw's mind was perhaps not quite as good as it used to be, but it was still better than anyone else's.
Alexander Woollcott, WHILE ROME BURNS 1934

21 The way Bernard Shaw believes in himself is very refreshing in these atheistic days when so many believe in no God at all.
Israel Zangwill

PERCY BYSSHE SHELLEY (1792–1822)
English poet

22 In his poetry as well as in his life Shelley was indeed "a beautiful and *ineffectual* angel", beating in the void his luminous wings in vain.
Matthew Arnold, LITERATURE AND DRAMA: *Shelley*

1 And did you once see Shelley plain / And
   did he stop and speak to you / And did you
   speak to him again? / How strange it seems
   and new!
   Robert Browning, MEMORABILIA

2 Poor Shelley always was, and is, a kind of
   ghastly object; colourless, pallid, tuneless,
   without health or warmth or vigour, the
   sound of him shrieky, frosty, as if a ghost
   were trying to sing to us; the temperament
   of him spasmodic, hysterical.
   Thomas Carlyle, REMINISCENCES   1871

3 The author of *Prometheus Unbound* has a
   fire in his eye, a fever in his blood, a maggot
   in his brain, a hectic flutter in his speech.
   William Hazlitt, ON PARADOX AND
   COMMONPLACE

4 Bysshe's dietary was frugal and independent, very remarkable and quite
   peculiar to himself. When he felt hungry he
   would dash into the first baker's shop, buy a
   loaf and rush out again bearing it under his
   arm; and he strode onward in his rapid
   course, breaking off pieces and greedily
   swallowing them. But however frugal the
   fare the waste was considerable, and his
   path might be tracked, like that of
   Hop-o'-my-Thumb through the woods, by a
   long line of crumbs.
   T. J. Hogg, LIFE OF SHELLEY   1906

5 A lewd vegetarian.
   Charles Kingsley

6 Shelley I saw once. His voice was the most
   obnoxious squeak I ever was tormented
   with.
   Charles Lamb, letter to Bernard Barton
   9 *Oct* 1822

7 He was a liar and a cheat; he paid no regard
   to truth, nor to any kind of moral
   obligation.
   Robert Southey

8 Shelley, lyric-lord of England's lordliest
   singers, here first heard / Ring from the lips
   of poets crowned and dead the Promethean
   word / Whence his soul took fire, and power
   to out-soar the sunward-soaring bird.
   Algernon Swinburne, ETON: *An Ode*

9 Swiftly gliding in, blushing like a girl, a tall
   thin stripling held out both his hands; and I
   could hardly believe it as I looked at his
   flushed, feminine and artless face, that it
   could be the Poet. Was it possible that this
   mild-looking, beardless boy could be the
   veritable monster at war with all the world?
   — excommunicated by the Fathers of the
   Church, deprived of his civil rights by the
   fiat of a grim Lord Chancellor, discarded by

every member of his family, and denounced
by the rival sages of our literature as the
founder of a Satanist school? I could not
believe it.
E. J. Trelawney, RECOLLECTIONS OF THE
LAST DAYS OF SHELLEY AND BYRON   1858

10 Mrs Williams asked Shelley what book he
   had in his hand. His face brightened and he
   answered briskly, "Calderon's Magico Prod-
   igioso. I am translating some passages in
   it." "Oh read it to us." Shoved off from the
   shore of commonplace incidents that could
   not interest him and fairly launched on a
   theme that did, he instantly became
   oblivious of everything but the book in his
   hand. The masterly manner in which he
   analysed the genius of the author, his lucid
   interpretation of the story and the ease with
   which he translated into our language the
   most subtle and imaginative passages of the
   Spanish poet, were marvellous, as was his
   command of the two languages.
   Ibid.

11 He was habited like a boy, in a black jacket
   and trousers, which he seemed to have out-
   grown, or his tailor, as is the custom, had
   most shamefully stinted him in his sizings.
   Ibid.

12 Shelley should not be read, but inhaled
   through a gas-pipe.
   Lionel Trilling. Quoted Clifton Fadiman,
   ENTER CONVERSING

RICHARD BRINSLEY SHERIDAN
(1751–1816)
Irish dramatist and politician

13 Good at a fight, but better at a play / God-
   like in giving, but the devil to pay.
   Lord Byron, ON A CAST OF SHERIDAN'S
   HAND

14 The flash of Wit, the bright Intelligence /
   The beam of Song, the blaze of Eloquence /
   Set with their Sun, but still have help behind /
   The enduring produce of immortal Mind /
   Fruits of a genial morn and glorious noon /
   A deathless part of him who died too soon.
   Lord Byron, ON THE DEATH OF SHERIDAN

15 The matchless dialogue, the deathless wit /
   Which knew not what it was to intermit /
   The glowing portraits, fresh from life that
   bring / Home to our hearts the truth from
   which they spring / These wondrous beings
   of his Fancy wrought / To fulness by the fiat
   of his thought.
   Ibid.

1 Long shall we seek his likeness — long in vain / And turn to all of him which shall remain / Sighing that Nature forms but one such man / And broke the die — in moulding Sheridan.
Ibid.

2 We have been to see the new comedy of young Sheridan, *The Rivals*. It was very unfavourably received the first night, and he had had the prudence to prevent total defeat, by withdrawing it and making great and various improvements; the event has been successful for it is now *better* though not *very* much liked. For my own part I think he ought to be treated with great indulgence; much is to be forgiven in an author of three-and-twenty whose genius is likely to be his principal inheritance. I love him for the sake of his amiable and ingenious mother.
Hannah More, letter to Mrs Gwatkin

3 During his last illness the medical attendants apprehending that they would be obliged to perform an operation on him, asked him if he had ever undergone one. "Never," said Sheridan, "except when sitting for my picture or having my hair cut."
Samuel Rogers, TABLE TALK 1856

4 Sheridan had fine eyes and was not a little proud of them. He said to me on his death-bed, "Tell Lady Bessborough that my eyes will look up at the coffin-lid as brightly as ever."
Ibid.

5 Sheridan worked very hard when he had to prepare himself for any great occasion. His habit was on these emergencies to rise at four in the morning, to light up a prodigious quantity of candles around him, and eat toasted muffins while he worked.
George Tierney

JEAN JULIAN CHRISTIAN SIBELIUS (1865–1957)
Finnish composer

6 Gentlemen, in the bass department you will observe in this movement a prolonged obbligato passage for the contra-bass, meandering through the lower reaches of the orchestra like an amiable tape-worm.
Sir Thomas Beecham, of Sibelius' Second Symphony. Quoted Humphrey Proctor Gregg, BEECHAM REMEMBERED

7 What you get in Sibelius, for the greater part of the time, is an extreme reticence and a slow delivery; and that, of course, is very popular in England. It is our tradition. We get it, possibly, from the Government.
Sir Thomas Beecham. Quoted Lord Boothby, MY YESTERDAY, YOUR TOMORROW

8 In this piece (Lemminkainen) you may find it a matter of some difficulty to keep your places. I think you may do well to imagine yourselves disporting in some hair-raising form of locomotion such as Brooklands, or a switchback railway. My advice to you is merely: hold tight and do not let yourselves fall off. I cannot guarantee to help you on again.
Sir Thomas Beecham. Quoted Bernard Shore, THE ORCHESTRA SPEAKS

SARAH SIDDONS (1755–1831)
Welsh-born actress

9 When Mrs Siddons came into the room there happened to be no chair ready for her, which Dr Johnson observing, said with a smile, "Madam, you who so often occasion a want of seats to other people, will the more easily excuse the want of one yourself."
Boswell, THE LIFE OF JOHNSON 1791

10 My friend Douglas Kinnard told a story, rather too long, about Mrs Siddons and Kean acting together at some Irish theatre. Kean got drunk and Mrs Siddons got all the applause. The next night Kean acted Jaffier and Mrs Siddons Belvidera, and then he got all the applause, and, said Sheridan, "she got drunk, I suppose".
Lord Broughton, RECOLLECTIONS OF A LONG LIFE 1909

11 I found her the Heroine of a Tragedy — sublime, elevated and solemn. In face and person truly noble, and commanding; in manners, quiet and stiff; in voice, deep and dragging; and in conversation, formal, sententious, calm and dry.
Fanny Burney, DIARY 15 Aug 1787

12 When Sir Joshua Reynolds painted the portrait of Mrs Siddons as the Tragic Muse he wrought his name in the border of her robe. The great actress, conceiving it to be a piece of classic embroidery, went near to examine it and seeing the words, smiled. The artist bowed and said, "I could not lose this opportunity of sending my name to posterity on the hem of your garment."
Allan Cunningham, LIVES OF THE MOST EMINENT BRITISH PAINTERS 1833

1 After her retirement she would give private readings. She acted *Macbeth* herself, better than either Kemble or Kean. It is extraordinary the awe this wonderful woman inspires. After her first reading the men retired to tea. While we were all eating toast and tinkling cups and saucers she began again. It was like the effect of a Mass bell at Madrid. All noise ceased and we slunk to our seats like boors, two or three of the most distinguished men of the day, with the very toast in their mouth, afraid to bite. It was curious to see Sir Thomas Lawrence in this predicament, to hear him bite by degrees, then stop for fear of making too much crackle, his eyes full of water from the constraint.
B. R. Haydon, JOURNAL   10 *Mar* 1821

2 She is out of the pale of all theories and annihilates all rules. Wherever she sits there is grace and grandeur, there is tragedy personified. Her seat is the undivided throne of the Tragic Muse. She has no need of robes, the sweeping train, the ornaments of the stage. In herself she is as great as any being she ever represented in the ripeness and plenitude of her power.
William Hazlitt, TABLE TALK   1821

3 Power was seated on her brow; passion radiated from her breast as from a shrine; she was Tragedy personified.
Ibid.

4 Combe, author of *Dr Syntax's Tours*, recollected having seen Mrs Siddons when a very young woman, standing by the side of her father's stage, and knocking a pair of snuffers against a candlestick, to imitate the sound of a windmill, during the representation of some Harlequin piece.
Samuel Rogers, TABLE TALK   1856

5 After she had left the stage Mrs Siddons, from want of excitement, was never happy. When I was sitting with her of an afternoon she would say, "Oh dear! This is the time I used to be thinking of going to the theatre; first came the pleasure of dressing for my part, then the pleasure of acting it, but that is all over now."
Ibid.

6 Mrs Siddons told me that one night as she stepped into her carriage to return home from the theatre Sheridan suddenly jumped in after her. "Mr Sheridan," she said, "I trust that you will behave with all propriety, if you do not I shall immediately let down the glass and desire the servant to show you

out." Sheridan did behave with all propriety. "But," continued Mrs Siddons, "as soon as we reached my house the provoking wretch bolted out in the greatest haste and slunk away as if anxious to escape unseen."
Ibid.

7 Mrs Siddons said, "Alas, after I became celebrated none of my sisters loved me as they did before."
Ibid.

SIR PHILIP SIDNEY (1554–1586)
English statesman, soldier and poet

8 Being thirsty with excess of bleeding, he called for a drink, which was brought to him; but as he was putting the bottle to his mouth he saw a poor soldier carried along, ghastly casting his eyes upon the bottle. Which Sir Philip took the bottle, before he drank, and delivered it to the poor man with these words, "Thy necessity is yet greater than mine."
Fulke Greville, of Sidney's death at Zutphen,
LIFE OF SIR PHILIP SIDNEY   1652

9 *Arcadia* is the most tedious, lamentable, pedantic pastime romance, which the patience of a young virgin in love cannot now wade through.
Horace Walpole

EDITH SITWELL (1887–1964)
English poet

10 Edith Sitwell, in that great Risorgimento cape of hers, looks as if she were covering a teapot, or a telephone.
Noël Coward. Quoted William Marchant,
THE PRIVILEGE OF HIS COMPANY   1980

11 Edith is a bad loser. When worsted in an argument she throws Queensberry Rules to the wind. She once called me Percy.
Percy Wyndham Lewis, BLASTING AND BOMBADIERING   1937

12 Then Edith Sitwell appeared, her nose longer than an anteater's, and read some of her absurd stuff.
Lytton Strachey, letter to Dora Carrington
28 *Jun* 1921

13 So you've been reviewing Edith Sitwell's latest piece of virgin dung, have you? Isn't she a poisonous thing of a woman, lying, concealing, flipping, plagiarising, mis-quoting, and being as clever a literary publicist as ever.
Dylan Thomas, letter to Glyn Jones   1934

1 I am as appreciatively indifferent to Edith
   Sitwell as I am to the quaint patterns of old
   chintzes, the designs on dinner plates, or the
   charm of nursery rhymes.
   H. G. Wells, AN EXPERIMENT IN
   AUTOBIOGRAPHY 1934

JOHN SKELTON (c. 1440–1529)
English poet

2 I praye Mayster John Skelton, lately created
   poet laureate in the Universitie of Oxen-
   forde to oversee and correct this sayed booke.
   And to addresse and expowne where as
   shall be fowned faulte to thym that shall
   requyre it. For hym I know for suffycyent to
   expowne and Wnglysshe every dyffyculte
   that is therein. For he hath late translated
   the Epystle of Tulle and diverse other
   workes out of Latyn into Englyshe, not in
   rude and olde language but in polysshed and
   ornate terms craftely.
   William Caxton, Preface to ENEYDOS 1490

3 Skelton's poems are all low and bad, there is
   nothing in them worth reading.
   *Alexander Pope. Quoted Rev. Joseph
   Spence,* OBSERVATIONS, CHARACTERS AND
   ANECDOTES 1829

ADAM SMITH (1723–1790)
Scottish political economist

4 He was the most absent man in company
   that I ever saw — moving his lips and
   talking to himself, and smiling in the midst
   of large companies. If you awakened him
   from his reverie he immediately began a
   harangue, and never stopped until he had
   told you all he knew about it.
   Alexander Carlyle. Quoted R. B. Haldane,
   ADAM SMITH

5 We shall never forget one particular evening
   when he put an elderly maiden lady, who
   presided at the tea-table, to sore confusion
   by neglecting her invitations to be seated
   and walking round and round the circle
   stopping ever and anon to steal a lump of
   sugar from the basin, which the venerable
   spinster was at last constrained to place on
   her own knee as the only method of
   securing it from his depredations.
   *Sir Walter Scott, Quarterly Review
   Jun* 1827

6 When walking in the street Adam had a
   manner of talking and laughing to himself,
   which often attracted the notice of the passengers. He used himself to mention the
   ejaculation of an old market woman,
   "Hegh, sirs!" shaking her head as she

uttered it to which her companion answered, having echoed the compassionate
sigh, "and he is well put on, too," expressing their surprise that a decided lunatic,
who from his dress appeared to be a gentleman, should be permitted to walk abroad.
Ibid.

TOBIAS GEORGE SMOLLETT (1721–1771)
Scottish novelist

7 The Doctor was a man of genius, but he
   certainly rated it to its full value. He was
   one, too, who abounded in generosity and
   good nature, but was at the same time extremely splenetic and revengeful.
   Thomas Davies

8 His touch was bold, but frequently coarse;
   his personages drawn with something of
   caricature; his humour broad, his wit, description and incidents sometimes licentious
   and even indecent; his satire shrewd, sarcastic, and often bitter.
   James Prior

9 You see somehow he is a gentleman
   through all his battling and struggling, his
   poverty, his hard-fought successes, and his
   defeats.
   William Makepeace Thackeray, ENGLISH
   HUMORISTS OF THE 18TH CENTURY 1858

SOCRATES (469–399 BC)
Athenian philosopher

10 'Tis he composes for Euripides / Those
    clever plays, much sound and little sense.
    Aristophanes, THE CLOUDS

11 O man that justly desirest great wisdom,
    how blessed will be thy life among
    Athenians and Greeks, retentive of memory
    and thinker that thou art, with endurance of
    toil for thy character, never art thou weary,
    whether standing or walking, never numb
    with cold, never hungry for breakfast; from
    wine and gross feeding and all other gross
    frivolities thou does turn away.
    Aristophanes

12 Socrates was the first to call philosophy
    down from the heavens and to place it in
    cities, and even to introduce it into homes
    and compel it to enquire about life and
    standards and good and ill.
    Marcus Tullius Cicero, TUSCULANAE
    DISPUTATIONES

13 He was so orderly in his way of life that on
    several occasions when pestilence broke out

in Athens he was the only man who escaped infection.
Diogenes Laertius, LIVES OF EMINENT PHILOSOPHERS

1 For the most part he was despised and laughed at, yet bore all the ill-usage patiently. So much so that, when he had been kicked, and someone expressed surprise at his taking it so quietly, Socrates rejoined, "Should I have taken the law of a donkey, supposing he had kicked me?"
Ibid.

2 Euripides gave him the treatise of Heraclitus and asked his opinion upon it, and his reply was, "The part I understand is excellent, and so too is, I dare say, the part I do not understand: but it needs a Delian diver to get to the bottom of it."
Ibid.

3 Socrates whom, well-inspired, the oracle pronounced, wisest of men.
John Milton 1671

4 Alcibiades offered him a large site on which to build a house: but he replied, "Suppose then I wanted shoes, and you offered me a whole hide to make a pair with, would it not be ridiculous in me to take it?" Often when he looked at the multitude of wares for sale he would say to himself, "How many things I can do without!" And he would continually recite the lines, "The purple robe and silver's shine more fits an actor's needs than mine."
Pamphilia, COMMENTARIES

5 Socrates is a doer of evil, who corrupts the youth; and who does not believe in the gods of the state, but has other new divinities of his own. Such is the charge.
Plato, DIALOGUE

6 Socrates acted wickedly, and is criminally curious in searching into things under the earth, and in the heavens, and in making the worse appear the better cause, and in teaching these same things to others.
The accusation against Socrates, quoted by him in his APOLOGIA 399BC

ROBERT SOUTHEY (1774–1843)
English poet

7 In the pathetic companionship of books lived Southey long after their beauty was shut out from him, passing his trembling hand up and down their ranks, and taking comfort in the certainty that they had not foresaken him.
Loris and Imogen Guiney, GOOSE-QUILL PAPERS

8 Southey had a great dislike to be "looked at" and although very regular in his attendance at church he would stay away when there were many tourists in the neighbourhood. One Sunday two strangers who had a great desire to see the poet besought the sexton to point him out to them. The sexton, knowing this must be done secretly, said, "I will take you up the aisle and in passing touch the pew in which he sits." He did so. A few days later the sexton met Southey in the street of Keswick. The poet looked sternly at him and said, "Don't do it again."
S. C. Hall, A BOOK OF MEMORIES

9 Southey gave a detailed account of his daily life to a certain literary Quaker lady. "I rise at five throughout the year. From six till eight I read Spanish, then French for an hour, Portuguese next for half an hour, my watch lying on the table. I give two hours to poetry. I write prose for two hours, translate so long, I make extracts for so long" and so the rest until the poor fellow had fairly fagged himself into his bed again. "And pray, when dost thou think, friend?" she asked drily, to the great discomforture of the future laureate.
Thomas Jefferson Hogg, LIFE OF P. B. SHELLEY 1858

10 I believe you are right about Southey's poetry, and cry mercy to it accordingly. He went to it too mechanically, and with too much nonchalance; and the consequence was a vast many words to little matter. Nor had he the least music in him at all. The consequence of which was that he wrote prose out into lyrical wild shapes, and took the appearance of it for verse.
Leigh Hunt

11 Beneath these poppies buried deep / The bones of Bob the bard lie hid / Peace to his 'mains, and may he sleep / As soundly as his readers did.
Thomas More, EPITAPH ON A WELL-KNOWN POET

12 Death, weary of so dull a writer, / Put to his books a *finis* thus. / Oh may the earth on him lie lighter / Then did his quartos upon us.
Ibid.

13 In all his domestic relations Southey was the most amiable of men; but he had no general philanthropy; he was what you call a *cold man.* He was never happy except when reading a book or making one, Coleridge once said to me, "I can't think of Southey without seeing him using or mending a pen."
Samuel Rogers, TABLE TALK 1856

1 He had fancy, imagination and taste — he is facile and flowing in his versification — most musical, if you will — but he is too smooth and level, he seldom or never rises with his subject; he will stand criticism as words go, but no further. He moves but does not touch the heart. One reads him with delight once, but never takes him up twice.
Percy Bysshe Shelley

HERBERT SPENCER (1820–1903)
English philosopher and social scientist

2 The most immeasurable ass in Christendom.
Thomas Carlyle

3 He was very thick-skinned under criticism and shrank from argument; it excited him overmuch and was really bad for his health. His common practice when pressed in a difficult position, was to finger his pulse saying "I must not talk any more", to abruptly leave the discussion unfinished. Of course, wicked people put a more wicked interpretation on this habit than it should in fairness bear.
Sir Francis Galton. Quoted David Duncan,
LIFE OF SPENCER

4 Spencer patented a special pin for binding sheets of music together. He also invented an invalid bed which worked well and a flying machine which did not work at all.
Frank Muir, THE FRANK MUIR BOOK 1975

EDMUND SPENSER (1552–1599)
English poet

5 He was always poor, though he had been secretary to the Lord Grey, Lord Deputy of Ireland. For he had scarcely fixed himself in his new retirement and had got a little leisure to pursue his studies, but the rebels rifled and threw him out of house and home, so that he returned into England in a bare condition, when he died not long after.
William Camden, ANNALS 1615

6 The Rubens of English poetry.
William Campbell

7 Spenser, presenting his poems to Queen Elizabeth, she highly affected therewith, commanded the Lord Cecil, her treasurer, to give him a hundred pounds. But Spenser received no reward, whereupon he presented this petition in a small piece of paper to the queen in her progress. "I was promised on a tyme, To have reason for my rhyme; From that tyme unto this season, I receiv'd not rhyme nor reason." Hereupon the queen gave strict order (not without some check to her treasurer) for the present payment of the hundred pounds.
Thomas Fuller, WORTHIES OF
ENGLAND 1662

8 This poet contains great beauties, a sweet and harmonious versification, easy elocution and a fine imagination. Yet does the perusal of his work become so tedious that one never finishes it from the mere pleasure it affords . . . Upon the whole Spenser maintains his place upon the shelves amid the English classics; but he is seldom seen on the table, and there is scarcely anyone, if he dares to be ingenuous, but will confess that, notwithstanding all the merits of the poet, he affords an entertainment with which the palate is soon satiated.
David Hume

9 A silver trumpet Spenser blows / And, as its martial notes to silence flee / From a virgin chorus flows / A hymn in praise of spotless Chastity / 'Tis still! Wild warblings from the Aeolian lyre / Enchantment softly breathe and trembling expire.
John Keats, ODE TO APOLLO

10 Spenser, though assuredly one of the greatest poets that ever lived, could not succeed in the attempt to make allegory interesting. It was in vain that he lavished the riches of his mind on the House of Pride and the House of Temperance. One unpardonable fault, the fault of tediousness, pervades the whole of the *Faerie Queene.* We become sick of cardinal virtues and deadly sins, and long for the society of plain men and women. Of the persons who read the first canto one in ten reaches the end of the first book, and not one in a hundred perseveres to the end of the poem. Very few and very weary are those who are in at the death of the Blatant Beast.
T. B. Macaulay, Edinburgh Review
Dec 1831

11 After my reading a canto of Spenser two or three days ago to an old lady between 70 and 80 she said that I had been showing her a collection of pictures. She said very right, and I know not how it is, but there is something in Spenser that pleases one as strongly in one's old age as it did in one's youth. I read the *Faerie Queene* when I was about twelve with a vast deal of delight; and I think it gave me as much when I read it over about a year or two ago.
Alexander Pope. Quoted Rev. Joseph
Spence, OBSERVATIONS, ANECDOTES AND
CHARACTERS 1820

1 The characteristics of this sweet and allegorical poet are not only strong and circumstantial imagery but tender and pathetic feeling, a most melodious flow of versification, and a certain pleasing melancholy in his sentiments, the constant companion of an elegant taste that casts a delicacy and grace over all his companions.
Thomas Warton, OBSERVATIONS ON THE FAERIE QUEENE 1754

JOSEPH VISSARIONOVICH STALIN
(1879–1953)
Russian Generalissimo

2 My father died a difficult and terrible death. God grants an easy death only to the just.
Svetlana Alliluyeva, Stalin's daughter, TWENTY LETTERS TO A FRIEND

3 He was clearly a pretty ruthless tyrant, but a man you could do business with because he said yes and no and didn't have to refer back. He was obviously the man who could make decisions, and he was obviously going to be difficult.
Clement Attlee. Quoted Francis Williams, A PRIME MINISTER REMEMBERS 1961

4 He turned Marxism on its head by making it fit his own theories.
George Lukacs

5 The huge, laughing cockroaches on his top lip.
Osip Mandelstam, POEMS: *Stalin Epigrams*

6 Stalin, that great lover of peace, a man of giant stature who moulded, as few others have done, the destinies of his age.
Jawaharlal Nehru, Obituary speech in Indian parliament 9 Mar 1953

7 Uncle Joe is my man.
Franklin D. Roosevelt. Quoted Robert Dallek, ROOSEVELT AND AMERICAN FOREIGN POLICY 1932–1945

8 I like old Joe Stalin. He's a good fellow but he's a prisoner of the Politburo. He would make certain agreements but they won't let him keep them.
Harry S Truman. Speech quoted News Review 24 Jun 1948

LADY HESTER STANHOPE (1776–1839)
Niece of William Pitt. Traveller in the Levant

9 She finally settled among the Druse of Mount Lebanon. Adopting Eastern dress and practising her own peculiar brand of religion, based partly on astrology, she gained such an influence over the half-civilised tribes by her prophecies and pronouncements that they believed her divinely inspired — a view that came to be shared by certain English mystics, and, eventually, by Lady Hester herself.
William Rose Benét, READER'S ENCYCLOPEDIA 1948

10 One day, when having dwelt a long time on the favourite subject of her own star, she got up from the sofa, and approaching the window, she called me. "Look," said she, "at the pupils of my eyes. There! My star is the sun. It is in my eyes." I looked and replied that I saw a rim of yellow round the pupil. "A rim!" cried she "It isn't a rim — it's a sun; there's a disc and from it go rays all round. 'Tis no more a rim than you are. Nobody has got eyes like mine."
Dr Meryon, MEMOIRS OF LADY HESTER STANHOPE 1846

11 Her habits grew more and more eccentric. She lay in bed all day and sat up all night, talking unceasingly for hour upon hour to Dr Meryon, who alone of her English attendants remained with her.
Lytton Strachey, BOOKS AND CHARACTERS: *Lady Hester Stanhope* 1922

12 Lady Hester's was a nose of wild ambitions, of pride grown fantastical, a nose that scorned the earth, shooting off, one fancies, to some eternally eccentric heaven. It was a nose, in fact, altogether in the air.
Ibid.

13 Brothers, the fortune-teller, told her that "she would one day go to Jerusalem, and lead back the chosen people; that on her arrival in the Holy Land mighty changes would take place in the world, and that she would pass seven years in the desert".
John Timbs, ENGLISH ECCENTRICS 1875

14 She had a remarkable talent for divining characters by the conformation of men. It was founded both on the features of the face and on the shape of the head, body and limbs. Some indications she went by were taken from a resemblance to animals; and wherever such indications existed, she inferred that the dispositions peculiar to these animals were to be found in the person.
Ibid.

SIR RICHARD STEELE (1672–1729)
Irish essayist, dramatist and politician

1 Steele, with considerable humour, had still more power in the pathetic; not indeed, that of the buskin, but of everyday life; hence his short narratives of domestic circumstances, often conveyed in imaginary letters which have much of this quality, were doubtless among the most attractive portions of *The Tatler* on its first appearance.
Lucy Atkins, LIFE OF ADDISON   1843

2 The comedies of Steele were the first that were written expressly with a view not to imitate the manners, but to reform the morals of the age. The author seems to be all the time on his good behaviour, as if writing a comedy was no very creditable employment, and as if the ultimate object of his employment was a dedication to the Queen. Nothing could be better meant, or more inefficient.
William Hazlitt, ENGLISH COMIC WRITERS   1819

3 The great charm of Steele's writing is its naturalness. He wrote so quickly and carelessly that he was forced to make the reader his confidant and had not the time to deceive him. He had a small share of book-learning, but a vast acquaintance with the world.
William Makepeace Thackeray, THE ENGLISH HUMORIST   1853

GERTRUDE STEIN (1874–1946)
American poet, novelist and critic

4 You would be surprised to know just how altogether American I found you.
Sherwood Anderson, letter to Gertrude Stein

5 Reading Gertrude Stein at length is not unlike making one's way through an interminable and badly printed game book.
Richard Bridgeman, GERTRUDE STEIN IN PIECES

6 While she believed that most writers failed to allow writing to express all that it could, in her own practice she scrupulously saw to it that writing expressed less than it would.
John Malcolm Brinnin, THE THIRD ROSE   1959

7 Gertrude Stein is the mama of dada.
Clifton Fadiman

8 What an old covered-wagon she is.
F. Scott Fitzgerald

9 Gertrude Stein's prose song is a cold, black suet-pudding. We can represent it as a cold suet roll of fabulously reptilian length. Cut it at any point, it is the same thing; the same heavy, sticky, opaque mass all through and all along . . . it is mournful and monstrous, composed of dead and inanimate material.
Percy Wyndham Lewis. Quoted John Malcolm Brinnin, THE THIRD ROSE   1959

10 Her voice was unlike anyone else's — deep, full, velvety like a great contralto's, like two voices. She was large and heavy with delicate small hands and a beautifully modelled and unique head. It was often compared to a Roman emperor's.
Alice B. Toklas, WHAT IS REMEMBERED   1963

11 She knew that she was the object of derision to many and to some extent the knowledge fortified her. Yet it is very moving to learn that on one occasion when a friend asked her what a writer most wanted she replied, throwing up her hands and laughing, "Oh praise, praise, praise."
Thornton Wilder, Magazine of the Year Oct 1945

12 She has outdistanced any of the symbolists in using words for pure purposes of suggestion — she has gone so far that she no longer even suggests.
Edmund Wilson. Quoted B. L. Reid, ART BY SUBTRACTION

STEPHEN (1097–1154)
King of England

13 In this King's time there was nothing but disturbance and wickedness and robbery for forthwith the powerful men who were traitors rose against him . . . The land was all ruined by such doings, and they said openly that Christ and his saints were weeping.
Anglo-Saxon Chronicle   1154

14 He was a man of great renown in the practice of arms, but for the rest almost an incompetent, except that he was rather inclined to evil.
Walter Map, DE NUGIS CURIALIUM   c.1200

15 Yet he was not broken in spirit by any man's rebellion but appeared suddenly now here, now there and always settled the business with more loss to himself than to his opponents, for after expending many great efforts in vain he would win a preference of peace from them for a time by the gift of honours and castles.
William of Malmesbury, HISTORICA NOVELLA   1142

16 When he was a count he had by his own good nature and the way he jested, sat and

ate in the company even of the humblest, earned an affection that can hardly be imagined.
Ibid.

GEORGE STEPHENSON (1781–1848)
English locomotive engineer

1 Stephenson, the great engineer, told Lichfield that he had travelled on the Manchester and Liverpool railroad for many miles at the rate of a mile a minute, that his doubt was not how fast his engines could be made to go, but at what pace it would be proper to stop. He had ascertained that 400 miles an hour was the extreme velocity which the human frame could endure.
Charles Greville, MEMOIRS   28 *Jan* 1834

2 My father knew several of the gentlemen most deeply interested in the undertaking of the Liverpool–Manchester railway, and Stephenson having proposed a trial trip permitted me to accompany them. He was a rather stern-featured man, with a dark and deeply-marked countenance; his speech was strongly inflected with his native Northumberland accent.
Fanny Kemble, RECORD OF A GIRLHOOD   1878

3 Mr Stephenson having taken me on the bench of the engine with him, we started at about ten miles an hour. You cannot imagine how strange it seemed to be journeying on thus, without any visible cause of progressing other than that magical machine, with its flying white breath, and rhythmical unwearying pace.
Ibid. Quoting a letter dated   26 *Aug* 1830

4 Every part of the scheme shows that the man has applied himself to a subject of which he has no knowledge and to which he has no science to apply.
Report of the Parliamentary Commission considering Stephenson's proposed Liverpool–Manchester railway   1825

5 A member of the House of Commons Committee on the Liverpool–Manchester Railway Bill put the following case to Stephenson. "Suppose, now, one of these engines be going along the railroad at the rate of nine or ten miles an hour, and that a cow were to stray on the line and get in the way of the engine, would not that, think you, be a very awkward circumstance?" "Yes," replied the witness, with a twinkle in his eye, "ver-r-y awkward indeed — *for the*

coo." The honourable member did not proceed further with his cross-questioning.
Samuel Smiles, LIFE OF GEORGE STEPHENSON   1857

6 I should say no railway ought to exceed 40 miles an hour on the most favourable gradient, but on a curved line that speed ought not to exceed 25 miles an hour.
Stephenson   1841

LAURENCE STERNE (1713–1768)
English novelist and clergyman

7 A bawdy blockhead.
Oliver Goldsmith, A CITIZEN OF THE WORLD   1762

8 Soon after *Tristram* had appeared Sterne asked a Yorkshire lady of fortune and condition whether she had read his book. "I have not, Mr Sterne," was the answer, "and to be plain with you, I am informed it is not proper for female perusal." "My dear good lady," replied the author, "do not be gulled by such stories; the book is like your young heir there", (pointing to a child of three years old, who was rolling on the carpet in his white tunic) "he shows a good deal of what is usually concealed, but it is all in perfect innocence."
Sir Walter Scott, LIFE OF LAURENCE STERNE

9 I begin with writing the first sentence — and trusting to God Almighty for the second.
Sterne, TRISTRAM SHANDY   1775

10 The man is a great jester, not a great humourist; he goes to work systematically in cold blood; paints his face, puts on his ruff and motley clothes, and lays down his carpet and tumbles on it.
William Makepeace Thackeray, THE ENGLISH HUMORISTS   1853

11 The third and fourth volumes of *Tristram Shandy* are the dregs of nonsense and have universally met the contempt they deserve.
Horace Walpole

ROBERT LOUIS BALFOUR STEVENSON (1850–1894)
Scottish author

12 Stevenson seemed to pick the right word up on the point of his pen, like a man playing spillikins.
G. K. Chesterton, THE VICTORIAN AGE IN LITERATURE   1913

13 I think of Mr Stevenson as a consumptive youth weaving garlands of sad flowers with pale, weak hands, or leaning to a large plate

glass window and scratching thereon exquisite profiles with a diamond pencil.
George Moore, CONFESSIONS OF A YOUNG MAN 1888

1 I, whom Apollo sometimes visited / Or feigned to visit, now, my day being done, / Do slumber wholly, nor shall know at all / The weariness of changes; nor perceive / Immeasurable sands of centuries / Drink up the blanching ink; or the loud sound / Of generations beat the music down.
Stevenson, EPITAPH FOR HIMSELF

JOHN STOW (1525–1605)
English antiquarian

2 In his eightieth year he was so reduced in his circumstances that he petitioned James I for a licence to collect alms, "as a recompense for the labour and travail of 45 years in setting forth the *Chronicles of England* and 8 years taken up in the *Survey of London.*" Letters patent under the great seal were granted and published by clergy from the pulpit. One entire parish in the city contributed seven shillings and sixpence. Such was the public remuneration of a man who had been useful to his nation, but not to himself.
Isaac D'Israeli, CALAMITIES OF AUTHORS 1812

3 He was tall of stature, lean of body and face, his eyes crystalline, of a pleasant and cheerful countenance; his sight and memory very good; very sober, mild, and courteous to any that required instructions; and retained full use of all his senses until the day of his death.
Edmond Howes, Stow's literary executor

4 He always protested never to have written anything either for malice, fear or favour, nor to seek his own particular gain or vain-glory, and that his only pains and care was to write *truth*. He could never ride, but travelled always on foot into divers cathedral churches, and other chief places of the land to search records. He was very careless of scoffers, back-biters, and detractors. He lived peacefully and died of the stone colic, being four-score years of age.
Ibid.

5 Stow early fell into a discord with the chronicler Grafton, and the two belaboured one another in print, sometimes having resort to bad puns. Grafton sneered at the "Memories of superstitious foundations, fables foolishly *stowed* together" and Stow

replied by alluding to *townes* and unfruitful *grafts* of Momus' offspring.
Henry B. Wheatley, Introduction to Everyman edition of SURVEY OF LONDON 1912

HARRIET ELIZABETH BEECHER STOWE (1811–1896)
American humanitarian, author of Uncle Tom's Cabin

6 The final proof of Mrs Stowe's power was that she created the Southern romance — and that, three generations later, Southern writers still had to reckon with her picture.
Van Wyck Brooks, THE FLOWERING OF NEW ENGLAND 1815–1865

7 Harriet Beecher Stowe, whose *Uncle Tom's Cabin* was the first evidence to America that no hurricane can be so disastrous to a country as a ruthless humanitarian woman.
Sinclair Lewis, Introduction to Paxton Hibben's, HENRY WARD BEECHER

8 Today I have taken my pen from the last chapter of *Uncle Tom's Cabin* and I think you will understand me when I say that I feel as if I had written some of it with my heart's blood. I look upon it almost as a despairing appeal to a civilised humanity.
Harriet Beecher Stowe, letter to Horace Mann Mar 1852

GILES LYTTON STRACHEY (1880–1932)
English author and historian

9 Lytton Strachey peered at everyone through thick glasses, looking like an owl in daylight. He is immensely tall and could be twice his height if he were not as bent as sloppy asparagus.
Cecil Beaton, DIARY 1923

10 Strachey had recently published *Eminent Victorians* and *Queen Victoria*. Someone incautiously asked him who would be the subject of his next biography. At the top of his small, weak but piercing voice he said "God".
Jacques-Emile Blanche, MORE PORTRAITS OF A LIFETIME 1918–1938

11 At a party the conversation turned to the question of which great historical figure the people there would most like to have gone to bed with. The men voted for Cleopatra, Kitty Fisher, and so on, but when it came to Lytton's turn he declared shrilly "Julius Caesar!"
Michael Holroyd, LYTTON STRACHEY: *A Critical Biography* 1968

IGOR FEDOROVICH STRAVINSKY
(1882–1971)
Russian composer

1 There is behind his façade of ingenious notes and patterns no continuous personality. I do not find in Stravinsky's newest production convincing signs that he has arrived at wisdom, even yet.
Sir Thomas Beecham. Quoted Neville Cardus, SIR THOMAS BEECHAM

2 In London Stravinsky was so entranced by the bells of St Paul's that he wrote down the changes on the back of an envelope. Another time, he noted down a song roared out by a couple of drunks on a French train and used it in his ballet *The Wedding*.
Alex Coleman, TV *Times* 2 *Apr* 1982

3 His music used to be original. Now it is aboriginal.
Sir Ernest Newman, Musical Times Jul 1921

4 I don't write modern music. I only write good music.
Stravinsky to journalists on his first visit to America 1925

5 My music is best understood by children and animals.
Stravinsky. Quoted Observer 8 *Oct* 1961

SIR JOHN SUCKLING (1600–1642)
English poet

6 He was the greatest gallant of his time, and the greatest Gamester, both for Bowling and Cards, so that no Shopkeeper would trust him for 6d a day. He was one of the best Bowlers of his time in England. He played at Cards rarely well and did used to practise by himself a-bed, and there studyed how the best way of managing the cards should be. His sisters would come to the Peccadillo bowling-green, crying for fear he should lose all their portions.
John Aubrey, BRIEF LIVES 1860

7 Sir John invented the game of Cribbage. He sent his cards to all the Gaming-places in the countrey, which were marked with private markes of his; he gott twenty thousand pounds by this way.
Ibid.

8 When the Expedition was into Scotland, Sir John Suckling, at his own charge, raysd a Troope of 100 very handsome proper men, whom he clad in white doubletts, and scarlett breeches, and scarlett Coats, hatts and feathers, well horsed and armed. They say 'twas one of the finest sights in those days butt . . . they made an inglorious charge against the Scots.
Ibid.

9 Sir John Suckling was an immoral man as well as debauched. The story of the French Cards (his getting certain marks affixed to all that came from the great makers in France) was told me by the late Duke of Buckingham, and he had it from old Lady Dorset herself.
Alexander Pope. Quoted Rev. Joseph Spence, OBSERVATIONS, ANECDOTES AND CHARACTERS 1820

10 His death was occasioned by a most uncommon accident. Sent over by the king to France he arrived late at Calais and in the night his servant ran away with his portmanteau in which were his money and papers. The servant, who knew his master's temper well and was sure he would pursue him, had driven a nail up into one of his boots in hopes of disabling him. Sir John's impetuosity made him regard the pain only just at first, and his pursuit hurried him from the thoughts of it for some time after. But after recovering his portmanteau one of his boots was full of blood and the wound was so bad, and so much inflamed, that it flung him into a violent fever which ended his life in a very few days.
Ibid.

EMMANUEL SWEDENBORG (1688–1772)
Swedish theologian, founder of the Swedenborgian sect

11 Swedenborg went into a little inn in Bishopsgate Street, and was eating his dinner very fast, when he thought he saw, in a corner of the room, a vision of Jesus Christ who said to him, "Eat slower". This was the beginning of all his visions and communications.
Caroline Fox, JOURNALS 7 *Apr* 1847

JONATHAN SWIFT (1667–1745)
Irish-born of English parents. Satirist, poet, clergyman

12 Gulliver was received but indifferently at first among us, but pleased after people got into the humour of the thing.
Abbé Boileau, at Tours 1787

13 What pleased before in Swift we now detest / Proscribed not only in the world polite / But even too nasty for a city knight.
Lord Byron

1   When Swift is considered as an author it is
    just to estimate his powers by their effects.
    In the reign of Queen Anne he turned the
    stream of popularity against the Whigs and
    must be confessed for a time to have
    dictated the political opinions of the English
    nation. In the succeeding reign he delivered
    Ireland from plunder and oppression; and
    showed that wit, confederated with truth,
    had such force as authority was unable to
    resist.
    Samuel Johnson

2   It was from the time he began to patronise
    the Irish that they may date their riches and
    prosperity. He taught them first to know
    their own interest, their weight and their
    strength, and gave them spirit to assert their
    equality with their fellow-subjects to which
    they have ever since been making vigorous
    advances, and to claim their rights which
    they have at last established. Nor can they be
    charged with ingratitude to their benefactor,
    for they reverenced him as a guardian, and
    obeyed him as a dictator.
    Ibid.

3   Swift has stolen all his humour from
    Cervantes and Rabelais.
    Lady Mary Wortley Montagu. Quoted
    Rev. Joseph Spence, OBSERVATIONS,
    ANECDOTES AND CHARACTERS   1820

4   He assumed more the air of a patron than a
    friend; he dictated rather than advised.
    With all this there was the greatest possible
    value set by Swift upon his own person. He
    was elated with the appearance of enjoying
    ministerial confidence. He enjoyed the
    shadow while the substance was withheld
    from him. He was employed, not trusted,
    and at the same time he imagined himself a
    subtle diver, who shot down into the pro-
    foundest regions of politics. He was suffered
    only to sound the shallows near the shore,
    and was scarce permitted to descend below
    the froth at the top. Perhaps the deeper
    bottom was too muddy for his inspection.
    Lord Orrery

5   Essentially he is an occasional poet who
    sings lightly about dandruff, drains, body-
    odour, dirty underclothes, and comic farts.
    Tom Paulin, Observer, The Dean's
    Bellyful   13 Feb 1983

6   Let Ireland tell how wit upheld her cause /
    Her trade supported and supplied her laws;
    / And leave on Swift this grateful verse en-
    grav'd. / "The rights a court attack'd, a poet
    saved / Behold the hand that wrought a
    nation's cure / Stretched to relieve the idiot

and the poor; / Proud vice to brand, or
injured worth adorn / And stretch the rays
to ages yet unborn."
Alexander Pope

7   Swift was delighted with the stir caused by
    the publication of *Gulliver's Travels* and
    from Dublin he wrote gaily to Pope about
    some of the first reactions to his book.
    Among the less favourable reactions he had
    to report were those of a real or apocryphal
    Irish bishop who said "The book is full of
    impossible lies and for my part I hardly be-
    lieved a word of it."
    Correspondence of Jonathan Swift   1721

8   Here lies the body of Jonathan Swift where,
    at last, savage indignation can no longer
    lacerate his heart.
    Translation of part of a Latin epitaph written
    by Swift and inscribed on his tomb,
    St. Patrick's Cathedral, Dublin

9   A monster gibbering, shrieking and
    gnashing imprecations against mankind,
    tearing down all shields of modesty, past all
    sense of manliness and shame, filthy in
    word, filthy in thought, furious, raging,
    obscene.
    William Makepeace Thackeray

ALGERNON CHARLES SWINBURNE
(1837–1909)
English poet

10 I attempt to describe Mr Swinburne, and lo!
    the Bacchanal screams, the sterile Dolores
    sweats, serpents dance, men and women
    wrench, wriggle and form in an endless
    alliteration of heated and meaningless
    words.
    Robert Buchanan, THE FLESHLY SCHOOL OF
    POETRY   1871

11 Swinburne entered a room where there was
    a mirror, and seeing his own twitching fig-
    ure and grimacing face reflected, smashed
    the glass in an attempt to chastise what he
    thought was some ill-conditioned fellow im-
    itating his own gait with intent to insult.
    S. M. Ellis, A MID-VICTORIAN PEPYS

12 A perfect leper and a mere sodomite.
    R. W. Emerson, in an interview in Frank
    Leslie's ILLUSTRATED   NEWSPAPER

13 Mr Swinburne is no longer writing poetry;
    he only makes a clattering noise.
    A. E. Housman. Quoted Laurence
    Housman, A. E. H.   1937

1   Swinburne has now said not only all he has
    to say about everything, but all he has to say
    about nothing.
    Ibid.

2   The product of Eton and Balliol, the re-
    volutionary republican poet, the lover of
    Ada Isaacs Menken, the enthusiast for
    lesbian love and frequenter of a St. John's
    Wood brothel that specialised in
    flagellation, was so tiny in stature and had
    such a frail constitution that the ladies who
    dispensed to Algernon his "potion of pain"

must have wielded the whip with a very light
hand.
*Paul Levy, Observer, reviewing Donald
Thomas's* SWINBURNE: *the Poet and his
World*   13 *Mar* 1979

3   While Jowett conducted his tutorials at
    Balliol Swinburne was stationed in an ante-
    room correcting Jowett's sometimes slapdash
    translation of Plato's Greek. "Another
    howler, master," Swinburne would shout
    with glee. "Thank you, Algernon," was the
    invariably chastened reply.
    Donald Thomas, SWINBURNE: *the Poet and
    his World*   1979

T

CHARLES MAURICE DE TALLEYRAND
(1754–1838)
French statesman and diplomat

1 Talleyrand was early destined for the church and in 1788 was appointed bishop of Autun by Louis XVI. He was gentle with the humble, haughty with the high.
Sir Henry Lytton-Bulwer, HISTORICAL CHARACTERS 1868

2 Vice leaning on the arm of crime, M.de Talleyrand supported by M. Fouché.
Francois-René, Vicomte de Chateaubriand, MEMOIRS 1849

3 He was not very exact in paying his debts, but very scrupulous in giving and breaking promises to pay them. For several days he saw, without recognising, a well-dressed individual, with his hat in his hand, and bowing very low as he mounted the steps of his coach. "And who are you my friend?" he asked at last. "I am your coachmaker, my lord,". "And what do you want, my coachmaker?" "I want to be paid, my lord." "You shall be paid, my coachmaker." "But *when* my lord?" "H'm," murmured the bishop, looking at his coachmaker very attentively, and at the same time settling comfortably in his new carriage. "You're very curious."
Ibid.

4 Such men as M. de Talleyrand are like sharp-edged instruments with which it is dangerous to play, but for great evils drastic remedies are necessary and whoever has to treat them should not be afraid to use the instrument that cuts the best.
Clement Metternich, when Austrian ambassador in Paris 24 Sep 1808

5 A lady wrote to Talleyrand, informing him, in high-flown terms of grief, of the death of her husband, and expecting an eloquent letter of condolence in return; his only answer "Hélas, Madame. Votre affectioné, Talleyrand." In less than a year another letter from the same lady informed him of her having married again; to which he returned an answer in the same laconic style.

"Oh, Oh, Madame. Votre affectioné, Talleyrand."
Tom Moore, JOURNAL

6 There are few individuals whose career appears to His Majesty to have been more disreputable, and although the king does not question his Talents, especially for Intrigue. He does not consider the selection of a Man of his Character to be either creditable to Himself, or complimentary to His Majesty.
William IV, *letter to Lord Aberdeen* 11 Sep 1830

TORQUATO TASSO (1544–1696)
Italian poet

7 Tasso's madness was, some think, only a pretended madness. He was caught making too free with a princess of the Duke of Ferreara's family, in which he lived. To save his honour, and himself, he from that time, so they say, began to play his melancholy tricks. There is a passage in his *Aminta* which may allude to this; it is in the end of the first act, and is spoken by Tersi, under which character Tasso meant himself.
Dr Cocchi. Quoted Rev. Joseph Spence, OBSERVATIONS, ANECDOTES AND CHARACTERS 1820

8 It is related of Torquato Tasso, the immortal author of *Jerusalem Divided,* that he spoke plain when only three months old. At the age of seven years he understood Latin and Greek, and composed several verses.
PERCY ANECDOTES 1823

9 At the age of nine he was condemned to death by Charles the Fifth, as was his father who was secretary to the Prince of Salerno, but both saved themselves by flight. The infant poet wrote a poem on their disgrace in which he compared himself and his father to Ascanius flying with Aeneas.
Ibid.

ALFRED LORD TENNYSON (1809–1892)
English poet

10 If Wordsworth is the great English poet of Nature Tennyson is the great English poet of the Nursery — i.e. his poems deal with

human emotions in their most primitive states, uncomplicated by conscious sexuality or intellectual rationalisation.
W. H. Auden, Introduction to SELECTED POEMS OF TENNYSON

1 In youth he looked like a gypsy, in age like a dirty old monk. He had the finest ear, perhaps, of any English poet since Milton, he was also, undoubtedly, the stupidest; there was little about melancholia that he didn't know; there is little else that he did.
Ibid.

2 Alfred is always carrying a bit of chaos round with him, and turning it into cosmos.
Thomas Carlyle. Quoted J. L. Lowes, CONVENTION AND REVOLT IN POETRY

3 We have had Alfred Tennyson here; very droll and very wayward; and much sitting up of nights with pipes in our mouths, at which good hour we would get Alfred to give us some of his magic music, which he does between growling and smoking; and so to bed.
Edward Fitzgerald, DIARY   4 *Apr* 1838

4 Tennyson is emerged half-cured, or half destroyed, from a water establishment; he's gone to a new doctor who gives him iron pills; and altogether this really great man thinks more about his bowels and nerves than about the Laureate's wreath he was born to inherit.
Edward Fitzgerald in 1848. *Quoted Edward Fitzgerald,* SELECTED WORKS *(edited by Joanna Richardson)*

5 In his later years his appearance was eccentric. He wore his hair long, flowing over his shoulders. He had a big black sombrero, a large, loose, soft Byronic collar; a big floppy tie and a cloak flung over one shoulder. He complained to a lady that it was one of the penalties of celebrity that he was stared at, and even sometimes followed. Her little girl of eight hoping to be helpful, suggested, "Perhaps, sir, if you cut your hair and dressed like other people they wouldn't stare so much." He was not pleased.
Sir George Leveson Gower, MIXED GRILL

6 The bower we shrined to Tennyson, Gentlemen / Is roof-wrecked; damps there drip upon / Sagged seats, the creeper-nails are rust / The spider is sole denizen / Even she who voiced these rhymes is dust / Gentlemen.
Thomas Hardy, AN ANCIENT TO ANCIENTS

7 Tennyson was not Tennysonian.
Henry James, THE MIDDLE YEARS

8 Not mine, not mine (O Muse forbid) the boon / Of borrowed notes, the mock-bird's modish tune, / The jingling melody of purloin's conceits / Outbraying Wordworth and outglittering Keats / Where all the airs of patchwork pastoral chime / To drowsy airs in Tennysonian rhyme.
Lord Lytton, THE NEW TIMES AND POETICAL ROMANCE OF LONDON   1846

9 Once a lady, who profoundly admired his genius, ventured to remonstrate with him on what she thought his undue eagerness for a peerage. He replied in a document called *My Wrath.* The entreaties of friends prevented him from despatching it; but he kept it handy in a drawer, and, if a visitor chanced to mention the lady's name, he would rejoin, "Oh, do you know that woman? Then you shall hear what I think of her" and would read the document aloud, while his hearers listened and trembled.
G. W. E. Russell, PORTRAITS OF THE SEVENTIES   1916

10 His manner was abrupt, his voice gruff, his vocabulary borrowed from the eighteenth century, and his whole demeanour that of a man who expected, and was accustomed, to be worshipped.
Ibid.

11 Now and then one caught sight of him in London and he certainly looked the poet to perfection. His long dark hair, mingled with the untrimmed luxuriance of beard, whiskers and moustache, his soft hat of Spanish mould, his loose cloak and clay pipe, all combined to give the world assurance of a Bard.
Ibid.

12 The Vivien of Mr Tennyson's idyll seems to me about the most base and repulsive person ever set forth in serious literature. Her impurity is actually eclipsed by her incredible and incomparable vulgarity. She is such a sordid creature as plucks men passing by the sleeve. The conversation of Vivien is exactly described in the poet's own phrase — it is "as the poached filth that flows the middle street".
Algernon Swinburne

13 What a *hog* that Alfred is, and what can you expect from a pig but a grunt?
Tennyson's cousin Edwin. Quoted LETTERS OF ALFRED TENNYSON *(edited Cecil V. Lang and Edgar F. Shannon Jnr)*   1982

14 When Tennyson entered the Oxford Theatre to receive his honorary degree of

D. C. L., his locks hanging in admired disorder on his shoulders, dishevelled and unkempt, a voice from the gallery was heard crying out to him, "Did your mother call you early, dear?" The allusion, of course, is to Tennyson's *May Queen*.
Julian Charles Young, DIARY   8 *Nov* 1863

DAME ALICE ELLEN TERRY (1847–1928)
English actress

1 She has a voice of plum-coloured velvet.
James Agate, EGO   1935

2 Henry James was complaining to us that Ellen Terry had asked him to write a play for her and now that he had done so, and read it to her, she had refused it. My wife, desiring to placate, asked, "Perhaps she did not think the part suited to her?" H. J. turned upon us both, and with resonance and uplifted voice replied. "Think? Think? How should the poor, chattering toothless hag THINK?"
John Bailey, letter to Edmund Gosse
14 *Apr* 1920

3 She has a charm, a great deal of a certain amateurish, angular grace, a total lack of that which the French call *chic* and a countenance very happily adapted to the expression of pathetic emotion.
Henry James, The Nation   12 *Jun* 1879

4 Her voice has a sort of monotonous, husky thickness which is extremely touching, though it gravely interferes with the modulation of many of her speeches.
Ibid.

5 She was an extremely beautiful girl and as innocent as a rose. When Watts kissed her she took it for granted she was going to have a baby.
George Bernard Shaw. Quoted Stephen Winston, DAYS WITH SHAW

WILLIAM MAKEPEACE THACKERAY
(1811–1863)
English novelist

6 I approve Mr Thackeray. This may sound presumptuous perhaps, but what I mean is that I have long recognised in his writings genuine talent, such as I admired, such as I delighted in and wondered at. No author seems to distinguish so exquisitely as he does dross from ore, the real from the counterfeit.
Charlotte Brontë, letter to W. S. Williams
28 *Oct* 1847

7 He had many fine qualities, no guile or malice against any mortal; a big mass of a soul, but not strong in proportion; a beautiful vein of genius lay struggling about in him. Nobody in our day wrote, I should say, with such perfection of style.
Thomas Carlyle

8 Thackeray doesn't sneer; he is really very sentimental; but he sees the silliness sentiment runs into, and so always tempers his with a little banter or ridicule. He is much farther into actual life than I am.
Arthur Hugh Clough. Quoted Ann Monsarrat, AN UNEASY VICTORIAN: *Thackeray the Man*   1980

9 People in general thought *Pendennis* got dull as it got on; and I confess I thought so too; he would do well to take the opportunity of his illness to discontinue it altogether.
Edward Fitzgerald, COLLECTED WORKS
(edited by Joanna Richardson)

10 Finished that brilliant, bitter book *Vanity Fair*. It shows great insight into the intricate badness of human nature, and draws a cruel sort of line between moral and intellectual eminence, as if they were commonly dissociated, which I trust is not a true bill.
Caroline Fox, JOURNALS   1849

11 Thackeray settled like a meat-fly on whatever one had got for dinner, and made me sick of it.
John Ruskin, FORS CLAVIGERA: *Letters to the Labourers and Working Men of Great Britain*   1889

12 Among all our novelists his style is the purest, as to my ear it is the most harmonious. Sometimes it is disfigured by a slight touch of affectation, by little conceits which smell of the oil; — but the language is always lucid. The reader, without labour, knows what he means, and knows all that he means.
Anthony Trollope, AUTOBIOGRAPHY   1883

MARGARET HILDA THATCHER
(1925–   )
British Prime Minister

13 She is trying to wear the trousers of Winston Churchill.
Leonid Brezhnev. Speech   1979

14 She slipped into her place as demurely tight-lipped as ever, and glossy with her best suburban grooming, fresh-flowered summer frock, and every wave of her hair in place. How *does* she keep her hair so unchangeably immaculate?
Barbara Castle, THE CASTLE DIARIES
1974–6

1 She has been beastly to the Bank of England, has demanded that the BBC "set its house in order" and tends to believe the worst of the Foreign and Commonwealth Office. She cannot see an institution without hitting it with her handbag.
Julian Critchley, The Times, Profile: Margaret Thatcher   21 June 1982

2 Mrs Thatcher is a woman of common views but uncommon abilities.
Ibid.

3 She has no imagination, and that means no compassion.
Michael Foot. Quoted John Mortimer, Sunday Times   18 Sep 1982

4 Attila the Hen.
Clement Freud, BBC Radio 4, News Quiz 26 Oct 1979

5 She approaches the problems of our country with all the one-dimensional subtlety of a comic-strip.
Denis Healey, House of Commons 22 May 1979

6 Mrs Thatcher is doing for monetarism what the Boston Strangler did for door-to-door salesmen.
Denis Healey, House of Commons 15 Dec 1979

7 For the past few months she has been charging about like some bargain-basement Boadicea.
Denis Healey. Quoted Observer, Sayings of the Week   7 Nov 1982

8 She is the Enid Blyton of economics. Nothing must be allowed to spoil her simple plots.
Richard Holme, Liberal Party Conference 10 Sep 1980

9 This woman is headstrong, obstinate, and dangerously self-opinionated.
Report by personnel officer at ICI when rejecting her as a possible employee   1948

10 She sounded like the Book of Revelations read out over a railway station public address system by a headmistress of certain age in calico knickers.
Clive James, of the 1979 election result in THE CHRYSTAL BUCKET   1981

11 She deserves credit for her iron guts, even if you think her brains are made of the same stuff.
Clive James, Observer, The Great Leap Homeward   3 Oct 1982

12 She is of such charming brutality.
Helmut Kohl, Chancellor of West Germany 23 Sep 1983

13 I am a great admirer of Mrs Thatcher — one of the most splendid headmistresses there has ever been.
Arthur Marshall, BBC Radio 4, Any Questions   22 Jan 1982

14 Mrs Thatcher has taken to power the way others take to the air at Colwyn Bay. It braces her. She is invigorated . She knocks people down.
Edward Pearce, Daily Telegraph 27 Jun 1979

15 The Queen Mother, visiting Halifax, Nova Scotia, was asked whether the election of Mrs Thatcher is having a significant effect on women in Britain. "More on the men," she replied with a laugh.
Peterborough, Daily Telegraph   2 Jul 1979

16 She is the best man in England.
Ronald Reagan to reporters   7 Jan 1983

17 Margaret Thatcher is David Owen in drag.
Rhodesia Herald   8 Aug 1979

18 I am extraordinarily patient — provided I get my own way in the end.
Margaret Thatcher, Observer, Sayings of the Years   2 Jan 1983

19 Don't forget Denis [her husband] when you're considering the influences on her. He sees her every morning at breakfast — far more often than any of us.
A Tory MP when Mrs Thatcher became Prime Minister. Quoted Laurence Marks, Observer   6 May 1979

DYLAN MARLAIS THOMAS (1914–1953)
Welsh poet

20 The crabbed and dark-eyed Welshman, Dylan Thomas, whose poems were strewn with wild, organic telescoped images under which, perhaps, ran a stream of poetic thought.
Robert Graves and Alan Hodge, THE LONG WEEKEND   1940

21 The fear of being unable to write was nearer the root of his trouble than the fear of not being able to pay the grocer.
New Yorker   21 Nov 1977

22 Dylan wore a "conscious Woodbine" on his lower lip, a check coat, and a porkpie hat, as he gathered more beer in his gut than news in his head. His beat was mainly the Swansea of the pubs.
Andrew Sinclair, POET OF THE PEOPLE

23 Dylan was a hidden puritan who expected women to be as neat as robins' eggs and was ever anxious about his wife's proper dressing

when they went to the shops, but equally he was the mighty drinker and rioter, heir of the ancient feasts and the dark pubs of Swansea, the pig in the middle between the new middle class and the old ways of farm and railway and mine.
Ibid.

1 Dylan was a complete chameleon and could adapt himself to any company and play any role. His favourite role was that of a Welsh country gentleman for which in later days he dressed in hairy tweeds and carried a knobbed walking stick.
Donald Taylor. Quoted Constantine Fitzgibbon, LIFE OF DYLAN THOMAS

2 He was a detestable man. Men pressed money on him, and women their bodies. Dylan took both with equal contempt. His great pleasure was to humiliate people.
A. J. P. Taylor, AUTOBIOGRAPHY 1983

3 His passion for lies was congenital; more a practice in invention than a lie. He would tell quite unnecessary ones, which did not in any way improve his situation; such as, when he had been to one cinema, saying it was another, and making up the film that was on.
Caitlin Thomas, LEFTOVER LIFE TO KILL

4 My method is this; I write a poem on innumerable sheets of scrap paper, write it on both sides of the paper, often upside down and criss-cross ways unpunctuated, surrounded by drawings of lamp posts and boiled eggs, in a very dirty mess, bit by bit I copy out the slowly developing poem into an exercise book; and when it is completed I type it out. The scrap sheets I burn.
Dylan Thomas, letter to Charles Fisher 1935

JAMES THOMSON (1700–1748)
Scottish poet

5 Thomson's *Seasons* — an enormously popular but diffuse and stilted poem being praised in his company, Samuel Johnson picked up a volume and read a passage from it with sonorous dignity. After the murmurs of applause had subsided he told the admirers he had omitted every other word.
Bergen Evans, DICTIONARY OF QUOTATIONS 1904

6 My own notion is that Thomson was a much wiser man than his friends are willing to acknowledge. His *Seasons* are indeed full of elegant and pious sentiments; but a rank

soil, nay, a dunghill, will produce beautiful flowers.
Samuel Johnson. Quoted Boswell, THE LIFE OF JOHNSON 1791

HENRY DAVID THOREAU (1817–1862)
American essayist and poet

7 He was a protestant *à outrance* and few lives contain so many renunciations. He was bred to no profession; he never married; he lived alone; he never went to church; he never voted; he refused to pay a tax to the State; he ate no flesh; he drank no wine, he never knew the use of tobacco, and though a naturalist he used neither trap nor gun.
W. R. Emerson, LECTURES AND BIOGRAPHICAL STUDIES: *Thoreau*

8 Whatever question there may be of his talent, there can be none I think of his genius. It was a slim and crooked one, but it was eminently personal. He was imperfect, unfinished, inartistic. He was worse than provincial — he was parochial.
Henry James, HAWTHORNE

9 I have been trying to read Thoreau, but after the subtlety, wisdom and beauty of the writings of Pater and his school I find the grave, didactic style of the old Puritan backwoodsman very slow and barren.
Llewelyn Powys, LETTERS

10 I love Henry, but I cannot like him; and as for taking his arm, I should as soon think of taking the arm of an elm tree.
An unknown friend of Thoreau. Quoted ibid.

TINTORETTO (1518–1594)
(Jacapo Robusti)
Italian painter

11 Some Flemish painters being at Rome showed Tintoretto two or three heads which they had painted and finished with great care. He asked how long they had taken to do them. They answered that they had taken several weeks. Tintoretto on this dipped his pencil in some black colour, and with a few strokes drew on a canvas a figure, which he filled in with white. Turning towards the strangers, "See", said he to them, "how we poor Venetian painters are accustomed to make pictures."
PERCY ANECDOTES 1823

12 I have been perfectly prostrated these two or three days back by my first acquaintance with Tintoretto; but then I feel as if I had got introduced to a being from a planet a

1,000,000 miles nearer the sun, not to a mere earthly painter. As for our little bits of R.A.s calling themselves painters, it ought to be stopped directly. One might make a mosaic of R. A.s perhaps; with a good magnifying glass, big enough for Tintoretto to stand with one leg upon — if he balanced himself like a gondolier.
John Ruskin, letter to Joseph Severn
21 *Sep* 1843

TITIAN (1489–1576)
(Tizlano Vecellio)
Italian painter

1 In the last three decades of his long career Titian did not paint man as if he were free from care and as fitted to his environment as a lark on an April morning. Rather did he represent man as acting on his environment and suffering from its reactions.
Bernard Berenson

2 When the Prado was on fire, on the fatal accident being reported to Philip IV he instantly demanded if the Titian Venus had escaped the conflagration. The messenger assured him it was safe. "Then", replied the king, "all other losses may be supported."
PERCY ANECDOTES   1823

3 There against the wall, without obstructing rag or leaf, you may look your fill upon the foulest, the vilest, the obscenest picture the world possesses — Titian's Venus . . . Without any question it was painted for a bagnio, and it was probably refused because it was a little too strong.
Mark Twain, A TRAMP ABROAD   1880

COUNT LEO NIKOLAIEVICH TOLSTOY (1828–1910)
Russian novelist and poet

4 In his wrestlings with God he behaved more with the authority of the aristocracy than the humility of the pilgrim. "Come and dwell within me," he demanded of God, and, as Gorky noted, the relationship of Tolstoy with God reminded him of "two bears in one den".
Simon Blow, Radio Times, Tolstoy: the eternal question 1 *Dec* 1979

5 Tolstoy towered above his age as Dante and Michelangelo and Beethoven had done. His novels are marvels of sustained imagination, but his life was full of inconsistencies. He wanted to be one with the peasants, yet he continued to live like an aristocrat. He preached universal love, yet he quarrelled

so painfully with his poor demented wife that at the age of 82 he ran away from her.
Sir Kenneth Clark, CIVILISATION   1969

6 I like Leo Tolstoy enormously, but in my opinion he won't write much of anything else. (I could be wrong.)
Dostoevsky, after the publication of
CHILDHOOD, BOYHOOD, YOUTH   1852

7 It has been said that a careful reading of *Anna Karenina*, if it teaches you nothing else, will teach you how to make strawberry jam.
Julian Mitchell, Radio Times   30 *Oct* 1976

8 Tolstoy, like myself, wasn't taken in by superstitions like science and medicine.
George Bernard Shaw

ANTHONY TROLLOPE (1815–1882)
English novelist

9 Have you ever read the novels of Anthony Trollope? They precisely suit my taste — solid and substantial, written on the strength of beef and through the inspiration of ale, and just as real as if some giant had hewn a great lump out of the earth, and put it under a glass case, with all its inhabitants going about their daily business and not suspecting they were being made a show of. And these books are just as English as beefsteak.
Nathaniel Hawthorne, letter to J. M. Field

10 He has a gross and repulsive face, but appears *bon enfant* when you talk to him. But he is the dullest Briton of them all.
Henry James, letter to his family
1 *Nov* 1875

11 A big, red-faced, rather underbred Englishman of the bald-with-spectacles type. A good roaring, positive fellow who deafened me till I thought of Dante's Cerberus.
James Russell Lowell, letter   20 *Sep* 1861

12 I called on Mrs Byles. She put into my hands a tale by Anthony Trollope called *The Warden*. A singular history. It is a sort of controversial tale with no object clearly made out. It is founded on Whiston's attack on the Deans and Chapters. There is a sharp satirical description of the *Times* newspaper, called *Jupiter*, and of the *Times* office, called *Olympus*. It is a singular book — a sort of wild goose flight.
Henry Crabb Robinson, JOURNAL
27 *May* 1857

13 Mr Trollope's success as a novelist for the time he was writing was almost wonderful because, as soon as death stopped his

prolific pen, the author and the books died at the same time, for no one reads or thinks about Mr Trollope's novels now.
William Tinsley, RECOLLECTIONS OF AN OLD PUBLISHER 1900

1 It was my practice to be at my table every morning at 5.30 a.m.; it was also my practice to allow myself no mercy. An old groom, whose business it was to call on me, and to whom I paid an extra £5 a year for the duty, allowed himself no mercy. During all those years at Waltham Cross he never once was late with the coffee which it was his duty to bring me. . . . By beginning at that hour I could complete my literary work before I dressed for breakfast.
Anthony Trollope, AUTOBIOGRAPHY 1883

IVAN SERGEVICH TURGENEV (1818–1883)
Russian novelist

2 Our old Turgenev is a true man of letters. A growth has just been removed from his stomach, and he said to Daudet, who went to see him, "During this operation I thought of our dinners, and I struggled to find words with which I could give you my exact impression of the steel cutting up my skin and entering my flesh — like a knife cutting up a banana."
Edmund de Goncourt, JOURNAL 21 *Apr* 1883

JOSEPH MALLORD WILLIAM TURNER (1773–1851)
English painter

3 Turner told me he had no systematic process for making drawings. He thinks it can produce nothing but manner and sameness. Turner has no settled process, but drives the colours about till he has expressed the idea in his mind.
Joseph Farrington, DIARY 21 *Jul* 1799

4 He knew more than anyone. He knew how a wave curled, how the spring of the branch of an elm differed from that of an ash, how a tree roots itself in the ground, what all kinds of cloud and rock form are like.
Roger Fry, REFLECTIONS ON BRITISH PAINTING

5 The vast total quantity of Turner's work is one of the marks of his genius. He had within him a spirit which forced him continually to paint. As Ruskin significantly

wrote of Turner's attitude towards nature, "It is intangible, incalculable, a thing to be felt, not comprehended — a music of the eyes, a melody of the heart, whose truth is only known by its sweetness."
Charles Johnson, ENGLISH PAINTING

6 He produced his effects as if by throwing handfuls of white and blue and red at the canvas, and letting what would stick, stick.
Literary Gazette May 1842

7 "Personally," said the publisher, "I find J. W. Turner rather a lovable person." Osbert Sitwell put his head on one side and smiled. "I know what it is," he said with an air of discovery. "You used to keep tadpoles."
Beverley Nichols, TWENTY-FIVE

8 A tortoiseshell cat having a fit in a platter of tomatoes.
Mark Twain, of Turner's Slave Ship

9 Sunsets are quite old fashioned. They belong to the time when Turner was the last note in art.
Oscar Wilde, THE DECAY OF LYING

MARK TWAIN (1835–1910)
(Samuel Langhorne Clemens)
American author

10 He had no notion of construction, and very little power of self-criticism. He was great in the subordinate business of decoration, as distinguished from construction; but he would mingle together the very best and the very worst decorations.
Arnold Bennett, Bookman Jun 1910

11 He combined syntactical elegance with tobacco-spitting raciness, and an exquisite ear with a healthy Philistinism which rejected Jane Austen, Scott, George Eliot and Henry James.
Anthony Burgess, Observer, Connecticut Yankee 4 Jul 1982

12 I love to think of the great and godlike Clemens. He was the biggest man you have on your side of the water by a damn sight, and don't you forget it. Cervantes was a relation of his.
Rudyard Kipling, letter to Frank Doubleday

13 Mark Twain and I are in very much the same position. We have to put things in such a way as to make people, who would otherwise hang us, believe that we are joking.
George Bernard Shaw

V

VINCENT VAN GOGH (1853–1890)
Dutch post-Impressionist painter

1 Here are pictures of potatoes, and of miners who have eaten potatoes until their faces are tuberous and dented and their skins grimed and unpeeled. They are hopeless and humble, so he loves them.
E. M. Forster, TWO CHEERS FOR DEMOCRACY; *The Lost Parade* 1951

2 I so often think how insane it would have been, how destructive for him, if Van Gogh had had to share the uniqueness of his vision with anyone, had had to examine the motives with someone before he had made his pictures out of them, those existences that justify him with their whole soul, that answer for him, that swear to his reality.
Rainer Maria Rilke, LETTERS 1892–1910

3 Van Gogh is the typical matoid and degenerate of the modern sociologist. *Jeune Fille au Bleuet* and *Cornfield with Blackbirds* are the visualised ravings of an adult maniac.
Robert Ross, Morning Post

4 You have Van Gogh's ear for music.
Billy Wilder

VICTORIA (1819–1901)
Queen of Great Britain and Ireland. Empress of India

5 Probably the most notable garment she ever wore was the nightdress in which she received, that early morning in Kensington Palace, the news of her uncle's death.
Alison Adburgham, A PUNCH HISTORY OF MANNERS AND MODES

6 Victoria has greatly improved, and has become very reasonable and good-natured.
Prince Albert, letter to his brother Ernst, three years after his marriage

7 You have again lost your self-control quite unnecessarily. There is no need for me to promise to *Trust* you, for it was not a question of trust, but of your fidgety nature.
Prince Albert, letter to Victoria. Quoted Robert Rhodes James, ALBERT PRINCE CONSORT 1983

8 She is a comely little lady with a pair of kind, clear and intelligent grey eyes; still looks plump and almost young (in spite of one broad wrinkle that shows in each cheek occasionally); has a fine low voice; soft indeed her whole manner is, and melodiously perfect; it is impossible to imagine a *politer* little woman.
Thomas Carlyle, letter to Mrs Aiken 11 Mar 1869

9 Queen Victoria in her eighties was more known, more revered, and a more important part of the life of the country than she had ever been. Retirement, for a monarch, is not a good idea.
Charles, Prince of Wales 1974

10 The Queen, Lady Cowley said, was excessively civil to everyone, had excellent manners, but was *Royal* (and quite right too, little Vic, I say). Nothing could be more agreeable than she was. Can you wish for a better account of a little tit of 18 made all at once into a Queen?
Thomas Creevey, letter to Elizabeth Orde 5 Aug 1837

11 In talking to Lady Cowper of Lord Melbourne and, as I suppose, of his health, Vic said, "He eats too much and I often tell him so. Indeed I do so myself and my doctor has ordered me not to eat luncheon any more." "And does your Majesty quite obey him?" "Why yes, I think I do," said Vic, "for I eat only a little broth." Now I think a little Queen taking care of her Prime Minister's stomach, he being nearly sixty, is everything one could wish.
Ibid. 9 Oct 1837

12 Today, 23 years ago, dear Grandmama died. I wonder what she would have thought of a Labour government?
George V, Diary entry on Ramsay Macdonald's appointment as Prime Minister 22 Jan 1924

13 It was much remarked that Victoria and Prince Albert were up very early on Tuesday morning walking about, which is very contrary to her former habits. Strange that a bridal night should be so short; and I

227

told Lady Palmerston that this was not the way to provide us with a Prince of Wales.
Greville, DIARY   13 *Feb* 1840

1   I don't know why, but the first sight of her in her coronation robes brought tears to my eyes; and it had this effect on many people; she looked almost like a child. She is very fond of dogs, and has one very favourite little spaniel, which is always on the look-out for her return when she has been from home. She had of course been separated from him on Coronation Day longer than usual and when the state coach drove up to the steps of the palace she heard him barking with joy in the hall and exclaimed, "There's Dash!" and was in a hurry to lay aside the sceptre and ball which she carried in her hands, and take off the crown and robes, to go and wash little Dash.
C. R. Leslie, letter to his sister   24 *Jul* 1837

2   An earnest clergyman described to Queen Victoria what he had seen in the East End of London and by way of showing how over-crowded the houses were said that in one house he visited he found that seven people slept in one bed. The Queen dryly remarked "Had I been one of them I would have slept on the floor."
Sir Frederick Ponsonby, RECOLLECTIONS OF THREE REIGNS

3   Nowadays a parlourmaid as ignorant as Queen Victoria was when she came to the throne would be classed as mentally defective.
George Bernard Shaw

VIRGIL (70–19 BC)
(Publius Vergilius Maro)
Latin poet

4   A crawling and disgusting parasite, a base scoundrel, and pander to unnatural passions.
William Cobbett

5   Thou art my master and my author, thou art he from whom alone I took the style whose beauty has done me honour.
Dante, DIVINE COMEDY, *Inferno, Canto* I 1321

6   Mantua bore me; Calabria captivated me; Naples now holds me. I sang of pastures, of country things, and of the leaders of war.
Epitaph. Quoted Claudius Donaties, LIFE OF VIRGIL

7   Virgil's great judgement appears in putting things together, and in his picking gold out of the dunghills of old Roman writers.
Alexander Pope. Quoted Rev. Joseph Spence, OBSERVATIONS, ANECDOTES AND CHARACTERS   1820

8   When the monk said of Virgil that it would make an excellent poem if it were only put into rhyme, is just as if a Frenchman should say of a beauty, "Oh what a fine woman that would be if only she were painted."
Baron Stoch (author of GEMMAE LITERATAE*) Quoted Rev. Joseph Spence,* OBSERVATIONS, ANECDOTES AND CHARACTERS   1820

VOLTAIRE (1694–1778)
(François Marie Arouet)
French philosopher, poet, dramatist and satirist

9   You know Voltaire is reckoned to have stolen a great deal from Shakespeare. It is supposed that his anger against the trans-lators is on account of the thefts aforesaid, which will soon be made manifest to all France.
Mrs Boscawen, letter to Hannah More   1776

10   He does not inflame his mind with grand hopes of the immortality of the soul. He says it may be, but he knows nothing of it. And his mind is in perfect tranquillity.
BOSWELL ON THE GRAND TOUR *(edited by F. A. Pottle)*   1953

11   At last M. de Voltaire opened the door of his apartment and stepped forth. I surveyed him with eager attention and found him just as his print had made me conceive him. He received me with dignity and that air of the world which a Frenchman acquires in such perfection. He had a slate-blue fine frieze nightgown, and a three-knotted wig. He sat erect upon his chair and simpered when he spoke. He was not in spirits, nor I neither. All I presented was the "foolish face of wondering praise".
Ibid.

12   With the fire of him whose tragedies have so often shone on the theatre of Paris he said, "I suffer much. But I suffer with patience and resignation; not as a Christian — but as a man."
Ibid.

13   When he talked our language he was animated with the soul of a Briton. He had bold flights. He had humour. He had an extravagance; he had a forcible oddity of style that the most comical of our *dramatis personae* could not have exceeded. He

swore bloodily as was the fashion when he was in England.
Ibid.

1 Built God a church and laugh'd his word to scorn / Skilful alike to seem devout and just, / And stab religion with a sly side-thrust.
William Cowper, RETIREMENT

2 I have done but very little but read Voltaire since I saw you. He is an exquisite fellow. One thing in him is peculiarly striking — his clear knowledge of the limits of human understanding. He pursues his game so far as the scent carries him, but no further. Where this fails, he turns off with a jest that marks distinctly where a wise man ought to stop.
Dr J. Currie, letter to Thomas Creevey 17 *Dec* 1798

3 I was born much too soon, but I do not regret it; I have seen Voltaire.
Frederick II, *King of Prussia* 1778

4 Jesus wept; Voltaire smiled.
Victor Hugo. Address at the centenary of Voltaire's death 30 *May* 1878

5 Here lies the child spoiled by the world which he spoiled.
Baronne de Montolieu, EPITAPH ON VOLTAIRE

6 I once said to the Abbé Delille, "Don't you think that Voltaire's *vers de société* are the first of their kind?" He replied, "Assuredly. The very first — and the last."
Samuel Rogers, TABLE TALK 1856

W

RICHARD WAGNER (1813–1883)
German composer

1 He disliked Wagner's music intensely. It
had, he said, the same effect on him as the
noise of a finger rubbed round the edge of a
piece of glass, and he said that he could
gauge from the intensity of his dislike how
keen the enjoyment of those who did enjoy
it must be.
Maurice Baring, quoting his friend Brewster,
THE PUPPET SHOW OF MEMORY 1922

2 Wagner was the most selfish man who ever
lived. Everything he wrote was too long.
Sir Thomas Beecham. Quoted Lord
Boothby, MY YESTERDAY, YOUR
TOMORROW

3 A genius, no doubt, but too often excessively theatrical and emotional. *Lohengrin*
was his only stylish work — the Germans
have no idea of style.
Sir Thomas Beecham. Quoted Neville
Cardus, SIR THOMAS BEECHAM

4 Damned German stuff. They've been at it
for two hours and they're still singing the
same bloody tune.
Sir Thomas Beecham. Quoted on BBC 2 TV
18 *Nov* 1979

5 Wagner has done undeniably good work in
humbling the singers.
Max Beerbohm

6 His music is like a beautiful sunset mistaken
for a dawn.
Debussy. Quoted Edward Lockspeiser,
DEBUSSY: *His Life and Mind*

7 Here we are again — weeping and sleeping.
Philip Hope-Wallace at the opera. Quoted
The Times obituary 17 *Dec* 1979

8 I remember a young man leaving in the middle of the last act of *Tristan*, apologising
loudly to the owners of the feet he trod on
with "You see, I've got some chaps coming
to breakfast."
G. W. Lyttelton, THE LYTTELTON
HART-DAVIS LETTERS 22 *Dec* 1955

9 This is demagogy, blasphemy, insanity,
madness! it is a perfumed fog, shot through

with lightning! It is the end of all honesty in
art.
Thomas Mann, of Tristan and Isolde,
BUDDENBROOKS 1901

10 The latest bore — but it is colossal — is
Tannhauser. I think I could compose something like it tomorrow, inspired by my cat
scampering over the keys of the piano.
Princess Metternich exerted herself hugely
in pretending to understand it.
Prosper Merrimée, letter 21 *Mar* 1861

11 Is Wagner a human being at all? Is he not
rather a disease? He contaminates everything he touches — he has made music sick.
I postulate this viewpoint: Wagner's art is
diseased.
Friedrich Nietzsche, DER FALL WAGNER

12 With Wagner amorous excitement assumes
the form of mad delirium. The lovers in his
pieces behave like tom-cats gone mad, rolling in contortions and convulsions over a
bed of valerian.
Max Nordau, DEGENERATION

13 What terrible harm Wagner did by inter-
spersing his pages of genius with harmonic
and modulatory outrages.
Nikolai Rimsky-Korsakov, LETTERS 1901

14 Wagner's music is better than it sounds.
Mark Twain

HORACE WALPOLE (1717–1797)
(Fourth Earl of Orford)
English author

15 He was a witty, sarcastic, ingenious
deeply-thinking, highly-cultivated quaint,
though evermore gallant and romantic,
though very mundane, old bachelor of other
days.
Fanny Burney, MEMOIRS OF DR BURNEY

16 His writings rank as high among the deli-
cacies of intellectual epicures as the
Strasburg pies among the dishes described
in the *Almanache Gourmands.* But as
the *paté de fois gras* owes its excellence to
the diseases of the wretched animal which
furnished it and would be good for nothing
if it was not made from the livers pre-
ternaturally swollen, so none but an un-
healthy and disorganised mind could have

produced such literary luxuries as the works of Walpole
T. B. Macaulay, Edinburgh Review, Walpole   Oct 1833

1   His original vein of playful humour and pleasantry runs through the whole of his works but it is mingled with a much larger proportion of profaneness and indelicacy than I should have expected from the casual intercourse and conversation which I have had with him, in which he was always decent and correct. I am sorry to say that he omits no opportunity of burlesquing the Scripture, religion and the clergy.
Bishop Porteus

SIR ROBERT WALPOLE (1676–1745)
(First Earl of Orford)
British Prime Minister

2   When Sir Robert Walpole was dismissed from all his employments he retired to Houghton and walked into the library; when, pulling down a book and holding it some minutes to his eyes, he suddenly and seemingly sullenly exchanged it for another. He held that about half as long, and looking out for a third returned that as instantly to its shelf and burst into tears. "I have led a life of business so long," said he "I have lost my taste for reading and now — what shall I do?"
Henry Fox, first Baron Holland

3   The whole system of his ministry was corruption, and he never gave bribe or pension without telling the receivers frankly what he expected from them, and threatening to put an end to his bounty if they failed to comply in every circumstance.
Jonathan Swift

IZAAK WALTON (1593–1683)
English author

4   And angling, too, that solitary vice, / Whatever Izaak Walton sings or says; / The quaint, old, cruel coxcomb, in his gullet / Should have a hook, and a small trout to pull it.
Lord Byron, Don Juan, Canto xiii   1824

5   It was wonderful that Walton, who was in a very low situation of life, should have been familiarly received by so many great men, and that at a time when the ranks of society were kept more separate than they are now. I suppose that Walton had given up his busi-ness as a linen-draper and sempster, and was only an author. He was a great panegyrist.
Samuel Johnson. Quoted Boswell, THE LIFE OF JOHNSON   1791

6   Did you ever light upon Walton's *Compleat Angler*? It breathes the very spirit of inno-cence, purity and simplicity of heart; there are many choice old verses interspersed in it; it would sweeten a man's temper any time to read it; it would Christianise every discordant, angry passion.
Charles Lamb, letter to Coleridge 28 *Oct* 1796

GEORGE WASHINGTON (1732–1799)
First President of the United States

7   While Washington's a watchword such as ne'er / Shall sink while there's an echo left to air.
Lord Byron, THE AGE OF BRONZE

8   Washington / Whose every battlefield is holy ground / Which breathes of nations saved, not worlds undone.
Lord Byron, DON JUAN   1824

9   Where may the wearied eye repose / When gazing on the great; / Where neither guilty glory grows / Nor despicable state? / Yes — one — the first — the last — the best — / The Cincinnatus of the West / Whom envy dares not hate / Bequeathed the name of Washington / To make men blush there was but one.
Lord Byron, ODE TO NAPOLEON BONAPARTE

10   The character, the counsels and example of our Washington will guide us through the doubts and difficulties that beset us; they will guide our children and our children's children in the paths of prosperity and peace while America shall hold her place in the family of nations.
Edward Everett. Address, Washington Abroad and At Home   5 *Jul* 1858

11   Washington is now only a steel engraving. About the real man who lived and loved and hated and schemed, we know but little.
Robert G. Ingersoll, LINCOLN

12   On the whole his character was, in its mass, perfect, in nothing bad, in few points in-different; and it may truly be said that never did nature and fortune combine more perfectly to make a man great.
Thomas Jefferson, WRITINGS, VOL XIV *(edited by P. L. Ford)*   1894

1 Were an energetic and judicious system to be proposed with your signature it would be a circumstance highly honourable to your fame and doubly entitle you to the glorious republican epithet, The Father of Your Century.
Henry Knox, letter to Washington
19 *Mar* 1787

2 First in war, first in peace, first in the hearts of his countrymen.
Henry Lee, addressing the House of Representatives on Washington's death
26 *Dec* 1799

3 Washington is the mightiest name on earth — long since mightiest in the cause of civil liberty, still mightiest in moral reformation. On that name no eulogy is expected. It cannot be. To add brightness to the sun or glory to the name of Washington is alike impossible. Let none attempt it. In solemn awe pronounce the name and in its naked deathless splendour leave it shining on.
Abraham Lincoln. Speech, Springfield
22 *Feb* 1842

4 The world will be puzzled to decide whether you are an apostate or an imposter, whether you have abandoned good principles, or whether you ever had any?
Thomas Paine

5 As to pay, Sir, I beg leave to assure the Congress that as no pecuniary consideration could have tempted me to accept this arduous employment at the expense of my domestic ease and happiness I do not wish to make any profit from it.
Washington to Congress, on being appointed Commander-in-Chief 16 *Jun* 1775

6 "George," said his father, "do you know who killed that beautiful cherry tree yonder?" Looking at his father with the sweet face of youth brightened with the inexpressible charm of all-conquering truth, he bravely cried out, "I cannot tell a lie, Pa; you know I can't tell a lie. I did cut it with my hatchet." "Run to my arms, you dearest boy," cried his father in transports, "run to my arms; glad am I, George, that you killed my tree, for you have paid me for it a thousand-fold. Such an act of heroism in my son is worth more than a thousand trees, tho' blossomed with silver and their fruits of purest gold."
M. L. Weems, THE LIFE OF GEORGE WASHINGTON: *With Curious Anecdotes, Equally Honourable to Himself and Exemplary to His Young Countrymen* 1806

7 The crude commercialism of America, its materialising spirit are entirely due to the country having adopted for its natural hero a man who could not tell a lie.
Oscar Wilde, THE DECAY OF LYING

JAMES WATT (1736–1819)
Scottish engineer

8 His aunt, Mrs Muirhead, sitting with him one evening at the tea-table, said, "James, I never saw such an idle boy! Take a book or employ yourself usefully. For the last half hour you have spoken no word, but taken off the lid of that kettle and put it on again, holding now a cup and now a silver spoon over the steam while it rises from the spout and counting the drops of water." It appears that when thus blamed his active mind was investigating the condensation of the steam. Who amongst us, if we had been placed in the same circumstances as Mrs Muirhead, would not in the year 1750 have resorted to the same language?
M. Arago, Perpetual Secretary of the French Academy of Scientists 1839

9 He devoured every kind of learning. Not content with chemistry and natural philosophy, he studied anatomy, and was one day found carrying home for dissection the head of a child that had died of some hidden disorder.
Henry, Lord Brougham, LIVES OF MEN OF LETTERS AND SCIENCE

10 I look upon him, considering the magnitude and the universality of his genius as perhaps the most extraordinary man this country has ever produced.
William Wordsworth, letter to his mother 1841

EVELYN ARTHUR ST. JOHN WAUGH
(1903–1966)
English novelist

11 He has the sharp eye of a Hogarth alternating with that of the ancient mariner.
Harold Acton, ADAM 1966

12 He was very conscious of what a gentleman should or should not do; no gentleman looks out of a window; no gentleman wears a brown suit.
Cecil Beaton, THE STRENUOUS YEARS

13 He drank port and put on weight, and attempted to behave in the manner of an Edwardian aristocrat. In fact Evelyn's abiding complex and the source of much of

his misery was that he was not six feet tall, extremely handsome, and a duke.
Ibid.

1 The satire of Evelyn Waugh in his early books was derived from his ignorance of life. He found cruel things funny because he did not understand them, and he was able to communicate that fun.
Cyril Connolly, ENEMIES OF PROMISE   1938

2 A contemporary undergraduate remembers him as "a prancing faun thinly disguised by contemporary apparel".
News Review, reviewing THE LOVED ONES
18 *Nov* 1948

DANIEL WEBSTER (1782–1852)
American politician

3 Daniel Webster struck me much like a steam-engine in trousers.
Sydney Smith. Quoted Lady Holland,
MEMOIRS

JOSIAH WEDGWOOD (1730–1795)
English potter

4 Whether, O Friend of Art! your gems derive / Fine forms from Greece, and fabled Gods revive; / Or bid from modern life the portrait breathe / And bind round Honour's brow the laurel wreath; / Buoyant shall sail, with Fame's historic page, / Each fair medallion o'er the wrecks of age / Nor time shall mar, nor Steel, nor Fire, nor Rust / Touch the hard polish of the immortal bust.
Erasmus Darwin, THE LOVES OF THE
PLANTS

5 The last Vases were not, some of them, what they were intended to be and it will very often happen so to Pebble Vases, but I have often noticed that what we have esteemed a *great fault* has been admired by some as a peculiar beauty, which makes me easier about such mishaps.
Josiah Wedgwood, DIARY   10 *Feb* 1770

ARTHUR WELLESLEY, DUKE OF WELLINGTON (1769–1852)
British soldier and Prime Minister

6 Friday half past two, the girls just returned from a ball at the Duke of Richmond's. Our troops are all moving from this place at present. Lord Wellington was at the ball tonight, as composed as ever.
Thomas Creevey, JOURNAL, *Brussels, the eve of Waterloo*   16 *Jun* 1815

7 The first thing I did was congratulate the Duke upon his victory. He made a variety of observations in his short, natural, blunt way, but with the greatest gravity all the time, and without the least approach to triumph or joy. "It has been a damned serious business," he said, "Blucher and I have lost 30,000 men. It has been a damned near thing — the nearest thing you ever saw in your life."
Thomas Creevey, JOURNAL   19 *Jun* 1815

8 In the course of the morning (Monday June 19, 1815) Wellington came over here to write his dispatch. Having shook hands he very gravely told me how very *critical* the battle had been, and with what incredible gallantry our troops had conducted themselves. He walked about uttering expressions of astonishment at our men's courage, and particularly at the Guards keeping their position in a Chateau and garden in front of left of his position.
Thomas Creevey, letter to Charles Ord
25 *Jun* 1815

9 I have taken to Wellington and his dispatches again, and the more I read of him the fonder I am of him.
Thomas Creevey, letter to Miss Ord
22 *Sep* 1837

10 The Duke of Wellington brought to the post of first minister immortal fame; a quality of success which would also seem to include all others.
Disraeli, SYBIL   1845

11 Arthur Wellesley, the future Duke of Wellington, was called in his youth "the fool of the family". His mother referred to him as "my awkward son", and his elder brother described him as "the biggest ass in Europe". But he won the Peninsular War, he defeated Napoleon, he was in parliament for 45 years and in the cabinet for more than 30; he became Prime Minister, and in his old age he was revered by many of his fellow-countrymen as the greatest living Englishman.
T. Charles Edwards and Brian Richardson,
THEY SAW IT HAPPEN   1958

12 It is incredible what popularity environs him in his latter days. He is followed like a show wherever he goes and the feeling of the people *for him* seems to be the liveliest of all popular sentiments, yet he does nothing to excite it, and scarcely seems to notice it.
Charles Greville, MEMOIRS   15 *Jul* 1847

13 I was marvellously struck (we rode together through St James's Park) with the profound respect with which the Duke was treated, everybody we met taking off their hats to

him, everybody in the Park rising as he went by. It is the more remarkable because it is not *popularity*, but a much higher feeling towards him.
Ibid.   19 *May* 1833

1 Went to Hullah's choral meeting at Exeter Hall. The finest thing was when the Duke of Wellington came in, near the end. The piece they were singing stopped at once; the whole audience rose, and a burst of acclamation and waving of handkerchiefs saluted the great old man, who is now the idol of the people. It was grand and affecting, and seemed to move everybody but himself.
Ibid.   *Jun* 1842

2 Waterloo is a battle of the first rank, won by a captain of the second.
Victor Hugo, LES MISÉRABLES   1862

3 The Duke, getting on for 80, wrote Baroness Burdett Coutts 850 letters, but was distinctly rattled when she proposed marriage. The Duke retreated in some disorder.
Diana Orton, A BIOGRAPHY OF ANGELA BURDETT COUTTS   1978

4 Of the Duke's perfect coolness on the most trying occasions, Colonel Gurwood gave me this instance. He was once in great danger of being drowned at sea. It was bed-time when the captain came to see him and said "It will soon be all over with us." — "Very well," said the Duke, "I shall not take off my boots".
Samuel Rogers, TABLE TALK   1856

5 The Duke of Wellington has exhausted nature and exhausted glory. His career was one unclouded longest day.
The Times, obituary   16 *Sep* 1852

HERBERT GEORGE WELLS (1866–1946)
English author

6 Mr H. G. Wells / Was composed of cells / He thought the human race / Was a complete disgrace.
E. C. Bentley, THE COMPLETE CLERIHEWS

7 All Wells' characters are as flat as a photograph. But the photographs are agitated with such vigour that we forget their complexities lie on the surface and would disappear if it was scratched and curled up.
E. M. Forster, ASPECTS OF THE NOVEL   1927

8 A history of humanity to the present time in which Shakespeare is not mentioned and

Jesus is dismissed in a page carelessly, if not with contempt, shocks me.
Frank Harris, of Wells' HISTORY OF THE WORLD *in* MY LIFE AND LOVES   1927

9 Whatever Wells writes is not only alive, but kicking.
Henry James. Quoted G. K. Chesterton, AUTOBIOGRAPHY

10 He is the old maid among novelists; even the sex obsession that lay clotted in *Anne Veronica* and *The New Machiavelli* like cold white sauce, was merely old maid's mania, the reaction towards the flesh of a mind too long absorbed in airships and colloids.
Rebecca West, reviewing MARRIAGE, FREEWOMAN   1912

JOHN WESLEY (1703–1791)
English founder of Methodism

11 John Wesley's conversation is good, but he is never at leisure. He is always obliged to go at a certain hour. This is very disagreeable to a man who loves to fold his legs and have out his talk.
Samuel Johnson. Quoted Boswell, THE LIFE OF JOHNSON   31 *Mar* 1778

12 As I was walking home from my father's bank I observed a great crowd of people streaming into the chapel in City Road. I followed them and saw, laid out upon a table, the dead body of a clergyman in full canonicals. It was the corpse of John Wesley; and the crowd moved slowly and silently round and round the table, to take a last look at that most venerable man.
Samuel Rogers, TABLE TALK   1856

13 A gentleman in the town [Bradford] desired me to preach at his door. The beasts of the people were tolerably quiet until I had nearly finished my sermon. Then they lifted up their voice, especially one, called a gentleman, who had filled his pocket with rotten eggs. But a young man coming unawares clapped his hands on each side and mashed them all at once. In an instant he was perfume all over, though it was not so sweet as balsam.
John Wesley, JOURNAL   19 *Sep* 1769

MAE WEST (1892–1980)
American film actress

14 By making sex a shared joke she defused the subject of much of its offensive power — though clearly not enough for many people in the 1920s and 1930s when she was constantly the target of outraged moralists,

even while she fortunately remained the darling of the public.
The Times obituary   24 Nov 1980

1   I've been in *Who's Who*, and I know what's what, but this is the first time I ever made the dictionary.
Mae West, on having a World War II life jacket named after her

JAMES ABBOTT MACNEILL WHISTLER (1834–1903)
American painter

2   To the question "Do you think genius is hereditary?" he replied, "I can't tell you. Heaven has granted me no offspring."
Hesketh Pearson, LIVES OF THE WITS

3   I have seen, and heard, much of cockney impudence before now but never expected to hear a coxcomb ask two hundred guineas for flinging a pot of paint in the public's face.
John Ruskin, of Nocturne in Black and Gold in FLORS CLAVIGARA: *Letters to the Labourers and Workers of Great Britain*   1889

4   I have never seen anything so impudent on the walls of any exhibition in any country, as last year in London. It was a daub professing to be a harmony in pink and white or some such nonsense, absolute rubbish, and which had taken a quarter of an hour or so to scrawl or daub. It had no pretence to be called a painting. The price asked for it was two hundred and fifty guineas.
Ibid.

5   I never saw anyone so feverishly alive as this little old man with his bright, withered cheeks, over which the skin was drawn tightly, his darting eyes under his prickly bushes of eyebrow, his fantastically creased black and white hair, his bitter and subtle mouth, and above all his exquisite hands, never at rest.
Arthur Symons, STUDIES IN SEVEN ARTS

GILBERT WHITE (1720–1793)
English naturalist

6   The mind and feeling which produced *Selbourne* is such a one as I have always envied. The single page alone of the life of Mr White leaves a more lasting impression on my mind than that of Charles V or any other renowned hero.
John Constable, DIARY   1 *Apr* 1821

7   Surely the serene and blameless life of Mr White, so different from the folly and quackery of the world, must have filled him with such a clear and intimate view of nature. It proves the truth of Sir Joshua Reynolds' idea that the virtuous man alone has true taste.
Ibid.

8   White was a prose Wordsworth . . . In his writings there is an entire absence of the eighteenth-century hankering after "Nature to advantage dressed"; He saw Nature plain, however lovingly, and his book is a prospectus rather than a rhapsody; the work of a scientist more than a poet. Yet through some miracle of single-heartedness and unblemished simplicity *Selbourne* has often the moving quality of poetry.
A. C. Ward, ILLUSTRATED HISTORY OF ENGLISH LITERATURE   1955

WALT WHITMAN (1819–1892)
American poet

9   W. W. is the Christ of the modern world — he alone redeems it, justifies it, shows it divine.
John Burroughs, journal entry on the death of Whitman

10   As Caesar Augustus found a Rome of brick and left it a Rome of marble so Walt Whitman found the everyday world around us a world of familiar substance and left it a world aureoled in mystery.
Benjamin de Casseres, THE PHILISTINE, VOL XV

11   This awful Whitman. This post-mortem poet. This poet with the private soul of him leaking out all the time. All his privacy leaking out in a sort of dribble, oozing into the universe
D. H. Lawrence, STUDIES IN CLASSICAL AMERICAN LITERATURE   1923

12   Always wanting to merge himself into the womb of something or other.
Ibid.

13   Whitman like a strange, modern American Moses. Fearfully mistaken. And yet the great leader.
Ibid.

14   A lofty, sturdy wind blows through his poems. There is a healing quality to his vision.
Henry Miller, THE BOOKS IN MY LIFE   1952

15   He is a writer of something occasionally like English, and a man of something occasionally like genius.
Algernon Swinburne, WHITMANIA

1 Under the dirty paws of a harper whose plectrum is a muck-rake anything will become a chaos of discords.
Ibid.

OSCAR FINGAL O'FLAHERTIE WILLS WILDE (1854–1900)
Irish dramatist and poet

2 From the beginning Wilde performed his life and continued to do so even after fate had taken the plot out of his hands.
W. H. Auden, FOREWORDS AND AFTERWORDS

3 The solution that he, deliberately or accidentally found, was to subordinate every other dramatic element to dialogue for its own sake and create a verbal universe in which the characters are determined by the kinds of things they say, and the plot is nothing but a succession of opportunities to say them.
Ibid.

4 Like a many-coloured humming top he was at once a bewilderment and a balance. He was so fond of being many-sided that among his sides he even admitted the right side. He loved so much to multiply his souls that he had among them one soul at least that was saved.
G. K. Chesterton, Daily News   19 *Oct* 1910

5 Oscar Wilde's talent seems to me essentially rootless, something growing in a glass in a little water.
George Moore

6 A ready means of being cherished by the English is to adopt the simple expedient of living a long time. I have little doubt that if Oscar Wilde had lived into his nineties, instead of dying in his forties, he would have been considered a benign, distinguished figure suitable to preside at a school prize-giving or to instruct and exhort scoutmasters at their jamborees. He might even have been knighted.
Malcolm Muggeridge, TREAD SOFTLY FOR YOU TREAD ON MY JOKES   1966

7 If with the literate I am / Impelled to try an epigram / I never seek to take the credit / We all assume that Oscar said it.
Dorothy Parker

8 It was rather amusing as it was a complete mass of epigrams, with occasional whiffs of grotesque melodrama and drivelling sentiment.
Lytton Strachey, of A WOMAN OF NO IMPORTANCE, *in a letter to Duncan Grant* 2 *Jun* 1907

9 — the great booby figure of Oscar Wilde. Even he was by no means as comic as his admirers have made him. He was over-dressed, pompous, snobbish, sentimental and vain. But he had an undeniable *flair* for the possibilities of the commercial theatre. He got himself into trouble, poor old thing, by an infringement of a very silly law, which was just as culpable, and just as boring, as an infringement of traffic or licensing regulations.
Evelyn Waugh, Harper's Bazaar   Nov 1930

10 What has Oscar in common with Art? Except that he dines at our tables and picks from our platters the plums from the puddings he peddles in the provinces.
J. M. Whistler, letter to The World   1886

11 Oscar — with no more sense of a picture than the fit of a coat — has the courage of the opinions — of others.
Ibid.

WILHELM II (1859–1941)
German Kaiser

12 Thou Blot / On the fair script of Time / Thou sceptred Smear across the Day
William Watson, TO THE GERMAN EMPEROR AFTER THE SACK OF LOUVAIN

JOHN WILKES (1727–1797)
English radical politician

13 Then Satan answered, "There are many; / But you may choose Jack Wilkes as well as any / A merry cock-eyed, curious-looking sprite / Upon the instant started from the throng / Dressed in a fashion now forgotten quite; / For all the fashions of the flesh stick long / By people in the next world, where unite / All the costumes since Adam's, right or wrong / From Eve's fig-leaf down to the petticoat / Almost as scanty, of days less remote.
Lord Byron

14 John Wilkes' death — awful event! talents how abused! Lord, who have made *me* to differ, but for they grace I might have blasphemed thee like him. In early youth I read Hume, Voltaire, Rousseau etc. I am a monument of mercy not to have made shipwreck of my faith.
Hannah More, JOURNALS   28 *Jan* 1798

1 One morning, when I was a lad, Wilkes came into our banking house to solicit my father's vote. At parting Wilkes shook hands with me and I felt proud of it for weeks after. He was quite as ugly, and squinted as much, as his portraits made him; but he was very gentlemanly in appearance and manners. I think I see him at this moment, walking through the crowded streets of the City, as Chamberlain, on his way to the Guildhall, in a scarlet coat, military boots and a bag-wig.
Samuel Rogers, TABLE TALK   1856

WILLIAM I (1027–1082)
(The Conqueror)
King

2 Chesse is a cholericke game and very offensive to him that loseth the Mate. William the Conqueror in his younger years, playing at chesse with the King of France, and losing a Mate, knocked the Chesseboard about his pate, which was a cause afterwards of much enmity between them.
Robert Burton, ANATOMY OF MELANCHOLY   1621

3 A French bastard landing with an armed banditti and establishing himself King of England against the consent of the natives is, in plain terms, a very paltry rascally original. The antiquity of the English monarchy will not bear looking at.
Tom Paine, COMMON SENSE   1776

WILLIAM II (c. 1056–1100)
(Rufus)
King

4 He was hated by almost all his people and abhorrent to God. This his end testified, for he died in the midst of his sins without repentance or any atonement for his misdeeds.
Anglo-Saxon Chronicle (c. 1120)

5 There exists no proof as / To who shot William Rufus / But shooting him would seem / To have been a sound scheme.
E. C. Bentley, MORE BIOGRAPHY

6 Dr Margaret Murray, in *God of the Witches* (1931), has argued that Rufus adhered to an exciting underground religion of the witches, that his death was the ritual murder of the king by fellow devil-worshippers. "Walter, do thou justice according to these things which thou hast heard." "So I will my lord," Walter Tirel answered, took an arrow

from the king and subsequently shot him with it.
Christopher Brooke, THE SAXON AND NORMAN KINGS   1963

7 This king, before he was slain with an arrow in hunting, told his company he dreamed the last night before then an extremely cold wind passed through his sides; whereupon some dissuaded him to hunt that day; but he resolved to the contrary, answering, "Thou art not good Christians that regard dreams." But he found the dream too true, being shot through the side by Walter Tyrell.
William Camden, REMAINS CONCERNING BRITAIN   1586

8 The King and Walter de Poix established themselves with a few companions in the wood and waited eagerly for the prey, with weapons ready. Suddenly a beast ran between them; the king jumped back from his place and Walter let an arrow fly. The arrow shaved the hair of the animal's back, sped on and wounded the king standing beyond. He soon fell to the ground and died instantly.
Orderic Vitalis, HISTORICA ECCLESIASTICA (c. 1240)

9 A few of the peasants carried his corpse to the cathedral in Winchester in a horse-drawn waggon with blood dripping from it the whole way. There in the cathedral crossing, under the tower, he was interred in the presence of many great men, mourned by few.
William of Malmesbury, DE GESTIS REGNUM ANGLORUM (c. 1140)

WILLIAM III (1650–1702)
(of Orange)
King of England

10 James II brought people to so desperate a pass as with uttermost expressions even passionately seen to long for and desire the landing of the Prince, whom they looked on as their deliverer from Popish tyranny, praying incessantly for an Easterly Wind.
John Evelyn, DIARY   6 Dec 1688

11 We who thought we should not be saved if we were Roman Catholics had the merit of maintaining our religion at the expense of submitting ourselves to the government of King William for it could not be done otherwise — to the government of one of the most worthless scoundrels that ever existed.
Samuel Johnson. Quoted Boswell, THE LIFE OF JOHNSON   1791

1 William and Mary for some reason was known as The Orange in their own country of Holland, and were popular as King of England because the people naturally believed it was descended from Nell Glyn. Finally the Orange was killed by a mole while out riding and was succeeded by the memorable dead queen, Anne.
W. C. Sellar and R. J. Yeatman, 1066 AND ALL THAT

2 There is one certain means by which I can be sure never to see my country's ruin; I will die in the last ditch.
William to the Duke of Buckingham 1672

WILLIAM IV (1765–1837)
King of Great Britain and Ireland

3 Altogether he seems a kind-hearted, well-meaning, not stupid burlesque, bustling old fellow, and if he doesn't go mad may make a very decent king.
Charles Greville, MEMOIRS   11 *Jul* 1830

4 The King was chief mourner at George IV's funeral and to my astonishment as he entered the chapel directly behind the body, in a situation in which he should have been apparently, if not really, absorbed in the melancholy duty he was performing, he darted up to Strathaven, who was ranged on one side below the Dean's stall, shook him heartily by the hand, and then went on nodding to the right and left.
Ibid.   18 *Jul* 1830

5 Once, when in company with William the Fourth I quite forgot it is against all etiquette to ask a sovereign about his health and on his saying to me "Mr Rogers, I hope you are well" I replied, "Very well, I thank you your majesty. *I trust that your majesty is quite well also*." Never was a king in greater confusion; he didn't know where to look, and stammered out "Yes — yes — only a little rheumatism."
Samuel Rogers, TABLE TALK   1856

JAMES HAROLD WILSON (1916–   )
(Lord Wilson of Rievelaux)
British Prime Minister

6 Harold Wilson grows fatter, more complacent and more evasive each time you meet him.
Richard Crossman, BACKBENCH DIARIES   7 *Nov* 1957

8 He is such an impersonal person. You don't feel you could be really close friends with him, or in fact that he would ever have close friends.
Hugh Gaitskell, DIARIES   1945–1956

8 I suppose Mr Wilson, when you come to think of it, is the 14th Mr Wilson.
Lord Home (fourteenth Earl Home), TV *interview*   21 *Oct* 1963

9 He always looks as though he were on the verge of being found out.
Rebecca West, interviewed by Frederic Raphael, Radio Times   21 *Oct* 1978

10 If Harold has a fault it is that he will smother everything with H. P. Sauce.
Mary Wilson in an interview   1962

THOMAS WOODROW WILSON
(1856–1924)
Twenty-eighth president of the United States

11 How can I talk to a fellow who thinks himself the first man in two thousand years to know anything about peace on earth.
Georges Clemenceau. Quoted Thomas A. Bailey, WOODROW WILSON AND THE LOST PEACE

12 The good Lord needed but ten commandments.
Georges Clemenceau of Wilson's Fourteen Points   1918

13 Like Odysseus, he looked wiser when seated.
John Maynard Keynes. Quoted Robert L. Heilbron, THE WORLDLY PHILOSOPHERS

14 The first thing that struck me about him was that he looked very clean. Immaculate. Not that I had expected to find him dirty. But there was something about the stiff white cuffs, the gleaming collar, the sparkling pince-nez, the beautifully pressed trousers, that he had dressed in a disinfected room with the assistance of a highly efficient valet, who had put on his clothes with pincers. Again the dentist feeling. He *was* like a dentist. Or a distinguished surgeon.
Beverley Nichols, TWENTY-FIVE

15 The air currents of the world never ventilated his mind.
Walter Hines Page. Quoted Patrick Devlin, TOO PROUD TO FIGHT: *Woodrow Wilson's Neutrality*

SIR PELHAM GRENVILLE WODEHOUSE (1881–1975)
English author

16 Literature's performing flea.
Sean O'Casey. Used by Wodehouse as the title of his autobiography   1973

1 There is no suggestion that either club men or girls would recognise a double bed except as so much extra sweat to make an apple-pie of.
Richard Usborne, WODEHOUSE AT WORK 1961

2 The failure of academic literary criticism to take any account of Wodehouse's supreme mastery of the English language or the profound influence he has had on every worthwhile English novelist in the past 50 years demonstrates in better and conciser form than anything else how the Eng. Lit. industry is divorced from the subject it claims to study.
Auberon Waugh, New Statesman 21 Feb 1975

3 There are almost as many quotations in Wodehouse as there are in Shakespeare.
Woodrow Wyatt, The Times, reviewing WODEHOUSE NUGGETS (*edited by Richard Usborne*) 24 Nov 1983

JAMES WOLFE (1727–1759)
English General

4 Oh, he is mad is he? Then I wish he would bite some other of my generals.
George II, *in* 1758. *Quoted Beckles Wilson,* LIFE AND LETTERS OF JAMES WOLFE

5 When no longer able to stand he whispered to an officer near him, "Support me, let not my brave officers see me drop. The day is ours. Keep it." The cry was heard, "They run! They run!" Wolfe demanded with great earnestness, "Who run?" "The enemy, sir. They give way everywhere." "Go one of you with all speed to Colonel Burton; tell him to march Webb's regiment down to Charles river and cut off their retreat." He then turned upon his side and his last words were, "Now God be praised, I die in peace."
Captain Knox, JOURNAL OF CAMPAIGNS 1769

6 The General repeated nearly the whole of Gray's *Elegy*, adding, as he concluded, that he would prefer being the author of that poem to the glory of beating the French tomorrow.
J. Robinson, account of the Quebec campaign 12 Sep 1759. *Published Transactions Royal Society, Edinburgh* 1814

THOMAS WOLSEY (c.1475–1530)
English cardinal and statesman

7 Being but a child he was very apt to learning, by means whereof his parents, or his good friends and masters, conveyed him to the University of Oxford where he prospered so in learning that, as he told me so in his own person, he was called the boy-bachelor, forasmuch as he was made a Bachelor of Arts at fifteen years of age, which was a rare thing and seldom seen.
George Cavendish, LIFE OF CARDINAL WOLSEY 1641

8 He was a scholar, and a ripe and good one; / Exceeding wise, fair-spoken and persuading; / Lofty and sour to them that loved him not; / But to those men that sought him, sweet as summer.
Shakespeare, HENRY VIII, *Act* IV, *Scene* ii

9 I see the matter against me, how it is framed. But if I had served God as diligently as I have done the King, he would not have given me over in my grey hairs.
Wolsey to Sir William Kingston, Constable of the Tower 3 Nov 1530

ADELINE VIRGINIA WOOLF (1882–1941)
English novelist

10 Clive Bell, back in London, wrote to Vanessa in May that the town seemed particularly dull. "Only Virginia is supremely happy as well she may be. Her book *To the Lighthouse* is a masterpiece". The view was generally held by critics, and a great many people wrote enthusiastically, although one complained that her description of flora and fauna in the Hebrides was totally inaccurate.
Quentin Bell, VIRGINIA WOOLF: *A Biography* 1972

11 Virginia Woolf seemed to have the worst defect of the Mandarin style, the ability to spin cocoons of language out of nothing. The history of her literary style has been that of form at first simple, growing more and more elaborate, the content lagging far behind and then catching up, till she produced a masterpiece in *The Waves*.
Cyril Connolly, ENEMIES OF PROMISE 1938

12 One of my *fears* — I don't think I was alone in this — was that one day she would speak to me (but she never did).
Hugo Dyson. Quoted Humphrey Carpenter, THE INKLINGS

13 I enjoyed talking to her, but thought *nothing* of her writing. I considered her "a beautiful little knitter".
Edith Sitwell, letter to G. Singleton 11 *July* 1955

14 I am now in the middle of Virginia's *To the Lighthouse*, which I like, so far, much better than *Mrs Dalloway*. It really is most unfortunate that she rules out copulation — not

the ghost of it visible — so that her presentation of things becomes little more than an arabesque — an exquisite arabesque, of course.
Lytton Strachey, letter to E. B. C. Lucas 7 May 1927

WILLIAM WORDSWORTH (1770–1850)
English poet

1 Time may restore us, in his course / Goethe's sage mind and Byron's force / But where will Europe's latter hour / Again find Wordsworth's healing power?
Matthew Arnold, MEMORIAL VERSES

2 The mild apostate from poetic rule / The simple Wordsworth, framer of a lay, / As soft as evening in his favourite May.
Lord Byron, ENGLISH BARDS AND SCOTTISH REVIEWERS 1808

3 A man of an immense head and great jaws like a crocodile, cast in a mould designed for work.
Thomas Carlyle. Quoted Sir Charles Gavan Duffy, CONVERSATIONS WITH CARLYLE 1892

4 The languid way in which he gives you a handful of numb, unresponsive fingers, is very significant.
Ibid.

5 One finds also a kind of sincerity in his speech. But for prolixity, thinness, endless dilution, it excels all the other speech I have heard from mortals.
Thomas Carlyle, ESSAYS, Wordsworth

6 Since Milton, I know of no poet with so many *felicities* and unforgettable lines and stanzas as you.
Samuel Taylor Coleridge. Quoted Henry Nelson, COLERIDGE, Memoir 1847

7 He was essentially a cold, hard, silent, practical man who, if he had not fallen into poetry, would have done effectual work of some sort in the world. This was the impression one got of him as he looked out of his stern blue eyes, superior to men and circumstances.
Sir Charles Gaven Duffy, CONVERSATIONS WITH CARLYLE 1892

8 We darted into Christies. In a corner of the room was a beautiful copy of the Cupid and Psyche statue kissing . . . catching sight of the Cupid as he and I were coming out, Wordsworth's face reddened, he showed his teeth, and then said in a loud voice "THE DEV-V-VILS!"
B. R. Haydon, letter to Miss Mitford

9 He reminds one of some of Holbein's heads, grave, saturnine, with a slight indication of sly humour, kept under by the manners of the age or by the pretensions of the person. He has a peculiar sweetness in his smile and great depth and manliness and a rugged harmony in the tones of his voice.
William Hazlitt, THE SPIRIT OF THE AGE 1825

10 The more I see of Mr Wordsworth the more I admire, and I may also say, I love him. It is delightful to see a life in such perfect harmony with all that his writings express, "true to the kindred points of heaven and home".
Mrs Hemans

11 He seems a very intelligent man — for a horse-couper.
James Hogg

12 Wordworth has left a bad impression wherever he has visited in town by his egotism, vanity and bigotry.
John Keats

13 What appears to have disturbed William Blake's mind is the preface to *The Excursion*. He told me six months ago that it caused him a bowel complaint that nearly killed him.
Henry Crabb Robinson, letter to Dorothy Wordsworth Feb 1826

14 Yesterday I had a melancholy letter from Wordsworth. He gives a sad account of his sister, and talks of leaving the country on account of the impending ruin to be apprehended from the Reform Bill.
Henry Crabb Robinson, Diary and Correspondence 24 Mar 1832

15 Speaking to me of *We Are Seven* Wordsworth said, "It is founded on fact. I met a little girl near Goderich Castle, who, though some of her brothers and sisters were dead, *would* talk of them in the present tense. I wrote that poem backwards — that is, I started with the last line."
Samuel Rogers, TABLE TALK 1856

16 In his youth Wordsworth sympathised with the French Revolution, went to France, wrote good poetry, and had a natural daughter. At this period he was a bad man. Then he became a good man, abandoned his daughter, adopted correct principles, and wrote bad poetry.
Bertrand Russell

17 This laurel greener from the brows / Of him that uttered nothing base.
Alfred Tennyson, TO THE QUEEN

1 Wordsworth went to the Lakes, but he never was a lake poet. He found in stones the sermons he had already put there.
Oscar Wilde, THE DECAY OF LYING

SIR CHRISTOPHER WREN (1632–1723)
English architect

2 Sir Christopher Wren was a man of small stature. When Charles II came to see the hunting place he had built for him at Newmarket he thought the rooms too low. Sir Christopher walked about them, and looking up replied, "Sir, and please your majesty, I think they are high enough". The king, squatting down to Sir Christopher's height, and creeping about in this whimsical posture cried, "Aye, Sir Christopher, I think they are high enough."
Anon. ANECDOTES OF DISTINGUISHED PERSONS 1804

3 When Sir Christopher Wren was at Paris about 1671 he dreamt he was in a place where Palm-trees grew (suppose Egypt) and that a woman in a romantic habit reached him dates.
John Aubrey, MISCELLANIES: *Dreams* 1696

4 Sir Christopher Wren / Said "I'm going to dine with some men / If anybody calls / Say I'm designing St. Paul's".
E. C. Bentley, BIOGRAPHY FOR BEGINNERS

5 What you whispered in my ear at your last coming hither is now come to pass. Our work at the West End of St. Pauls is fallen about our ears. We most earnestly desire your presence and assistance with all possible speed.
William Sancroft, Dean of St. Paul's, letter to Wren reporting failure to repair St. Paul's after the Great Fire 25 *Apr* 1668

6 He was not only in his profession the greatest man of that age, but had given more profits of it than any other man ever did; yet for want of that natural freedom and audacity which is necessary in commerce with men, his personal modesty overthrew all his public actions.
Richard Steele, The Tatler 9 *Aug* 1709

7 Concerning the Repair of St. Paul's, some may possibly aim at too great a Magnificence, which neither the Disposition nor extent of this Age will probably bring to a Period. Others again may fall so low as to think of piecing up the old Fabrick. I

suppose your Lordship may think proper to take a Middle Way.
Wren, submitting plans for the repair of St. Paul's, before it was destroyed in the Great Fire

8 By a judicious Regularity and Temperance (having acquired good knowledge in Physick) he continued healthy, with little Intermission, even to his extreme old Age. Further 'tis observable, that he was happily endued with such an Evenness of Temper, a steady Tranquillity of Mind, and Christian Fortitude, that no injudicious Incidents, or Inquietude of human Life, could ever ruffle or discompose; and was in Practice a *Stoick*.
Christopher Wren Jr, PARENTALIA *(published by Wren's grandson, Stephen)* 1750

WILLIAM WYCHERLEY (c. 1640–1716)
English dramatist

9 His misfortunes were such that he was thrown into the Fleet and lay there seven years. It was then that Colonel Brett got his *Plain Dealer* to be acted, and contrived to get King James II to be there. He was much pleased with the play, asked who was the author of it; and upon hearing it was one of Wycherley's enquired what had become of him. The colonel improved the opportunity so well that the king gave orders that his debts should be discharged out of the privy purse.
John Dennis. Quoted Rev. Joseph Spence, OBSERVATIONS, ANECDOTES AND CHARACTERS 1820

10 Wycherley was in a bookshop, at Bath, or Tonbridge, when Lady Drogheda came in and happened to enquire for *The Plain Dealer*. A friend of Wycherley's, who stood by him, pushed him towards her and said, "There's the Plain Dealer, madam, if you want him." Wycherley made his excuses and Lady Drogheda said that "she loved plain dealing best". He afterwards visited that lady, and in some time married her.
Ibid.

11 He appears to have led, during a long course of years, that most wretched life, the life of a vicious old boy about town.
T. B. Macaulay, Edinburgh Review, Comic Dramatists of the Restoration *Jan* 1841

12 Wycherley had this odd peculiarity in him from the loss of his memory that the same chain of thought would return into his mind at the distance of two or three years, without remembering that it had been there before. Thus perhaps one year he would write an encomium on Avarice (for he loved

paradoxes) and a year or two after in dispraise of Liberty, and in both the words only would differ, and the thoughts be as much alike as two medals of different metals out of the same mould

Alexander Pope. Quoted Rev. Joseph Spence, OBSERVATIONS, ANECDOTES AND CHARACTERS 1820

JOHN WYCLIFFE (1320–1384)
English religious reformer

1 What Heraclitus would not laugh, or what Democritus would not weep? For though they digged up his body, burned his bones and drowned his ashes, yet the word of God and truth of his doctrine, with the fruit and success thereof, they could not burn.

John Foxe, BOOK OF MARTYRS. *Referring to the Council of Constance* 1428, *which ordered Wycliffe exhumed, and the burnt remains scattered on a nearby stream*

2 Thus this brook hath conveyed his ashes into Avon, Avon into Severn, Severn into narrow seas, they into the main ocean. And thus the ashes of Wycliffe are the emblem of his doctrine, which now is dispersed the world over.

Thomas Fuller, CHURCH HISTORY 1655

3 The devil's instrument, church's enemy, people's confusion, heretic's idol, hypocrite's mirror, schism's broacher, hatred's sewer, lies' forger, flatteries' sink; who at his death despaired like Cain. And, stricken by the horrible judgement of God, breathed forth his wicked soul to the dark mansion of the black devil!

Thomas Walsingham, YPODIGMA NEUSTRIAE

4 As thou these ashes, little brook will bear / Into the Avon, Avon to the tide / Of Severn, Severn to the narrow seas / Into main ocean they, this deed accursed / An emblem yields to friends and enemies / How the bold teacher's doctrine, sanctified / By truth shall spread, through the world dispersed.

Wordsworth, ECCLESIASTICAL SONNETS

Y

WILLIAM BUTLER YEATS (1865–1939)
Irish poet and dramatist

1 Earth, receive an honoured guest / William Yeats is laid to rest / Let the Irish vessel lie / Emptied of its poetry.
W. H. Auden, IN MEMORY OF
W. B. YEATS 1940

2 He was the real original rationalist who said that the fairies stand to reason. He staggered the materialists by attacking their abstract materialism with a completely concrete mysticism.
G. K. Chesterton, AUTOBIOGRAPHY

3 I left him in my room to himself and at lunch time he told me he had done an excellent morning's work; having written four lines and destroyed them.
John Drinkwater, DISCOVERY

4 I am too old for Yeats, just as I am too old to hear the cry of a bat.
G. W. Lyttelton, THE LYTTELTON
HART-DAVIS LETTERS 30 *Nov* 1955

5 He talked a great deal about the spirits to whom his wife, being a medium, had introduced him. "Have you ever seen them?" Dodds asked. Yeats was a little piqued. No, he said grudgingly, he had never seen them, but — with a flash of triumph — he had often *smelt* them.
Louis MacNeice, THE STRINGS ARE FALSE

6 Yeats always seemed to move in a mist. He was like "men as trees, walking". He would wander along the street with his head in the air and his hands behind his back, always wearing an overcoat, even in the hottest weather, with a long loose bow, and a mouth perpetually open. To walk behind him was in itself an adventure for when he crossed the street he never took the slightest notice of any traffic that might be bearing down on him, but dawdled over, oblivious of the stream of cars, bicycles, horses and motor-lorries that were rushing past.
Beverley Nichols, TWENTY-FIVE

7 He was fastidious in his person and his choice of friends; he loathed pretentiousness in others, and so had none

himself. The only art to which he was almost wholly insensitive was music.
Lennox Robinson. Quoted A. N. Jeffares and K. G. W. Cross, IN EXCITED REVERIE

CHARLOTTE MARY YONGE (1829–1901)
English novelist

8 I feel deep gratitude towards you for the pleasure and real moral benefit derived from your books. My royal pupil, Princess Margaret, too, owes very much to you. With children, although gifted as my princess is, in a high degree there must be some *tempting inducements* to make them study more willingly.
Rose Arbesser, governess to Princess Margaret of Italy, in a letter to Charlotte M. Yonge.

9 Devout and charitable, sentimental and narrow, Miss Yonge herself stands as an epitome of Victorian property.
William Rose Benét, READER'S
ENCYCLOPEDIA 1948

10 She practised definitely and on purpose many self-denials, of which she never spoke, and which only gradually became obvious to her friends. Until the necessities of the trade forced it on her, she never wrote stories in Lent.
Christabel Coleridge, C. M. YONGE

11 The only trait in her character which astounded me was that painful shyness which consumed and transfigured her in the presence of strangers.
Mrs M. E. Sumner. Quoted ibid.

EDWARD YOUNG (1683–1765)
English poet

12 When Young was writing a tragedy Grafton is said by Spence to have sent him a human skull, with a candle in it, as a lamp; and the poet is reported to have used it.
Herbert Croft. Quoted Samuel Johnson,
LIVES OF THE POETS 1781

13 He had no uniformity of manner; one of his pieces has no great resemblance to another . . . His plan seems to have started in his mind at the present moment, and his thoughts appear the effect of chance, some-

times adverse and sometimes lucky, with
very little operation of judgement.
Samuel Johnson, LIVES OF THE
POETS 1781

1 I was dining in a parliamentary party with
Lord Castlereagh and he produced for our
amusement in the evening some volumes of
original letters curiously preserved by Lady
C. My curiosity was immediately fixed by
that of Dr Young. I professed my enthusiastic admiration for his *Night Thoughts* and
begged to see and admire as a relic the
original letter of such a man. My request
was immediately granted with a significant
smile; and what had I the mortification to
read? *Horrsco referens!* It was the most
fawning, servile, mendicant letter, perhaps,
that was ever penned by a clergyman, im-
ploring the mistress of George II to exert
her interest for his preferment.
Hannah More, MEMOIRS

2 *Night Thoughts* (1744), in spite of much
fustian sublimity and artificial melancholy
has never ceased to be popular, and many of
its sententious lines have passed into pro-
verbial use.
David Patrick and F. Hindes Groome,
CHAMBERS BIOGRAPHICAL
DICTIONARY 1897

3 He was the author of many more or less
feeble lyric poems, now never read. He also
wrote tragedies of passion, ending in
suicide.
Angus Ross, COMPANION TO LITERATURE
(edited by David Daiches) 1971

Z

EMILE ZOLA(1840–1902)
French author

1 In Victor Hugo we have the average sensual man impassioned and grandiloquent, in Zola we have the average sensual man going near the ground.
Matthew Arnold, DISCOURSES IN AMERICA 1834

2 That he is a sexual psychopath is betrayed on every page of his novels. His consciousness is peopled with the images of unnatural vice, bestiality, passivism, and other aberrations.
Max Nordau, DEGENERATION 1893

3 His instinctive inclination is to depict demented persons, criminals, prostitutes and semi-maniacs. His symbols, his passivism and his coprolalia, and his predeliction for slang, sufficiently characterize M. Zola as a high-class degenerate.
Ibid.

4 The accuser Zola is a man who has gained for himself a very prominent place in French literature as a writer of fiction of a peculiar kind, but he has not hitherto shown, so far as we are aware, any very special care for public justice, or any special interest in the fate of the oppressed.
The Times, editorial on the Dreyfus Affair 14 *Jan* 1898

Index

Authors of quotations are referenced by page number followed by the number of the quotation on that page. (The subjects of their quotations are listed in the contents.)

Beardsley, Mabel, 27:2

Beatles, The, 27:8

Beaton, Cecil, 31:7, 110:8, 156:14, 157:1, 216:9, 232:12, 232:13

Beatty, Dr, 168:13, 169:1, 169:2, 169:3, 169:4

Beaverbrook, Lord, 23:7, 72:15, 73:1, 114:1, 172:12

Beckett, Sanuel, 18:1

Bede, 60:1

Bee, Brigadier-General Barnard E., 128:1

Beecham, Sir Thomas, 21:6, 31:15, 31:16, 51:17, 91:9, 91:10, 164:10, 208:6, 208:7, 208:8, 217:1, 230:2, 230:3, 230:4

Beerbohm, Max, 27:3, 31:8, 57:10, 63:4, 64:11, 127:3, 157:13, 164:6, 202:14, 206:1, 206:2, 230:5

Beery, Wallace, 101:8

Beethoven, Ludwig van, 114:7, 167:2

Bell, Kenneth, 18:12, 40:5

Bell, Quentin, 239:10

Belloc, Hilaire, 71:11, 206:3

Benét, William Rose, 30:2, 30:8, 35:12, 35:13, 35:14, 38:2, 40:15, 61:10, 61:11, 66:6, 66:7, 66:8, 79:1, 182:1, 200:2, 213:9, 243:9

Bennett, Alan, 84:5

Bennett, Arnold, 143:7, 146:8, 148:8, 226:10

Bennett, Rodney, 101:3

Benson, A. C., 51:10

Benson, E. F., 109:3, 109:4, 109:5

Bentley, E. C., 22:6, 33:6, 40:6, 82:10, 83:15, 85:1, 104:12, 120:3, 122:4, 183:14, 234:6, 237:5, 241:4

Berenson, Bernard, 181:3, 225:1

Berger, John, 156:12

Berkeley, Grantley, 52:2

Berlin, Sir Isaac, 196:6

Berlioz, Hector, 21:7, 202:15

Berry, Adrian, 90:17

Best, H. D., 107:13

Bevan, Aneurin, 15:13, 15:14, 23:8, 67:19, 67:20, 73:2, 73:3, 73:4, 88:1, 100:9

Bevin, Ernest, 142:3

Bierce, Ambrose, 22:7

Bigelow, Poultney, 64:4, 64:5

Billington, Rachel, 165:13

Binkley, W. E., 195:13

Birkenhead, First Earl of, 23:9, 73:5

Birkenhead, Second Earl of,

6:12, 39:19, 39:20, 39:21, 40:1, 40:2

Birrell, Augustine, 95:7

Bismarck, 168:5

Bizet, Georges, 72:2

Blackman, John, 119:1, 119:2, 119:3, 119:4

Blackwood, Captain, 135:8, 169:5

Blackwoods Magazine, 125:9, 135:9, 135:10

Blake, William, 190:15, 196:13

Blanche, Jacques-Emile, 216:10

Blatchford, Robert, 54:4

Blessington, Lady, 57:11

Blom, Eric, 186:4

Blow, Simon, 225:4

Blunden, Edmund, 116:4

Blunt, Wilfrid Scawen, 90:6

Boer description of Churchill, 73:6

Boileau, Abbé, 217:12

Bompas, George C., 53:10

Bonaparte, Lucien, 167:3

Bonham Carter, Mark, 14:11

Booker, Christopher, 124:3

Boothby, Lord, 31:3

Borrow, George, 95:8

Boscawen, Mrs, 228:9

Boswell, James, 35:15 36:1, 56:12, 95:9, 102:2, 102:3, 107:14, 131:7, 131:8, 184:4, 208:9, 228:10, 228:11, 228:12, 228:13

Bowden, B. V., 21:1, 136:7

Bowen, Elizabeth, 126:1

Bowers, Lieutenant, 200:10

Bowles, Caroline, 162:14

Boyd-Carpenter, John, 156:6

Bracken, Brendan, 88:2

Bradbury, Malcolm, 33:9

Bradford, Sarah, 44:3, 44:4, 44:6

Bradley, Ian, 60:5

Bradshaigh, Lady Dorothy, 95:10

Brahms, Caryl, 18:13, 22:8, 103:15

Braybrooke, Lord, 179:4

Brendon, Piers, 111:10, 111:11

Brennan, Gerald, 158:10

Brennan, Robert E., 79:14, 177:3

Brewster, Sir David, 36:2

Brezhnev, Leonid, 222:13

Bridgeman, Richard, 214:5

Bridges, Robert, 156:8

Bridges, Sir Samuel Egerton, 131:9

Briggs, Asa, 47:10, 47:11

Bright, John, 47:12

Brinnin, John Malcolm, 214:6

Britten, Benjamin, 47:16, 47:17

Broad, C. D., 148:14

Brontë, Charlotte, 19:1, 19:2, 48:1, 49:7, 103:5, 222:6

Brooke, Christopher, 7:11, 10:7, 62:7, 62:8, 62:9, 237:6

Brooks, Van Wyck, 149:7, 216:6

Brophy, Brigid, 19:3

Brophy, James D., 16:14

Brougham, Henry Lord, 232:9

Broughton, Lord, 172:5, 208:10

Brown, John, 50:2, 50:3

Brown, Peter, 27:9

Browne, Sir Thomas, 10:14, 66:2, 134:2, 186:10

Browning, Elizabeth Barrett, 12;11, 58:1, 70:7, 138:3, 200:1

Browning, Robert, 24:14, 51:2, 207:1

Bryant, Arthur, 30:9, 157:6, 176:5

Brydges, Sir E., 80:1

Buchan, John, 28:13, 142:7

Buchanan, Robert, 17:14, 218:10

Bullock, Alan, 28:14, 39:5, 39:6, 39:7, 39:8, 39:9, 122:5

Bulwer, Sir Henry Lytton, 106:4, 220:2, 220:3

Bunyan, John, 54:5

Burgan, Wanda, 84:15

Burgess, Anthony, 32:14, 32:15, 66:10, 86:5, 131:10, 133:7, 133:8, 185:9, 188:1, 188:2, 188:3, 226:11

Burke, Sir Bernard, 52:3

Burke, Edmund, 81:3, 154:6, 154:7, 182:7, 196:7

Burne-Jones, Sir Edward, 27:4, 190:16

Burnet, Gilbert, 26:8, 29:7, 45:11, 53:4, 69:6, 69:7, 86:11, 128:12, 128:13, 128:14, 178:14

Burney, Dr Charles, 95:11, 106:5, 186:6

Burney, Fanny, 12:8, 44:8, 104:13, 104:14, 121:6, 131:11, 149:13, 208:11, 230:15

Burns, J. M., 195:1

Burns, Robert, 184:5

Burroughs, John, 235:9

Burton, Richard, 56:10

Burton, Robert, 4:2, 11:11, 84:13, 124:10, 187:1, 237:2

Busoni, Feruccio, 21:8, 31:17

Butler, Josephine, 8:7

Butler, Lord, 38:9, 38:10, 38:11, 38:12, 88:3

248

250

251

254

O'Connor, Daniel, 85:10
O'Connor, T. P., 2:1
Ogilvy, Mrs David, 51:5, 51:6
Oldham, John, 57:3
Oliver, F. S., 148:10
Ollard, Richard, 179:6
Opie, John, 145:1
Orderie Vitalis, 237:8
Orrery, Lord, 218:4
Orton, Diana, 234:3
Orwell, George, 16:7, 17:6,
   77:12, 125:5, 126:6
Osborn, H. F., 126:8
Osborne, Charles, 17:7, 17:8,
   17:9
Osborne, John, 79:15, 206:14
Owen, Mary, 147:8

P

Packenham, Thomas, 23:4, 23:5
Page, Walter Hines, 238:15
Paget, Reginald, 88:4
Paine, Thomas, 55:5, 232:4,
   237:3
Palais Royal guide, 79:6
Pamphilia, 211:4
Parker, Dorothy, 14:13, 78:12,
   97:3, 110:9, 177:5, 236:7
Parker, Michael, 180:12
*Parliamentary Commission
   report*, 215:4
Parr, Samuel, 55:6
Parton, James, 130:1
Pascal, Blaise, 74:11
Pater, Walter, 145:16
Patmore, P. G., 42:9
Patrick, David, 50:12, 60:3, 61:7,
   65:9, 65:10, 73:17, 73:18,
   127:10, 180:2, 184:1, 185:7,
   244:2
Pattison, Mark, 159:14
Paulin, Tom, 218:5
Pearce, Edward, 223:14
Pearson, Hesketh, 235:2
Pepys, Samuel, 45:15, 57:4,
   94:14, 113:1, 113:2, 123:7,
   179:2, 204:16
Percy Anecdotes, 11:3, 11:6,
   26:15, 27:1, 43:10, 43:11, 45:16,
   46:1, 46:6, 46:7, 98:12, 171:2,
   175:11, 180:6, 180:7, 190:13,
   196:16, 197:1, 220:8, 220:9,
   224:11, 225:2
Percy, Thomas, Bishop of
   Dromore, 132:5
Perelman, S. J., 177:6
Pericles, 180:3
Perles, Alfred, 158:12
Personnel officer, ICI, 223:9

Peterborough, *Daily Telegraph*,
   223:15
Peterborough, Lord, 179:3
Petrie, Sir Charles, 62:4
Philip, Prince (Duke of
   Edinburgh), 180:13, 181:1
Picasso, Pablo, 91:4, 181:9,
   181:10
Picasso, Mme, 181:8
Pilley, W. Charles, 144:2
Pinero, Arthur, 135:6
Piozzi, Mrs Hester, 132:6, 132:7,
   191:8, 201:7, 201:8
Plato, 183:9, 211:5
Pliatsky, Leo, 124:6
Plomer, William, 19:15, 78:7,
   97:12
Plumb, J. H., 57:7, 182:4
Plutarch, 6:6, 6:7, 11:4, 11:5,
   84:14, 134:7, 134:8, 150:5
Pollock, John, 174:6
Pompadour, Marquise de, 184:2
Ponsonby, Sir Frederick, 139:4,
   192:3, 228:2
Poole, A. J., 192:7, 192:8
Pope, Alexander, 3:11, 9:9,
   22:16, 53:9, 70:17, 73:19,
   81:11, 83:2, 87:1, 87:2, 103:1,
   103:10, 103:11, 103:12, 139:9,
   139:10, 145:10, 154:10, 171:3,
   171:4, 183:10, 188:6, 188:7,
   202:5, 204:17, 204:18, 204:19,
   204:20, 210:3, 212:11, 217:9,
   217:10, 218:6, 228:7, 241:12
Pope, Wilson, 6:8
Porteous, Bishop, 231:1
Porter, Peter, 51:13
Pound, Ezra, 27:7, 34:8, 94:13,
   96:9, 158:1, 158:13
Pound, Reginald, 14:14, 29:3
Powell, Anthony, 96:10, 144:3,
   144:4
Powys, Llewelyn, 224:9
Prawdin, Michael, 5:1
Previn, André, 32:9
Priestley, J. B., 8:11, 11:7, 11:8,
   13:2, 17:10, 25:1, 25:2, 26:6,
   26:7, 27:16, 27:17, 41:4, 49:17,
   66:12, 82:4, 123:13, 175:2,
   197:12, 206:15, 206:16
Pringle, Sir John, 186:1
Prior, James, 86:2, 87:3, 210:8
Pritchett, V. S., 84:10, 175:8
Proctor, Edna Dean, 50:4
Prynne, Abraham de la, 174:7
Puckler-Moskau, Prince von,
   62:5
Puttenham, George, 93:9

Q

Quarterly Review, 116:9,
   116:10
Quennell, Peter, 64:9, 64:13,
   64:14
Quinton, Anthony, 40:11

R

Raban, Jonathan, 33:4, 33:5
Racket, Mrs, 184:17
Ralph, Abbot of Coggeshall,
   130:11
Rankin, Hugh, 2:7
Raphael, Frederic, 4:1
Ratcliffe Michael, 171:5, 171:6,
   171:7, 196:1
Ravel, Maurice, 199:4
Raven, J. E., 12:3
Read, Herbert, 197:2
Reagan, Ronald, 223:16
Redding, Cyrus, 42:10
Rees, C. B., 32:10
Rees-Mogg, William, 137:14
Reeve, Henry, 152:7
Reni, Guido, 197:3
Renoir, Auguste, 146:1
Retz, Cardinal de, 194:3
Reynolds, Sir Joshua, 103:13,
   145:2, 184:18, 197:4
Rhodesia Herald, 223:17
Richard of Devizes, 192:9
Richardson, Sir Arthur, 2:2
Richardson, Brian, 61:13,
   154:8, 168:11, 233:11
Richardson, John, 181:11
Richmond, William, 171:12
Richmond, W. R., 162:16,
Rieff, Philip, 144:5
Rienow, Robert and Leona,
   195:7
Rilke, Rainer Maria, 227:2
Rimsky-Korsakov, Nikolai,
   230:13
Ritchie, Anne, Lady, 48:13
Robertson, Alec, 83:14
Robertson, W., 140:3
Robespierre, Maximilien, 150:3
Robinson, Henry Crabb, 41:5,
   116:11, 141:10, 225:12, 240:13,
   240:14
Robinson, Sir Hercules, 67:15
Robinson, J., 239:6
Robinson, John (Bishop of
   Woolwich), 144:6
Robinson, Lennox, 243:7
Rochester, Earl of, 87:4
Rockefeller, John Davison,
   194:9

258

Sphere Reference

HANDBOOK OF 20th CENTURY QUOTATIONS

DEATH ('on the plus side, death is one of the few things that can be done as easily lying down'), **CELIBACY** ('is not an inherited characteristic'), **CHILDREN** ('It is no wonder people are so horrible when they start life as children'), **GERTRUDE STEIN** ('the mama of dada'), **POETRY** ('the stuff in books that doesn't quite reach the margins'), **VIRGINIA WOOLF** ('a beautiful little knitter'), **LONGEVITY** ('the revenge of talent upon genius'), **BOGNOR** ('Bugger Bognor!') . . . .

Sphere Reference

ROGET'S THESAURUS

Never be at a loss for the right word.
Fully updated to meet the demand for technical terms,
Americanisms and slang.